ESSAYS IN THE HISTORY OF IDEAS

PUBLISHED FOR THE HISTORY OF IDEAS CLUB OF
THE JOHNS HOPKINS UNIVERSITY

LONDON: GEOFFREY CUMBERLEGE
OXFORD UNIVERSITY PRESS

ESSAYS IN THE HISTORY OF IDEAS

BY

ARTHUR O. LOVEJOY

BALTIMORE

THE JOHNS HOPKINS PRESS

1948

PRINTED IN THE UNITED STATES OF AMERICA

30337

CONTENTS

PREFATORY NOTE

At its meeting in January, 1947, the History of Ideas Club of Johns Hopkins University, in anticipation of the twenty-fifth anniversary of its founding, voted to invite its originator, Professor Arthur O. Lovejoy, to publish a collection of his historical papers, under the Club's sponsorship. Professors D. C. Allen, George Boas and Ludwig Edelstein were appointed a committee to make the necessary arrangements for the printing of the volume. The articles have been selected and revised by Professor Lovejoy. Most of them have previously been published; the original place of publication is indicated in the first reference of each article. The Committee and the author gratefully acknowledge their indebtedness to the Editors of journals for permission to reprint.

FOREWORD

TWENTY-FIVE YEARS ago the author of these essays joined with some of his colleagues to found the History of Ideas Club at the Johns Hopkins University. Unlike so many societies established at universities, the new organization shunned parochialism. To be a member one need not be a professor at Johns Hopkins; indeed, one need not be a professor anywhere. The purpose of the club was for "the historical study of the development and influence of general philosophical conceptions, ethical ideas, and aesthetic fashions, in occidental literature, and of the relations of these to manifestations of the same ideas and tendencies in the history of philosophy, of science, and of political and social movements." Anyone who had something to say towards this end was sure of an audience, but it was an audience that examined everything critically and did not hesitate to inform the speaker about his hits and misses.

At the first meeting, Professor Gilbert Chinard read a paper on "Volney and Jefferson" and, as has often happened since, Professor Lovejoy opened the discussion with a penetrating question that stimulated the other listeners to an enlightening commentary. Since that date in 1923, the club has met six times a year and listened to lectures by students of ideas from all parts of the world. The memoirs of the meetings are an interesting barometer of the fluctuations of scholarly taste for the last quarter century. But the History of Ideas Club has been more than a weather glass of rising and falling intellectual interests; it has been a sort of seminar where mature men and women learned new and valuable lessons.

The importance of the club for the further education of its members is due to the genius of Professor Lovejoy, who is not only the father of the club but also the chief inspirer of the modern study of the history of ideas. The investigation of the genesis and career of human notions has, of course, been with us for a long time. Philosophers and, to some extent, historians have often pointed out the course of an idea, especially the faulty ideas of their predecessors. One also remembers that the tracking down of human concepts or the revelation of the ideological pattern of a given generation became a form of intellectual pastime and pleasure in the nineteenth century. But one can now see how uncritical and narrow most of these early attempts were and how much more interested the historians of those days were in supporting a particular bias than in producing an unprejudiced verdict. That we have this new insight is largely the work of Professor Lovejoy, who brought to this wavering and unfruitful study an amazing practice of analysis, a special feeling for terminology, and a careful ritual of self-examination that protects the student from his own inherent narrowness, from his own emotional weaknesses.

The product of Professor Lovejoy's talents and energy is a new discipline that has many practitioners and has given the academic study of philosophy a new range and vitality. But others have also profited, for by his own studies Professor Lovejoy has indicated how useful the application of his principles is to the study of literature and art. One has only to go back some twenty years to see what has happened. In the 1920's most students of art and letters were engaged in frenzied pursuits after minor historical facts or in the production of vapours and inane descriptions. The fine points were being ground finer, and yet a surprising number of works of art and a large area of world literature were either misunderstood or inadequately comprehended, because the climate of ideas in which they had come to life and grown and blossomed was utterly unknown. This is no place to present a series of demonstrations, for one only need recall how many tangling places in poetry and art have been elucidated by Professor Lovejoy's work on primitivism or by his exploration of the doctrines of hierarchy and plentitude, and one only need remember how many so-called knotty places in verse or motifs in art that baffled the experts of the first part of the century are now immediately clear to the modern student because of Professor Lovejoy's studies.

It is, then, with a full consciousness of the debt that most students of the humanities owe to Professor Lovejoy, and with a keen sense of individual obligation, that the present members of the History of Ideas Club bring out this selection of his papers.

DON CAMERON ALLEN

AUTHOR'S PREFACE

In the first of the following essays some reflections on the nature, methods, and difficulties of the historiography of ideas are briefly set down. To these general observations, originally designed for another occasion, it may now (since a preface is the postscript of a book) be appropriate to add some explanation of the *raison-d'être* of—I should perhaps rather say, an *apologia* for—the present publication of a collection of papers already, for the most part, printed elsewhere. My fellow-members of the History of Ideas Club of Johns Hopkins University are, in a sense, primarily responsible; but for their kind proposal that such a volume be issued under the Club's auspices I should hardly have ventured to publish it. But—deeply grateful as I am for the honor conferred by the proposal, and despite my deference to the judgment of so distinguished a body of colleagues—I had some initial misgivings about the needfulness, or the expediency, of bringing together, from the various more or less specialized journals in which most of them appeared, a group of papers seemingly so miscellaneous in their subjects and so diverse in the classes of readers to whose interests they might be supposed to appeal. Further consideration, however—really prompted, no doubt, by an author's natural desire to get his lucubrations before as wide a public as possible—has encouraged me to think that there may be a certain advantage in combining in a single volume attempts to apply some of the general conceptions about the history of ideas which I have expressed in Essay I and elsewhere, to a considerable variety of special topics and "fields." The general conceptions, I may be permitted to say, grew out of rather than preceded most of the inquiries into special topics; the essays are not examples of a deliberate effort to impose a predetermined "method" upon refractory material. But on re-reading them, I seem to find in many of them some underlying common assumptions and procedures. Whether these are valid can only be judged by their results in the differing specific instances in which they are applied.

It may, at any rate, be worth while to indicate to the reader in advance, so that he may note them as he reads, some *general* or frequently recurrent phenomena in the history of ideas, of which the various essays may be regarded as offering particular illustrations.

1. *The presence and influence of the same presuppositions or other operative "ideas" in very diverse provinces of thought and in different periods.* "The Parallel of Deism and Classicism" is (if I have succeeded in establishing the parallel) the most explicit example of this; but the underlying idea-complex, summed up in the word "nature" in one of its senses, which is there exhibited as shaping both religious heterodoxy and æsthetic orthodoxy in the eighteenth century, is also shown, in the concluding essay, as at work in the mind of a third-century Christian apologist, and as constituting one conspicuous (though much neglected) side of his thought and teaching. The fundamental identity of the idea, and of the logic of the reasonings to which it gave rise, is not annulled by the dissimilarity of the concomitant ideas with which it was associated, nor by the differing preoccupations and temperamental biases of the writers into whose thinking it entered. The identity *in* the differences, and the differences against the background of the identity, serve to bring out more clearly the significance of each; and the recognition of both is essential to an understanding of the historic rôle of the idea in question. In this case we have one of the major and persistent ideas of Western thought, which, since the fourth century B. C., has scarcely ever disappeared altogether, though in some periods it has been dominant and in others highly recessive. In two other of the essays we see a much shorter-lived and less pervasive idea— the association of the notion of "irregularity" and "wildness" with that of "beauty"—manifesting itself first in the theory and practice of two arts—landscape-design and landscape painting—where it appeared especially appropriate, and then passing over into other arts.

2. *The rôle of semantic transitions and confusions, of shifts and of ambiguities in the meanings of terms, in the history of thought and of taste.* That "man lives not by bread alone, but

chiefly by catchwords," is not precisely the whole truth, but it is a large and, for the historian, an extremely important part of the truth, about *homo sapiens*; and nearly all of the great catchwords have been equivocal — or rather, multivocal. The supreme example of this is, of course, to be seen in the most potent, pervasive, and persistent of all catchwords — "nature." Behind any given use of it there is usually — though, it is to be feared, not always — some determinable idea or association of ideas, sometimes of a more or less logical sort; but since the word is one and the ideas it may express are prodigiously numerous and various, it is, for the historian, often a task of difficulty and delicacy to determine what, in a given writing or passage, the idea behind the word is; and when this task of discriminating its meanings in particular texts is accomplished, if it can be—in some cases, I think, it cannot be—the analytic historian must be alert to observe the ways in which the multivocality of the word sometimes facilitates or promotes (though it doubtless seldom or never solely causes) changes—some of them revolutionary changes—in the reigning fashions in ideas. More than half the essays in the present volume are pertinent to this theme, and may be considered as, among other things, contributions (supplementary to previous studies of the same subject) to the history of the normative ideas which have been associated with and expressed (or concealed) by the word "nature." Several of the essays are also attempts to show the diversity of meanings, and the resultant confusions of thought, which have come, in the course of a century and a half, to characterize the use of the words "Romantic" and "Romanticism." The confusion here has arisen mainly, not in the minds of the authors, or in the writings, dealt with by historians and literary critics, but in the minds of the historians and critics; they have — in this case and in others — done a good deal unconsciously to exemplify a process — and a danger — against which their studies might have been expected to make them peculiarly alert.

3. *The internal tensions or waverings in the mind of almost every individual writer—sometimes discernible even in a single writing or on a single page—arising from conflicting ideas or*

incongruous propensities of feeling or taste, to which, so to say, he is susceptible. I suppose most careful interpreters of particular writings or authors have some realization of this phenomenon; but I have long felt that it is often insufficiently realized, or at all events insufficiently made evident to the reader. Many expositions of an author's views and his reasonings seem to me not merely over-simplified but over-unified. It appears often to be assumed that his thinking, in general or at least on a particular subject or question, is all-of-a-piece; or, if the expositor himself observes some inner discrepancies, some cross-currents in his author's mental processes, he tends to minimize them or to ignore them altogether, selecting for exclusive presentation only what he considers (sometimes quite erroneously) the most " important," or the most " permanently valuable," or the " most characteristic," idea, or consistent scheme of ideas, of the author. But it is only the narrowest or the dullest minds that are—if any are—completely in harmony with themselves; and the most important and most characteristic thing about many a great author is the diversity, the often latently discordant diversity, of the ideas to which his mind is responsive, and which manifest themselves at one and another point in what he writes. To "read" an author, in any but a superficial and mechanical manner, is to be aware of the import of the idea which he is expressing in each passage and of the *relations* (not always explicit, often even unconscious) of the ideas in one passage to those in another, whether they be relations of simple congruity or mutual implication or mutual incongruity; and to be constantly observant of the transitions from one strain of thought to another. It is possible—and is not, I think, very uncommon—to harmonize the thought of a reflective writer in such a fashion that what is, historically considered, precisely the most interesting and most noteworthy fact about him—the impact upon him of traditions of differing origins and opposite tendencies, or the dim emergence in his thinking of new ideas destined to be seized upon and made much of by his successors—is wholly concealed. It must not, of course, be assumed *a priori* that this is true in the case of any given writer; whether it is true or not can only be determined by careful and unprejudiced analysis. But there should be no tacit assumption, in the mind of the expositor, that it is not true; the question whether it is true should always be raised and considered; and a fairly extensive reading in the course of half a century has inclined me to the belief that it is more often true than not. In the present volume, examples of what appear to me to be such inner tensions — fluctuations or hesitancies between opposing ideas or moods, or the simple and more or less unconscious embracing of both sides of an antithesis — may be found especially in the essays dealing with one of Rousseau's *Discourses*, with Herder, Friedrich Schlegel, Schiller, Coleridge, Milton, and Tertullian.

The papers included in the volume (after the first) are all, in intention, historical, in accordance with what I believe to be the wish of my colleagues of the History of Ideas Club; I have not taken advantage of the opportunity to introduce discussions of contemporary metaphysical and epistemological questions. I have also excluded a few historical studies dealing with technical philosophical issues, and a group of articles on the history of the theory of organic evolution before Darwin, which now need extensive revision and should, if eventually published, appear as a separate volume. As excursions, or border-raids, of a philosopher into provinces—chiefly of literary history — in which he is not a specialist, the essays doubtless illustrate the risks of error inherent in any such enterprise; but they would have been still more imperfect if I had not had the advantage of much converse with, and of assistance from, colleagues, both at Johns Hopkins and Harvard, who are eminent experts in the fields into which I have ventured to wander. I cannot conclude without expressing my gratitude to Professors D. C. Allen, George Boas, and Ludwig Edelstein who, on behalf of the History of Ideas Club, looked after all the arrangements for the publication of the book, and my further particular thanks to Professor Edelstein for his generous sacrifice of time in sharing in the tedious labors of proof-reading.

ARTHUR O. LOVEJOY.

Johns Hopkins University,
    May 29, 1948.

ESSAYS IN THE HISTORY OF IDEAS

I. THE HISTORIOGRAPHY OF IDEAS [1]

TO EXPLAIN what is meant in the title by the word ' ideas ' would demand a long preamble, and I have attempted the explanation at some length elsewhere; [2] for both reasons I shall dispense with a preliminary definition, hoping that the meaning of the term, for the present purpose, will become fairly evident from its context in what follows.

Historical study having to do, more or less, with ideas and their rôle in human affairs is now actively pursued in our universities and by non-academic scholars under at least twelve different labels:

1. The history of philosophy.

2. The history of science.

3. Folklore and some parts of ethnography.

4. Some parts of the history of language, especially semantics.

5. The history of religious beliefs and theological doctrines.

6. Literary history, as it is commonly presented, namely, the history of the literatures of particular nations or in particular languages—in so far as the literary historians interest themselves, as some do in but small degree, in the thought-content of literature.

7. What is unhappily called " comparative literature," which is apparently, by its most competent investigators, understood to be the study of international intellectual relations, of the transfer of tendencies of thought and taste, and of literary fashions, from one country to another, with especial attention to the modifications or metamorphoses which these undergo when transplanted into a new milieu.

---

[1] First published in *Proceedings of the American Philosophical Society*, Vol. 78, No. 4, March, 1938.
[2] *The Great Chain of Being* (1936), 7-20.

1

8. The history of the arts other than literature, and of changes of taste in these arts.

9. Economic history and the history of economic theory, which, though they are not the same thing, are so closely related that they may here, for brevity, be grouped together.

10. The history of education.

11. Political and social history, and

12. The historical part of sociology, in so far as specialists in these subjects take account, as they now increasingly do, of intellectual or quasi-intellectual processes, of " ruling ideas " or " climates of opinion," either as causal factors in, or as consequences or " rationalizations " of, the political institutions, laws, *mores*, or social conditions prevalent in a given period—the subject sometimes designated as *Wissenssoziologie*. The enumeration might be extended and further subdivided; but these twelve appear to be the principal recognized divisions of the general field.

These subjects have usually in the past been studied in relative, though scarcely ever in complete, isolation. They are assigned in universities to separate departments, between which there frequently has not, I suspect, been much consultation concerning the interrelations of their respective provinces. Those who investigate them have their separate journals and their special learned societies, and, for the most part, do not and, indeed, cannot give much time to reading the journals or attending the meetings of their brethren in other fields— unless they have the good fortune of membership in some non-specialized society. This division of the general domain of intellectual history has, of course, been inevitable and highly useful. Increasing specialization, and with it the development and refinement of distinctive techniques of inquiry, is obviously a necessary condition of progress in all branches of knowledge, and not least in the historical disciplines. Nevertheless the divisions—in so far as these several disciplines are concerned with the historiography of ideas—are artificial, though not, in general, arbitrary; that is to say, they correspond to no lines of absolute cleavage in the historical phenomena under investigation. They are in part temporarily convenient isolations of certain objects from their contexts, to facilitate more minute scrutiny; and in part they are fortuitous, results of accidents in the history of educational institutions or of the idiosyncratic limitations of the intellectual interests of influential scholars. And in the present phase of the development of, at least, several of these nominally distinct disciplines the lines of division are breaking down.   They are breaking down because questions originally raised within the traditional limits of one or another of these subjects prove incapable of adequate and accurate answer without going beyond those limits.   Ideas are commodities which enter into interstate commerce.   One notable example of the growing recognition of this has been the emergence, out of the study of separate national literatures, of the study of comparative literature.   But the observation of what happens to ideas when they cross national or linguistic boundary lines is but a small part of the process of which I am speaking, even in the specific case of the history of literature.

This may be illustrated by recent tendencies in the study of English literature.   Scholars who primarily set out to be specialists in that field, and even in a limited part of it, have found themselves compelled to confess, not only how little they know of English literature who only *English* literature know— that has long been obvious—but also how little they know of English literature who only literature know.   A scholar, for example, decides to attempt a special study of Milton, or, narrowing his subject of investigation still further, of *Paradise Lost*.   It is, of course, possible to treat that work from an exclusively aesthetic point of view, as " pure literature," without raising any historical questions about it—though, if I may thus parenthetically dogmatize, a great part even of the aesthetic values of the poem will thereby be lost.   In any case *Paradise Lost* is, *inter alia*, an extremely interesting phenomenon in the history of the activities of the human mind; and it is, in part, as such that most scholars in English literature now approach it.   Now *Paradise Lost* is not merely, as the schoolboy noted with surprise, full of familiar quotations; it is also full of ideas, which, if only as a means to the understanding of what Milton meant, and of the movement of his mind as he composed, need to be seen in their historical perspectives. Scarcely one of them is original with him, though many of them receive a special twist or coloring, or enter into novel combinations, in consequence of personal characteristics of his. Even to recognize what is distinctive of either his style or his thought *as* distinctive, it is necessary to have both an extensive and a fairly intimate acquaintance with manifestations of the same ideas elsewhere, especially among his contemporaries and among those of his predecessors with whom he is known, or can be fairly presumed, to have been acquainted. It is as impossible to appreciate the characteristic qualities of a poet's mind and art, when he is expressing a general idea, without knowing the idea and also other expressions of it, as it is to appreciate the art of a painting of the Annunciation without knowing the first chapter of the Gospel of Luke and without having seen any other paintings of the same subject. But the history of the ideas in Milton in great part does not, by the conventional classification of " subjects," lie in the field of English literature; it belongs to the history of philosophy, of theology, of religious poetry in other languages, of science, of æsthetic doctrines, and of taste.

For example, in the Eighth Book, it will be remembered, Adam and the Archangel Raphael engage—somewhat oddly— in a long discussion of the theories of seventeenth-century astronomy. Even for the exegesis of Milton's text—for the mere identification of the hypotheses referred to, which are by the poet sometimes rather loosely expressed—it is necessary to be extensively acquainted with the doctrines and reasonings of the astronomers from Copernicus's time to Milton's concerning the arrangement and motions of the celestial bodies; and this is the more plainly necessary if any competent judgment is to be formed as to Milton's knowledge of and attitude towards the new science of his age. The student of *Paradise Lost*, therefore, is forced by the nature of the historical inquiry in which he is engaged to turn to a part of the history of science. And if he is a cautious and critical scholar, he will not be content to get up a little information on the subject from Dreyer, Duhem, or other general survey, scarcely even to review the more recent monograph-literature on the history of early modern astronomy—especially as this will often not give him what he needs for his special purpose. He will feel constrained to study the relevant astronomical texts themselves, and to attempt to make himself really at home in the theories of the period; and he may be enabled, in consequence, to make fresh contributions to the history of that science, of interest to those who know not Milton and are indifferent to the reputed astronomical opinions of the Archangel Raphael.

I am not describing a hypothetical case; I am describing what has actually been happening in a single part of recent Miltonic study [3] directed upon a passage of some two hundred lines in one Book. If the meaning and the background of the ideas in the whole of *Paradise Lost* are dealt with in a similar manner, the student will find a wide range of other conceptions the history of which, once more, is not a part of what has commonly been considered the province of the historian of English literature, but lies within the domains of the specialists in many other branches of learning. When, for one brief example, Milton's Adam quotes Aristotle (without acknowledgment) to his Creator, observing that while the deity is self-sufficient and "best by himself accompanied," *he* (Adam) needs a human companion even in so agreeable a place as Eden, it is desirable that the careful student of the poem, as a historical phenomenon, should know this fact. For, in the first place, without a knowledge of it, it is not impossible for the reader to miss much of the point of Milton's lines. In the second place, the identification of self-sufficiency with the supreme good—which, however, Adam is here made to declare, is a good for God but not for man—is one of the most influential and widely-ramifying ideas in Western thought; [4] and in this larger historical vista Milton's expression of the idea gains a great enrichment of interest—an increase, so to say, of voluminosity. In the third place, Milton's particular way of employing the Aristotelian theorem, on the one hand illuminates his conception of God and on the other hand comes close to a denial of the proposition—which had been assumed as axiomatic in most orthodox

---

[3] As examples among American scholars in this field I may mention the work of Dr. Marjorie Nicolson, Dr. F. R. Johnson and Dr. Grant McColley.

[4] See the writer's *The Great Chain of Being* (1936), 161, and 42 f., 48 f., 62, 83, 159, 300, 351.

Christian theology—that man's chief good is the imitation or the ecstatic contemplation of God. And finally, a recognition of the Aristotelian source of Adam's theology lends to the passage, I can't but think, an agreeable touch of humor—not, I admit, probably intended by the poet. But all this appears not to have been generally known to the earlier Milton-commentators. They have, no doubt, usually been too little acquainted with Aristotle, and with the history of philosophy in general, and the Aristotelian specialists have been too little concerned with Milton, for either to establish the connection. Similar examples might be multiplied by the hundred, all illustrating the general fact that the quest of a historical understanding even of single passages often drives the student into fields which at first seem remote enough from his original topic of investigation. The more you press in towards the heart of a narrowly bounded historical problem, the more likely you are to encounter in the problem itself a pressure which drives you outward beyond those bounds.

If, instead of literary history, we had taken as a starting-point any one of several other fields of historical inquiry, we should have encountered similar, and in many cases more important, illustrations of the necessity of this sort of correlation; and we should, if I am not mistaken, have found among the keener-minded specialists in those fields a growing sense of that necessity. It is perhaps not too much to say that, in the history of historiography itself, we have now reached a juncture at which the indispensability of a closer and wider *liaison*—or, to better the metaphor, of a great deal more cross-fertilization—between primarily distinct disciplines, is much more apparent and more urgent than it has ever been before. It would be wholly false to say that the phase of increasing minute specialization in these studies is over—though in some of them, I suspect, the period of diminishing returns from the customary methods of cultivation has been reached; it would not, I believe, be false to say that increasing specialization has actually " passed over," like a category in the Hegelian logic, into its own apparent opposite, and now manifests itself as a demand for more historical synthesis—for the establishment of concrete and fruitful interconnections at a large number of specifiable points. And if this is so, we are confronted with a difficult situation pertinent to what may be called the general strategy of historical inquiry, and in some degree also to the organization of advanced instruction in universities, which demands practical consideration.

The nature of the difficulties is, I suppose, evident; explicit consideration of it may perhaps suggest some alleviations, if not a complete remedy. The divisions of the total domain having to do in any degree with the rôle of ideas in history exist; and it is neither possible nor desirable to abolish them in favor of any vague "universal history." Yet it is now plain that the scholar who wishes to understand sufficiently the material within almost any one of these divisions must take account of material lying, according to the conventional boundary-lines, in other—often in several other—divisions. But no man, obviously, can be a competent original investigator in many provinces even of history. Yet the specialist often—and, I am disposed to think, usually—cannot get what he needs even from the more substantial general treatises or manuals in the subjects which he finds his own overlapping. One reason, though not the only one, why he cannot is that the authors of those works, having preoccupations different from his, may have left out precisely the portions of their subjects which are most pertinent to his. It would be possible to cite, if time permitted, specific instances, in which the initial specialized interest of investigators in one province has produced a kind of blindness to aspects of the historical material with which they deal that are of great significance in relation to other parts of intellectual history. That it is easy, in observing any object—including historical sources—to overlook a good deal of what is there, and is important, unless you know what to look for, is a truism sufficiently illustrated by the classic anecdote of the student who, being required to describe a fish-skeleton placed before him, faithfully enumerated all the features of the object except the most conspicuous—bilateral symmetry. Learned historians of literature, philosophy, religion, science, or social or political movements, sometimes fall into comparable omissions, simply because, knowing only their own subjects, they do not know all that is to be looked for *in* those subjects.

But it is time to pass on to the question how the difficulties of this situation can be diminished. Upon this question I submit three observations.

1. The first will perhaps be the most repugnant, and may seem only the expression of a professional bias, of the tendency of a specialist to fancy his own subject to be of peculiar interest and importance. However that may be, I think one of the desiderata in the juncture I have described is a more general recognition of the fact that in the history of philosophy is to be found the common seed-plot, the *locus* of initial manifestation in writing, of the greater number of the more fundamental and pervasive ideas, and especially of the controlling preconceptions, which manifest themselves in other regions of intellectual history. To offer proof of this here, for those, if there be such, who doubt it, is manifestly impossible. But if it is a fact, it has two practical implications: first, that in the preparation of scholars for competent investigation in most other historical fields, a sound training both in the history of philosophical ideas and—what is not less important—in the methods of philosophical analysis—of taking idea-complexes apart—is especially needful; and second, that the history of philosophy needs to be studied with more attention to the repercussions of philosophic ideas outside the great technical systems, and to be presented in a manner rather different from the usual one, which will make it more digestible and nutritious for non-philosophers. In explanation and justification of this last thesis I might, but I shall not here, expatiate at length; but what I mean by it may in part be gathered from what I shall say under the next head.

2. The history of *individual* ideas as such—or the ideas entertained by men on individual *questions* which have seemed to them significant—is in great part still to be adequately investigated and the results to be written. On this I have gone into print elsewhere [5] and shall on this occasion speak only sum-

[5] In the introductory lecture of *The Great Chain of Being*, the rest of the volume being an attempt to give, so far as the author's resources and the limitations of a single course of lectures permitted, an illustration of such a study of a single idea, in its interactions with others. Professor George Boas and the writer have attempted a similar study, by a somewhat different method, in *Primitivism and Related Ideas in Antiquity* (1935).

marily. There are, I have suggested, many " unit-ideas "—types
of categories, thoughts concerning particular aspects of common
experience, implicit or explicit presuppositions, sacred formulas
and catchwords, specific philosophic theorems, or the larger
hypotheses, generalizations or methodological assumptions of
various sciences—which have long life-histories of their own,
are to be found at work in the most various regions of the
history of human thinking and feeling, and upon which the
intellectual and affective reactions of men—individuals and
masses—have been highly diverse. There is here another distinct realm of historiography, which needs to be added to the
dozen mentioned at the outset, partly because it is concerned
with a class of historical phenomena of extraordinary interest
in themselves, which the others do not wholly cover, and partly
(which is the point that I here wish to make) because their
progress depends greatly upon it—as its progress, not less truly,
depends upon theirs. Until these units are first discriminated,
until each of them which has played any large rôle in history
is separately pursued through all the regions into which it has
entered and in which it has exercised influence, any manifestation of it in a single region of intellectual history, or in an
individual writer or writing, will, as a rule, be imperfectly
understood—and will sometimes go unrecognized altogether.
" There are few things in the world more interesting," Professor Lowes has remarked, " than the disclosure of facts which
throw into fresh perspective a mass of other historic facts." [6]
Through the sort of study of which I am now speaking, the
study of the (so far as possible) total life-history of individual
ideas, in which the many parts that any one of them plays upon
the historic scene, the different facets which it exhibits, its interplay, conflicts and alliances with other ideas, and the diverse
human reactions to it, are traced out with adequate and critical
documentation, with analytical discrimination, and, finally, with
imagination—through this, I am persuaded, are to be disclosed
many facts which will throw into fresh perspective, and thereby
invest with heightened interest and greater intelligibility, facts
in other branches of intellectual history which, lacking such

[6] In his " Teaching and the Spirit of Research," *The American Scholar*, 1933.

perspective, sometimes appear dull, unrelated, and more or less incomprehensible.

I do not mean to imply that this form of the historiography of ideas is as yet non-existent; some excellent examples of it, or at least approximations to it, have long been in our libraries, and numerous scholars in different quarters are now contributing to it. But if it is not in its infancy, it is still, I think, barely in its adolescence; and its methods, its requirements, its aims, and its interest, are less generally understood than could be desired. Its program is one of both isolation and synthesis— the provisional isolation of an idea for separate study, but the bringing together, for that study, of material from all the historical provinces into which the idea has penetrated.

3. From all that has so far been said, one conclusion seems to me to emerge almost too plainly to require statement. It is that in almost all of the branches of historiography which deal with the history of men's thoughts or opinions, and the affective attitudes and behavior associated with these, there is imperative need of more definite, responsible, organized collaboration between specialists in these several branches than has hitherto been customary—collaboration too, in some cases, between historians and specialists in non-historical disciplines, notably the natural sciences. Trustworthy historical synthesis is not a one-man job. If the pieces that are to be put together—even for the understanding of one part of one subject—are to be sound pieces, they must be provided, or at least be critically inspected, by those having special training and up-to-date technical knowledge in the fields to which the pieces primarily belong. And by coöperation I do not mean the sort of thing exemplified by the *Cambridge Modern History* and *History of English Literature*, admirable and useful as those great works are. What I have in mind is not simply the parcelling-out of the subdivisions of a large subject among specialists in those subdivisions; it is the convergence upon *each* of them of all the special knowledge from all of these subdivisions which is genuinely pertinent to it. The indispensability of such coöperation is especially evident if we consider possible large enterprises of scholarship which now wait to be undertaken. I will briefly mention only two such

enterprises, of different types and scales of magnitude, and in quite dissimilar provinces, either of which might well be sponsored by a great learned society or a great university. The first is a book of annotations on *Paradise Lost* and of studies on special historical and literary aspects of that poem. Such books were fairly frequent in the eighteenth century, though usually very badly done. I am unable to discover, through some bibliographical search and inquiries of English scholars, that there exists any modern work of this character, bringing together all the knowledge needed for placing that great English classic in its historical relations, and for the adequate illumination of the ideas which it contains. And the reason, no doubt, is that such a work cannot now decently be done by one man, unaided; it needs, as what I have earlier said implies, the coöperation not only of a number of specialists in English, but also of a classical scholar, a patristic scholar, a medievalist, a philosopher, a student of rabbinical and other Jewish literature, a theologian versed in early Protestant divinity, special students both of French and Italian literature of the sixteenth and seventeenth centuries, and a historian of science especially at home in early modern astronomy. I do not, once more, mean to imply that no studies in these fields, pertinent to Milton, as yet exist. Much valuable work on them has been and is being done, chiefly by English scholars who have found themselves compelled, in the manner already mentioned, to deviate into provinces not primarily their own.[7] The task to which I am referring would consist in part in bringing together in a connected and synoptic way the results of these previous

---

[7] Some further recent examples of this may be given: Mr. Harris F. Fletcher's *Milton's Rabbinical Studies* (1930); Miss Kathleen E. Hartwell's *Milton and Lactantius* (1929), both of which convincingly demonstrate the relevance and interest, for the student of Milton, of such excursions into other branches of learning; the cooperative enterprise of a group of scholars at the University of North Carolina, under the leadership of Professor U. T. Holmes, who, in order to contribute to the definitive clarification of one important question concerning the background and sources of *Paradise Lost*, and Milton's way of using his sources, have undertaken a carefully documented biography of Du Bartas and a critical edition of *La Semaine*; and the work of Professor G. C. Taylor on the same subject (*Milton's Use of Du Bartas*, 1934). What promises to be an important study of the " analogues of *Paradise Lost* in all languages and from all periods " has been announced by Mr. Walter Kirkconnel; see his article in *Transactions of the Royal Society of Canada*, 1946.

studies now scattered through many scores of monographs, books, and articles. But those studies are, as a rule, sound and dependable precisely in the degree in which the English specialists have been able to obtain collaboration and criticism from specialists of thorough competence in the other provinces in question; some of them would be of more value if considerably more such cooperation could have been had by their authors; and in any case, much further research is needed in some of these collateral fields, as well as a better correlation and cross-illumination between them. If such a piece of work could be cooperatively carried out, there could be focussed upon Milton's text a mass of facts which would, we may be confident, throw many parts of it into fresh perspectives of great and of diverse interest.

To turn to the history of (primarily) scientific conceptions: there as yet exists, so far as I know, no historically and philosophically respectable account of the total development of the idea of evolution before Darwin—using the term even in its narrower sense of the theory of the transformation of species; and we have certainly no adequate history of the idea in its broader sense, i. e., of developmental conceptions in astronomy, geology, anthropology, social philosophy, cosmology and theology, and the influence of all of these in other provinces of thought.[8] Historically, the various phases of the progress of what may be called the genetic way of thinking—which has been a long, complex, and extremely gradual process—are closely related. The reason why there exists no adequate history of the process as a whole is, in part, that much of the *grundlegend* detailed study of sources still remains to be done; but the task, in any case, can scarcely be executed properly by any one scholar. For it requires a competent acquaintance with many special fields—not only with the several natural sciences mentioned, and with the history of particular subdivisions of these—in biology, for example, of taxonomy, comparative

---

[8] Substantially the same opinion is expressed by Professor P. T. Sorokin in his *Social and Cultural Dynamics*, II, 371 (published since this paper was presented), with especial reference to the medieval part of the story: " The real history of the idea of progress . . . is not written yet. Works like J. B. Bury's *The Idea of Progress*, or Delvaille's work, . . . only most superficially touch the problem."

anatomy, paleontology, embryology and genetics—but also with an extremely wide range of the philosophical, theological and general literature of the seventeenth, eighteenth, and early nineteenth centuries, and with the history of ideas *about* history and its general movement. A part of the story, for example, can be verified only through a thorough study of the works of Leibniz; and another part demands an intimate acquaintance with the literature, the metaphysics, and even the aesthetic theories and fashions, of the German Romantic period. And all of these need to be illuminated from the special history of certain relevant individual ideas—for instance, of the principle of continuity and of the concept or pseudo-concept of ' species.' The thing can be done, and it could be wished that American scholarship would undertake it. But unless it is undertaken in the manner suggested, through large-scale, planned, and articulated coöperation, it is likely to be much more imperfectly done than even the present state of knowledge in the numerous special fields pertinent to it would make possible.

It may be that the kind and measure of coöperation needed, at these and at many other points in the historiography of ideas, is unattainable. There are undeniably great obstacles to it, both in the organization and traditions of most of our universities, and in human nature. Natural scientists have, if I am not mistaken, realized earlier than historians the necessity for planned team-work, and have thus far developed it more skillfully and on a much greater scale. But in a number of historical disciplines encouraging beginnings of it are now discernible. The difficulty of realizing it, however, is still so considerable that I have thought it perhaps not wholly useless to take this occasion to emphasize its necessity in the present phase of that large business which is the endeavor to investigate the history, and thereby, it may be hoped, to understand better the nature, of the workings of the human mind.

II. THE SUPPOSED PRIMITIVISM OF ROUSSEAU'S
DISCOURSE ON INEQUALITY *

THE NOTION that Rousseau's *Discourse on Inequality* was essentially a glorification of the state of nature, and that its influence tended wholly or chiefly to promote " primitivism," is one of the most persistent of historical errors. Many examples of it might be cited; I limit myself to one, chosen because it is found in what is likely to be for many years to come the standard English treatise on the history of political theories, a monumental work by a scholar of admirable learning. In the *Discourse on Inequality*, wrote the late Professor W. A. Dunning,

the natural man was first the solitary savage, living the happy, care-free life of the brute. The steps by which men emerged from their primitive state are depicted with fascinating art, but the author's regret at their success pervades the picture. . . . Throughout the fluctuations of his usage, one idea alone appeared unmistakable, viz., that the natural state of man was vastly preferable to the social or civil state, and must furnish the norm by which to test and correct it.[1]

This is an exceptionally moderate statement of the traditional view of the *Second Discourse*; but it appears to me to be highly misleading, especially in what it implies as to the sort of ideas which that writing tended to encourage in Rousseau's contemporaries. The actual doctrine of the *Discourse*, its relation to other conceptions of the state of nature, the character of the influence upon opinion which it must have had in its time, and the features of it which must be regarded as constituting its chief historic significance, I shall attempt to show in what follows.

As in so many other cases, confusion has arisen in this matter partly through a neglect to note the ambiguity of the terms employed in the discussion. The term " state of nature " has at

* First published in *Modern Philology*, XXI (1923), 165-186.
[1] *History of Political Theories*, III (1920), pp. 8-9.

least three easily distinguishable senses. It may have a merely
chronological signification and refer to the primeval condition
of man, whatever its characteristics. In the terminology of
political theory it means the status of human individuals or
groups who in their relations to one another are not subject
to the authority of any government. Finally, it may be used—
and in the eighteenth century was often used—in what may be
called a cultural sense, to designate the state in which the arts
and sciences—civilization in its non-political elements—had
made least progress. These three senses were not necessarily
identical in denotation. It was, indeed, usually assumed that
the earliest stage was a pre-political one; but it did not follow
that the primitive stage, in the cultural sense, was coextensive
with the pre-political stage. The period preceding the organization of the political state might have been a very long one, in
the course of which mankind might have departed very widely—
whether for better or worse—from its primeval condition. The
confusion of these senses is, indeed, an old one. Pufendorf's
definition, for example, combines the cultural with the juristic
criteria; the " state of nature," in contrast with the " adventitious state," is for him not only " such a state as we may
conceive man to be placed in by his bare nativity, abstracting
from all rules and institutions, whether of human invention or
of the inspiration or revelation of heaven "; it is also " a state
in which the divers sorts of arts, with all the commodities of
life in general," are lacking.[2] In Locke, on the other hand,
the conception of " the natural state of mankind " is mainly a
juristic one. It was, moreover, a commonplace of political philosophy in these centuries that the juristic " state of nature "—
whether or not it had ever actually existed in the past, in the
relations between individuals—certainly existed at that very
time in the relations to one another of sovereign states having
no common law or government. This obviously implies nothing as to the cultural condition of the countries concerned.

   The oddly neglected facts which I wish to point out, with
regard to Rousseau's Discourse, are that the juristic state of
nature—the period prior to the establishment of civil govern-

---

[2] Law of Nature and of Nations, Book I, chap. i.

ment—was by him divided into four distinct cultural stages, all of them of long duration; that in his terminology in this writing the term " state of nature " usually refers, not to the pre-political state as a whole, but to the *first* of these cultural stages; that this first stage—the " state of nature " in his own sense—is not regarded by him as an ideal state; that the third stage, which is for him no more primitive culturally than chronologically, is the condition in which he regrets that mankind did not remain; that he cannot properly be said to maintain the excellence of the state of nature in the purely juristic sense, inasmuch as that state, according to his argument, inevitably works itself out into a final stage of intolerable conflict and disorder; and that the *Discourse* in general represents a movement rather away from than towards primitivism. I shall also show that the characteristics of three of these stages closely correspond to, and are probably borrowed from, three different " states of nature " described by earlier writers: that his first stage, namely, is similar to the state of nature of Voltaire and substantially identical with that of Pufendorf; that the third stage is, in its cultural characteristics, approximately the same as the state of nature of Montaigne and of Pope; and that the fourth stage is the state of nature of Hobbes.

That the first phase of human history, the life of man *tel qu'il a dû sortir des mains de la nature*, was not for Rousseau an ideal condition is evident, in the first place, from the picture which he gives of it. If he had really intended to set up what *he* called the " state of nature " as a norm, or as " the age at which one could have wished the race had remained," his ideal would have been explicitly that of a purely animal existence; his gospel would have been that it would be better for the featherless biped if he lived the life of a solitary wild beast. For the *Discourse* maintains with all possible definiteness that in the true state of nature man differed from other animals, not at all in his actual mode of life, but only in his yet undeveloped potentialities. *L'homme sauvage commencera par les fonctions purement animales. Apercevoir et sentir sera son premier état, qui lui sera commun avec tous les animaux.* His life, in short, was " that of an animal limited at first to mere sensation, scarcely profiting by the gifts which nature held out

to him, and not even dreaming of seizing anything from her."
He lived only in and for the moment, having almost no power
of forethought, as little memory, and consequently no ability
to learn from experience.   He possessed no language and had
no use of tools or weapons.   No social bonds united men; not
even the herd, to say nothing of the family, as yet existed.
The young remained for a relatively brief period (compared
with the prolonged helplessness of children under civilization)
with the mother, but once strong enough to forage for themselves, they left her and were thereafter unable to recognize
even this tie of kinship.   The individual, in short, lived a life
oisive, errante et vagabonde, developing only " those faculties
which were needed in attack or defense, either to overcome
his prey or to protect himself from becoming the prey of other
animals "—a danger always at hand.   And lest there be any
doubt about his meaning, Rousseau expressly contends (Note
10) that the gorilla and the chimpanzee,[3] whose manner of
existence had been described by travelers in Africa, are probably a portion of the human species who still remain *dans l'état
primitif de nature*, are " veritable savage men whose race, dispersed at some early period in the forest, has never had occasion
to develop any of its latent faculties."   The only difference,
indeed, between primitive man and the gorilla discoverable in
Rousseau's pages is favorable to the latter animal, since, as
described by Rousseau's authorities, it represents a stage definitely higher than the truly primeval condition of mankind,
as described by Rousseau himself.   Those who set forth the
doctrine of the *Discourse* in the manner still usual in histories
of literature, philosophy, and political theory, must be supposed
to have neglected to read, or to have entirely forgotten, Rousseau's Note 10.   In this same note, it is worth remarking,
Rousseau appears as the herald of the science of anthropology.
He laments that the knowledge of his day concerning both
gorillas and savage tribes is derived mainly from travelers'

---

[3] It is clearly to these animals that Rousseau refers, though he supposes them
to be the same as " the animals called *orang-outangs* in the East Indies."   His
knowledge of these African apes is derived mainly from the original description of them by the English sailor Battel, given in *Purchas his Pilgrimage* (1614)
and reproduced in the *Histoire générale des voyages*.

tales and the relations of missionaries; the former are pro-
verbially mendacious, and the missionaries, however well-inten-
tioned, are scarcely *bons observateurs*; "for the study of man
there are requisite gifts which are not always the portion of
the saints." Rousseau therefore calls upon the scientific
academies to send expeditions composed of trained and genuinely "philosophical" observers to "all savage countries," in
order that, upon their return, such investigators "may compose at leisure an *histoire naturelle, morale et politique* of what
they have seen." By such a study a whole "new world," he
declares, would be disclosed, and by means of it we should
"learn to understand our own." [4]

It was, then, a primary object of the *Discourse* to identify
the state of nature with the state of the brute. The sketch of
the manners and customs of the natural man drawn by Rousseau is, when analyzed, no more attractive than that given in
the principal early eighteenth-century satire upon primitivism,
Voltaire's *Le Mondain* (1736):

> Quand la nature était dans son enfance,
> Nos bons aïeux vivaient dans l'ignorance,
> Ne connaissant ni le *tien* ni le *mien*:
> Qu'auraient-ils pu connaître? ils n'avaient rien. . . .
> Il leur manquait l'industrie et l'aisance:

---

[4] Note 10 and much more of the same kind throughout the *Discourse* seem to
me fatal to a view expressed by M. Durkheim (*Rev. de Métaphysique*, XXV, 4)
and apparently given some support by Mr. Vaughan—viz., that Rousseau was
not attempting a hypothetical reconstruction of the early history of civilization,
and was therefore not interested in historical facts, but was merely presenting
in a picturesque way a psychological analysis of certain permanent factors in
human life. The term "state of nature," according to this view, does not designate a stage in social evolution; it is an expression for "those elements of
human nature which derive directly from the psychological constitution of the
individual" in contrast with those which are of social origin. The only evidence for this is the passage near the beginning in which Rousseau disclaims any
pretension to offer *vérités historiques*. The context, however, shows that this
disclaimer is merely the usual lightning-rod against ecclesiastical thunderbolts;
it would, says Rousseau, be inadmissible to regard the state of nature as a fact
"because it is evident from a reading of the sacred books that the first man was
not in this state,". etc. In reality, Rousseau was keenly interested in tracing
the succession of phases through which man's intellectual and social life has
passed; but he recognized that the knowledge of his time permitted only
raisonnements hypothétiques on the subject.

Est-ce vertu? c'était pure ignorance. . . .
Le repas fait, ils dorment sur la dure:
Voilà l'état de la pure nature.

Rousseau's *état primitif* differed from this only in that it was a still more brutish condition. It is almost identical with the unfavorable picture of the state of nature presented by Pufendorf, of the French translation of whose work a new edition had appeared only a few years before.[5] Many philosophers, as Rousseau justly enough points out, had arrived at their conception of man in the state of nature by a pure process of idealization, had conceived of him as " himself a philosopher discovering unaided the most sublime truths." Rousseau prides himself upon his adherence to a more realistic method, upon a more faithful and less flattering picture of the genuinely natural and truly primitive. And such a picture shows us, not the benignant primeval sage animated by *maximes de justice et de raison tirés de l'amour de l'ordre en général*; shows us not even beings like Montaigne's " Cannibals," who were " less barbarous than we, *eu esgard aux regles de la raison*"; it shows us, says Rousseau, creatures characterized by the last degree of *pesanteur et stupidité*, and destitute of moral ideas of any kind.

True, Rousseau points out certain very real advantages enjoyed by the human species in this initial phase of its evolution. If primitive man was merely a lazy and stupid animal, he was at least a healthy, a happy, and a comparatively harmless animal. It is when rhapsodizing over the physical superiority of early man that Rousseau falls into the often-quoted language which probably has done most to give hasty readers the impression that he identifies the state of nature with the ideal state. After tracing the physical disorders of modern mankind to the luxuries and artificialities of civilization, Rousseau continues:

Such is the melancholy evidence that we might have avoided almost all the ills we suffer from, if we had kept to the simple, uniform, and

---

[5] *Droit de la Nature et des Gens* (6th ed., 1750), Book II, chap. i, §2. The similarity has been pointed out by Morel, *Ann. de la Soc. J.-J. Rousseau* (1909), 163. Pufendorf, however, is less thorough and consistent than Rousseau in the

solitary existence prescribed to us by nature. If she intended us to be healthy, I venture almost to affirm that the state of reflection is a state contrary to nature and that the man who thinks (*médite*) is a vitiated animal.

But the proposition, it must be noted, is hypothetical, and in the final summing-up Rousseau does not assert the hypothesis; he does not hold that physical health is the sole or chief end of nature with regard to man. That the sentences quoted refer only to physical well-being is made certain by Rousseau's own remark at the end of the passage: " I have thus far been considering only *l'homme physique*."

Primitive man was also happier than his civilized successors, Rousseau undeniably maintains. He maintains it on the grounds on which many would still maintain that the animals in general experience less suffering than man. The primeval *bête humaine*, living in the moment, was untroubled either by regrets or by fears of coming evil. His powers and satisfactions, though few and meager, were commensurate with his few and simple desires. Since self-esteem had not yet waked in him, it was his body alone that was vulnerable; he knew nothing of the deeper and more septic wounds of vanity, or of the torment of unsatisfied ambition. Having no ideas of moral obligation, he was as little subject to the reproaches of conscience as he was disturbed by its incitements. Having no affections, he was untouched by sorrow. There is nothing particularly paradoxical about this. That men are, in Rousseau's sense, less happy than dogs or sheep, is a familiar, almost a platitudinous, conjecture, and not lacking in plausibility, though somewhat difficult of proof. Rousseau's thesis about the happiness of the state of nature has essentially the same meaning. And just as the admission of the former conjecture does not imply that one would, on the whole, prefer to be a dog or a sheep, so Rousseau's thesis does not necessarily imply a preference for the condition of the truly natural man. Later in the *Discourse* he expressly declares that for man " to place himself on

recognition of the pure animality of man in this state. " L'usage de la raison," he writes in a later passage, is " inséparable de l'état de nature" (*ibid.*, § 9).

the level of the beasts, which are the slaves of instinct," would be to " degrade his nature."

True it is, also, that Rousseau asserts the " goodness " of man in his primitive state; but how little this means has been shown by others, notably by Professor Schinz.[6] That in the state of nature man has not the status of a moral agent, Rousseau plainly tells us: *les hommes dans cet état n'ayant entre eux aucune sorte de relation morale ni de devoirs connus.* The doctrine of *la bonté naturelle,* so far as the *Second Discourse* is concerned, could best be expressed in English by the proposition that man was originally a non-moral but good-natured brute. He was not *méchant,* not malicious nor wantonly cruel. Against Hobbes's assertion that " all men in the state of nature have a desire and will to hurt," Rousseau maintains that primitive man (like some other animals) had " an innate repugnance to see others of his kind suffer." [7] In the course of social development, Rousseau finds, if man has learned more about the nature of the good, he has lost much of his primitive good nature; his progress in moral knowledge has been accompanied by a weakening of his animal instinct of sympathy—and the former has unhappily, Rousseau is persuaded, proved a less efficacious means of preventing men from injuring their fellows. Primitive man killed when necessary to procure food or in self-defense; but he invented no instruments of torture and he waged no wars.

In spite of these desirable aspects of the state of nature, it would be scarcely conceivable—even if we had no direct statement of Rousseau's upon the point—that he should have wished his readers to understand that he regarded as the ideal existence for man a state of virtual idiocy—the life of a completely unintelligent, unsocial, and non-moral though good-natured beast, such as was realistically portrayed in *his* version of the natural state of man.[8] Jean-Jacques was doubtless more or less mad,

---

[6] A. Schinz, " La notion de vertu dans le Premier Discours de J.-J. Rousseau," *Mercure de France,* XCVII (Ier, juin, 1912), 532-55; cf also " La théorie de la bonté naturelle de l'homme chez Rousseau," *Revue du XVIIIᵉ siècle,* I (Oct.-déc., 1913), 433-47.

[7] As will be shown below, however, Rousseau does not really join issue with Hobbes here, for he was not dealing with the *same* " state of nature."

[8] Since writing the above I find that M. Lanson has made substantially the same

but he was not so mad as that; and if he had been, it is certain that no such teaching would have been taken seriously by his contemporaries.

The *Discourse*, it is true, is characterized by a great deal of wavering between conflicting tendencies. There was, on the one hand, the tendency (which had been dominant, though not unchallenged, for some two centuries among thinkers emancipated from theological tradition) to employ the adjective " natural " as the term of highest possible eulogy, and to assume that man " as he came from the hands of nature " must have been the model of what " nature " intended, a being of uncorrupted rationality, knowing intuitively all essential moral and religious truths, and completely furnished for all good works:

> Nor think in Nature's state they blindly trod;
> The State of Nature was the reign of God:
> Self-love and social at her birth began,
> Union the bond of all things, and of man.[9]

This sort of philosophy of history was of the essence of deism: no religious beliefs could be true, or at all events none could be important, which could not be supposed to have been evident to man from the beginning. This was the meaning of the thesis embodied in Tindal's title: " Christianity," identified with natural religion, was " as Old as the Creation," i. e., known to the earliest men; it would not have been " natural " if it had not been. The idea of the " noble savage," whether primitive or contemporary, was a natural and usually recognized corollary from this assumption. Now Rousseau, even when writing of his first stage, was not unaffected by this tradition, though he was working himself free from it; though *his* " state of nature " was essentially different from the older conception, and was not likely to be taken seriously by anyone as an ideal, he was not yet wholly emancipated from the assumption of the excellence of the " natural " as such. And thus, with his characteristic eagerness to put the point he is at the

remark: " If we are to conceive of the man of nature as resembling the orang-outang, can we suppose that Rousseau seriously desired to make us retrogress to that point? " (*Ann. de la Soc. J.-J. Rousseau,* VIII [1912], 12).

[9] Pope, *Essay on Man,* III, 147-50.

moment making as forcibly as possibly, he sometimes writes what, taken apart from their general context, sound like enthusiastic eulogies of the primitive state. The opposition between this and the contrary tendency consequently sometimes approaches, perhaps in one passage in the preamble reaches, the point of actual contradiction. But the historian of ideas has performed but a small part of his task when he points out such an opposition of tendencies, or even a direct contradiction, in a historically important writing. What is essential is to see from what influences and prepossessions the opposing strains in the author's thought arose; to observe their often complex interplay; to note which was the prevailing and more characteristic tendency; above all, to determine when the author is merely repeating current commonplaces, and when he is expressing new insights not yet perfectly disentangled from traditional ideas. It is, in short, needful to know not only where a writer stands, but in which direction he is heading. Now it was the primitivistic strain that was (contrary to the usual supposition) the traditional and imitative side of the content of the *Discourse*. The relatively innovating side of it consisted in a repainting of the portrait of the true child of nature so that he appeared in a much less pleasing guise, even though a few of the old features were left.

How far from idyllic is Rousseau's picture of the state of nature may be seen, finally, from his account of the causes which brought this phase of the history of our race to an end. The explanation is couched in somewhat Darwinian terms, a hundred years before Darwin. As the species increased in numbers, Rousseau observes, there arose between it and other species a formidable struggle for existence. He clearly distinguishes the three aspects of such a *concurrence vitale*: the growing insufficiency of readily accessible food-supply, the competition of other animals, both frugivorous and carnivorous, for the means of subsistence which they shared with man, and the direct attacks of carnivorous animals. This struggle, Rousseau intimates, might have ended in the elimination of our species, if man had been able to fight only with tooth and claw. But under the pressure of necessity, another endowment, which is *le caractère spécifique de l'espèce humaine*, began to manifest itself—intelligence, in its several elements and manifestations; a power which, meager enough at first, is yet capable of an "almost unlimited" development. Because it is thus the distinguishing character of man among the animals, and because its unfolding is gradual and progressive, Rousseau calls it the *faculté de se perfectionner*, or, for short, "perfectibility." At the outset its functions were purely practical; it was simply a means of survival. It enabled man to invent primitive weapons and rudimentary tools, to discover the art of making fire, and to adapt himself to diversities of climate and food in the new environments to which he was forced by increase of population to migrate. Thus the moment at which man first manifested the previously latent attribute distinctive of the nature of his species was, in Rousseau's terminology, the moment at which his emergence from the state of nature began.

From this account of the first stage alone it is easy to see that the *Discourse*, so far from strengthening the primitivistic illusion, tended to weaken it. Though it shows sufficiently plain vestiges of the older habit of mind, it nevertheless insists that the historian of mankind must begin by supposing the human race in a state, not of primitive perfection from which it has degenerated, but in a state of pure animality, with all its *lumières*, both moral and intellectual, still to attain, through an immensely long, slow process, due primarily to environmental necessities working upon an originally dormant capacity for the exercise of intelligence. Thus to the conviction of the undesirability of the true state of nature, already found in Voltaire and Pufendorf, was added the idea of a law of necessary and gradual progress through natural causes. This combination of ideas was not new in 1755. It had, indeed, been the central issue in a celebrated controversy which had lately agitated the learned world, the affair of the Abbé de Prades; and as M. Morel has well shown,[10] Rousseau in this part of the *Discourse* is simply developing conceptions presented by Diderot in his *Apologie de l'Abbé de Prades*, 1752, and in the *Pensées sur l'interprétation de la nature*, 1754. What was significant in the *Discourse* was that through it Rousseau aligned himself

[10] *Ann. de la Soc. J.-J. Rousseau* (1909), pp. 135-38.

with the partisans of a new movement, a veritable *philosophie nouvelle*, as Diderot had called it—a movement essentially antagonistic to the current primitivism as well as to religious orthodoxy. The *Discourse*, in short, is chiefly notable in the history of ideas as an early contribution to the formulation and diffusion of an evolutionary conception of human history. It has other aspects, some of them partly incongruous with this; but this is obviously the most significant, since it was a manifestation of a new tendency which was destined to revolutionize modern thought.

That the *Discourse* helped to undermine the primitivistic prepossession in the minds of eighteenth-century readers may be gathered from some of the comments made upon it by Mme de Staël in 1788. "With how much finesse," she exclaims, " does Rousseau follow the progress of man's ideas! How he inspires us with admiration for the first steps of the human mind!" That his own admiration did not extend to the later steps, Mme de Staël notes; but she intimates that this was an inconsistency arising from a peculiarity of Rousseau's temperament, not a consequence of the principles which he adopted. "Rousseau ought perhaps to have acknowledged that this ardor to know and to understand was also a natural feeling, a gift of heaven, like all other faculties of men; means of happiness when they are exercised, a torment when they are condemned to inactivity." [11] The term " perfectibility " to which—though it was apparently invented by Turgot in 1750—Rousseau probably did more than anyone else to give currency, became the catchword of Condorcet and other subsequent believers in the reality, necessity, and desirability of human progress through a fixed sequence of stages, in both past and future.

Rousseau's own thought, however, is more complex and many-sided than that of his successors who drew from these conceptions an amiable confidence in the speedy " perfecting of the species." For, in addition to the two conflicting tendencies already noted, there is in the *Discourse* a third strain which modifies and deflects both the others in a curious way, to which Rousseau's commentators have given too little attention. This

[11] *Lettres sur les écrits de Rousseau*, 1788; *Œuvres*, I (1820), 15.

was the influence of Hobbes's conception of human nature, and in particular his account of the " passion " which is dominant in and distinctive of man. Hobbes finds that the object of our characteristically *human* desires, the sole " pleasure of the mind " (as distinct from those of the senses, which he sums up under the word " conveniences "), " is either glory (or to have a good opinion of oneself), or refers to glory in the end "; and glory " consists in comparison and precellence." " All the pleasure and jollity of the mind," he writes again, " consists in this, even to get some with whom comparing, it may find somewhat wherewith to triumph and vaunt itself." It is this craving chiefly which makes men social animals. " Men delight in each other's company " that they may " receive some honor or profit from it," may " pass the more current in their own opinion " or " leave behind them some esteem and honor with those with whom they have been conversant." " All society," in short, " is either for gain, or for glory; that is, not so much for love of our fellows as for love of ourselves." [12] But while " vain glory " thus engenders a kind of self-seeking and even malicious sociability, it is also the most frequent cause of quarrel among men. While conflicts between individuals or nations sometimes arise from actual oppositions of material interest, they arise much oftener, Hobbes thought, from this passion of self-esteem, which causes men to attack one another " for trifles, as a word, a smile, a different opinion, or any other sign of undervaluing, either direct in their persons or by reflection in their kindred, their friends, their nation, their profession, their name."

This social psychology of Hobbes, with its implication of the inherent *méchanceté* of man, we have seen Rousseau rejecting, so long as he is describing the *pur état de nature*. The original gorilla was not interested in nor conscious of the sort of figure he cut in the eyes of other animals of his kind, nor in that which, in comparison with others, he cut in his own. But the " pure state of nature " for Rousseau, it must be remembered, is precisely the stage in which that which is distinctive of

[12] *Leviathan,* chap. xlll; *Philosophical Rudiments concerning Government,* chap. i; in Woodbridge's *The Philosophy of Hobbes in Extracts,* pp. 233-37, 240-48.

human nature has not yet manifested itself. When, however, man becomes differentiated from the other animals, his ruling passion and his general disposition, according to the *Discourse*, are precisely such as the philosopher of Malmesbury had described. Rousseau's theory of human nature here, in short, is identical with and manifestly derived from that of Hobbes. " It is easy to see," he too declares, " that all our labors are directed upon two objects only, namely, for oneself, the commodities of life, and consideration on the part of others." *Amour-propre*—" a sentiment which takes its source in comparison "—is " not to be confused with *l'amour de soi-même.*" The latter is a natural concern for one's own interest, which is common to man and other animals; the former is a " factitious feeling, arising only in society, which leads each man to think more highly of himself than of any other." This passion began to show itself with the first moment of human self-consciousness, which was also that of the first step of human progress: as he emerged from the state of nature, man came to feel a racial pride in his superiority over the other animals.

C'est ainsi que le premier regard qu'il porta sur lui-même y produisit le premier mouvement d'orgueil; c'est ainsi que, sachant encore à peine distinguer les rangs, et se contemplant au premier par son espèce, il se préparoit de loin à y prétendre par son individu.

The same passion has ever since been, and still is, Rousseau declares, the principal source of all that is most characteristic of us, both good and bad—but chiefly bad.

It is to this universal desire for reputation, honors, and preferment, which devours us all, . . . this ardor to make oneself talked about, this rage to be distinguished, that we owe what is best and worst in men— our virtues and our vices, our sciences and our errors, our conquerors and our philosophers—in short, a vast number of evil things and a small number of good.

It is this, Rousseau in one passage goes so far as to say, " which inspires men to all the evils which they inflict upon one another." It is the cause of the boundlessness of human desires; for while the normal desires for " commodities," for means of sensuous gratification, are limited, the craving for

" distinction," for that which will feed the individual's sense of importance, pre-eminence, power, is insatiable, and infinite in the variety of the forms in which it manifests itself. Man— once he becomes truly man—is thus by his own constitution (so long as he fails to become aware of and to restrain this impulse) condemned to endless dissatisfaction, to a ceaseless pursuit of goals which when attained leave him no more content than before. Finally, *l'amour-propre* is the source of that insincerity which Rousseau finds especially odious in the emotional life and behavior of civilized men—the elaborate structure of pretense and accommodation, "keeping up appearances," simulated good will or admiration, the tribute which the vanity of one leads him to pay to the vanity of another, in order that he may receive a return in kind. Through this exclusively human type of desire, men have finally developed a strange sort of mutual parasitism in their inner existence; they have come to be beings who *savent être heureux et contents d'eux-mêmes sur le témoignage d'autrui plutôt que de leur propre.* "The savage has his life within himself; social man outside himself, in the opinion of others." [18]

It is therefore as true to say that Rousseau teaches the *méchanceté naturelle,* as to say that he teaches the *bonté naturelle,* of man; and the former teaching is the more significant of the two, since it alone relates to what is *distinctive* in man's nature. It is thus evident that the doctrine of the *Discourse* is almost completely contrary to that which Professor Irving Babbitt sets forth as characteristic of Rousseau:

> He puts the blame of the conflict and division of which he is conscious in himself upon the social conventions that set bounds to his temperament and impulses; once get rid of these purely artificial distinctions, and he feels that he will be one with himself and nature.[14]

The real source of our evils Rousseau here finds in human nature itself, and in the most characteristic of its propensities.

---

[18] This idea has been wittily elaborated by Henry James in his short story, "The Private Life." One of its characters, though a master of all the social graces, had *no* private life; he ceased to exist altogether when not in society— when no longer an object of the admiring attention of others.

[14] *Rousseau and Romanticism,* p. 79.

But though he holds that intellect and iniquity made their début together and have since developed together, he does not represent them as developing *pari passu*. In the earlier stages of cultural evolution, after men's emergence from the state of nature, their animal instinct of sympathy was still relatively strong, their *amour-propre* relatively weak, or lacking in means of expression; so that the progress in knowledge and power made possible by man's intellectual perfectibility was only slightly offset by the effects of his egotism. The characteristics of these stages, as Rousseau pictures them, must now be recalled.

The second stage in his *Outline of History* is a long transitional period—covering, he says, a "multitude of centuries"—in the course of which men little by little learned the use of the simpler tools and weapons, united in herds for mutual protection and for procuring food, invented language, finally developed the permanent family, and with it a first and very limited stage of the institution of property—in the form of recognized ownership by each individual of his weapons and other personal belongings, and by each family of its own cabin. The culmination of this process is Rousseau's third period, which he calls the stage of *société naissante* and (as I have indicated) clearly and repeatedly distinguishes from the pre-social "state of nature." [15]   It is the patriarchal stage of human society; the only government was that of the family. Men lived in loose, unorganized village groups, gaining their subsistence by hunting or fishing and from the natural fruits of the earth, and finding their amusement in spontaneous gatherings for song and dance. That so many learned historians of literature and of political thought, and even writers of works on Rousseau, have failed to point out that this third stage, and not the state of nature, was regarded by him as the most desirable,

[15] There is, however, some variation in Rousseau's use of *état de nature*, which is doubtless partly responsible for the common misinterpretation. I have counted forty-four instances of the term in the *Discourse*; in twenty-nine of these it designates exclusively the first stage, that of complete animality; in four it is used in a merely juristic sense, without reference to any distinction of cultural stages; in two it covers the first three stages, and in nine cases the context does not permit a certain determination of the meaning.

is rather amazing, since he is perfectly explicit on the point.[16]
The passage ought to be the most familiar in the *Discourse*;
but as it is usually neglected, it seems needful to recall it here:

> Though men had now less endurance, and though natural sympathy
> (*pitié*) had suffered some diminution, this period of the development
> of human faculties, holding a just mean between the indolence of the
> primitive state and the petulant activity of our self-esteem, must have
> been the happiest and the most lasting epoch.   The more one reflects
> upon it, the more one perceives that it was the state least subject to revo-
> lutions, the best state for man; and that he can have departed from it
> only by some unhappy chance, which in the interest of the general good
> (*utilité*) ought never to have occurred.   The example of the savages,
> who are nearly all found to be at this point, seems to afford further
> evidence that this state is the veritable youth of the world; and that
> all subsequent advances have been, in appearance so many steps towards
> the perfection of the individual, in reality towards the decrepitude of
> the species.

It is to be borne in mind, however, that this patriarchal and
communistic society, supposed to correspond to the cultural condition of existing savage tribes, was what a number of writers
before Rousseau had meant by the " state of nature." Rousseau's account of it is not very dissimilar to the passage—
quoted in part by Shakespeare in *The Tempest*—in which Montaigne describes the pleasant life of the " Cannibals "—i. e.,
the Carib Indians—except for the anthropophagy, which Montaigne treats as a trifling peccadillo of his children of nature.
Pope's " state of nature," though it confusedly mingles several
stages which Rousseau definitely distinguishes, in the main also
corresponds broadly to Rousseau's third stage.

It may, therefore, perhaps appear at first that the distinction
between Rousseau's view and that of such precursors is merely
terminological—that his ideal is what *they* called the state of
nature, though he prefers to apply that expression to another
condition of human life.   And it is, indeed, true that in his

---

[16] It should be said, however, that Professor Dunning (*op. cit.*) mentions this,
but treats it as a mere contradiction of the dominant contention of the *Discourse*.
The fact is duly recognized by Mr. Vaughan.   The original misconception is
well exemplified by Voltaire's famous letter to Rousseau on receiving the *Discourse* (Moland ed., XXXVIII, 446-50).

praise of the third stage Rousseau is merely singing an old song, which all the long line of sentimental eulogists of the noble savage had sung before him. Yet the distinction between his position and theirs is much more than verbal. What the *Discourse* asserted was that this best condition of mankind was *not* primitive and was *not*, properly speaking, " of nature," but was the product of art, i. e., of a conscious exercise of man's contriving intelligence, in its slow and arduous development. The third stage was not invested with the glamor of the sacred adjective " natural "; you could not say of it, as Montaigne had said of the savage *moeurs* which he so enthusiastically depicted,

> Hos natura modos primum dedit.

For Rousseau, in short, man's good lay in departing from his " natural " state—but not too much; " perfectibility " up to a certain point was desirable, though beyond that point an evil. Not its infancy but its *jeunesse* was the best age of the human race. The distinction between such a view and a thoroughgoing primitivism may seem to us slight enough; but in the mid-eighteenth century it amounted to an abandonment of the stronghold of the primitivistic position.

Nor is this the whole of the difference. As compared with the then-conventional pictures of the savage state, Rousseau's account even of his third stage is far less idyllic; and it is so because of his fundamental unfavorable view of human nature *quâ* human. Though the coloring is not uniform, there is a large admixture of black in *his* picture; his savages are quite unlike Dryden's Indians—

> Guiltless men, that danced away their time,
> Fresh as their groves and happy as their clime—

or Mrs. Aphra Behn's natives of Surinam who " represented [to her] an absolute idea of the first state of innocence, before man knew how to sin." The men in Rousseau's " nascent society " had *déjà bien des querelles et des combats; l'amour propre* was already manifest in them, as a necessary consequence of their transcendence of the purely animal stage; and slights or affronts were consequently visited with *vengeances terribles.*

Already, too—from the same motive—men had begun to desire objects, not for their real utility, but merely to feel the pride of possession—objects, therefore, " privation of which was much more cruel than the possession of them was enjoyable."

Here, once more, it is true, there is in Rousseau a conflict of tendencies which approaches self-contradiction. But here also it is not difficult either to determine which tendency is the more distinctive, or to see how, in a measure, he reconciles the conflict. It is the dark part of the picture, resulting from his assumption of a radically evil element in human nature, which is the exceptional and significant aspect of his account of the third stage; the other part represents a more conventional strain of eighteenth-century thought. And the reason why he regards this stage, not as perfect, but as the best actually attainable condition of human life is that the two characteristic assumptions of the *Discourse* forced him to a compromise. Those assumptions, as we have seen, are that primitive man was healthy, placid, and good-natured, but absolutely stupid, non-social, and non-moral; and that civilized man is highly intelligent and morally responsible, but profoundly *méchant*, insincere, restless, and unhappy. Rousseau could not bring himself to accept either extreme as his ideal; the obvious way out, therefore, was to regard the mean between these extremes as the best state possible. In the third stage, men were less good-natured and less placid than in the state of nature, but were also less stupid and less unsocial; they were less intelligent and had less power over nature than civilized man, but were also less malicious and less unhappy. In thus regarding the state of savagery, which some had called the " state of nature," not as a kind of natural perfection, an absolute norm, but as a mixed condition, intermediate between two extremes equally undesirable, Rousseau once more differed profoundly from his primitivistic predecessors.

With the causes which brought the third stage to a close we are not concerned here; Rousseau, as everyone knows, found them in the introduction of agriculture and metallurgy, which led to the establishment of private property in land, to the accumulation of capital, and to an ever increasing inequality in the wealth and power of individuals. What is pertinent to the theme of this paper is to point out that his fourth phase of human evolution, thus unhappily ushered in, was in essentials the same as the "natural condition of mankind" which had been described by Hobbes. Rousseau differed from Hobbes merely in holding that this condition was not primitive; in tracing the gradual process through which mankind had come into it; and in definitely placing it after the invention of agriculture and the beginning of private property. But these were minor considerations from Hobbes's point of view; his essential contention was that the *state immediately preceding the establishment of political society through a social compact*—the state into which any civilized society would revert if all law and government were removed—is one in which men, animated by "a mutual will of hurting," would necessarily be involved in universal conflict, latent or overt—in a *bellum omnium contra omnes.* Similarly Rousseau tells us that in the fourth, or last pre-political, stage, "devouring ambition, eagerness to improve their relative fortune, less through real need than to make themselves superior to others," inspired in all men *un noir penchant à se nuire mutuellement.* "The state of nascent society gave place to a most horrible state of war," in which "none, whether rich or poor, found any security." The implications, in short, of the conception of human nature which Rousseau had learned from Hobbes become fully evident only in his description of his fourth stage; they have hitherto, so to say, been held in abeyance, but are now permitted to work themselves out, with the natural consequence that we have in this part of the *Discourse* little more than a replica of the state of nature pictured in the *Leviathan.*

In the end, then, it is this Hobbesian (and partly Mandevillian) social psychology that—even more than the primitivistic tradition represented by Montaigne and Pope—prevented the evolutionistic tendency in the thought of the *Discourse* from issuing in a doctrine of universal progress, in a faith in *perfectibilité.* Man being the kind of creature that he is, the inevitable culmination of the process of social development is a state of intolerable evil. For the violence and universal insecurity characteristic of the fourth stage, the political state was, says Rousseau, invented as a remedy. But it was not invented in good faith; it was a trick of the rich, designed merely to protect their property and still further extend their power. Its final effect was to add political inequality, and thus new occasions of rivalry and conflict between classes, to the economic inequality already existing—a consistent deduction from Hobbes's premises, though very different from Hobbes's own. The remedy, in short, Rousseau held, served only to aggravate the disease. Such is the pessimistic conclusion of the *Discourse*. But in his next writing on the subject—the *Contrat Social*, especially the first draft of it, which according to Vaughan " probably goes back to a date shortly before or shortly after the *Discourse* "—the evolutionary conceptions conspicuous in the latter, but there entangled with incongruous tendencies, reach clear and unqualified expression. *Never* in the past, Rousseau now declares, has there been an ideal condition of human society:

La douce voix de la nature n'est plus pour nous un guide infaillible, ni l'indépendance que nous avons reçue d'elle, un état désirable; la paix et l'innocence nous ont échappé pour jamais, *avant que nous en eussions goûté les délices*. Insensible aux stupides hommes des premiers temps, échappée aux hommes éclairés des temps postérieurs, *l'heureuse vie de l'âge d'or fut toujours un état étranger à la race humaine*.[17]

No exception, it will be observed, is made even for the third stage of the *Discourse on Inequality*. As for the state of nature—already repudiated, as we have seen, in the *Discourse*— Rousseau now still more emphatically declares that man's emergence from it was the beginning of his long march towards his highest good. The continuance of such a condition would have been *nuisible au progrès de nos plus excellentes facultés*. So long as men lived without definite and lasting social ties their *entendement* could never have developed:

Nous vivrions sans rien sentir, nous mourrions sans avoir vécu; tout notre bonheur consisterait à ne pas connaitre notre misère; il n'y aurait ni bonté dans nos coeurs ni moralité dans nos actions, et nous n'aurions jamais goûté le plus délicieux sentiment de l'âme, qui est l'amour de la vertu.

[17] First draft of *Contrat Social*; in Vaughan, *Political Writings of Rousseau*, I, 448. Internal evidence seems to me to make it improbable that this preceded the *Discourse*.

The premises of the argument here, it should be noted, lie wholly in the two ideas which I have pointed out as the significant and relatively novel features of the *Discourse:* (*a*) the identification of the *état primitif*, not with a state of idyllic savagery, but with one of utter stupidity and animality; (*b*) the conception of the subsequent stages of human history as a process of gradual *perfectionnement* of man's distinctive faculty of intelligence. But the Hobbesian influence, though it has not entirely disappeared, has greatly diminished; Rousseau no longer insists that man's intellectual progress is evitably accompanied by an intensification of his *amour propre*, and therefore by an increasing and incorrigible *méchanceté*. The pessimism of the concluding passage of the *Discourse* has thus been overcome by the more hopeful implications of the evolutionistic strain in that writing; and Rousseau, having now ceased to idealize *any* past stage of social development, finds his ideal in the future:

Far from thinking that there is no longer any virtue or happiness attainable by us, and that Heaven has abandoned us without resource to the depravation of the species, let us endeavor to draw from the very evil from which we suffer the remedy which shall cure it.

This remedy consists, of course, in the reorganization of society upon the basis of a properly drawn social compact. Let us then, he concludes, show the eulogist of the state of nature *toute la misère de l'état qu'il croyait heureux* and teach him to find *dans l'art perfectionné la réparation des maux que l'art commencé fit à la nature.*[18] The repudiation of primitivism in the published text of the *Contrat Social,* though less striking in expression, is not less explicit; and it too has its basis in that relatively new conception of primitive man which Rousseau had presented in the *Discourse.* The transition—of which the several intermediate stages are not now distinguished—from the *état de nature* to the *état civil* is described as a benign process,

qui, d'un animal stupide et borné, fit un être intelligent et un homme . . . en substituant dans sa conduite la justice à l'instinct, et donnant à ses actions la moralité qui leur manquait auparavant.[19]

[18] *Ibid.*, p. 454.   [19] *Contrat Social*, Book I, chap. viii.

Yet it remains for the future to show whether the original doctrine of the *Discourse* did not contain the more profound insight into human nature and offer the truer account of the general course of human affairs. For that doctrine, as has been shown, declares that there is a dual process going on through history: on the one hand, an indefinite progress in all those powers and achievements which express merely the potency of man's intellect; on the other hand, an increasing estrangement of men from one another, an intensification of ill-will and mutual fear, culminating in a monstrous epoch of universal conflict and mutual destruction. And the chief cause of the latter process Rousseau, following Hobbes and Mandeville, found, as we have seen, in that unique passion of the self-conscious and social animal—pride, self-esteem, *le besoin de se mettre au-dessus des autres.* A large survey of history does not belie these generalizations, and the history of the period since Rousseau wrote lends them a melancholy verisimilitude. Precisely the two processes which he described have, during that period, been going on upon a scale beyond all precedent: immense progress in man's knowledge and in his power over nature, and at the same time, a steady increase of rivalries, distrust, hatred, and at last *le plus horrible état de guerre.* At the present moment Europe and a great part of Asia offer a vivid illustration of Rousseau's fourth stage; and of the seats of older civilization, at least, it is not yet certain that he did not draw a prophetic picture, when he described how

le genre humain, avili et désolé, ne pouvant renoncer aux acquisitions malheureuses qu'il avait faites et ne travaillant qu'à sa honte, par l'abus des facultés qui l'honorent, se mit à la veille de sa ruine.

Nor was his determination of the principal cause of the second and sinister process mistaken, except in a detail. Though he did not overlook the fact altogether, he failed to realize fully how strongly *amour-propre* tends to assume a collective form. Its more extreme individual manifestations being sharply repressed within any compact and homogeneous social group, it finds an effective substitute in group-vanity and intergroup animosity—in pride of race, of nationality, of class. This

" pooled self-esteem," as a recent writer has aptly termed it,[20] is at once more difficult to control and infinitely more powerful for mischief than the individual form of the passion.   But subject to this qualification, recent history and the present state of things all too abundantly confirm Rousseau's account of the part played by this motive in human events and of its potency to generate in men a *penchant à se nuire mutuellement.*

[20] Mr. A Clutton-Brock in *Atlantic Monthly* (December, 1921), pp. 722-31.

III. MONBODDO AND ROUSSEAU [1]

O N THE thirtieth of September, 1769, Boswell and his hero were dining at the Mitre. Boswell had for some time been subject to intermittent yearnings to return to the state of nature. There were few of the intellectual diseases epidemic in his day which he did not catch. As Miss Lois Whitney's researches have shown, certain forms of primitivism seem in the 1750's and 1760's to have ravaged Boswell's native region more extensively than they did the southern portions of the island,[2] and though his earlier hero-worship of Rousseau had now abated, some of its effects persisted. In any case, scarcely any topic could have been more serviceable to what for Boswell, when in London, was the chief end of life—to find subjects of conversation sufficiently provocative to stir the Great Bear to one of his best outbursts. Boswell, therefore, on this occasion, as he tells us, " attempted to argue for the superior happiness of the savage life, upon the usual fanciful topics."

JOHNSON. ' Sir, there can be nothing more false. The savages have no bodily advantages beyond those of civilized men. They have not better health; and as to care or mental uneasiness, they are not above it, but below it, like bears. No, Sir; you are not to talk such paradox: let me have no more on't. It cannot entertain, far less can it instruct. Lord Monboddo, one of your Scotch Judges, talked a great deal of such nonsense. I suffered *him*; but I will not suffer *you*.'—BOSWELL. ' But, Sir, does not Rousseau talk such nonsense? '—JOHNSON. ' True, Sir, but Rousseau *knows* he is talking nonsense, and laughs at the world for staring at him.'

BOSWELL. ' How so, Sir? '—JOHNSON. ' Why, Sir, a man who talks nonsense so well, must know that he is talking nonsense. But I am

---

[1] First published in *Modern Philology*, XXX (1933), 275-296.
[2] " English Primitivistic Theories of Epic Origins," *Mod. Phil.*, XXI (1924), 337-78. For an example of Boswell in a primitivistic mood, cf. *Letters of James Boswell*, ed. Tinker (1924), I, 98 (February 1, 1767): "You are tempted to join Rousseau in preferring the savage state. I am so too at times. When jaded with business, or when tormented with the passions of civilized life, I could fly to the woods," etc.

afraid (chuckling and laughing), Monboddo does *not* know that he is talking nonsense..' [3]

Boswell, it need not be added, was not wholly crushed, even by this, and he presently observed that he had himself sometimes "been in the humor of wishing to retire to a desert." Than the retort which this pose drew there are few more perfectly Johnsonian: "Sir, you have desert enough in Scotland." [4]

When, then, Johnson and Boswell fell to talking of what we now call "primitivism," the two contemporaries whose names

---

[3] *Boswell's Life of Johnson*, ed. G. B. Hill (Oxford, 1887), II, 73-74. For Dr. Johnson's view of the savage life, cf. also the *Adventurer*, No. 67 (1753). On the other hand, in the *Rambler*, No. 33 (1750), Johnson had drawn a picture of a primitive Golden Age which was brought to an end when men began to desire private property. "Then entered violence and fraud, and theft and rapine. Soon after pride and envy broke out in the world, and brought with them a new standard of wealth, for men, who till then thought themselves rich when they wanted nothing, now rated their demands, not by the calls of nature but by the plenty of others; and began to consider themselves poor, when they beheld their own possessions exceeded by those of their neighbors." In this version of the Golden Age, however, "Rest" takes the place of Astraea. In this passage Johnson had thus anticipated the so-called primitivistic and communistic strain in Rousseau's discourses. But this is, of course, not in the least surprising, since the opening part of the essay was simply a new mixture of bits from Aratus, Ovid, and Seneca, while Rousseau's discourses, in so far as they were primitivistic, were for the most part only further variations upon the same classical themes.

[4] Monboddo did not take Johnson's jokes in good part; in his *Origin and Progress of Language* (hereafter cited as *O. and P.*) (2d ed., 1789), V, 262-75, he assails the taste, the learning, and even the character of the Great Cham with a good deal of venom. Johnson was "neither a scholar nor a man of taste"; he was not "the twentieth part of the tythe of a critic"; he was "the most invidious and malignant man I have ever known, who praised no author or book that other people praised, and in private conversation was ready to cavil at and contradict every thing that was said, and could not with any patience hear any other person draw the attention of the company for ever so short a time." The explicit ground of this outburst, however, lay not in Johnson's attacks upon Monboddo (which Boswell had not failed to report to his countryman), but, on the one hand, in Johnson's disparagement of Milton's English and Latin style, and, on the other hand, in his remark that "*Paradise Lost* is not the greatest of heroic poems, only because it is not the first." In Monboddo's opinion, "the subject of the *Paradise Lost* is much too high for poetical imitation; whereas the story of Homer's *Iliad* is the best subject for an epic poem that ever was invented, or to speak more properly, that ever was chosen." Some of Monboddo's strictures on Johnson's literary criticism and his scholarship are not without point. The mutual esteem manifested by them, as host and guest, on the occasion of Johnson's visit to Monboddo in 1773—one of the most engaging passages in Boswell's *Tour to the Hebrides*—evidently did not last.

first occurred to them as representatives of that "paradox" were the author of the two *Discours de Dijon* and a Scottish Lord of Session whose theories were not to be published to the world until four years later, but were already notorious in the circles in which he moved in Edinburgh and London—the difference between the two, in Johnson's opinion, being merely that the Scot was a sincere, and the French writer an insincere, primitivist.

The truth was, however, that this, though not wholly groundless, was a seriously misleading conception of both; and the student of the history of ideas today who simply sets down Rousseau and Monboddo as " primitivists " misses the really important and interesting fact about them. That both sometimes dilated on the felicities of the savage life cannot, of course, be denied. Monboddo—or James Burnet, as he was before his elevation to the bench—had entered Marischal College of the University of Aberdeen in 1728, being then fourteen years old, and had thus early come under the influence of Thomas Blackwell the younger; and some favorite ideas of the Aberdeen primitivists, with which he may have been indoctrinated at this tender age, continued throughout his life to influence his opinions on certain matters. Yet his chief significance in the intellectual history of Great Britain is not as a spokesman of primitivism, but as one of the initiators (in that country) of a new way of thinking which tended to destroy primitivism. And in this his position was parallel to that of Rousseau—at least of the Rousseau of the *Discourse on the Origin of Inequality*. That the comparatively original, innovating, historically momentous thing in that discourse was precisely the reverse of what many of the historians of French literature and of philosophy have represented it as being, I have shown in the preceding essay. Though a good deal of the long-traditional primitivism still survived in the *Second Discourse*, the feature of it whereby it helped to introduce a new phase in the history of thought consisted in a sort of sociological evolutionism—and evolutionism is in essence, of course, the logical opposite of primitivism, though in the middle of the eighteenth century the two appear in several curious combinations. In the present paper I shall show that what I have previously observed with respect to Rousseau is also true of Monboddo; shall incidentally inquire whether the similarity between their ideas is attributable to Rousseau's influence upon the Scottish writer; and shall indicate the reasons for thinking that Monboddo went even farther in this way than Rousseau.

In Monboddo's chief work, as in Rousseau's *Discourse*, the following six theses, all of them unusual and some of them startling novelties in the third quarter of the eighteenth century, are to be found.

1. That the state of nature, or original condition of mankind, was a condition of pure animality, in which our ancestors possessed no language, no social organization, almost no practical arts, and in general were in no way distinguished from the apes by intellectual attainments or mode of life.

2. That, therefore, the state of nature, properly so called, was not an ideal state, except with regard to the physical condition of the human animal. It was a phase from which it was not only inevitable but desirable that mankind should emerge. On this point, however, the utterances of both Rousseau and Monboddo are not wholly free from inconsistency; and both, though not truly primitivists, might be called " retrospectivists "; they both saw the best chapter of human history in an earlier, though by no means in the earliest, phase of man's development, though Rousseau found it in the pastoral stage of cultural evolution and Monboddo in ancient Greece.

3. That man and the " orang-outang " are of the same species; in other words, that the orang-outangs are a portion of the human race who, for some reason, have failed to develop as the rest of it has done; and that, therefore, we may see in these animals approximate examples of the characteristics of our early ancestors and of their manner of life.

4. That, as the foregoing propositions suggest, the chief psychological differentia of the human species consists not in any mental attributes or powers discoverable in mankind throughout its history and therefore present from the beginning, but solely in a capacity for the gradual unfolding of higher intellectual faculties—what Turgot and Rousseau called *perfectibilité*. Thus man's history begins in a stage in which,

in a sense, he was not yet human, in which he was essentially differentiated from other animals only by a latent potency of progress. It was not until he emerged from the state of nature that he began to be truly man.

5. That, therefore, human history—at least up to a certain point—should be regarded, not as it had very commonly been regarded, as a process of decline from a primitive perfection, a gradual dimming of the pure light of nature by which men had at first been illumined, but rather as a slow, painful ascent from animality, though savagery, to the life of a rational and social being.

6. That, consequently, there was needed a new historical science which should trace out the successive stages of this process of intellectual development and social evolution, and that for this purpose what was chiefly requisite was a far more thorough study than had ever yet been made of the life of contemporary savages—that is, of races who still remained at one or another of the typical cultural stages through which the ancestors of civilized peoples must be supposed to have passed.

That all of these theses are to be found in Rousseau's second *Discourse* I have previously shown; I shall now cite some illustrations of them from Monboddo—chiefly from the first volume of his *Origin and Progress of Language* (1773), and from some of his letters published in Professor Knight's volume, *Lord Monboddo and Some of His Contemporaries* (1900).

1. *Character of the state of nature.*—It is, says Monboddo, an established fact

that there have been in the world, and are still, herds of men (for they do not deserve the name of nations) living in a state entirely brutish, and, indeed, in some respects, more wild than that of certain brutes, as they have neither government nor arts. . . . Wherever there is progress, there must be a beginning; and the beginning in this case can be no other than the mere animal. For in tracing back the progress, where else can we stop? If we have discovered so many links of the chain, we are at liberty to suppose the rest, and conclude, that the beginning of it must hold of that common nature which connects us with the rest of the animal creation. From savage men we are naturally led to consider the condition of the brutes; between whom and the savages there is such a resemblance, that there are many who will hardly admit of any difference; and even betwixt us and them at the time of our birth, and for some considerable time after, there is not any material difference.[5]

Monboddo wrote similarly to his friend James Harris, the author of *Hermes*, in 1772:

I believe that I shall be thought by many to have sunk our nature too low. For though nobody has a higher idea than I of Human Nature, when it is improved by the arts of Life and exalted by Science and Philosophy, I cannot conceive it—before the invention of language— to have been in a state much superior to that of the brute. In short the *mutum ac turpe pecus* of Horace is my notion of man in his natural and original state; and in support of my philosophy, I have appealed to History—both ancient and modern—for proof of the brutal condition in which many nations have been found and are still to be found even though they have some use of speech. From which we may justly infer how much more abject and brutish their condition must have been before they had the use of speech at all.[6]

2. *Undesirability of the state of nature.*—Obviously it is inconceivable that Monboddo should have lamented man's emergence from this " abject and brutish condition " or have wished the race to return to it; on the contrary, he has expressly told us that human nature attains its high estate only " when it is improved by the arts of Life, and exalted by Science and Philosophy." Yet there are in Monboddo, as in Rousseau, passages which might easily be taken for eulogies of this state of nature which they had both depicted in such unalluring terms. With respect to Rousseau the apparent incongruity between these two positions was pointed out by Voltaire: " Pour raisonner conséquemment, tout ennemi du luxe doit croire avec Rousseau que l'état de bonheur et de vertu pour l'homme est celui, non de sauvage, mais d'orang-outang." [7] The explanation of the supposed incongruity is, in great part, that both writers, when extolling the " natural condition of mankind," were referring primarily to the bodily superiority of the primeval brute and lamenting the physical deterioration of our

---

[5] *O. and P.* 2d ed. (1774), I, 147.
[6] Knight, *op. cit.*, p. 73.
[7] *Dict. philos.*, art. " Luxe."

species, which they believed to be due to the luxuries of civilized life. Thus Monboddo:

> If it be true, as I most firmly believe it is, that the state in which God and Nature have placed man is the best, at least so far as concerns his body, and that no art can make any improvement upon the natural habit and constitution of the human frame; then, to know this natural state is of the highest importance and most useful in the practice of the several arts, and in the whole conduct of life. The object, for example, of the physician's art must be to restore, so far as possible, the body to that natural state, which must therefore be the standard of perfection of his art. The political philosopher, in like manner, will study to preserve the natural strength and vigor of the animal . . . by proper diet, exercise, and manner of life. . . . And lastly, every private man . . . if he is wise, will, if he knows this natural state, endeavor to bring himself back to it, as much as is consistent with the state of society in which we live; and will, after the example of the great men of antiquity, endure thro' choice, those hardships, such as they are commonly thought, which the savage only endures through necessity, without knowing that they are absolutely necessary to his happiness.[8]

Monboddo's passages on the advantages of the state of nature, then, were a way of expressing an ideal rare in his age and, doubtless, greatly in need of propaganda—that of physical fitness. He inveighs against the " constant intemperance in eating and drinking " of his contemporaries, and laments that " athletic exercises, at least such as are proper to give any great degree of strength and agility to the body, are almost entirely disused." [9] He was, in short, an early and zealous, if ineffectual, prophet of physical culture and a preacher of the hygienic value of a rather Spartan regimen.[10] His occasional praises

[8] *O. and P.*, I, iii; also p. ii: " The political philosopher . . . will study to preserve the natural strength and vigour of the animal (human art can do it), by proper exercise, and manner of life, and to prevent, as much as possible, the indulgence of ease and bodily pleasure, by which the race of civilized men, in all nations, has been constantly declining from the earliest times."

[9] *Ibid.*, III, 453; cf. also I, 447 n.: " The fact no doubt is true, that man is at present more liable to disease than any other animal; but the blame ought to be laid where it truly lies, upon bad manners and institutions, and the many ingenious arts we have invented for the destruction of our bodies, not upon God and nature."

[10] The need for such preaching in Scotland at this period is illustrated in Dean Ramsay's *Reminiscences of Scottish Life and Character* (1858).

of the state of nature are to be explained partly as survivals of an old convention, but chiefly as inspired by nothing more paradoxical than the laudable aim of improving the physical condition of eighteenth-century mankind. But of the ethical naturalism which was a frequent concomitant of primitivism and of the general philosophy of history which it implied, Monboddo was rather an adversary than an advocate. He believed in the deteriorating influence of the arts and sciences only in so far as they make for luxury and physical softness; and, unlike Rousseau, he did not think this an inevitable consequence of the cultivation of them. On the contrary, he maintained that " it is only by means of our arts and sciences that we have any advantages over savages." [11]

There cannot be virtue, properly so called, until man is become a rational and political animal; then he shows true courage, very different from the ferocity of the brute or savage, generosity, magnanimous contempt of danger and of death; friendship and love of the country, with all the other virtues which so much exalt human nature, but which we can as little expect to find in the mere savage as in the brute, or infant of our species.[12]

3. *Man and the orang-outang.*—Rousseau had buried his suggestion of our kinship with the apes in a note, where it doubtless escaped the attention even of many readers of his own time, as it has apparently eluded that of most subsequent historians. But Monboddo devoted more than a hundred pages to the defense of this hypothesis; and it was probably above all with this doctrine that his name was associated in the minds of most of his contemporaries, after the first volume of the *Origin and Progress* appeared in 1773.[13] Here was an even richer theme than Monboddo's notions about savages for Johnson's gibes: " Sir, it is as possible that the *Ouran-Outang* does

[11] *O. and P.*, III, 455; cf. also pp. 463-66.
[12] *Ibid.*, I, 440.
[13] Rousseau and Monboddo are the " recent writers " referred to by the "founder of anthropology," J. F. Blumenbach, in his doctoral dissertation, *De generis humani varietate nativa* (1775), as having " not blushed at advancing the doctrine of man's kinship with the oran-utan "—which Blumenbach here treats cavalierly as " needing no long refutation *apud rei peritos.*" An English version of this may be found in Blumenbach's *Anthropological Treatises*, trans. T. Bendyshe (1865), 95.

not speak, as that he speaks. However, I shall not contest the point. I should have thought it not possible to find a Monboddo; yet *he* exists." "It is a pity," said Johnson again, " to see Lord Monboddo publish such notions as he has done; a man of sense, and of so much elegant learning. There would be little in a fool doing it; we should only laugh; but when a wise man does it, we are sorry. Other people have strange notions, but they conceal them. If they have tails, they hide them; but Monboddo is as jealous of his tail as a squirrel." The history of science and philosophy in the ensuing century was to turn the edge of *this* jest very cruelly against Dr. Johnson. " Sir," he said to Boswell, about a month after the publication of the first volume of the *Origin and Progress*—" Sir, it is all conjecture about a thing useless, even were it known to be true. Knowledge of all kinds is good. Conjecture, as to things useful, is good; but conjecture as to what it would be useless to know, such as whether men went upon all four, is very idle." [14] Johnson too was a man of uncommon sense and of much elegant learning; but that remark was perhaps the most profoundly stupid thing said by any man of his generation. To *reject* what Boswell calls " Lord Monboddo's strange speculation about the primitive state of human nature " was but natural conservatism, such as was to be expected of a man of Johnson's time and temper; but to pronounce the question raised unimportant and idle was to betray a strange blindness to the significance of ideas, a singular lack of the scientific and philosophic imagination. How Monboddo shines by comparison, in the conclusion—stated with the moderation of the scientific spirit—of his two chapters on the orang-outang!

That my facts and arguments are so convincing as to leave no doubt of the humanity of the orang-outang, I will not take upon me to say; but thus much I will venture to affirm, that I have said enough to make the philosopher consider it as problematical, and a subject deserving to be inquired into.[15]

The term " orang-outang " for Monboddo was apparently a generic one, applicable also to the gorilla and the chimpanzee,

---

[14] *Boswell's Life of Johnson*, ed. Hill, V, 46, 111; II, 259-60 (May 8, 1773).
[15] *O. and P.*, I, 360.

and, indeed, usually referring rather to these African apes than to the orang-outang of Borneo or Sumatra. His primary reason for asserting our probable consanguinity with these anthropoids was, so far as it went, of an entirely legitimate scientific sort: it consisted in the facts of comparative anatomy then recently set forth by Buffon and Daubenton in the *Histoire naturelle*. From these it appeared, Monboddo says, that

as to his body, he [the orang-outang] is altogether man, both outside and inside, excepting some small variations, such as cannot make a specific difference between the two animals, and I am persuaded are less considerable than are to be found betwixt individuals that are undoubtedly of the human species. And, more particularly, he has, says Mr. Buffon, the tongue and the other organs of pronunciation the same as those of man; and the brain is altogether of the same form and the same size. He and man have the same viscera . . . exactly of the same structure, and they alone have buttocks and calfs of the leg, which make them more proper for walking upright than any other animal.[16]

Monboddo, however, was more interested in the "inward principle" of the orang, the "habits and dispositions of the mind," than he was in the animal's anatomy; and in these, even more than in the homologies of physical structure, he found evidence of the identity of species between these apes and ourselves. On the manners and customs of the gorilla and the chimpanzee he diligently collected evidence from many sources; upon some of the witnesses he relied rather more confidingly

[16] *Ibid.*, 271. Monboddo was apparently acquainted also with Edward Tyson's *Orang-outang, sive homo sylvestris; or, the anatomy of a Pygmie compared with that of a Monkey, an Ape, and a Man* (1699), the first competent study of the anatomy of a chimpanzee; and Tyson's description of the organs of speech of that animal was, for Monboddo, important evidence in favor of his theory; cf. Ashley Montagu's admirable work on the English anatomist, *Edward Tyson* (1943), 270. Tyson also provided a comprehensive review of previous descriptions of the anthropoid apes, which was doubtless useful to Monboddo. Tyson was an ardent believer in the continuity of the Chain of Being, and therefore approximated, without actually reaching, Monboddo's conclusion: " in this Chain of Creation, as an intermediate link between an Ape and a Man, I would place our Pygmie," *i. e.*, chimpanzee. "The animal of which I have given the anatomy seems the nexus of the Animal and Rational." Nevertheless Tyson in the end pronounces him "to be wholly a Brute." (*Orang-outang*, pp. iii, 5.) The anatomical resemblance between man and the chimpanzee was, of course, less than was usually supposed in Monboddo's time, and did not justify the theory of identity of "species."

than might have been expected of an experienced Scots advocate and judge. From all of the descriptions available to him, he concludes:

The sum and substance of all these relations is, that the Orang Outang is an animal of the human form, inside as well as outside: That he has the human intelligence, as much as can be expected of an animal living without civility and the arts: That he has a disposition of mind mild, docile and humane: That he has the sentiments and affections common to our species, such as the sense of modesty, of honour, and of justice; and likewise an attachment of love and friendship to one individual so strong in some instances, that the one friend will not survive the other: That they live in society and have some arts of life; for they build huts, and use an artificial weapon for attack and defence, *viz.*, a stick; which no animal merely brute is known to do. . . . They appear likewise to have some civility among them, and to practise certain rites, such as that of burying the dead. It is from these facts that we are to judge whether or not the Orang-Outang belongs to our species. Mr. Buffon has decided that he does not. Mr. Rousseau inclines to a different opinion. The first seems to be sensible of the weight of the facts against him. . . . There are some of our naturalists . . . who having formed systems without facts, adjust the facts to their prejudicated opinions, believing just as much of them as suits their purpose, and no more. Of this number, I take Mr. Buffon to be, who has formed to himself a definition of man, by which he makes the faculty of speech a part of his essence and nature; and having thus defined man, he boldly avers, that the pure state of nature, in which man had not the use of speech, is a state altogether ideal and imaginary, and such as never had any real existence.[17]

Monboddo has often been ridiculed, in his own time and since, for his affecting picture of the gentlemanly gorilla and the civil chimpanzee; and it can hardly be denied that he had

[17] *O. and P.*, I, 289-93. Monboddo is here probably referring chiefly to Buffon's passage on this subject in *Histoire naturelle*, Tome XIV (1766); cf. especially pp. 3-4, 30-33, 37-38, 41-42. Buffon's conclusion is " Je l'avoue, si l'on ne devoit juger que par la forme, l'espèce du singe pourroit être prise pour une variété dans l'espèce humaine." Neverthless, " quelque ressemblance qu'il y ait entre l'Hottentot et le singe, l'intervalle qui les sépare est immense, puisqu'à l'intérieur, il est rempli par la pensée, et au dehors par la parole." Monboddo seeks to eliminate this twofold " interval " by asserting the fairly considerable intelligence of the orang-outang, and by arguing that man was originally devoid of speech. On the variations in Buffon's views on the theory of organic evolution in general, see the writer's " Buffon and the Problem of Species," *Popular Science Monthly*, LXXIX (1911), 464-473 and 554-567.

formed a somewhat too exalted conception of the intellectual parts and the charm of temperament of our cousins of the Simiidae. Of the refinement of the female of the species, in particular, he cites some rather surprising examples from " Bontius the Batavian physician " [18] and others; it would seem that the apes of the gentler sex are modest to the point of prudery, and of a somewhat excessive sensibility. Yet Monboddo, while exaggerating on one side, was nearer to the truth than most later writers until a very recent time. A number of the accomplishments which he attributed to the higher anthropoids they have now been shown—after a century and a half of scientific skepticism—actually to possess. Köhler has proved that chimpanzees are not only tool-using but tool-fabricating animals; and the " almost human " traits of these apes have been shown by the careful studies of Yerkes and Kearton.[19]

So considerable, however, are the attainments credited to the orang-outang by some of the observers whom Monboddo quotes, that the necessary inference, from his own point of view, would be that the orang-outang does *not* represent to us the primitive condition of mankind—as Monboddo elsewhere depicts it, and as Rousseau had done before him—but a more advanced stage; and, indeed, he draws this inference himself. In the pure state

[18] Jakob de Bondt, whose *Historia Naturalis et Medica Indiae Orientalis* (1658) contained a chapter (Bk. V, ch. 32) on the " *orang-outang sive homo silvestris,* which concluded *nihil ei humani deesse praeter loquelam.* Bontius's ape was not the chimpanzee, but the orang-outang of Borneo and Sumatra, where he had for a number of years resided.

[19] Köhler, *The Mentality of Apes* (1924); Koffka, *The Growth of the Mind* (1924), chap. iv; Yerkes, *Almost Human* (1925); C. Kearton, *My Friend Toto* (1925). Some of the observations of Yerkes may be cited as close parallels to some passages of Monboddo's: " Again and again it has been demonstrated in connection with tests of intelligence that the orang-utan, the chimpanzee and the gorilla can and do use objects effectively to attain such desired ends as foods, freedom, and opportunity to play. The results of experiments . . . are indicative of an order of intelligence which certainly suggests the human, if it does not closely approach it." " The primates exhibit in varying forms the principal types of emotion which appear in man. . . . It is not at all surprising that scientists should feel that the chimpanzee is more nearly human in its emotional life than in any other way. . . . This picture of the tender aspect of the emotional life of the monkeys and great apes may give the reader reason to pause and reflect. Are we humans after all so nearly unique in our flaunted altruism? " Kearton's young chimpanzee Toto was hardly at all less " human " than Monboddo's " orang-outangs."

of nature, Monboddo holds, with Rousseau, that man was a
" solitary wild beast " having " no natural propensity to enter
society," and therefore living neither in herds nor in family
groups.   But since the orang-outangs, according to Monboddo's
informants, sometimes

live together in society; act together in concert, particularly in attacking
elephants; build huts, and no doubt practice other arts, both for sustenance and defence: . . . they may be reckoned to be in the first stage
of human progression, being associated, and practising certain arts of
life; but not so far advanced as to have invented the great art of
language.[20]

Like Rousseau, it will have been noted, Monboddo believed
in the *bonté naturelle* of the orang-outang; that animal, though
not capable of morality properly so called, has, and *a fortiori*
the truly primitive members of our species had, a " mild " and
" gentle " disposition.   And like Rousseau, again, Monboddo
takes occasion, in this connection, to emphasize his dissent from
Hobbes:

I would not have it understood, that I believe, as Mr. Hobbes does,
that man is naturally the enemy of man; and that the *state of nature*
is a state of *war* of every man against every man.   This is such a state
as neither does exist, nor ever did exist, in any species of animals.   And,
however ingenious Mr. Hobbes may have been, (and he certainly was a
very acute man, and much more learned than those who now-a-days
set up for masters of philosophy), it is plain to me, that he did not
know what man was by nature, divested of all the habits and opinions
that he acquires in civil life; but supposed that, previous to the institution of society, he had all the desires and passions that he now has.[21]

This, obviously, implied that the desires and ambitions which
make man pugnacious and set him at variance with his fellows
have been developed since he adopted the habit of living in
society, and that his antisocial passions are thus in some sense
a product of the social state.   This idea plays a great part in
Rousseau's *Second Discourse*; as I have pointed out, while he
rejects Hobbes's psychology when picturing man in the state of
nature, he accepts it as true—and increasingly true—of man in

[20] *O. and P.*, I, 268-80.   [21] *Ibid.*, p. 222.

civilized society, so that the stage which in Rousseau is at four removes from *his* " state of nature " corresponds pretty exactly to the " state of nature " of the philosopher of Malmesbury.[22] But Monboddo does not make a great deal of the point; he takes a much less unfavorable view than Rousseau of human nature under the conditions of social life.

Was Monboddo, unlike Rousseau, an evolutionist in the biological as well as in the anthropological sense—i. e., did he accept the general hypothesis of the transformation of species which had already been propounded by Maupertuis and Diderot?[23] So far as his published treatise is concerned, the answer would at first seem to be in the negative. The importance he attaches to showing that man and the orang-outang are of the same species might naturally be taken to imply that animals of different species cannot be descended one from the other or from common ancestors. And in one passage he expressly denies intending to suggest that we are akin to the monkeys as well as to the great apes:

Though I hold the Orang Outang to be of our species, it must not be supposed that I think the monkey or ape, with or without a tail, participates of our nature; on the contrary, I maintain that, however much his form may resemble ours, yet he is, as Linnaeus says of the Troglodyte, *nec nostri generis, nec sanguinis.*[24]

The principal reason he gives for this is that " neither monkey, ape nor baboon, have anything mild or gentle, tractable or docile, benevolent or humane, in their dispositions; but on the contrary, are malicious and untractable, to be governed only by force and fear, and without any gravity or composure in their gait and behaviour, such as the Orang Outang has." Thus those traits of the *bandarlog* which to some have seemed rather to indicate their kinship with humanity are cited by Monboddo as evidence that they cannot be related to the orang-outang, nor, therefore, to us.

Yet there are reasons for thinking that his real belief inclined

[22] See the preceding essay.
[23] See my " Some Eighteenth Century Evolutionists," *Popular Science Monthly,* (1904), 240-51, 323-27.
[24] *O. and P.,* I, 311.

to the wider hypothesis which in the passage last cited he disclaims. In a letter of June, 1773—that is, very shortly after the publication of the first volume of his book—he writes:

I think it is very evident that the Orang-Outang is above the simian race, to which I think you very rightly disclaim the relation of brother, though I think that race is of kin to us, though not so nearly related. For the large baboons appear to me to stand in the same relation to us, that the ass does to the horse, or our gold-finch to the canary-bird.[25]

This, apparently, can only mean that all the apes, the monkeys and man are descended from common ancestors. As Monboddo would not have classified all of these as belonging to a single species, he implied that the descent of one species from another is possible. And even in the *Origin and Progress of Language* the same belief is more than hinted at. Monboddo introduces into that work several accounts of the existence, in various parts of the world, of men with tails.[26] There was, for example, a Swedish naval lieutenant, whose good faith was vouched for by no less a person than Linnaeus, who had reported that, when sailing in the Bay of Bengal, he had " come upon the coast of one of the Nicobar Islands, where they saw men with tails like those of cats, and which they moved in the same manner." [27] A similar story had been recorded by the great Harvey. It was not, however, necessary to go to the remote parts of the earth for examples; Monboddo offered " to produce legal evidence by witnesses yet living " concerning a teacher of mathematics in Inverness who " had a tail half a foot long," which he carefully concealed during his life, " but was discovered after his death, which happened about twenty

---

[25] Knight, *Lord Monboddo and His Contemporaries*, p. 85.

[26] The existence of tailed men had been asserted by Pliny *Nat. hist.* vii. 2 and not rejected by Linnaeus, *System naturae* (2d ed., 1766), I, 33; and Robinet had devoted a chapter of his *Gradation naturelle des formes de l'être* to the evidence for the reality of *hommes à queue*, which to him illustrated how *finement nuancée* is the scale of being. The (tailless) pongo " is connected with man by an infinity of similarities; man must be connected by other characteristics with species far below the pongo " (*De la nature*, V [1768], 160). Robinet, however, held the pongo and orang-outang to be " not truly men " but " an intermediate species which fills up the transition from the ape to man " (*ibid.*, p.151). He has a place with Maupertuis and Diderot among the French pioneers of evolutionism.

[27] *O. and P.*, I, 258.

years ago." What is certain, at any rate, as Monboddo points out, is that we all have rudimentary tails, in the form of the *os coccygis*. Now the anthropoids, as Monboddo knew, have no tails, or at least none much more developed than man's, and his stories of *homines caudati*, therefore, were without pertinency in an argument for our kinship with the orang-outang. He himself remarks that he relates " this extraordinary fact concerning our species as a matter of curiosity, though it belong not to [his] subject, except in so far as it tends to give us more enlarged views of human nature." But the occasional existence of tailed men, and the presence of vestigial tails in both man and orang-outang, would tend to indicate that both are descended from remote ancestors who were endowed with that pleasing and useful member. And that Monboddo meant, by these considerations, to suggest that hypothesis may be seen from a remark in one of his footnotes:

Those who have not studied the variety of nature in animals, and particularly in man, the most various of all animals, will think this story, of men with tails, very ridiculous; and will laugh at the credulity of the author for seeming to believe such stories; But the philosopher, who is more disposed to inquire than to laugh and deride, will not reject it at once, as a thing incredible, that there should be such a variety in our species, as well as in the simian tribe, which is of so near kin to us.[28]

Now " the simian tribe " meant, in Monboddo's terminology, not the orang-outangs, but the monkeys; so that he here affirms the probable truth of the view which on another page he seems to deny. One may conclude, therefore, that he accepted in principle the general possibility of the transformation of species and that he definitely asserted, as a probable hypothesis, the community of descent of most or all of the Anthropoidea. He was thus (so far as I know) the first British proponent of evolutionism, or near-evolutionism, in biology; he anticipated Erasmus Darwin's *Zoönomia* by twenty years.[29]

[28] *Ibid.*, 262.
[29] Akenside had, however, somewhat obscurely foreshadowed the theory of descent in *Pleasures of the Imagination* (1744), Book II; cf. G. R. Potter in *Mod. Phil.*, XXIV (1926), 55-64, and Lovejoy, *The Great Chain of Being*, 263-5.

Monboddo, of course, was well enough aware of the sort of sentimental objection which his hypothesis would evoke—the objection against evolutionism which a Bishop of Oxford repeated on a famous occasion nearly a century later. But he met it stoutly, with virtually the reply which the contemporary evolutionist usually employs:

As to the vulgar, I can never expect that they should acknowledge any kinship with those inhabitants of the woods of Angola; but that they should continue, thro' a false pride, to think highly derogatory from human nature, what the philosopher, on the contrary, will think the highest praise of man, that, from the savage state, in which the Orang Outang lives, he should, by his own sagacity and industry, have arrived at the state in which we now see him.[30]

4. *The specific differentia of " homo sapiens."*—Whatever room for dispute there may be—Rousseau had said in the *Discourse on Inequality*—respecting the differences between men and other animals,

there is one very specific quality which distinguishes them, and about which there can be no controversy: this is the *faculté de se perfectionner,* a faculty which, with the aid of circumstances, gives rise one after another to all the rest, . . . whereas an animal is, at the end of a few months, what he will be all his life, and his species at the end of a thousand years is what it was the first year of the thousand.

To the same theme Monboddo frequently recurs.

There is no *natural* difference between our minds and theirs [the brutes'] and the superiority we have over them is *adventitious.* . . . Allowing that . . . we can go farther than the brute with any culture can go (which I believe to be the case), this is saying no more than that . . . we have by Nature greater capabilities than they. . . . I deny that there is any other difference betwixt us and them.[31]

Man is called a " rational animal," but " this specific difference of *rational* does not consist in the energy or actual exercise of the faculty of reason, nor even in the possession; else the newborn infant would not be a man." And what is true of the individual is true of the race; the species had at the outset a mere

[30] *O. and P.*, I, 360; cf. also pp. 437-41.
[31] *Ibid.*, 147-49.

"*capability* of intellect and science," which long ages were required to develop. Monboddo as well as Rousseau had been anticipated in this remark in an anonymous writing published before 1740, whose author remarks:

I cannot but look on the common definition of man as *animal rationale*, to be somewhat *defective*. I think it might be altered for the better, though that would not be compleat, to define him *animal rationabile*, if *rationabile* may be allowed to signify the capacity of receiving, and not the actual exercise, of reason. . . . This definition is proper, whereas Aristotle's is not which makes him *animal rationale*, as if he were actually and not only potentially so, by his specific nature, without any foreign help or culture.[32]

5. *The ascent of man.*—As all the foregoing implies, the attributes commonly regarded as distinctive of humanity were not created ready-made, but were arduously and slowly attained. Monboddo happily sums up the most significant thesis of his doctrine by an adaptation of a line of Vergil's: "Tantae molis erat *humanam* condere gentem." In short, nothing that is distinctive of man was primitive, and nothing that is most excellent in him comes by nature alone.

Monboddo was thus an evolutionist in a profounder sense than is implied by a belief in the identity of primitive man with the orang-outang. He was one of the few men of his time who really had what may be called the genetic habit of mind. The Aristotelian distinction "between the power of becoming anything, and the actually *being* that thing," or "between *capacity* and *energy*," is fundamental to his whole doctrine. And he declares that

this distinction runs through all nature, in which there is a perpetual progress from one state to the other, and that nothing *is* at first what it

---

[32] *A Philosophical Dissertation upon the Inlets to Human Knowledge* (reprinted; Dublin, 1740), 47, 57. Forty years after Monboddo Destutt de Tracy was still enunciating the same doctrine with the enthusiasm of a preacher of a new insight: "We have received from this admirable Nature—that is to say, from our own organization—only the possibility of perfecting ourselves. When we came from her hands, . . . we possessed only the germ of the means of attaining knowledge. . . . Thus we are entirely works of art, that is, of our own labor; and we have to-day as little resemblance to the man of nature, to our original mode of existence, as an oak has to an acorn or a fowl to an egg" (*Elémens d'idéologie* [1814; 3d ed., 1817], chap. xv, p. 289).

afterwards becomes. Now if anyone says that the human mind is an exception from this law of nature, he must prove it. But this he will never be able to do.[33]

Monboddo therefore did not shrink from saying—however much " some pious and well disposed persons " might " take offence "—that " the chief prerogative of human nature, the rational soul," is " of our own acquisition, and the fruit of industry, like any art and science, not the gift of nature." Whatever such a doctrine be called, it certainly cannot be called " primitivism." Yet even in our own day learned authors may be found declaring that Monboddo was " a primitivist of the extremest type." [34]

This way of thinking, moreover, struck at the heart, not merely of primitivism, but also of that uniformitarian conception of human nature with which from the sixteenth to the eighteenth centuries primitivism was commonly associated.[35] This was, indeed, already being undermined by the " theory of climates," especially through the influence of Montesquieu. But a still more serious attack upon it was that made by these early social evolutionists, Rousseau and Monboddo. Commenting upon the theories of certain political philosophers, Monboddo writes:

I must enter a caveat against the manner of reasoning which I observe is very common on this subject. In the first place, an hypothesis is laid down that man was from the beginning, in all ages and nations of the world, the same, or nearly the same, with what he is at present in Europe, or other civilized parts of the world. For it is a maxim constantly in the mouths of such reasoners, that human nature is and always has been the same. And, secondly, supposing this maxim to be undeniable, they argue, from the manners and customs of such men as we are; and because such and such institutions are practised by civilized nations, they conclude that they must have been always in use, and as old as the human race. . . . But I think I am at liberty to set hypothesis against hypothesis, and to suppose that man, so far from continuing the same creature, has varied more than any other being

---

[33] O. and P., I, 438.
[34] H. N. Fairchild, The Noble Savage, p. 331. Mr. Fairchild also notes, however, that Monboddo (incongruously) " anticipated the theory of evolution."
[35] On this see " The Parallel of Deism and Classicism," below.

that we know in Nature.   And tho' his nature may in some sense be
said to be the same, as he has still the same natural capabilities as he
had from the beginning; yet this nature is, by its original constitution,
susceptible of greater change than the nature of any other animal
known.   And that, in fact, it has undergone the greatest changes, is
proved, I say, first from the general history of mankind, by which it
appears, that there has been a gradual progress in arts and manners
among the several nations of the earth; . . . and secondly, from particular relations of the customs and manners of barbarous nations, both
antient and modern.[36]

In such a passage we may see one of the foreshadowings of
that distrust of universal formulas, that distinctively evolutionary relativism in political and social philosophy, which was
to be among the traits chiefly differentiating the thought of the
nineteenth century from that of the earlier modern centuries—
but which has been but imperfectly acquired even yet by a
large part of mankind.

6.   *Conception of an evolutionary universal history.*—Monboddo's original grand design had been to do on a large scale
what Rousseau had attempted in a brief, sketchy way in the
Discourse on the Origin of Inequality.   In 1766 Monboddo
wrote to Harris that he projected

a *History of Man* in which I would trace him through the several stages
of his existence; for there is a progression of our species from a state
little better than mere brutality to that most perfect state you describe
in ancient Greece, which is really amazing, and peculiar to our species.[37]

This plan he was compelled regretfully to abandon, finding it
" too extensive for [his] abilities and the time [he] had to
bestow on it "; and he therefore only attempted a part of the
original program, consisting chiefly of an account of the origin
and evolution of language.   On this narrower theme he contrived to write some three thousand pages in the intervals of his
judicial duties, and when about fifty years of age and upward.
With his linguistic speculations we are not here concerned;
what is to the point is merely that, like Rousseau, he had caught
a vision of a possible new sort of history—and that he insisted

[36] *O. and P.*, I, 443-44.
[37] *Lord Monboddo and His Contemporaries*, p. 50.

that such a science must rest upon a careful study of the actual life of peoples in the earlier stages of social evolution:

Those who have studied the history of *man*, not of particular nations only, that is, have studied history in the liberal and extensive view of discerning the nature of *man* from fact and experience, know very well, that all nations, even the most polished and civilized, of which we read in history, were originally barbarians. . . . Whoever, therefore, would trace human nature up to its source, must study very diligently the manners of barbarous nations, instead of forming theories of *man* from what he observes among civilized nations. Whether we can, in that way, by any discoveries hitherto made, trace man up to what I suppose his original state to have been, may perhaps be doubted; but it is certain that we can come very near it.[38]

Of the possibility of accomplishing such a task in his own time, Monboddo was unduly sanguine; but he expressed a just conception of the program to be followed, if a too favorable one of his actual achievement even with regard to the history of language, when he declared: " My system is founded, not upon hypothesis, but on the history of man, collected from facts, in the same manner as we collect the history of any other animal." [39]

Much of Monboddo's doctrine, then, and the part of it which was most revolutionary in his time, may fairly be said to be an elaboration of a group of interrelated ideas to be found in Rousseau's *Discourse on the Origin of Inequality*, published twenty years before the *Origin and Progress of Language*. Was the similarity due to the spontaneous occurrence of the same thoughts to two contemporary minds, or to the direct influence of the earlier works of the one writer upon the other? The question cannot be answered with certainty. Both were, of course, familiar with the Epicurean accounts of primeval man and of the gradual evolution of society, in Lucretius, Cicero, and Horace, especially the passage in Horace's *Satires* i. 3 (ll. 99 ff.) which Monboddo took as the motto of his book. Much of Rousseau's *Second Discourse* may be described as an ingenious combination of this anti-primitivistic strain in the classical tradition with the primitivistic strain in it represented,

[38] *O. and P.*, I, 145.
[39] *Ibid.*, 444.

in different ways, by Ovid and Seneca.[40] As Monboddo was primarily a classical scholar and an enthusiast for antiquity, it is entirely possible that, as Knight has assumed, his ideas on these matters were first suggested to him through his reading of ancient authors.[41] Both, also, were familiar with the facts disclosed by the progress of comparative anatomy in their century, and both were eager readers of descriptions, some of them recent, of primitive peoples and of the anthropoid apes. In particular, the increasingly numerous descriptions of those by no means noble savages, the Hottentots, by voyagers of the late seventeenth and eighteenth centuries tended strongly to suggest an unfavorable view of the "original condition of mankind."[42]

[40] Cf. *Primitivism and Related Ideas in Antiquity*, 43-49 and 263-286.

[41] Monboddo himself writes: "My opinion on this subject will, I know, be thought new and singular; but it is only an antient opinion revived; for I have shown that it was the opinion of the antient philosophers, as many as have treated of the original state of man before society or civilization" (*O. and P.*, I, v). The classical writers cited in support of this (*ibid.*, 368 ff.) are Horace, Lucretius, Plato (*Laws*, Book i; *Theaetetus* 186 c; *Timaeus* 47a), Diodorus Siculus, Cicero. Cf. also I, 298: "I have endeavored to support the antient definition of man, and to shew that it belongs to the Orang Outang, though he have not the use of speech."

[42] The combination of the almost universally current conception of nature as a continuum of forms (chain of being) with the facts reported about the Hottentots had long since led some writers of the late seventeenth and early eighteenth centuries to approximate, without actually anticipating, the doctrine which was to be propounded by Rousseau and Monboddo. Cf. the remark of Sir John Ovington, *Voyage to Surat* (1696), cited in *Modern Philology* by R. W. Frantz (XXVIII [1931], 55-57): The Hottentots are "the very Reverse of Human kind . . . so that if there's any medium between a Rational Animal and a Beast, the Hottentot lays the fairest claim to that species." Monboddo's theory had been still more nearly adumbrated by Blackmore and Hughes in the *Lay Monastery*: "Nothing is more surprising and delightful than to observe the Scale or gradual Ascent from Minerals to Plants, from Plants to Animals, and from Animals to human Nature. 'Tis easy to distinguish these Kinds, till you come to the highest of one, and the lowest of that next above it; and then the Difference is so nice, that the Limits and Boundaries of their Species seem left unsettled by Nature to perplex the curious, and to humble the proud Philosopher. As Man, who approaches nearest to the lowest class of Celestial Spirits (for we may justly suppose a subordination in that excellent Order), being half body and half Spirit, becomes the *Aequator*, that divides in the Middle the whole Creation, and distinguishes the Corporeal from the Invisible Intellectual World; so the Ape or Monkey, that bears the greatest Similitude to Man, is the next Order of Animals below him. Nor is the Disagreement between the basest Individuals of our species and the Ape or Monkey so great, but that were the latter endow'd with the Faculty of Speech, they might perhaps as justly claim

On the other hand, it is certain that Monboddo had read Rousseau's *Discourse* before writing his book; that the latter contains a number of passages very similar to some of Rousseau's; and that Monboddo was one of the most enthusiastic admirers whom Rousseau found among his own generation. " Even the philosophers (one only excepted) seem to know nothing of this state" of nature, Monboddo declares; the one exception is identified in a footnote as " Mr. Rousseau, a very great genius, in my judgment, but who has been thought whimsical and odd, for having said so much in commendation of the natural state of man." [43] Again, when insisting upon the indispensability of a study of existing savages if we would know the early condition of all mankind, instead of attempting " to form a system of *human* nature from what" we " observe among civilized nations only," Monboddo refers to " Mons. Rousseau, in his Treatise on the *Inequality of Men*, where he ridicules the folly of those who think they understand human nature, because they know the character and manners of their own nation, and perhaps some of the neighboring nations; and very wisely tell us that *man* is the same in all ages and in all nations." " I am very happy," adds Monboddo, " to find that my notions, both with respect to the original state of human nature, and the origin of language, agree so perfectly with the notions of an author of so much genius and original thought, as well as learning." [44] Monboddo, however, does not say that he derived his theory of the humanity of the orang-outang from Rousseau, and rather implies that he hit upon the great idea independently.

the Rank and Dignity of the human Race, as the savage *Hottentot*, or stupid native of Nova Zembla. . . . The most perfect of this Order of Beings, the *Orang Outang*, as he is called by the natives of *Angola*, that is, the Wild Man, or Man of the Woods, has the Honour of Bearing the greatest Resemblance to Human Nature. Tho' all that Species have some Agreement with us in our Features, many Instances being found of Men of Monkey Faces; yet this has the greatest Likeness, not only in his Countenance, but in the Structure of his Body, his Ability to walk upright, as well as on all fours, his Organs of Speech, his ready Apprehension, and his gentle and tender Passions, which are not found in any of the Ape Kind, and in various other respects " (No. 5 [1714], p. 28. This was a new edition of the *Lay Monk* [1713]).

[43] *O. and P.*, I, iii. That Rousseau had not represented " the natural state of man " as, on the whole, the ideal one, Monboddo was, of course, well aware.

[44] *Ibid.*, 152; cf. p. 381: " that singular genius which our age has produced, Mr. Rousseau."

Mons. Rousseau, in his work above quoted, note 10, has collected the several accounts given of this animal by travellers, and seems to agree with me in opinion that he belongs to our species, rejecting with great contempt the notion of those who think that speech is natural to man. Now, if we get over that prejudice, and do not insist, that other arts of life, which the Orang Outangs want, are likewise natural to man, it is impossible we can refuse them the appelation of *men*.[45]

All that can be confidently asserted on the matter is that Rousseau and Monboddo were brothers-in-arms, the two chief champions in their age of the six connected theses set down at the beginning of this paper, and that Rousseau's priority in the enunciation of all of them renders Monboddo's originality in these points somewhat questionable. He developed them, however, far more fully; by most educated persons in Great Britain in the eighties he was probably looked upon as their originator; and he with some wavering extended Rousseau's doctrine of the identity of species of man and the chimpanzee into the hypothesis of the common descent of all the anthropoids, and suggested by implication a general law of organic evolution. In this last he had already been anticipated by at least three French writers (Maupertuis, Diderot, Robinet) and by Leibniz; but of this he was apparently unaware, as were most of his British contemporaries—and as most historians of science continued to be for more than a century. It is not surprising, therefore, that a countryman of his has claimed for him—and therefore for Scotland—the credit usually given to the author of *The Origin of Species*:

> Though Darwin now proclaims the law,
>   And spreads it far abroad, O!
> The man that first the secret saw
>   Was honest old Monboddo.
> The architect precedence takes
>   Of him that bears the hod, O!
> So up and at them, Land o' Cakes,
>   We'll vindicate Monboddo.[46]

[45] *O. and P.*, I, 189.
[46] From lines " To the Memory of Lord Monboddo " by Lord Neaves (1800-1876), a judge of the same bench, cited by Knight, *op. cit.*, p. 20.

IV. "PRIDE" IN EIGHTEENTH-CENTURY THOUGHT

IT HAS doubtless been noted by most students of modern literature that satirists and moralizing writers in the late seventeenth and the eighteenth centuries were much preoccupied with a vice which they called "pride," and were usually given to denouncing it with peculiar vehemence. It has not always been noted that two different—though not unrelated—conceptions, or rather, groups of conceptions, were expressed by the word. On the one hand, it designated a "passion," or set of passions, which was recognized by many, not to say most, of the more acute literary psychologists of the period as the most powerful and pervasive motive of men's behavior, the "spring of action" which differentiates *homo sapiens* from all the other animals, and by which all his most distinctive human propensities and performances, good or bad, are to be explained. There is a long series of passages, in prose and verse, which dilate upon the diversity of the manifestations of this motive in the conduct of various types of individuals and upon its innumerable disguises, discuss the question—then deemed a highly important question—whether its consequences for society in general are preponderantly harmful or benign, and deduce conclusions pertinent to social ethics, politics and education from the assumption of its ubiquity and singular potency in the affective constitution of man. The term, even as the name for a determinant of men's behavior in their social relations, was equivocal; for it was often used to designate two distinct, though kindred, types of feeling or desire: self-esteem, or the craving to think well of oneself, in its many degrees and forms, especially its emulative form; and the desire for, and pleasure in, the esteem, admiration or applause of others, especially the craving for "distinction," the *fureur de se distinguer*. But in

62

one or the other, or both, of these senses, " pride " was one of
the most frequent and pregnant themes of what may be called
the social psychology of the period.[1]

But the pride to which such a typical writer as Pope, in the
Essay on Man, most frequently refers is not primarily the pride
of the individual human creature comparing himself with others
of his species, but the generic pride of man as such. The
featherless biped, it was observed, has a strange tendency to
put himself in the centre of the creation, to suppose himself
separated by a vast gap from all other and " irrational " creatures, to credit himself with the possession of virtues of which
he is inherently incapable, and to attempt tasks, especially intellectual tasks, which he has in reality no power to accomplish.
A sense of the dignity and importance of the *genus homo* had
been fostered by the medieval Christian view of man's place in
the universe. Though the Church had bidden the individual
man walk humbly with his God, and had dwelt upon the inner
corruption of unregenerate human nature, it had nevertheless
given its sanction to certain conceptions flattering to men's
racial self-esteem. Upon his own planet, at least, man reigned
supreme over the brute creation, infinitely removed in dignity
from even the highest animals by his sole participation in the
intellectual light of the divine Reason; all other terrestrial
creatures existed solely for his use and benefit; upon the acts
of will of individual men inexpressibly momentous issues depended; and the good which man was capable of attaining
immeasurably transcended all that could be experienced in this
temporal world of matter and sense. But there were certain
ideas especially current in (though not original with) the
eighteenth century which forbade mankind to hold any such
flattering opinion of itself; and it was these ideas which
underlay many of the recurrent invectives against " pride."

---

[1] The material for the history of this phase of seventeenth and eighteenth-
century thought is both rich and complicated. The author has attempted a survey
and analysis of it in a course of lectures on the Cooper Foundation given at
Swarthmore College in 1942, now (1947) being amplified and revised for
publication. Most of what follows in the present essay, dealing with another
aspect of the idea of " pride," was published in *Modern Language Notes*, 1921,
pp. 31 ff.

1. The first of these, which I need only briefly recall here,[2] was among the most characteristic and influential of all eighteenth-century ideas: the so-called "principle of continuity," *lex continui*, one of the components of the conception of the Great Chain of Being. According to this conception, the world is necessarily a *plenum formarum*, a system

> Where all must full or not coherent be,
> And all that rises, rise in due degree.

In other words, every logically possible kind of being, through all the infinite graded scale of conceivable "natures" between Deity and nonentity, must necessarily exist; and between any two adjacent links in the chain there can be only infinitesimal differences. One of the principal events in European thought in the eighteenth century was the rapid growth of a tendency towards a deliquescence of all sharp distinctions, resulting from the introduction of this assumption that all things must be regarded as parts of a qualitative continuum—the assumption embodied in the maxim *Natura non facit saltus*. Since all gaps thus disappeared from nature, there could be none between man and the other animals. He could differ from them only in degree, and from the higher animals in an almost insensible degree, and only with respect to certain attributes.[3] No link in the Chain of Being, moreover, is more essential than another, or exists merely for the sake of another. The lower creatures are no more means to the convenience of man than he is a means to their convenience.[4] Thus, so long as man remained normal, *i. e.*, in the state of nature, he assumed no grand airs of superiority to the creatures of the field and wood:

> Pride then was not, nor arts that pride to aid;
> Man walked with beast joint-tenant of the shade.[5]

---

[2] The topic has been dealt with at greater length in the writer's *The Great Chain of Being* (1936), pp. 186-203.

[3] *Essay on Man*, I, 173 ff.

[4] *Id.*, III, 22-70, I, 53-68; *cf.* Voltaire, *Discours sur l'homme*, VI.

[5] *Essay on Man*, III, 151-2. Pope's lines are the probable source of Rousseau's remark, in his second *Discours*, that man's emergence from the pure state of nature began with his invention of certain practical arts, which was followed by "le premier mouvement d'orgueil," in the form of a feeling of superiority to the other animals.

In its most significant aspect, then, " pride " gets its meaning for eighteenth-century thought from this group of conceptions. It is, in Pope's words, the " sin against the laws of order," *i. e.,* of gradation; it is the vice which causes man to set up pretensions to a place higher in the Scale of Being than belongs to him.

> Pride still is aiming at the blest abodes,
> Men would be angels, angels would be gods.

The virtue which is its opposite lies in a contented recognition of the limitations of the human lot and the littleness of man's powers;

> The bliss of man (could pride that blessing find)
> Is not to act or think beyond mankind.[6]

Thus the eighteenth-century denunciations of pride are often, at bottom, expressions of a certain disillusionment of man about himself—a phase of that long and deepening disillusionment which is the tragedy of a great part of modern thought. True, the conception of the Chain of Being owed its vogue largely to its use in the argument for (so-called) optimism; and it had its cheerful aspects. But it clearly implied the dethronement of man from his former exalted position. In the bitter spirit of Swift this disillusionment, though for other reasons, already touched its extreme; the Yahoo is not merely brought nearer to the other animals, he is placed below them. The most detestable and irrational of beings, he crowns his fatuity by imagining himself the aim and climax of the whole creation. Yet Swift had been anticipated in his opinion of the Yahoo by Robert Gould:

> What beast beside can we so slavish call
> As *Man?* Who yet pretends he's Lord of all.
> Whoever saw (and all their classes cull)
> A dog so snarlish, or a swine so full,
> A wolf so rav'nous, or an ass so dull?
> Slave to his passions, ev'ry several lust
> Whisks him about, as whirlwinds do the dust;
> And dust he is, indeed, a senseless clod
> That swells, and yet would be believ'd a God.[7]

---

[6] *Essay on Man*, I, 189-190.
[7] Gould's " Satire against Man " (*ca.* 1708), *Works*, II, 149 f. It should be

Two further aspects of the eighteenth-century notion of
" pride " are in part special applications of the principle of continuity, in part consequences of the vogue of certain other
conceptions.

2. It was upon his rational faculty and his intellectual
achievements that modern man had been wont most to plume
himself. But the conception of the graded scale of being tended
to fix attention especially upon the limitations of man's mental
powers. Moreover, the primitivism which had long been associated with the cult of the sacred word ' nature ' had expressed
itself, among other ways, in the disparagement of intellectual
pursuits and the depreciation of man's intellectual capacity. In
the sixteenth century both Erasmus and Montaigne had dilated
upon the vanity of speculation and the corrupting influence of
science.

In the first golden age of the world," wrote Erasmus, " there was no
sort of learning but what was naturally collected from every man's
common sense improved by an easy experience. They were not so
presumptuous as to dive into the depths of Nature, to labor for the
solving all phenomena in astronomy, or to wreak their brains in the
splitting of entities and unfolding the nicest speculations, judging it to
be a crime for any man to aim at what is put beyond the reach of his
shallow comprehension.[8]

This strain, less in evidence in the seventeenth century, the
age of great systems in philosophy and science, became in the
eighteenth one of the most popular of commonplaces. Finally,
the reigning philosophy of the period, in England and France,
that of Locke, had as its characteristic aim to fix the boundaries
of human knowledge; and it ostensibly found those boundaries
to be very narrow.[9] In consequence, chiefly, of the convergence

added that, as an orthodox churchman, Gould elsewhere, not too consistently,
insists upon man's superiority, as evidenced by his possession of a conscience
and an immortal soul. The poem is one of a number of imitations of Boileau's
Eighth Satire (1667).

[8] *Moriae Encomium.* For the equation of " pride " with the spirit of science
in Montaigne, *cf.* the following: " Le soing de s'augmenter en sagesse et en science, ce feut la premiere ruyne du genre humain; . . . l'orgueil est sa perte et sa
corruption " (*Apologie de Raimond Sebond*). Note also how closely much of
Swift's contrast of the Yahoos and the Houyhnhnms follows Montaigne's comparison of man with the other animals, in the same essay.

[9] *Essay Concerning Human Understanding,* I, chap. i, §§ 5-7.

of these three lines of influence, it became customary to berate
and satirize all forms of intellectual ambition, and to ascribe
to it a great part in the corruption of the natural innocence of
mankind. So Pope exhorts:

> Trace science, then, with modesty thy guide,
> First strip off all her equipage of pride, etc.[10]

The condemnation of " pride," then, is frequently, in the
eighteenth century, one of the ways of expressing a primitivistic
anti-intellectualism. Rousseau was but repeating a current
commonplace when he wrote in the *Premier Discours* that
" toutes les sciences, et la morale même, sont nées de l'orgueil
humain," and that " le luxe, la dissolution et l'esclavage ont
été de tout temps, le châtiment des efforts orgueilleux que nous
avons faits pour sortir de l'heureuse ignorance où la sagesse
éternelle nous avait placés."

3. In ethical as in intellectual endeavor, typical moralists of
the early eighteenth century believed in a program of limited
objectives. Here, again, the tradition of ethical naturalism
which had been handed down especially through Erasmus and
Montaigne readily combined with the idea of the graded scale
of being. Man must not attempt to transcend the limitations
of his " nature "; and his nature, though not the same as that
of the animals below him in the scale, is close to it. " Reason "
has a part in the conduct of human life, but it is an ancillary
part. Pope devotes many lines of versified argumentation to
showing that the motive-power and the principal directive force
in man's life is—and should be—not reason, but the complex
of instincts and passions which make up our " natural " constitution.[11] " Pride," then, in an especially important sense,
meant a sort of moral overstrain, the attempt to be unnaturally
good and immoderately virtuous, to live by reason alone.

---

[10] *Essay on Man*, II, 43 ff.; *cf*. Robert Gould's satirical picture of the scholar's
life (" Satire against Man," 167-9) and his praise of the ignorance of the state
of nature (170 ff.). In the mid-eighteenth century it is, of course, true that
this sort of anti-intellectualism co-existed—sometimes even in the same minds—
with that enthusiasm for the " study of nature," *i. e.*, of empirical physical science, of which M. Mornet has admirably written the history in his *Les sciences
de la nature en France au 18ᵉ siècle.*
[11] *Essay on Man*, II, 59-202.

Erasmus and Montaigne had come to have an antipathy to this lofty and strenuous moral temper through a direct revulsion against the revived Stoicism in fashion in the late Renaissance; and the Stoics passed in the eighteenth century for the proverbial embodiments of "pride" in this sense. Thus Pope describes man as a being "with too much weakness for the Stoic pride"; and Wieland in his *Theages* (1760) remarks that the Stoic pride and self-sufficiency "departs very widely from nature" and "can be possible only in God." "Eben so wenig," he adds, "konnte ich die Unterdrückung des sinnlichen Teils unsers Wesens mit der Natur reimen."

I have dwelt upon this and the preceding aspect of the conception of pride especially because it has become customary seriously to exaggerate the rationalism of the period, its "extravagant claims to reason," its confidence in "the dry light of reason." Unless "reason" is carefully and somewhat peculiarly defined, such expressions are misleading. The authors who were perhaps the most influential and the most representative in the early and mid-eighteenth century made a great point of reducing man's claims to "reason" to a minimum, and of belittling the importance of that faculty in human existence; and the vice of "pride" which they so delighted to castigate was exemplified for them in any high estimate of the capacity of the human species for intellectual achievement, or in any of the more ambitious enterprises of science and philosophy, or in any moral ideal which would make pure reason (as distinguished from natural "passions") the supreme power in human life. "Pride" was, indeed, exemplified, for some such writers, in everything "artificial"; and in the homilies against it the whole gospel of the Return to Nature was sometimes implicit.

V. "NATURE" AS AESTHETIC NORM [1]

"**D**ER BEGRIFF und das Wort 'Natur' ist ein wahrer Scherwenzel," observed Friedrich Nicolai more than a century and a half ago. The remark was then obvious, and has by this time become trite; yet there have been few, and, so far as I know, no adequate attempts to exhibit completely and connectedly the manifold historic rôles played by this verbal jack-of-all-trades. Nothing, however, is more needful, especially for the student of the literature and philosophy of the seventeenth and eighteenth centuries, than a thorough understanding of the diversity of meanings of the word, at once the most sacred and most protean in the vocabulary of those periods. What is requisite is, of course, not a mere list of lexicographer's definitions, but such an analytical charting of the senses of the term as will make clear the logical relations and (what is historically still more important), the common confusions between them, the probable semasiological development of one out of another, and the doctrines or tendencies with which they are severally associated. To read eighteenth-century books (in particular) without having in mind such a general map of the meanings of "nature" is to move about in the midst of ambiguities unrealized; and it is to fail to observe an important causal factor in certain of the most momentous processes of change in opinion and taste. For "nature" has, of course, been the chief and the most pregnant word in the terminology of all the normative provinces of thought in the West; and the multiplicity of its meanings has made it easy, and common, to slip more or less insensibly from one connotation to another, and thus in the end to pass from one ethical or aesthetic standard to its very antithesis, while nominally professing the same principles.

In what follows I have attempted to give in concise form such an analytical enumeration of the purely aesthetic uses of

[1] Published in *Modern Language Notes*, 1927, pp. 444-450.

the term— [2] *i. e.*, its meanings in the formulas that art should
" imitate " or " follow " or " keep close to Nature." The references given under I, A. B. D. and E. are, with a few exceptions,
limited to the seventeenth and eighteenth centuries, and are
not, of course, intended to be exhaustive. Under C illustrations seem hardly necessary. The list of senses is, no doubt,
incomplete, and some of the distinctions indicated may be
inexact. The appended " Remarks " are merely fragments of
the skeleton of what should have been, and perhaps may some
day be, a somewhat extensive study in the history of the appeal
to " nature " for the norms of art. The evidence available in
support of the generalizations propounded is, I think, abundant,
but a volume would be needed to present it.

I. *Senses of " Nature " as Aesthetic Norm.*

A. *" Nature " as objects to be imitated (in the sense of " reproduced " or " represented ") in art.*
   1. " Nature " as empirical reality. *E. g.*, D'Alembert, *Disc.
      Prélim.*; Goldsmith, *Cultivation of Taste*; Granville,
      Essay upon Unnatural Flights in Poetry; Reynolds, *Disc.
      on Painting*, XII, *ad fin.* Especially:
      (a) Human nature, *i. e.*, possible or usual human be-
          havior, the " natural " expression of the passions,
          in possible situations. *E. g.*, Shakespeare, *Hamlet*,
          III, 2; Dryden, Pref. to *Tyrannic Love*; Pref. to
          Fables (on Chaucer); Molière, *Misanthrope*, I,
          388; Boileau, *Art poét.* III, 360-370, 414-420;
          Fénelon, *Lettres sur les occupations*, VI; Diderot,
          Lettre à Mlle Jodin (*Oeuvres*, XIX, 388); Johnson,
          Lives (*ed.* Hill, 1908) III, 255; H. Walpole, Pref.
          to second ed. of *Castle of Otranto.*
      (b) Real interconnections between facts, especially the
          relations of cause and effect in human experience.

---

[2] A tentative discrimination and enumeration of the historic senses of the
term not primarily aesthetic in their reference has been given by the writer in
Primitivism and Related Ideas in Antiquity, 1935, Appendix (pp. 447-456). See
also the same volume, pp. 11-22; and for the eighteenth century especially, *cf.*
Professor Basil Willey's *The Eighteenth-Century Background*, 1941.

E. g., Dryden, Pref. to *The Rival Ladies*; cf. Diderot, *Encyclopédie*, art. "Beau."

2. "Nature" as the essence or Platonic Idea of a kind, imperfectly realized in empirical reality; hence, idealized type-form, *la belle nature*. E. g., Sidney, *Apology for Poetry*; Du Fresnoy, *De arte graphica*; Molière, *La gloire du Dôme de Val-de-Grâce*; Dryden, *Parallel of Poetry and Painting*; Addison, *Spectator*, 418; Mingard, Art. "Beau" in *Encyclopédie*. éd. d'Yverdun (1777); Batteux, *Les Beaux Arts réduits*, etc.; Diderot, *Avant-propos du Salon de 1767;* Hurd, *Notes on the Art of Painting*; Arteaga, *La Bellezza Ideal considerada como objeto de todas las artes de imitación.* (For another sense of imitation of *la belle nature*, cf. Diderot, *Encyclopédie*, art. "Beau"). Quatremère de Quincy, *On the nature, the end and the means of imitation in the fine arts.* Cf. Helen T. Garrett, "The Imitation of the Ideal," *PMLA* (1947), 735 ff.

3. "Nature" as the generic type, excluding the differentiae of species and individuals. E. g., Johnson, *Rasselas*, ch. X.; Pref. to *Shakesp.*; Reynolds, *Discourses*, III and VII.

4. "Nature" as the average type, or statistical "mode," of a kind (no. 2 interpreted in a way which makes it approximate no. 1). E. g., Reynolds in *Idler*, 79 and 82; cf. Buffier. *Tr. des premières, vérités* I, ch. 13, and Lessing, *Hamburgische Dramaturgie*, 95.

5. "Nature" as antithetic to man and his works; the part of empirical reality which has not been transformed (or corrupted) by human art; hence, the out-of-doors, "natural" sights and sounds. E. g., Shaftesbury, *Char.*, "The Moralists," III, § 2 (ed. Robertson, II, p. 125); Akenside, *Pleasures of the Imagination*, first ed., III, *passim*; Langhorne, *Vision of Fancy*, El. 3, and *Inscription, etc.*; Beattie, *Minstrel*, I, 9; Fr. Schlegel, *Werke* (1825) VI, 223, 280; X, 71.

B. *"Nature" (i. e., the "nature of things") as the system of necessary and self-evident truths concerning the properties and relations of essences*; hence, with respect to aesthetic judgments:

6. Intuitively known principles or standards of " taste " (analogous to the " law of nature " in morals), whereby that which is objectively and essentially (*i. e.*, " by nature ") beautiful is recognized. *E. g.*, Shaftesbury, *Char.* (ed. Robertson, " Soliloquy," III, 3 (vol. I, pp. 216-220) ; " Moralists," III, 2 (vol. II, p. 137) ; " Inquiry," II, 3 (vol. I, p. 251) ; André, *Essai sur le Beau*, I; Balguy, *Foundation of Moral Goodness*, II, a. 21.

C. *" Nature " in general, i. e., the cosmical order as a whole, or a half-personified power (natura naturans) manifested therein, as exemplar, of which the attributes or modes of working should characterize also human art.*

These attributes have been variously conceived to be:

7. Uniformity (*cf.* 6 and 17).
8. Simplicity.
9. Economy of means in achieving a given end.
10. Regularity: nature as " geometrizing."
11. Irregularity, " wildness."
12. " Fullness," abundance and variety of content, insatiable fecundity—and as consequence of these, as sometimes conceived, juxtaposition of sharply contrasting features.
13. (In the later eighteenth century only). Progressive diversification of types in the order of time, continuous evolution.

D. *" Nature," i. e., naturalness, as an attribute of the artist.*

This commonly conceived as consisting in:

14. Freedom from influence of convention, rules, traditions (antithesis of " nature " and " custom "). *E. g.*, J. Warton, *The Enthusiast*.
15. Self-expression without self-consciousness; freedom from premeditation or deliberate and reflective design, artlessness (antithesis of " nature " and " art "; cf. 5). *E. g.*, Boileau, *Épitre* IX, 81-90. Hence:
16. The qualities exemplified by primitive man or primitive

art. *E. g.*, Dryden, *Essay on Satire*; Addison, *Spect.* 209; Johnson, *Rasselas*, Ch. X; J. Warton, *The Enthusiast*; Diderot, *De la poésie dramatique*, xviii.

E. "*Nature*" *as manifested in the artist's public, and therefore as determining the appeal or aesthetic validity of the work of art.*

Sometimes with the same implications as 14, 16, but much more commonly, in this use, with the following connotations:

17. The universal and immutable in thought, feeling and taste; what has always been known, what everyone can immediately understand and enjoy; usually connected with the assumption that the universally valued is also the objectively beautiful (cf. 6, 7). *E. g.*, Boileau, Pref. vi (*Oeuvres*, ed. Gidel, i, 19); Dryden, *Parallel of Poetry and Painting*; Pope, *Essay on Crit.*, 297-300; Addison, *Spect.*, 253; Fénelon, *Lettre sur les occupations*, v; Diderot, *Oeuvres*, xiv, 432; Hurd, *Disc. on Poetical Imitation*; Johnson (*lcc. cit.* under 3); J. Warton, *Essay on Genius and Writings of Pope*, i, 86, 1806 ed.); Rousseau, *Émile*, iv (*Oeuvres*, ed. Auguis, iv, 317-320); Reynolds, *Disc.*, iii; T. Warton, *On Sir Joshua Reynolds's Window, etc.*; Schiller, *Ueber Matthisons Gedichte.*

18. The familiar and intimate: the "natural" as that which is most congenial to, and immediately comprehensible and enjoyable by, *each* individual—this conceived not as uniform in all men, but as varying with time, race, nationality, and cultural tradition (*cf.* 12). *E. g.*, Alfonso Sanchez in Saintsbury, *Loci Critici*, 137; Herder, "Shakespeare" in *Von deutscher Art und Kunst; Ideen zur Philos. der Gesch. der Menschheit*, ix, ch. 4, § 3. *Cf.* Fr. Schlegel, *Werke* (1825), vi 253; x, 103; Scott, *Misc. Prose Works* (1847), i, 749.

II. *Implied Desiderata in Works of Art* (if they are to "accord with Nature" in one or another of the above senses):

    a. Literal realism, fidelity of reproduction of objects or events imitated; usually in the sense of adherence to probability (sense 1).

b. Verisimilitude, adherence to apparent or supposed probability. (Modification of *a* under the influence of the assumption that a work of art must be judged by its effect on the beholder, reader, *etc.* Associated in thought with 17.)

c. Restriction of employment of supernatural apparatus or mythological figures to " that which is universally agreed upon "; or inner consistency even in the portrayal of the unreal. Cf. Granville, *Unnatural Flights*, n. 1; Addison, *Spect.*, 419; Hurd, *Letters on Chivalry*, X. (An extreme attenuation of *a*; cf. also *o*, below.)

d. Restriction of (all or certain) arts or *genres* to depiction of ideal types (sense 2).

e. Depiction of general types only, not of individuals (sense 3).

f. Depiction of average types (sense 4).

g. Adherence to standards of " objective " beauty (sense 6); these commonly identified with one or both of the two following.

h. Simplicity, *i. e.*, sparseness of ornament and avoidance of intricacy in design (senses 8, 9).

i. Symmetry, balance, definiteness and regularity of form (sense 10).

k. Irregularity, avoidance of symmetry, of fixed, recurrent forms, *etc.* (sense 11).

l. Preponderance of feeling (as the spontaneous and therefore more " natural " element in human nature) over intellection or deliberate aesthetic design (sense 15).

m. Naïveté, unsophistication, likeness to the primitive; or representation of the life and emotions of primitive or unsophisticated persons or societies (sense 16; *cf.* also 11 and 17).

n. Disregard of rules and precedents, free self-expression of the artist—often, but not necessarily, identified with *m* (sense 14).

o. Universal aesthetic validity, capacity for being immediately understood and enjoyed by all men (whose "natural" taste has not been corrupted) (sense 17). Often construed as equivalent to *g*.

p. Adherence to rules and precedents or imitation of models of which the "conformity to nature" (*i. e.*, their universal validity, and appeal to that which is immutable in human nature) has been shown by their general and long-continued acceptance (sense 17).

q. Expression of that which is most distinctive of, or most intimately familiar to, the artist and his immediate public; hence (1) racialism or nationalism in art; or (2) expression by modern art of ideas or feelings that are distinctively Christian; or (3) expression by the art of each period of its own distinctive *Zeitgeist* (sense 18).

r. Completeness of representation of human life or of the aspects of the sensible world; expression of their "fullness," diversity and richness of contrasts. Conceived as a program for art as a whole, this included both *a* and *n* among its implications; it also suggested the doctrine of the greater value of "content" than of "form" in art. Conceived as an ideal to be approximated in an individual work of art, it implied, *inter alia*, the mixture of *genres* (sense 12).

s. Progressive diversification and expansion of the content and forms of art, continuous aesthetic evolution. Hence the cult of originality and novelty (sense 13).

t. *Naturgefühl*, expression of emotions derived from the contemplation of the sensible world external to man, especially when this is conceived as a source of moral teaching or as a manifestation of, or means of contact with, some pervasive spiritual Presence ("Nature" as in sense 5; but the function of the artist is here conceived to be, not "imitating" the external world, but expressing his subjective response to it or interpreting its supposed inner meaning).

III. *Remarks.*

(1) The principle of "imitating" or "following" or "keeping close to nature" was primarily the maxim of neo-classicism; but it was also fatal to that creed, since nearly all forms of the revolt against neo-classical standards invoked the same catchword. The justification of new tendencies by the old rule was made possible partly by the substitution (conscious or unconscious) of other meanings of the multivocal terms "nature" and "natural," partly by the emergence of latent logical implications of certain already accepted neo-classical senses of the formula.

(2) The strictly neo-classical meanings of the rule were o (often with the implication of g), p, h, i.[3]

(3) While neo-classical theorists often tended to construe the rules as implying d or e (*i. e.*, the duty of art to portray ideal types not found in empirical reality, or to represent only the generic characters of things, not individuals) these tendencies were counteracted by the realistic connotation (a or b) implicit in the traditional formula as commonly construed. Much neo-classical criticism constantly wavers between a and d or e or f.

(4) Sense 1, and the corresponding conceptions of the "imitation" of nature (a or b), are to be found in orthodox neo-classicists and in their opponents. *E. g.*, the unities and other features of the classical drama were by the one side defended on the ground that they were favorable to realism or verisimilitude, by the other side attacked as inconsistent therewith. But the preponderant influence of this sense of the formula was adverse to neo-classical standards, and especially to the assumption that imitating ancient models was equivalent to imitating "nature" (*i. e.*, empirical reality) at first hand. The same sense was also conducive to nationalism in art, on the ground that only the life and the

---

[3] On these, see the two essays following.

types of feeling most familiar to the artist can be faithfully represented by him.

(5) Sense 16, and the primitivistic strain associated therewith (*m*), were deeply implanted in the neo-classical tradition, especially in the theory of the epic and the assumption of the superiority of Homer in that *genre*. They were also closely connected logically with the fundamental neo-classical ideal of immutability and universal aesthetic validity (*o*); primitive man must, it was generally assumed, have manifested most clearly, simply, and uncorruptedly those elements in human nature which are universal and fundamental. But this element of the tradition (becoming increasingly identified with *k* and *l*, *sc*. the ideas of irregularity, wildness and uncontrolled feeling) was at variance with *i* and *p*, and in general with the high valuation of "elegance" and "correctness"; and this opposition in the eighteenth century became acute. Aesthetic primitivism even in its later forms was thus not a direct reaction against neo-classicism but a natural development of one of the elements of that complex compound of aesthetic ideas.

(6) The conceptions of the characteristics of "nature" which were relatively novel in the eighteenth century were 12, 13, 18; and the aesthetic ideals associated with these (*q*, *r*, *s*), together with *n*, were (though all but *s* had found some earlier expressions) essentially revolutionary, since they implied a rejection of the most fundamental of the neo-classical meanings of the formula (*o*, *p*, *g*, *h*, *i*). The former ideals were the essential novelties of early German Romanticism and were embodied in Fr. Schlegel's definition of *die romantische Poesie* as *eine progressive Universal poesie* (*Athenaeum*, *Frag.* 116), and in other manifestos of the school; and, if the term "Romantic" is to be given any one historical meaning, these four ways of conceiving of an art in harmony with Nature best deserve to be called the essentials of the aesthetic creed of Romanticism.

---

[4] On this last, *cf.* the essays on "The Meaning of Romanticism," etc., "Schiller and the Genesis of Romanticism," "On the Discrimination of Romanticisms," and *The Great Chain of Being*, Lectures VII and X.

VI. THE PARALLEL OF DEISM AND CLASSICISM [1]

IF THERE is in this paper anything not generally familiar to students of the history of modern literature, it is likely to consist, not in the parts, but in their interconnection. I wish to attempt three things. First, I shall outline briefly the characteristic idea-complex which constitutes what is commonly called the "rationalism of the Enlightenment," the purpose of the outline being to bring out the essential unity of this complex, the way in which the distinguishable ideas composing it are related to one another and, indeed, are, or might naturally be taken to be, all implications of a single fundamental assumption. This scheme of ideas in its *systematic* character is not, I think, always so well understood or so steadily kept in mind by scholars who have to do with the thought of the sixteenth to eighteenth centuries as it with advantage might be. It is not a system which you will find connectedly set forth by any one philosopher; it is rather a set of preconceptions which you will find taken for granted by most philosophers, and determining the opinions, on all manner of subjects, of the majority of educated men for more than two centuries, in so far as they were emancipated from the dominance of tradition and authority. There were, of course, numerous contrary tendencies, not a few of them springing from latent implications of one or another of the same group of assumptions which they were to oppose or undermine; and the system in question was perhaps consistently and undeviatingly held by no one writer. Nevertheless, scarcely anything that goes on in the thought of the *Aufklärung* can be rightly understood, nor can its significance be justly appraised, unless it is considered in its relation to this coherent body of underlying assumptions, widely accepted as too self-evident to need, as a whole, formal exposition or defense. Second, I shall

[1] Read at the annual meeting of the Modern Language Association of America at Washington, D. C., December, 1930; first published in *Modern Philology*, February, 1932.

point out that deism is simply the application of this complex of ideas to religion. It is not a peculiarly English development; its appearance in many writers does not need to be—though, no doubt, it in some cases may be—attributed to specific influences of one upon another; it was merely the manifestation, in a field of reflective thought in which they were especially apposite, of presuppositions having a much wider potential applicability and actual application. And, third, I shall point out that the neo-classical theory of poetry, and of the other arts, was in great part the application of the same set of preconceptions to aesthetics. Such a detailed parallel of deism and neo-classicism seems well fitted to illustrate how identical general ideas may be operative, not only in provinces of thought seemingly remote from one another, but even in movements which, at first sight, appear very unlike in their temper and orientation. Most people, I suppose, are accustomed to think of deism as the seventeenth-eighteenth century form of religious radicalism or progressivism, and in particular as a rejection of all authority and tradition, and a complete emancipation of the private judgment of the individual, in matters of religion; while neo-classicism, on the other hand, is often conceived to be a species of aesthetic conservatism or reactionism, and a return to authoritarianism and traditionalism in matters of taste. In so far as the two movements are thus conceived as, in their respective spheres, antithetic, both are to some degree misconceived; and their common relation to the general background of ideas, in the period in which both arose and developed, is missed.

For brevity's sake, and for convenience of cross-reference, I shall have to introduce some rather unlovely terms to designate certain of the elements of this complex; and, also in the interest of brevity, I have illustrated its specific manifestations in deism in the course of the general summary of it.

1. *Uniformitarianism.*—This is the first and fundamental principle of this general and pervasive philosophy of the Enlightenment. The reason, it is assumed to be evident, is identical in all men; and the life of reason therefore, it is tacitly or explicitly inferred, must admit of no diversity. Dif-

ferences in opinion or in taste are evidences of error,[2] and universality of appeal or of acceptance tends to be taken, not merely as an effect, but as in itself a mark or criterion, of truth. Anything of which the intelligibility, verifiability, or actual affirmation is limited to men of a special age, race, temperament, tradition, or condition is *eo ipso* without truth or value, or at all events without importance to a reasonable man. The object of the effort of the religious, moral, or social reformer, as of the literary critic, is therefore to standardize men and their beliefs, their likings, their activities, and their institutions. Typical is a remark of Spinoza's, reported by one of his early biographers: " The purpose of Nature is to make men uniform, as children of a common mother."[3] So Fénelon: " Les hommes de tous les pays et de tous les temps, quelque éducation qu'ils aient reçue, se sentent invinciblement assujettis à penser et à parler de même. . . . Ainsi, ce qui paraît le plus à nous, et être le fond de nous-mêmes, je veux dire notre raison, est ce qui nous est le moins propre."[4] That which is " according to nature" meant, first and foremost, that which corresponds to this assumption of uniformity; it is perhaps still necessary to repeat that in the most frequent of the normative uses of the term " nature" in the Enlightenment, the principal element in the signification of the word *is* uniformity. Despite its sixty-odd other senses, it was primarily and chiefly because of *this* connotation that " nature" was the sacred word of the Enlightenment.[5] And the campaign of which it was thus the

---

[2] Cf. Voltaire, *Poème sur la loi naturelle*, Part I (of the conception of God):
" Est-ce le peuple altier conquérant de Byzance,
Le tranquille Chinois, le Tartare indompté,
Qui connaît son essence, et suit sa volonté?
Différents dans leurs mœurs, ainsi qu'en leur hommage,
Ils lui font tenir tous un différent langage;
Tous se sont donc trompés."

[3] Lucas de la Haye, *La vie de M. Benoît de Spinoza*, cited by Brunschvicg, *Spinoza et ses contemporains*, 333.

[4] *De l'existence de Dieu* (1718), in *Œuvres philosophiques* (1863), 55.

[5] Cf. Selden, *De jure naturali ac gentium* (1640): " Iam vero Naturalis vocabulum . . . id tantum indicat quod, ex Ebraeorum, seu Ecclesiae aut Reipublicae veteris Ebraicae, Placitis, Sententiis, Moribusque, tam in Foro quam in Scholis, receptis avitisque, pro Jure Mundi seu omnium hominum omnimodarumque tam gentium tam aetatum communi, etiam ab ipso rerum conditu est habitum, ut

war cry, the general attack upon the *differentness* of men and
their opinions and valuations—this, with the resistances to it
and the eventual revulsion against it, was the central and domi-
nating fact in the intellectual history of Europe for two hundred years—from the late sixteenth to the late eighteenth
century.[6]

Now this assumption seemed of especially evident validity in
the case of religion.   In matters of minor consequence or of a
purely speculative interest, local variations of opinion might
perhaps be permissible, or at least negligible.   But there should
surely, it was felt, be only one religion—as, indeed, the Church
had always insisted.   Yet Christianity, in all its forms, manifestly contained much that was not of universal acceptance,
and it expressly demanded belief in many dogmas which the
natural light of reason could admittedly never have discovered—and which after they were revealed it could not
understand.   The Christian creed, as interpreted by the
churches, seemed to be but a sort of local custom of the European peoples, and therefore, on that ground alone, it was
suspect to those who were resolved to be rid of all merely
local customs.   It contained, moreover, numerous historical
propositions; it made salvation conditional upon the acceptance
of assertions concerning events supposed to have happened at
particular times " in a little corner" of a particular planet.
Such propositions were trebly incapable of universal verification: they could not be known to persons living before the
events occurred; they could not be known to races living on
this or other globes whom the report of such events did not
reach; and their truth could not be determined by simple means
of knowledge in every man's possession, but only by the difficult and technical investigations of historians.   The only re-

scilicet a Totius Naturae creatae Autore seu Numine sanctissimo, Humano generi,
simulatque creatum est, indicatum infusum imperatumque."
    [6] In the foregoing I have merely repeated what a number of students of the
history of ideas have said before; cf., e. g., K. Schück's dissertation, *Studien über
Johannes von Müller* (1912), 13 f.: " Bei aller dieser Mannigfaltigkeit . . . aber
hat die Aufklärung, die deutsche wie die ausserdeutsche, einen gemeinen Grund-
zug, die Richtung auf das *Allgemeine* der natürlichen Gesetzmässigkeit. Dieser
Naturalismus, gleichgültig ob er in empiristischer, metaphysischer oder idealis-
tischer Form auftrat, ist ihr Wesen und der Ausgangspunkt der Epoche welche
sie überwand." Cf. also Dilthey, *Schriften*, II, 90 ff.

ligion, therefore, which could claim credence from any man must be the religion of nature—" of nature " here signifying primarily and most essentially uniformity and universality.

Now, assuming that the non-universal was to be rejected, there were two ways in which the positive content of the truly catholic creed might be sought. They were seemingly incongruous, but were nevertheless commonly associated. The more characteristic, on the whole, was:

2. *Rationalistic individualism.*—The term " individualism " has been a pregnant source of confusion and false generalizations in the historiography of ideas; for it has often been applied to two precisely opposite tendencies, one of them highly characteristic of the Enlightenment, the other equally characteristic of the Romantic age. By rationalistic individualism I mean the belief that—precisely because all individuals, *quâ* rational, are fundamentally alike, and because this uniform element in them is the only important element—truth is to be attained by every individual for himself, by the exercise of his private judgment uninfluenced by tradition or external authority; in other words, by " the pure light of nature " which shines in all alike. To defer to tradition or to submit to authority was to turn away from that light. It is thus that Voltaire, after bidding men ignore the fine-spun reasonings of the great theologians, concludes: " Et pour nous élever, descendons dans nous-mêmes." [7] Rousseau in the *Vicaire Savoyard* finds the source of the religion of nature rather in " the heart " than the reason, but the antithesis is more verbal than real; the emphasis is still upon the idea of uniformity. " Le culte que Dieu demande est celui du cœur; & celui-là, quand il est sincère, est toujours uniforme." [8] Antithetic to this is the Romantic individualism, in which the value of individuals is conceived to lie chiefly, not in what is uniform, but in what is diverse or unique in them, in which the object aimed at is the revelation, or the cultivation, of idiosyncrasy, personal, racial, or temporal.

Yet the fundamental preconception of rationalism suggested

---

[7] *Poème sur la loi naturelle*, Exorde.
[8] Ed. Masson, p. 309.

that there is another way to the attainment of those truths which
are attested by the uniform reason of man, namely:

3. *The appeal to the "consensus gentium."*—Since that
which is " according to nature " should be common to all mankind, you cannot, it should seem, miss it if you accept the beliefs
and valuations which have in fact *been* common to all mankind.
" The general and perpetual voice of men," said the judicious
Hooker, " is as the sentence of God himself. For that which
all men have at all times learned, Nature herself must needs
have taught; and God being the author of Nature, her voice is
but his instrument." [9] This the scholastic philosophers and
orthodox divines of the more rationalistic sort had often said;
the deist merely added " nothing but " to the proposition, and
applied it to the special case of religion. *Only* that which
could be shown, or plausibly be assumed, to be uttered by " the
general and perpetual voice of men " could be taken as the
voice of God, and therefore the content of the true religion,
Bodin's *religio generis humani* could be ascertained by survey-
ing all the historic religions, discarding all beliefs not to be
found in every one of them, and retaining the common resi-
duum. Precisely this was the ostensible procedure of Herbert
of Cherbury. *Summa veritatis norma est consensus universalis;*
true religion consists solely of *notitiae communes*, things that
everybody knows; and to judge how far a " particular faith "
coincides with this norm you must ask, among other things,
whether any of its articles " be not controverted among foreign
nations, among whom other faiths are received." Thus alone
is to be determined the doctrine of the *Ecclesia vere catholica
sive universalis*, the only church *quae errare non potest*, because
it alone utters the judgment of all mankind with respect to
those truths of which they have self-evident knowledge by the
light of nature. As Voltaire said, " Sans doute [Dieu] a parlé;
mais c'est à l'Univers." [10]

4. *Cosmopolitanism.*—From the assumption that all the best
gifts of nature are equally distributed, that there can be nothing of real value in human life which is not in widest com-

[9] *Laws of Ecclesiastical Polity* (1594), I, viii, 3.
[10] *Poème sur la loi naturelle*, Part I.

monalty spread, the condemnation of every form of nationalism or racialism obviously followed. *Natura* and *natio* were words of profoundly antithetic connotation; to be true to the one, you must emancipate yourself from all special predilection for the other. And deism being, when full-blown, not merely cosmopolitan but cosmical in its outlook and temper, could admit the claim of no people and no planet to an exceptional or even distinctive rôle in religious history.

5. *Antipathy to " enthusiasm" and originality.*—Similarly, it could not be admitted that anything of substantial importance to mankind could have been communicated either through the private supernatural revelations claimed by " enthusiasts " or through any special insights attained by individuals of exceptional endowment, of original genius in matters of morals or religion. The function of the benefactor of mankind was not to proclaim to men truths which they had never known before, but to purge their minds of " prejudices " and so to fix their attention upon the central, simple truths which they had really always known. The

> Follow'r of God, or friend of human kind,
> Poet or patriot, rose but to restore
> The faith and moral, Nature gave before,
> Relum'd her ancient light, not kindled new.[11]

6. *Intellectual equalitarianism.*—This preoccupation with the quest of universally valid yet individually and inwardly verifiable truths, tended necessarily to produce an *intellectual equalitarianism*—a democratic temper in matters of religion and morals and taste, even in persons not democratic in their political views. If the light of nature is universal, and if the knowledge which it affords is alone truly requisite for the guidance of life, then one man's intelligence is—literally, for all *practical* purposes—as good as another's; and it followed, when this preconception was consistently carried out, that nothing can be a valid or at least a needful belief which is beyond the comprehension of the plain man. " Les choses que si peu de personnes peuvent se flatter de comprendre sont inutiles au reste du genre humain," declared Voltaire in *Le philosophe*

[11] *Essay on Man*, III, 284-87.

ignorant. An "internal proof of the divine original of the law of nature," wrote Bolingbroke, "is the plainness and simplicity which renders it intelligible in all times and places, and proportions it to the meanest understanding. It has been made intricate by casuistry, that of lawyers and divines. . . . [But] these principles want neither paraphrase nor commentary to be sufficiently understood."[12]   And thus deism professed to be a religion "level with every man's mother-wit," and—as Swift not altogether unfairly said, in attacking it—to contain "nothing which cannot be presently comprehended by the weakest noddle."

7. *Rationalistic anti-intellectualism.*—The term sounds paradoxical, but it designates with precision a view perfectly consistent with the fundamental preconceptions of the type of rationalism with which we are concerned . The presumption of the universal accessibility and verifiability of all that it is really needful for men to know implied that all subtle, elaborate, intricate reasonings about abstruse questions beyond the grasp of the majority are certainly unimportant, and probably untrue. Thus any view difficult to understand, or requiring a long and complex exercise of the intellect for its verification, could be legitimately dismissed without examination, at least if it concerned any issue in which man's moral or religious interests were involved. A "system" was a legitimate object of suspicion simply because it *was* a system.

> Ne pouvons-nous trouver l'auteur de notre vie
> Qu'au labyrinthe obscur de la Théologie?
> Origène et Jean Scot sont chez vous sans crédit.
> La nature en sait plus qu'ils n'en ait jamais dit.
> Écartons ces romans qu'on appelle systèmes.[13]

Voltaire's "Ingénu" argues with his Jansenist friend: "If there were but one truth hidden in your load of arguments, it would without doubt have been discovered, and all the world would have been unanimous with respect to it. . . . It is an absurdity, an insult to human nature, an affront to the Infinite and Supreme Being, to say that there is one truth essential to

---

[12] *Fragments or Minutes of Essays,* viii, *Works* (Dublin, 1793), V, 103-4.
[13] Voltaire, *Poème sur la loi naturelle,* Exorde.

the well-being of man which God conceals "—that is, which is too recondite for any man to discover for himself. And in his numerous expressions of this idea Voltaire was but repeating what Lord Herbert and many others had said long before him.

8. *Rationalistic primitivism.*—The entire logic of this type of rationalism implied that the truths of " reason " or " nature," since they were universal, must have been at least *as well* known to the earliest and least sophisticated men as to any other members of the race; and, what is more, that early men were really in a better position to apprehend such truths than men of later periods. For the minds of the men of the first ages were not corrupted by " prejudices " at all; there were no traditions and no crystallized social forms to hinder the workings of common sense in them. What is universal and uniform in man, then, but has been overlaid and obscured by historic accretions in the unhappy diversities of belief and practice of modern and civilized peoples, *must*—according to this logic—have been exemplified in the earliest age, " Ere wit oblique had broke the steady light " of nature, and must have persisted with least contamination among savages. The true religion, Bodin's deist in the *Colloquium Heptaplomeres* maintains, must be the oldest, whereas " new religions, new sacrifices, new customs, new conceits, new churches, new opinions, new morals—these have brought flourishing states to ruin." " Nec aliam religionem habuisse videmus antiquissimos humani generis principes ac parentes, qui aurei saeculi memoriam posteritati reliquerunt, non docti, sed facti, non instituti, sed imbuti, ab ipsa natura." Of English eighteenth-century deism the most typical and most systematic single expression is the book of Tindal, of which the title tells almost the whole story: *Christianity as Old as the Creation, or the Gospel a Republication of the Religion of Nature.* Since God—so runs Tindal's principal argument—exists and is good, he must have been " willing that all men should come to a knowledge of his truth." He must, accordingly, have from the beginning " given mankind some rule or law for their conduct," and a rule equally clear and evident to all. The doctrine of special revelations, or of a gradual and cumulative disclosure of religious truth, is therefore itself an irreligious

doctrine. The religion which " God from the beginning gave men " must have been " absolutely perfect," and it therefore " cannot admit of any alteration, or be capable of addition or diminution." So Voltaire in the *Profession de foi des théistes* (the word is, of course, a synonym of " deist ") :

> Notre religion est aussi ancienne que le monde. . . . Il faut que le juif et le chrétien avouent que, suivant leurs propres livres, le théisme a régné sur la terre juqu'au déluge . . . et qu'ainsi le théisme a été la seule religion divine pendant 2513 années, jusqu'au temps où les Juifs disent que Dieu leur donna une loi particulière dans un désert.

In short, as Voltaire elsewhere puts it, " un déiste est de la religion d'Adam, de Seth, de Noé." [14] Consequently, " il faut ramener les hommes, autant qu'on le peut, à la religion primitive." And of this church, as Haller observed, the American Indian and the African are members:

> Die Kraft von Blut und Recht erkennen die Huronen
> Die dort an Mitchigans beschneyten Ufern wohnen,
> Und unterm braunen Sud fühlt auch der Hottentot
> Die allgemeine Pflicht und der Natur Gebot. [15]

The combination of uniformitarianism with a less thoroughgoing form of primitivism—and also, somewhat incongruously, with a touch of patriotic *amour-propre*—is illustrated in Henry Brooke's Prologue to his *Gustavus Vasa* (1739), when he describes those who follow only

> Great Nature's law, the law within the breast:
> Formed by no art, and to no sect confined,
> But stamped by Heaven upon th' unlettered mind.
>   Such, such of old, the first born natives were
> Who breathed the virtues of Britannia's air,
> Their realm when mighty Caesar vainly sought,
> For mightier freedom against Caesar fought,
> And rudely drove the famed invader home,
> To tyrannize o'er polished—venal Rome.
>   Our bard, exalted in a freeborn flame,
> To every nation would transfer this claim:
> He to no state, no climate, bounds his page,
> But bids the moral beam through every age.

---

[14] *Défense de Milord Bolingbroke* (1752).
[15] *Ueber den Ursprung des Uebels* (1750 ed.), II, 184. For numerous illus-

The same general thesis was a favorite one of Lessing's in his early period; for example, in the *Gedanken über die Herrnhuter* (1750): "Turn back to the earliest ages. How simple, easy, and living was the religion of Adam! But how long did such religion continue? Each of his descendants added something to it, according to his own liking. The essential was submerged in a deluge (*Sündflut*) of arbitrary doctrines. All were disloyal to the truth, though a few men, the posterity of Abraham, less so than others." And the mission of Christ, adds Lessing, was only "to restore religion to its original purity, and to confine it within those limits in which it brings forth effects the more holy and universal, the more narrow the limits. God is a spirit, ye shall worship him in spirit and in truth; upon what beyond this did he insist? and what truth is more capable than this of binding together all the varieties of religion?" The deist, if not precisely, in the usual sense of the term, a conservative, was manifestly the arch-reactionary in religion.

9. From all this followed *a negative philosophy of history.*— A uniform standard must obviously be an immutable standard; and all the changes in beliefs, cultures, institutions that have occurred in the course of the ages—all that we, under the influence of the opposite illusion, are accustomed to describe pleasantly as "progress"—must have been changes for the worse. The examples of this way of thinking are innumerable, and many of them extremely familiar; it is the more striking when it appears in an anti-deistic writer, as in the following passage of Hamann's:

Alle natürliche Erkenntis [*i. e.*, all knowledge which is "natural" in the eulogistic sense of the adjective] ist offenbart: die Natur der Dinge giebt den Stoff, und die Gesetze, nach denen unsere Seele empfindet, denkt, schliesst, urteilt, vergleicht, geben die Form. Alle natürliche Erkenntis ist daher so alt als die Natur selbst; und weil diese unveränderliche bleibt, so kann keine Neuigkeit in den Empfindungen derselben im eigentlichen Verstande Statt finden.[16]

When consistently applied to religion, as it was by the deists,

trations of the belief in the currency of the religion of nature among savages, cf. Atkinson, *Les relations de voyage au 17e siècle*, chap. vii.

[16] *Biblische Betrachtungen* (1758), in *Schriften* (1821), I, 115.

this meant that the entire moral and religious history of civilized mankind, most of all in the West, had been worse than barren— had not only yielded no enrichment of ethical insight or religious understanding or experience, but had been a long tale of multiplying error and increasing departure from the uniformity and simplicity of " nature."

Now substitute " poetry," or " art in general," for " religion " in the foregoing propositions, and you have an outline, not of all, but of much of the more general and fundamental part, of the neo-classical aesthetics. The actual subjective *motivation* of neo-classicism was, no doubt, a complex affair; and in it the force of tradition and the habit of deference to ancient authority undeniably had a large part. But the " rationalization " of these motives is what here concerns us. As a theory, resting upon a coherent, or supposedly coherent, body of principles, neo-classicism was, at bottom, neither traditionalist nor authoritarian; it was an expression of the same rationalism of the Enlightenment which was manifesting itself in deism; and in taking " nature " as *its* sacred word also, it was, in the main, using the word in the same primary sense which it had for the deist.

That neo-classicisim in theory—though happily not quite always in practice—was fundamentally an aesthetic uniformitarianism can hardly need argument. The fact is writ large in all the most famous expositions of neo-classic doctrine; and it is amply demonstrated in some admirable pages of M. René Bray's *La Formation de la doctrine classique en France* (1927). The artist is simply the spokesman of the reason, and it is exclusively to the reason in other men that he must appeal; and " reason " here is not chiefly synonymous with intellect and antithetic to feeling—which, indeed, it may include—but is a name for that which is fundamental and constant in the generic constitution of man. The aim of the poet is to express—in the words of Chapelain (*ca.* 1638), cited by Bray—" cette beauté qui doit plaire à tout le monde," for " la raison n'est pas sujette au changement "; " il est certain," as Balzac and all the neo-classic writers, in one or another form of words, had declared, " que la raison est de tout pays." " Le beau," wrote Fénelon, " ne perdrait rien de son prix quand il serait commun à tout le genre humain; il en serait plus estimable. La rareté est un défaut et une pauvreté de la nature. . . . Je veux un beau si naturel, qu'il n'ait aucun besoin de surprendre par sa nouveauté; je veux que ses grâces ne vieillissent jamais." [17] Pope's rule for literary criticism is the same as the deist's rule for religion:

> First follow Nature, and your judgment frame
> By her just standard, which is still the same:
> Unerring Nature, still divinely bright,
> One clear, unchang'd, and universal light.

Pope accordingly indicts the belief that Nature's gift of " wit," as manifested in literature, is confined to some particular portion of the human race, just as the deists denounced the belief that the knowledge of religious truth is to be found in any creed so confined—and himself points the parallel:

> Some foreign writers, some our own despise;
> The Ancients only, or the Moderns prize.
> Thus wit, like faith, by each man is apply'd
> To one small sect, and all are damn'd beside.
> Meanly they seek the blessing to confine,
> And force that sun but on a part to shine,
> Which not alone the southern wit sublimes,
> But ripens spirits in cold northern climes;
> Which from the first has shone on ages past,
> Enlights the present, and shall warm the last.[18]

The similar passages in Johnson, Reynolds, and other late eighteenth-century English theorists need not be recalled. It was, as I have pointed out elsewhere,[19] the same uniformitarian creed that the future initiators of the Romantic Movement in Germany were still preaching in the belated German classicism of the early 1790's when they inveighed against *interessante* and *charakteristische Poesie*.

An English expression of the principle late in the century is to be found in the *Looker-On*, No. 74 (1792):

---

[17] *Lettre sur les occupations de l'Académie française*, V, " Projet de poétique " (1693).

[18] *Essay on Criticism*, 394-403.

[19] " On the Meaning of ' Romantic ' in Early German Romanticism," and " Schiller and the Genesis of German Romanticism," below.

All the great rules in the fine arts have fixed foundations in our general nature. . . . These principles, I am convinced, are throughout human nature the same in kind, though different in degree according to the primary organization of different minds. . . . The constancy and uniformity of human feelings form the only ground of connexion between those arts which appeal to the imagination and the passions. But the minds of individuals may be discolored and perverted by prejudice, by interest, and by false associations; we are therefore not to consider how particular men are affected, but the general course, the average, if I may so say, of human feelings is to be taken in forming rules and principles for the conduct of those arts which found their claim of excellence upon the power they possess over the heart and fancy. [Again in No. 77, the essayist proposes to convince his readers] that by a right analysis of the human mind, they may come at a system of rules which will exactly coincide with the genuine unperverted sentiments of mankind, . . . that the general approbation of a particular conjuncture is not a standard of taste, though the true standard be founded on general approbation, that is, on an observation of what has at all times been pleasing or displeasing to our uncorrupted feelings; that this standard results from a consideration of the general qualities of objects, and not of the particular accidental sensations which objects produce.

This requirement of universality of appeal was, it must be remembered, the express ground of the neo-classic demand for limitation and approximate invariability of content and description. To be comprehended and appreciated by everybody, the poet must introduce into his imitation of human or physical nature only those traits of either which could have fallen under the observation of all men, even—as Dr. Johnson added in substance, in the notorious passage about the streaks of the tulip—of the least observant of men. It is put even more clearly in the almost equally familiar passage in the *Preface to Shakespeare* in which Shakespeare is declared to be " above all modern writers the poet of nature" *because* " his characters are not modified by the customs of particular places unpractised by the rest of the world; by the peculiarities of studies or professions, which can operate upon but small numbers; or by the accidents of transient fashions or temporary opinions "; but " are the genuine progeny of common humanity, such as the world will always supply, and observation will always find."

There is, it need hardly be said, plenty of the opposite sort of thing also to be found in Johnson; but it is in such passages that he is uttering the pure neo-classic doctrine that the work of art (like the religion of nature) should *express* only what everybody already knows. This had been applied to the content of literature by Boileau in a remark which is obviously the original of Pope's definition of " true wit."

> Qu'est-ce qu'une pensée neuve, brillante, extraordinaire? Ce n'est point, comme se persuadent les ignorants, une pensée que personne n'a jamais eu, ni dû avoir, c'est au contraire, une pensée qui a dû venir à tout le monde, et que quelqu'un s'avise le premier à exprimer. Un bon mot n'est un bon mot qu'en ce qu'il dit une chose que chacun pensait, et qu'il la dit d'une manière vive, fine et nouvelle.[20]

How widely this passed for a self-evident proposition in aesthetics in the mid-eighteenth century is perhaps best illustrated by the assurance of Warburton's comment on Young's *Conjectures*: " Dr. Young is the finest writer of nonsense of any of this age. And had he known that original composition consisted in the manner and not the matter, he had wrote with common sense." A French poet (Delille) as late as the first decade of the nineteenth century was, as Fusil has noted, able to take pride in a couplet in which the propositions that five and four make nine, and two from nine is seven, were poetically expressed. " Everybody," he remarked, " knows that addition and subtraction are two rules of arithmetic, which, being so happily put into verse, *produce a great effect*." [21]

Uniformitarianism is, moreover, worked out in the same dual way in the neo-classical aesthetics as in deism: on the one hand, the reader or beholder is sometimes bidden to rely solely upon his own judgment or feeling—once it has been purified of prejudices and is a genuine expression of " common nature "—in judging of the value or " beauty " of a work of art; on the other hand, he is bidden to accept the *consensus gentium* as the test of merit, and to allow himself to like only what everybody else has always liked. The former way of developing the idea may be illustrated from Hurd's *Discourse on Poetical Imita-*

---

[20] *Preface* to edition of 1701, cited by Vial and Denise, *Idées et doctrines littéraires du XVIIᵉ siècle*, 166.
[21] Fusil, *La poésie scientifique*, 59.

tion: " The perceptions of these inward commotions [i. e., the passions] are uniformly the same in all; and draw along with them the same, or similar, sentiments and reflections.   Hence the appeal is made to every one's own consciousness which declares the truth or falsehood of the imitation." But Hurd (who elsewhere expresses himself in precisely the opposite sense) here forgets that nearly everyone's own consciousness, at least in modern times, was supposed to have been vitiated by false conventions.   To discover the " natural " taste within oneself a corrective process is first necessary, as Batteux points out:

If men were sufficiently attentive to recognize promptly in themselves this natural taste, and if they thereupon labored to extend and develop it, and to render it more acute by observation, comparison and reflection, they would have an invariable and infallible rule for judging of the arts. But since most think on these matters only when they are filled with prejudices, they are unable, in so great a confusion, to distinguish the voice of Nature.[22]

Thus the safer method for arriving at a universally valid standard of taste is to study the classics as, supposedly, the only writings which have aesthetic catholicity, which have been enjoyed and approved *semper, ubique et ab omnibus*; " hence," as Pope wrote—

>   Hence learn for ancient rules a just esteem;
>   To copy nature is to copy them.

The passages on this theme in Reynolds and Johnson are familiar; I will cite rather its expression by a minor writer, William Melmoth the younger, in his *Letters of Sir Thomas Fitzosborne* (1749):

By observing the peculiar construction of those compositions of genius which have always pleased, we perfect our idea of fine writing in particular. It is this united approbation, in persons of different ages and of various characters and languages, that Longinus has made the test of the true sublime; and he might with equal justice have extended the same criterion to all the inferior excellencies of elegant composition. Thus the deference paid to the performances of the great masters of antiquity is based upon just and solid reasons; it is not because Aristotle and Horace have given us the rules of criticism that we submit to

---

[22] *Les beaux arts réduits à un seul principe* (1747), p. 66.

their authority; it is because those rules are derived from works that have been distinguished by the uninterrupted admiration of all the more improved part of mankind, from their earliest appearance down to the present hour. For whatever, through a long series of ages, has been universally esteemed beautiful, cannot but be conformable to our just and natural idea of beauty.[23]

It is this impress of the *general* uniformitarian principle, of the ideal of standardization, upon poetry which chiefly explains why, as Mr. F. L. Lucas [24] has remarked, almost every eighteenth-century poet—and not Gray merely—" never spoke out," never expressed " all those intimate sadnesses and agonies which have given life to the utterances of so many minor poets in other eras." It was not that, as Mr. Lucas suggests, they were restrained by a sense of decorum, a shrinking from the " emotional immodesty " of such behavior. There were plenty of eighteenth-century poets, major and minor, who were little hampered by a sense of decorum. The reason for their restraint was that it still generally passed for an aesthetic axiom that " speaking out " is not art, that the poet who wishes to become a classic must never be himself, except to the extent that he is— aside from a greater gift for putting things—the same as every other man.

The aesthetic cosmopolitanism implicit in this is obvious. An art that accords with a reason which is *de tout pays* could as little give place to national as to personal idiosyncrasy of character or taste. Racine expressed the gratification which he had experienced in discovering that, in imitating the the dramatic art of ancient Greeks and Romans, he had the more surely reached the minds and hearts of Parisians of the seventeenth century: " Le goût de Paris s'est trouvé conforme à celui d'Athènes; mes spectateurs ont été ému des mêmes choses qui ont mis autrefois en larmes le plus savant peuple de la Grèce." [25] When one orthodox critic wished to say something peculiarly unpleasant of another, he accused him of betraying his nationality in his writings; it was thus that Fréron, in his *Lettres sur quelques écrits de ce temps* (1749), belittled Voltaire:

[23] P. 130. These letters were long taken very seriously: there were at least twelve London editions, and at least two in America, in 1805 and 1815.

[24] *The New Statesman*, February 28, 1925, p. 599.

[25] Preface to *Iphigénie en Aulide*.

M. de Voltaire is really a French author; that is to say, he belongs to his own nation and his own age, whereas the true poets are of all times and countries.   Often the slave of the ruling taste, he has preferred the advantage of being known to his contemporaries to the glory of being admired by our remote descendants.

The neo-classic antipathy to originality and to private intuitions in matters of taste is, again, analogous to the deist's usual antipathy to " enthusiasm."   And a complete aesthetic equalitarianism was inherent in the neo-classic principles.   It is true that there was often to be found in writers commonly classified as neo-classicists another strain—a cultivation of the pose of the connoisseur, a restriction of the right to pronounce judgment on works of art to the " improved " or " refined " part of mankind.   But in so far as its fundamental logic was consistently carried out, neo-classicism was the doctrine that artistic merit is to be determined by universal suffrage; and this democratic tendency in it is nowhere more strikingly and amusingly made evident than in its expression by a stout Tory, such as Dr. Johnson.   Detesting levelers in politics and society, he was himself, in more than one way, a preacher of leveling in art: as in a passage of the *Life of Gray:*

By the common sense of readers uncorrupted by all the refinements of subtilty and the dogmatism of learning must be finally decided all claim to poetical honors.   The " Churchyard " abounds with images which find a mirror in every mind, and with sentiments to which every bosom returns an echo.

The artist must thus smooth out all differences and lower his observation or his dream or his emotion (so far as they are given expression) to the plane of common sensibility and of the average understanding.

The strict neo-classicist's high valuation of simplicity and regularity in all the arts is akin to what I have called " rationalistic anti-intellectualism "; though it certainly had other causes, it was in part a manifestation of a general dislike for intricacy and complexity.   A complex design does not reveal itself to the eye at once; it imposes upon the beholder, hearer, or reader a special effort of comprehension, an effort difficult for all, and probably impossible for some; and it is sufficiently condemned by that fact alone.[26]

With respect to primitivism, the analogy may seem to break down; but it does so only in part. The modern literary theorist could not well go back for his models to the poetry, as the deist supposed himself to be going back to the religion, of Adam, Seth, and Noah; for if those worthies wrote any epics, odes, or tragedies, they unfortunately did not transmit them to posterity. Literature presupposed a certain degree of civilization, and, so far as was known, had made its appearance only at a time considerably removed from the earliest age. And the primitivistic preconception certainly was less potent in the shaping of the neo-classic creed than it was in the case of deism. Nevertheless, it was, of course, of the essence of rigorous neo-classicism to maintain that each *genre* attained its ideal form almost at its birth; the oldest known epic, the oldest known tragedies, comedies, and odes, the earliest criticism, were the standards of excellence in their respective kinds; and to observe the truest examples of what is in accord with " universal nature " in each kind the modern poet or the modern critic must turn to these primitives. And so far as the epic was concerned, those classicists who placed Homer above Vergil as well as all the moderns, were committed to a fairly thoroughgoing primitivism, often of the rationalistic sort; and it definitely tended, as Miss Lois Whitney has shown,[27] through the writings of scholars learned in the classics, such as Blackwell, Blair, and Robert Wood, to transform itself into the " romantic " type of primitivism and to promote the enthusiasm for Ossian. Other traits of ancient poetry were not seldom eulogized on primitivistic grounds: so Fénelon writes: " on gagne beaucoup en perdant tous les ornements superflus pour se borner aux beautés simples, faciles, claires, et négligées en apparence. Pour la poésie,

---

[26] Cf. Fénelon, *Lettre sur les occupations de l'Académie française*, V: " Il faut une diction simple, précise et dégagé, où tout se développe de soi-même et aille au-devant du lecteur. Quand un auteur parle en public, il n'y a aucune peine qu'il ne doive prendre pour en épargner à son lecteur. . . . Un auteur ne doit laisser rien à chercher dans sa pensée; il n'y a que les faiseurs d'énigmes qui soient en droit de présenter un sens enveloppé. . . . En effet, le premier de tous les devoirs d'un homme qui n'écrit que pour être entendu, est de soulager son lecteur en se faisant d'abord entendre."

[27] " English Primitivistic Theories of Epic Origins," *Mod. Phil.*, May, 1924.

comme pour l'architecture, il faut que tous les morceaux néces-
saires se tournent en ornements naturels.   Mais tout ornement
qui n'est qu'ornement est de trop; retranchez-le, il ne manque
rien, il n'y a que la vanité qui en souffre." Quoting a passage
from one of Vergil's *Eclogues*, Fénelon exclaims: "Combien
cette naïveté champêtre a-t-elle plus de grâce qu'un trait subtil
et raffiné d'un bel esprit." And a little later: in reading the
Odyssey, "on croit être dans les lieux qu' Homère dépeint, y
voir et y entendre les hommes. Cette simplicité de moeurs
semble ramener l'âge d'or.   Le bonhomme Eumée me touche
bien plus qu'un héros de *Clélie* ou de *Cléopatre*.   Les vains
préjugés de notre temps avilissent de telles beautés; mais nos
défauts ne diminuent point le vrai prix d'une vie si raisonnable
et si naturelle." [28]   Bishop Hurd, in his *Notes on the Art of
Poetry*, defended the practice of the Greek dramatists in "moralizing so much" by observing that "in the virtuous simplicity
of less polished times this spirit of moralizing is very prevalent."

Finally, just as the deist saw in the greater part of the religious history of mankind merely a long aberration from "nature," the strict neo-classicist saw the same in the greater part
of the history of all the arts.   They all began well; they all
were soon corrupted; and the way of salvation lay, not in an
advance, but in a reversion.   "The Gothick" was, in the
orthodox classical critic's vocabulary, what "revealed religion"
or "superstition" was in that of the deist; and the most interesting thing about Thomas Warton's familiar lines on Sir Joshua
Reynolds's window at New College is the way in which they
illustrate this parallelism between classicism in art and in religion.   The defect of Gothic art, according to Warton, it will
be remembered, was that it did not conform to that truth
which is

by no peculiar taste confined,
Whose universal pattern strikes the mind.

"Gothick" and "non-universal" were assumed to be equivalent; and both were antithetic to "natural" for the same reason.   But this was, in principle, precisely the fundamental reason why the deist rejected all positive, historical, or ostensibly
revealed, religion.

[28] *Lettre sur les occupations de l'Académie française*, "Projet de poétique."

Of the latent contradictions in all this, and of its bearing upon the causes of the ultimate fate of both the deistic movement and the neo-classical aesthetics a good deal might be said; but that is another story—part of which I have already attempted to tell elsewhere.[29]

[29] *The Great Chain of Being*, chaps. VII, X.

VII. THE CHINESE ORIGIN OF A
ROMANTICISM *

1

THE SANCTITY of the notion of "regularity" in the typically neo-classical aesthetic doctrines is well known; but three examples of it are worth recalling, to serve as background for the principal theme of this essay. The first is Sir Christopher Wren's definition of beauty:

Beauty is a Harmony of Objects, begetting Pleasure by the Eye. There are two Causes of Beauty—natural and customary. Natural is from Geometry, consisting in Uniformity (that is Equality). . . . Always the true test is natural or geometrical Beauty. Geometrical Figures are naturally more beautiful than any other irregular; in this all consent, as to a Law of Nature.[1]

In the same vein John Dennis wrote of poetry in 1704:

If the end of poetry is to instruct and reform the world, that is, to bring mankind from irregularity and confusion to rule and order, how this should be done by a thing that is in itself irregular and extravagant, is difficult to be conceiv'd. . . . The work of every reasonable creature must derive its beauty from regularity, for Reason is rule and order, and nothing can be irregular . . . any further than it swerves from rules, that is from Reason. . . . The works of man must needs be the more perfect, the more they resemble his Maker's. Now the works of God, though infinitely various, are extremely regular. The Universe is regular in all its parts, and it is to that exact regularity that it owes its admirable beauty.[2]

It was, however, rather difficult to make this last proposition appear plausible when one actually observed the visible appear-

* Published in part in *The Journal of English and Germanic Philology*, January, 1933; Pt. 2 has been revised and expanded, and Pt. 4 has been added.
[1] *Parentalia*, cited in L. Weaver, *Sir Christopher Wren* (1923), 150.
[2] "The Grounds of Criticism in Poetry," in Durham, *Critical Essays, 1700-1725*.

ances of nature. It is therefore interesting to note the delight
with which the disclosure of previously unknown examples of
regularity in nature's architecture was sometimes hailed. As
late as 1772 Sir Joseph Banks, on his expedition to Iceland,
discovered the grotto now known as Fingal's Cave on the Island
of Staffa, in which basaltic pillars, "almost in the shape of
those used in architecture, rise in natural colonnades on either
side with remarkable regularity." What seems most to have
pleased the discoverer was that Nature was thus aesthetically
vindicated and shown to furnish the model for classical architecture. For after describing the scene he bursts into this
rhapsody:

Compared to this, what are the cathedrals or palaces built by men! mere
models or playthings, diminutive as his works will always be when
compared to those of Nature. Where is now the boast of the architect! Regularity, the only part in which he fancied himself to excel his
mistress, Nature, is there found in her possession, and here it has been
for ages undescribed. Is not this the school where the art was originally
studied, and what had been added to this by the whole *Grecian* school?
A capital to ornament the column of Nature, of which they could
execute only a model; and for that very capital they were obliged to a
bush of Acanthus: how amply does Nature repay those who study her
wonderful works! [3]

It is no longer needful to dwell upon the many-sided importance of that change in aesthetic standards which took place,
chiefly in the course of the eighteenth century, when regularity,
uniformity, clearly recognizable balance and parallelism came
to be regarded as capital defects in a work of art, and irregularity, asymmetry, variety, surprise, an avoidance of that simplicity and unity which render a whole design comprehensible
at a glance, took rank as aesthetic virtues of a high order. It
is also, by this time, pretty generally known that the change

[3] "Account of Staffa, communicated by Joseph Banks, Esq." in Thomas
Pennant's *A Tour of Scotland and Voyage to the Hebrides*, 1774. That actual
observation of nature would not lead one to suppose that God "always geo-
metrizes" had been admitted by the botanist John Ray in his *Three Physico-
Theological Discourses* (3d ed., 1713, pp. 34-5). But, desiring to justify God's
ways to man, he maintained that "the present Face of the Earth, with all its
Mountains and Hills, as rude and deformed as they appear," is a more "beautiful and pleasant Object" than it would be without these "Inequalities."

first appeared on a considerable scale in other arts and only gradually spread to the aesthetics of literature. In these other arts this incipient Romanticism manifested itself in, and was promoted by, four new phenomena in eighteenth-century taste and artistic practice: (a) the enthusiasm for the landscape-painting of Claude Lorrain, Poussin and Salvator Rosa; (b) the introduction and wide diffusion of the English or so-called "natural" style in gardening, which was perhaps the eighteenth-century art *par excellence*; (c) the Gothic revival which began in England with the not very happy efforts of Batty Langley and Sanderson Miller in the 1740s; (d) the admiration for the Chinese garden and, in a less degree, for the architecture and other artistic achievements of the Chinese. These, and especially the last three, were very intimately associated in the eighteenth-century mind; the second and fourth, indeed, were so completely fused that, as is well known, they came to bear a single name, *le goût anglo-chinois*. They were associated because they all exemplified, or were supposed by *virtuosi* and critics of the first half of the century to express, the same set of fundamental aesthetic principles. They were differing applications of the gospel of irregularity, diverse modes of returning to the imitation of nature conceived, not as geometrical, orderly and uniform, but as distinguished by freedom from formal patterns, "wildness," and inexhaustible diversity.

Of these four related movements, three have been dealt with and their significance in the history of general aesthetic ideas pointed out in recent and excellent studies—the first in Miss Manwaring's *Italian Landscape in Eighteenth Century England*, the second in Mr. Christopher Hussey's book on *The Picturesque*, and to some extent in Mr. Draper's life of William Mason. The story of the third, the Gothic revival, has been told interestingly but not altogether adequately in Sir Kenneth Clark's work on this topic. The fourth, though its external history, chiefly in separate countries, has more than once been written, has not, so far as I know, been comprehensively treated from the standpoint of the student of the history of ideas—certainly not in its English manifestations. Mr. Hussey has devoted three or four lively and sometimes illuminating pages to it, but he has not traced the fashion to its real source, nor distinguished the phases of its history, nor done full justice to its historical significance.

I shall in this essay show that the Chinese style in gardening began to exercise its influence upon aesthetic ideas and fashions earlier than the new models in gardening given by Switzer, Kent, Brown, and Bridgman, earlier even than the literary expression of the new ideal of gardening by Pope and Addison in the first decade of the century; that the general idea of a " beauty without order " was apparently first definitely presented by an important English writer as a Chinese idea, actually realized in Chinese gardens; that the taste for the *jardin anglais* owed much to the earlier idealization of the Chinese garden; that through the first seven or eight decades of the century the admiration for these gardens—or for what they were supposed to be—continued to exercise an influence which was probably little, if at all, less potent than that of the other three new aesthetic fashions mentioned, in promoting the variety of Romanticism to which I have referred; that for a time Gothicism and the *goût chinois* were especially closely related; and that in the seventeen-seventies a new conception of the aesthetic aims and principles of Chinese gardening (and other arts) and of its relation to the English style was introduced, which was apparently fatal to the enthusiasm for Chinese gardens in England.

2

The general fact which lies behind the particular episode with which I shall deal is, of course, the enormous reputation which Chinese civilization had in Europe from the late sixteenth until the late eighteenth century.[4] In the very earliest reports by voyagers and missionaries who had visited China, even before the establishment of the Jesuit mission in Peking, the writers dilate with surprise and admiration upon the excel-

---

[4] On this see Reichwein, *China und Europa*, 1923 (Engl. tr., 1925) ; G. Atkinson, *Les relations de voyages du 17e siècle* (n. d.), chap. V; and the following, which have appeared since this essay was written: V. Pinot, *La Chine et la formation de l'esprit philosophique en France, 1640-1740* (1932) ; A. H. Rowbotham, *Missionary and Mandarin* (1942), chaps. XVI-XVII; Lewis S. Maverick, *China a model for Europe* (1946). Pinot's and Maverick's volumes contain extensive bibliographies.

lence of the Chinese system of government and of their administration of justice, which, it is usually remarked, Europeans might imitate with advantage; by 1590 the assumption of the superiority of the Chinese political system was apparently already a commonplace.[5] The earliest substantial treatise on China, by Father Gonzalez de Mendoza, which was speedily translated into the principal European languages,[6] evoked the first enthusiastic eulogy of the Chinese by a great European writer: Montaigne, who had never mentioned China in the editions of the *Essais* published during his lifetime, read this book sometime between 1588 and his death in 1592, and prepared a new paragraph which was inserted in the posthumous edition (1595):

. . . la Chine, duquel royaume la police et les arts, sans commerce et cognoissance des nostres, surpassent nos exemples en plusieurs parties d'excellence, et duquel l'histoire m'apprend combien le monde est plus ample et plus divers que ny les anciens ny nous ne penetrons.[7]

Thus, by the beginning of the seventeenth century, the Chinese already figured in European eyes as, above all, masters in the great practical art of government. And as such they continued to figure for nearly two hundred years. When, after 1615, the long succession of Jesuit reports and descriptions of China began to flow into Europe,[8] its reputation in

[5] Cf. *An excellent treatise of the kingdome of China, and of the estate and government thereof written in Latin* . . . (Macao, 1590); English tr. in Hakluyt's *Voyages* (1589-1598): "their manner of government, wherein the Chinians are said greatly to excell" (1904 ed., VI, 363).

[6] *Historia de las cosas mas notables, ritos y costumbres del Reyno de la China,* Lisbon, 1584; Spanish tr., 1585; Italian, 1586; French, 1588; English, 1588.

[7] *Essais,* III, 13: "De l'expérience." Montaigne proceeds to dwell upon the feature of Chinese "justice" which he especially admired: it rewards officials who perform their functions well, and does not merely punish those who perform them ill. This, he had already insisted in the original version of the essay, is requisite for real justice; he now discovered, with gratified surprise, that—in contrast with *notre justice à nous*—the Chinese actually embodied his own conception in their institutions and laws.

[8] The first of these was the general descriptive account by Father Nicolas Trigault prefixed to his story of the early years of the mission, based upon the diary of its founder, Father Matteo Ricci: *De christiana expeditione apud Sinas suscepta* . . . Libri V, 1615. Trigault's account (Bk. I) was partially translated in *Purchas his Pilgrimes* (1625), Bk. III. A not always accurate translation of it by Father L. J. Gallagher, S. J. has been published (1942)

this respect was only confirmed, as various more specific grounds for it were set forth. A stereotyped list of points in which the Chinese political institutions and practice were superior to those of the West was repeated again and again. In that country even the highest state offices (below the Emperor) were " open for all men, without any respect of degree or parentage." [9]   Admission to the public service required definite and exacting educational qualifications, tested by examinations, and evidence of personal character and competence: " the holding of any political office depends upon proved knowledge, virtue, prudence and ability." [10]   There was a seeming constant insistence, through periodic visitations of inspectors, upon efficiency and a regard for the public interest in the operation of the entire political mechanism. China was the realization of Plato's dream—a state ruled by " philosophers "; the great Jesuit polymath, Athanasius Kircher, in his *China illustrata* (1670)—a sort of encyclopedia of information about the Middle Kingdom—though, naturally, disapproving of the popular religions of the Chinese and of much in their private behavior, wrote:

. . . cet État est gouverné parles Doctes, à la mode des Platoniciens, et selon le désir du Philosophe divin: en quoy j'estime ce Royaume heureux, lequel a un Roy qui peut philosopher ou qui souffre du moins qu'un philosophe le gouverne et le conduit.[11]

Exemplary also were the Chinese in their conduct towards neighboring countries: "' neither the king nor his subjects ever think of conquering other nations. They are content with what is theirs and do not covet what belongs to others." [12]   They were, in fact, the least militaristic of all peoples: " no

under the title: *The China that was: China as discovered by the Jesuits of the sixteenth century.*

[9] *An excellent treatise*, etc., in Hakluyt, *op. cit.*, VI, 363.

[10] Trigault, *op. cit.*, 50.

[11] *Op. cit.*, French tr., 226. In general, Kircher observes, " de toutes les Monarchies qu'il y ait dans l'Univers, il n'y a pas une de si célèbre ny de si recommandable " (*ibid.*, 223).

[12] Trigault, *op. cit.*, 64. " In this respect," Trigault adds, " they appear to me to differ most widely from the peoples of Europe, . . . who seem eaten up with an insatiable lust of domination."

mortals have ever had an abhorrence of everything military equal to that of the Chinese." [13]

Admittedly preëminent in the science and art of politics, the Chinese soon acquired an almost equally great reputation as moralists. Trigault had remarked that they have a peculiar preoccupation with the *science des moeurs*, " to a knowledge of which they have attained "—though he did not think highly of their achievements in the natural sciences. But it was especially to the growing fame of Confucius in the seventeenth century that the recognition of their merit in moral philosophy was due; and for this the Jesuit writers were almost wholly responsible, at first through brief summaries of his teachings, after 1687 through a small volume containing Latin translations from his (actual or reputed) writings, *Confucius Sinarum philosophus*, by a group of Jesuit Fathers. The Introduction to this reached the high-water mark of Western eulogy of the Chinese sage; it boldly declared that Confucius's is " the excellentest Morality that ever was taught, a Morality which might be said to proceed from the School of Jesus Christ." [14]

By the end of the century, then, it had come to be widely accepted that the Chinese—by the light of nature alone—had surpassed Christian Europe both in the art of government and in ethics. To illustrate this, it will here suffice to quote the observations concerning them of the greatest mind among their admirers. Leibniz in his *Novissima Sinica* (1699) makes a detailed comparison of the achievements of the Chinese with those of Europeans. The latter, he concludes, excel in logic and metaphysics, the knowledge of " incorporeal things," in astronomy and geometry, and in military science.

In these, then, we are superior. But who would formerly have believed that . . . there is a people which surpasses us in its principles of civil life? And this, nevertheless, we now experience in the case of the Chinese, as they become better known to us. And so, if in the mechanical arts we are their equals, if in the contemplative sciences we beat them, certainly in practical philosophy—be it said almost with shame—we are beaten by them—that is, in the principles of Ethics and Politics. For it is impossible to describe how

[13] Isaac Voss (Vossius) in *Variarum observationum liber* (1685), 66.
[14] Quoted from the English translation, 2nd ed., 1724.

beautifully everything in the laws of the Chinese, more than in those of other peoples, is directed to the achievement of public tranquillity, to that good order in the relations of men to one another whereby each is in the least degree injurious to others. Certain it is that the greatest evils which men suffer come from themselves, and are inflicted by them upon one another, so that the saying *homo homini lupus*, every man is a wolf to his neighbor, was all too truly spoken. Great indeed is our folly (but it is universal folly) with which we, exposed as we are to so many natural ills, heap upon ourselves miseries from which we should otherwise be free. If reason anywhere provides a remedy for this evil, certainly the Chinese more than others attain to a better standard (*norma*), and, in a vast society of men, they achieve it in almost a higher degree than do, among us, the founders of religious societies in their small establishments (*familiae*).[15]

Both China and Europe, Leibniz held, have something to learn from one another, and he was zealous in promoting the project of a joint Chinese-European Academy of Science, in which the scientific knowledge of the West, especially the " mathematical arts," and also " our doctrine of Philosophy," should be investigated and taught:

If this should be carried out, I fear lest we soon be inferior to the Chinese in everything that is deserving of praise. I say this, not because I envy them any new light—on that I should rather congratulate them—but because it is to be desired that we, on our side, should learn from them those things which hitherto have, rather, been lacking [16] in our affairs, especially the use of practical philosophy and an improved understanding of how to live (*emendatior vivendi ratio*)—to say nothing at present of other arts. Certainly the state of our affairs, as corruptions spread among us without measure, seems to me such that it would appear almost necessary that Chinese missionaries should be sent to us to teach us the use and practice of natural religion (*theologia naturalis*), just as we send missionaries to them to teach them revealed religion. And so, I believe that if a wise man were chosen to pass judgment, not upon the shapes of goddesses, but upon the excellence of peoples, he would award the golden apple to the Chinese—except that we should have the better of them in one supreme, but superhuman, thing, namely, the divine gift of the Christian religion.[17]

[15] *Op. cit.*, preface.
[16] I take *essent* in the Latin text to be a misprint for *deessent*.
[17] *Ibid.*

All this, however, was bound to produce a reaction among the watch-dogs of religious, especially of Catholic, orthodoxy. To admit that the heathen Chinese, guided only by the light of nature, had been able to attain the best ethics and the best government in the world, was to cast doubt upon the indispensability of the Christian teaching and of the guidance of human affairs by the Church. The theologians had never denied the needfulness of the use of the natural reason; but to say that, even for this life, it was sufficient, and that those who relied upon it alone were better moralists than Christians, whose minds were illumined by supernatural grace, was too much. The Jesuit mission, as is now notorious, had had a paradoxical outcome. It had not converted many Chinese, but it had done much to strengthen the position of sceptics and deists in Europe. As Rowbotham remarks, in his admirable and sympathetic history of the mission, " the outstanding ironic fact of early Jesuit history is that, perhaps more than any other organization, the members of the Society put into the hands of the anti-Christian forces one of their most effective weapons against the Church." [18] The danger had been noted by some of the Jesuits themselves in the seventeenth century; about the beginning of the eighteenth century the ecclesiastical reaction against Sinomania became marked. The legend of Chinese superiority must be destroyed. In the first decade of the century Fénelon led the attack. He devoted the longest of the *Dialogues des Morts* to an argument between Confucius and Socrates in which the latter belittles " la prééminence tant vantée des Chinois." The belief in the virtues of the Chinese, Socrates is made to argue, arises from an idealization born of ignorance; Europeans know too little of Chinese history, literature and life, to justify the customary eulogies. Nor does Fénelon content himself with mere scepticism upon the point; on the evidence available he, through the mouth of the Greek sage, pronounces the Chinese to be " the vainest, the most superstitious, the most selfish (*intéressé*), the most unjust, and the most mendacious people on earth." [19]

But this effort to check Sinomania was unavailing. The

[18] *Missionary and Mandarin* (1942), 294.
[19] *Oeuvres*, 1823 ed., XIX, 146-161.

most sensational incident in the history of the German universities in the first half of the century contributed to its growth. The philosopher Christian Wolff in an academic oration at the University of Halle in 1721, *De Sinarum philosophia practica*, declared that " the ancient Emperors and Kings of *China* were men of a *philosophical* Turn," and that " to their Care it is owing, that their Form of Government is of all others the best, and that as in Antiquity, so in the Art of Governing, this Nation has ever surpassed all others without exception." [20] The result may best be told in the words of Wolff's contemporary English translator:

This Speech so alarmed the Divines of the *University* at *Halle*, that without regard to Truth or common Justice, they fastened on him the blackest of imputations and the most impious Notions possible; tho' he asserted nothing other in it but that the *Chinese Manner of Philosophy* had a great affinity with his own. *Francke* and *Lange*, both Doctors in Divinity, and the greatest Enemies Mr. *Wolffius* ever had, exclaimed against him on this Occasion in their publick Sermons. And the *Odium Theologicum* went so far as to brand him with the appellation of Heathen and Atheist: Nor was their Rancour thus satisfied, but they represented him to the late King of *Prussia* as a Man of the most dangerous and pernicious, and so far their black Calumny prevailed, that the King ordered him under *Pain of immediate Death to quit the University of Halle* in twenty-four hours and his Dominions in forty-eight.[21]

The Chinese cult thus had a martyr—and the martyrdom was highly advantageous to it as well as to the victim, who was promptly called to Marburg, where he was rapturously received by the students as a hero of the cause of enlightenment.[22] Wolff's political and moral gospel according to the Chinese appeared in English as a dissertation: *The Real Happiness of a People under a Philosophical King Demonstrated; Not only from the Nature of Things, but from the undoubted Experience of the Chinese, under their first Founder Fo Hi, and his illustrious successors, Hoam Ti and Xin Num.*

The chorus of praise of Chinese government and ethics was

[20] From Wolff's own summary in the English translation of his book (1750).
[21] *Ibid.*, preface.
[22] There is in the *aula* of the University of Marburg a striking mural painting depicting Wolff's triumphal arrival in that town.

swelled in the course of the eighteenth century by numerous
and powerful voices: by Dr. Johnson (in his youth, though
not in his later years),[23] the Marquis d'Argens,[24] Quesnay [25]
(who believed the Founding Fathers of the Chinese polity and
economy were Physiocrats *sans le savoir*), Goldsmith, whose
Citizen of the World is an imitation of a series of French
Lettres Chinoises by various writers; [26] and above all by Voltaire. Among their higher classes, at least, he declared, deism,
the pure religion of nature, which Europe, and most civilized
peoples, had lost, had been preserved uncorrupted.

Worship God and practise justice—this is the sole religion of the
Chinese *literati*. . . . O Thomas Aquinas, Scotus, Bonaventure, Francis,
Dominic, Luther, Calvin, canons of Westminster, have you anything
better? For four thousand years this religion, so simple and so noble,
has endured in absolute integrity; and it is probable that it is much
more ancient.

True, "the common people are foolish and superstitious in
China, as elsewhere." But the "wise and tolerant government,
concerned only with morals and public order," has never inter-
fered with these beliefs of the populace: " il ne trouva pas mau-
vais que la canaille crût des inepties, pourvu qu'elle ne troublât
point l'État et qu'elle obéit aux lois." Thanks to this rational
and tolerant régime, " Chinese history has never been disturbed
by any religious disorders," and " no mystery has ravaged their
souls." [27]   In the *Dictionnaire Philosophique*, while admitting
their backwardness in the natural sciences and the mechanic
arts, Voltaire insisted upon their superiority in more important
things:

One may be a very poor physicist and an excellent moralist. Thus it is

[23] *Gentleman's Magazine*, VIII (1738), 365. This and other passages of
Johnson on China have been brought together by a Chinese writer, Mr. Fan
Tsen-chung: *Dr. Johnson and Chinese Culture* (*Occasional Papers of the China
Society*, N. S., No. 6), London, 1945.
[24] *Lettres chinoises* (1739) ; *Histoire de l'esprit humain* (1767), 30.
[25] Quesnay's *Du despotisme de la Chine* has been translated, with an introduction, by Maverick, *China a model for Europe*, 1946. Cf. also Reichwein,
op. cit., 101 ff.
[26] Cf. R. S. Crane and H. J. Smith: "A French Influence on Goldsmith's
Citizen of the World," *Modern Philology* (1921), 183.
[27] *Dieu et les hommes*, 1769.

in morals, in political economy, in agriculture, that the Chinese have perfected themselves. We have taught them all the rest; but in these matters we ought to be their disciples. . . . The constitution of their empire is in truth the best that there is in the world . . . [In spite of the superstitions of the lower classes] the fact remains that four thousand years ago, when we did not know how to read, they knew everything essentially useful of which we boast today.[28]

When, then, a new criterion of excellence in the arts was also introduced as an importation from China, and supported by a constant appeal to Chinese examples, its acceptance was obviously facilitated by the widely current assumption—of which I have given a few illustrations—of the excellence, or the actual superiority, in the chief essentials of civilization, of the Chinese ways of doing things.

3

In England apparently the earliest, and certainly the most zealous, enthusiast for the Chinese was Sir William Temple. In his essay *Upon Heroick Virtue* (1683) he devoted a long chapter to them, and described their government as " framed and policed with the utmost force and reach of human wisdom, reason and contrivance; and in practice to excel the very speculations of other men, and all those imaginary schemes of the *European* wits, the Institutions of *Xenophon*, the Republic of *Plato*, the Utopias and Oceanas of our modern writers." He was also a passionate garden-lover, and liked to philosophize about beauty in general in connection with the problem of garden-design. His ideas on the subject are expressed in his essay *Upon the Gardens of Epicurus*, written about 1685, published in 1692, in the second volume of his *Essays*. He observes that

in the laying out of gardens, great sums may be thrown away without effect or honour if there want sense in proportion to money; or if nature be not followed; which I take to be the great rule in this, and perhaps in everything else, as far as the conduct not only of our lives, but our governments. And whether the greatest of mortal men should attempt the forcing of nature, may best be judged by observing how

[28] Art.: " De la Chine."

seldom God Almighty does it himself, by so few true, and undisputed miracles as we see or hear of in the world.

Temple is nevertheless so far subject to the older convention that his recommendations to the English designer as to " the best forms of gardens " relate only to " such as are in some sort regular." But he adds a paragraph which, in describing and extolling the gardens of the Chinese, foreshadows the new English style of the following century:

There may be other forms wholly irregular that may, for aught I know, have more beauty than any of the others; but they must owe it to some extraordinary dispositions of nature in the seat, or some great race of fancy or judgment in the contrivance, which may reduce many disagreeing parts into some figure, which shall yet, upon the whole, be very agreeable. Something of this I have seen in some places, but heard more of it from others who had lived much among the Chineses; a people whose way of thinking seems to be as wide of ours in Europe as their country does. Among us, the beauty of building and planting is placed chiefly in some certain proportions, symmetries, or uniformities; our walks and our trees ranged so as to answer one another, and at exact distances. The Chinese scorn this way of planting, and say, a boy that can tell a hundred, may plant walks of trees in straight lines, and over-against one another, and to what length and extent he pleases. But their greatest reach of imagination is employed in contriving figures, where the beauty shall be great, and strike the eye, but without any order or disposition of parts that shall be commonly or easily observed: and though we have hardly any notion of this sort of beauty, yet they have a particular word to express it, and, where they find it hit their eye at first sight, they say the sharawadgi is fine or admirable, or any such expression of esteem. And whoever observes the work upon the best India gowns, or the painting upon their best screens or porcelains, will find their beauty is all of this kind (that is) without order.[29]

Temple, however, little realizing that he was laying down the principles of the future *jardin anglais*, thought the attainment of this subtler beauty of the irregular too difficult for his countrymen to aspire to:

[29] *Works* (1757), III, 229-230. The NED declares that " Chinese scholars agree that the word *sharawadgi* cannot belong to that language." Mr. Y. Z. Chang, who has considered the problem at my request, finds the probable original of the word in the syllables *sa-ro-(k)wai-chi*, which may have the meaning " the quality of being impressive or surprising through careless or unorderly grace." (Cf. his article in *Modern Language Notes* (1930), 221-224).

I should hardly advise any of these attempts in the figure of gardens among us; they are adventures of too hard achievement for any common hands; and though there may be more honour if they succeed well, yet there is more dishonour if they fail, and 'tis twenty to one they will; whereas, in regular figures 'tis hard to make any great and remarkable faults.[30]

This, however, must obviously have affected an ambitious designer of a later generation less as a discouragement than as a challenge. " Fortunately "—as Walpole long afterwards remarked in quoting the passage—" Kent and a few others were not so timid."

As bearing upon the degree of importance to be attached to these observations of Temple's it is to be borne in mind that he was universally read by persons of taste in the eighteenth century; he was regarded as one of the great masters of English prose and his essays " were used as exercises and models." [31]

Mason in *The English Garden*, Bk. II (1777), recognized Temple's priority in the apostolic succession of English garden-theorists; but (in consequence of a political-literary feud which had by that time broken out, to which I shall later refer), he suppressed the fact that the one doctrine of Temple which he applauded was derived from the Chinese. After satirizing the artificiality and formality of the garden at Moor Park which Temple had pronounced " perfect," Mason adds:

> And yet full oft
> O'er TEMPLE'S studious hour did Truth preside,
> Sprinkling her lustre o'er his classic page:
> There hear his candour own in fashion's spite,
> In spite of courtly dullness, hear it own
> " There is a grace in wild variety
> Surpassing rule and order."
>   TEMPLE, yes,
> There is a grace; and let eternal wreaths
> Adorn their brows who fixt its empire here.
> The Muse shall hail the champions that herself
> Led to the fair achievement.[32]

---

[30] *Ibid.*
[31] *DNB*, XIX, 531.
[32] *The English Garden*, II, 483-494.

Now Temple's enunciation—definite, though made with the timidity of one who feels himself to be advancing a radical novelty—of the ideal of beauty without order (or manifest order) antedates by more than two decades Addison's praise of artificial wildness in gardens in the *Tatler* and *Spectator*. Miss Manwaring gives Addison the credit of being "the most influential early advocate of . . . escape from the artificial in gardening." [33]   But in his most noteworthy expression on the subject (*Spectator*, No. 414, June 25, 1712), Addison expressly sets up the Chinese as the actual exemplars of the ideals which he is preaching; and most of the passage is taken from Temple without acknowledgment:

Writers who have given us an account of *China*, tell us that the inhabitants of that country laugh at the Plantations of our *Europeans*, which are laid out by rule and line; because they say any one may place Trees in equal Rows and uniform Figures.   They choose rather to show a Genius in Works of Nature, and thereby always conceal the Art by which they direct themselves.   They have a Word it seems in their Language, by which they express the particular Beauty of a Plantation that thus strikes the Imagination at first Sight, without discovering what it is that has so agreeable an Effect.   Our *British* gardeners, on the contrary, instead of humouring Nature, love to deviate from it as much as possible.   Our Trees rise in Cones, Globes, and Pyramids. We see the Marks of the Scissors upon every Plant and Bush.

Next to Addison chronologically in the revolt against symmetry in garden-design, Pope is usually placed in the histories of the movement; but in his earliest manifesto against the modern practice of gardening (in *The Guardian*, No. 17, 1713) Pope quotes with approval from Temple's essay; and much of the famous passage about gardens in the *Epistle to the Earl of Burlington*, 1731, reads like a metrical paraphrase of some of Temple's remarks—though without mention of the Chinese.

We must, then, I think, see in Temple's account of the peculiarities and underlying principles of Chinese gardening the probable effective beginning (in England) of the new ideas about that art which were destined to have consequences of such unforeseen range.   It will, further, be observed that the

[33] *Italian Landscape in Eighteenth Century England*, 124.

passage introduces a Chinese word to express approximately the notion of the " picturesque "—an aesthetic category distinct from both the sublime and the beautiful, in the neo-classical sense—for which no English term except the vague, and still to many ears disparaging, " romantic " was yet available. " Picturesque " apparently did not come into use until the first decade of the eighteenth century (the first reference to it in *NED* is of 1703); and Pope employs it in 1712 somewhat apologetically, as a Gallicism. The concept of " the picturesque " as such a distinct property—not limited to the visual arts—had its formal definition and elaboration from Uvedale Price just a century after Temple (*Essay on the Picturesque*, 1794). To follow Mr. Hussey's abridgment:

While the outstanding qualities of the sublime were vastness and obscurity, and those of the beautiful smoothness and gentleness, the characteristics of the picturesque were ' roughness and sudden variation joined to irregularity ' of form, color, lighting, and even sound.[34]

Now, as Mr. Hussey justly remarks, " the picturesque phase through which each art passed, roughly between 1730 and 1830, was in each case a prelude to Romanticism "—or at least, as I should qualify, to one of the Romanticisms. What I am suggesting is that this prelude definitely began nearly half a century before 1730, and that the first clearly audible notes of it appear in Temple's account of the nature of the beauty sought and attained by the Chinese designers of pleasure-gardens. The recognized significance of this passage of Temple's may be further gathered from an essay of Richard Owen Cambridge in *The World*, 1755. After depreciating the gardens of " Le Nantre " (i. e., Le Nôtre) Cambridge writes:

This forced taste, aggravated by some Dutch acquisitions, for more than half a century deformed the face of Nature in this country, though several of our best writers had conceived nobler ideas, and prepared the way for improvements which have since followed. Sir William Temple, in his gardens of Epicurus, expatiates with great pleasure on that at More Park in Hertfordshire; yet after he has extolled it as the pattern of a perfect garden for use, beauty, and magnificence, he rises to nobler images, and in a kind of prophetic spirit points out a higher

[34] *The Picturesque*, p. 14.

style, free and unconfined. . . . It is the peculiar happiness of this age
to see these just and noble ideas brought into practice, regularity
banished, prospects opened, the country called in, Nature rescued and
improved, and art decently concealing herself under her own perfections.[35]

But Addison, in *Spectator*, No. 414, undeniably added to
the notion of the qualities of Chinese gardens an element which
it had not explicitly had in Temple. Natural landscape is usually
ungeometrical, irregular, highly diversified, without obvious
plan; Chinese gardens had been represented by Temple as ungeometrical, irregular, highly diversified, without obvious plan;
but it did not follow—nor, though he demanded that Nature
be followed in garden-design, had he expressly said—that
Chinese gardens resemble natural landscape or that they are
free from all artificialities except an artificial naturalness. Addison, however, supposed that since both had certain abstract
qualities in common, they must be essentially similar—and
therefore assumed that the Chinese gardeners sought and
achieved the imitation of " natural wildness." This assumption long continued to be widely current; and it was partly
because of it that the Chinese and English styles were so generally conceived to be essentially identical. But the " naturalness " of the Chinese garden, either in fact or intent, was
subsequently denied—sometimes by its critics but also by the
most zealous of its later champions. The supposition that the
Chinese gardeners aimed at the reproduction of natural effects
did not, at all events, rest wholly upon the authority of Addison—who probably knew nothing whatever of the matter.
Some actual observers testified to the same effect. Father Le
Comte in 1696 wrote that " the Chineses, who so little apply
themselves to order their Gardens, and to manage the real
Ornaments, are nevertheless taken with them, and are at some
cost about them; they make Grotto's in them, raise pretty little

---

[35] *The World*, No. 18. Cambridge adds in the essay: "Whatever may have
been reported, whether truly or falsely, of the Chinese gardens, it is certain that we are the first of the Europeans who have founded this taste. . . . Our
gardens are already the astonishment of foreigners, and in proportion as they
accustom themselves to consider and understand them, will become their
admiration."

Artificial Eminences, transport thither by piecemeal whole
Rocks, which they heap upon one another, without any further
design then to imitate Nature." [36]   A later example, in which
the notion of *sharawadgi* is already equated with the imitation
of nature, is to be found in one of the *Lettres édifiantes* written
in 1767 by le Père Benoist:

> The Chinese, in the ornamentation of their gardens, employ art to per-
> fect nature so successfully that an artist is deserving of praise only if
> his art is not apparent and in proportion as he has the better imitated
> nature. Here there are not, as in Europe, alleys drawn out till they are
> lost to sight, or terraces disclosing an infinity of distant objects which
> by their multitude prevent the imagination from fixing upon any one in
> particular. In the gardens of China the eye is not fatigued; views are
> almost always confined within a space proportioned to its reach. You
> behold a whole of which the beauty strikes and enchants; and a few
> hundred paces farther on new objects present themselves to you and
> cause in you new admiration.[37]

The gardens are traversed by numerous canals winding
amongst artificial mountains, sometimes falling in cascades,
sometimes spreading out into the valleys in lakes. The irregular banks of the canals and lakes are provided with parapets,
but, contrary to the European custom in such cases, the parapets
are formed of seemingly natural rocks. " Si l'ouvrier emploie
beaucoup de temps à les travailler, ce n'est que pour en augmenter les inégalités et leur donner une forme encore plus
champêtre."   Amongst the rocks are introduced caves which
" seem natural and are overgrown with trees and shrubbery." [38]
Of the prevalence in the second half of the century of the
belief in the identity of the Chinese and English styles in gardening, and in the derivation of the latter from the former, I
give a few examples; others may be found in Mr. Hussey's
book. Goldsmith lent it support in *The Citizen of the World*
(1760); he makes his Chinese philosopher in London say
(Letter XXXI):

[36] English tr. (1697) of Le Comte's *Nouveaux mémoires sur l'état présent de
la Chine* (1696), 162.
[37] *Lettres édifiantes et curieuses*, ed. of Aimé-Martin, IV (1877), 120.
[38] For an illustration of some of these effects of artificial naturalness, see
Mrs. Kerby's *An Old Chinese Garden*: " The ' Let-Go ' Bower."

The English have not yet brought the art of gardening to the same perfection with the Chinese, but have lately begun to imitate them.
Nature is now followed with greater assiduity than formerly; the trees
are suffered to shoot out with the utmost luxuriance; the streams, no
longer forced from their native beds, are permitted to wind along the
valleys; spontaneous flowers take the place of the finished parterre, and
the enamelled meadow of the shaven green.

A French writer in the *Gazette littéraire* observes that the English were not really the originators of the new style:

Though Kent had the glory of being the first to introduce into his own
country the most natural method of laying out gardens, he cannot be
said to have been the inventor of it; for aside from the fact that this
method has always been practised in Asia, among the Chinese, the
Japanese, . . . it was anticipated in France by the celebrated Dufresnoy.[89]

The Abbé Delille in a footnote to *Les Jardins* (1782) repeats
this, with the exception of the claim of priority for the French.
While Kent was the first European " who attempted with success the free style which has begun to spread throughout all
Europe, the Chinese were without doubt the first inventors of
it." In the text of the poem Delille had, indeed (following
Walpole) suggested another source of this horticultural primitivism, the description of Eden in *Paradise Lost.*

> Aimez donc des jardins la beauté naturelle.
> Dieu lui-même aux mortels en traça le modèle.
> Regardez dans Milton. Quand ses puissantes mains
> Préparent un asyle au premier des humains,
> Le voyez-vous tracer des routes régulières,
> Contraindre dans leurs cours les ondes prisonnières?
> Le voyez-vous parer d'étranges ornemens
> L'enfance de la terre et son premier printemps?
> Sans contrainte, sans art, de ses douces prémices
> La Nature épuisa les plus pures délices.

In the prose note, however, Delille explains that while, since
*plusieurs Anglois prétendent que c'est cette belle description du
paradis terrestre, et quelques morceaux de Spencer, qui ont*

---

[89] *Gazette littéraire* (1771), VI, 369. The term " le jardin anglo-chinois "
still distinguished one of the main divisions of the history of gardening in
A. Lefèvre's *Les parcs et les jardins*, 2d ed., 1871.

donné l'idée des jardins irréguliers, he has, in the poem, " preferred the authority of Milton as more poetic," it is not that he really questions "that this *genre* comes from the Chinese." Gray had, some time before, in a letter to a friend, complained with some bitterness of this current assumption, which seemed to him to rob the English of their chief distinction in the arts:

Count Algarotti is very civil to our nation, but there is one point on which he does not do us justice; I am the more solicitous about it, because it relates to the only taste we can call our own; the only proof of our original talent in the matter of pleasure, I mean our skill in gardening, or rather laying out grounds: and this is no small honour to us, since neither France nor Italy have ever had the least notion of it, nor yet do at all comprehend it when they see it. That the Chinese have this beautiful art in high perfection seems very probable from the Jesuits' letters, and from Chambers's little discourse published some years ago; but it is very certain we copied nothing from them, nor had anything but Nature for our model. It is not forty years since the art was born among us, and as sure we then had no information on this head from China at all.[40]

But Gray was mistaken. He had, oddly, forgotten Sir William Temple and *sharawadgi*. There is, it is true, no reason, so far as I can recall, for supposing that the earliest practitioners of the new English style directly imitated Chinese models in detail. But they had probably all read Temple; they had certainly read Addison and Pope on gardens; in these writers they found set forth certain general aesthetic principles pertinent to garden-design, which they proceeded to carry out, according to their several lights; and these principles Temple, by whom Addison and Pope were unmistakably influenced, professed to have learned from the Chinese.

Chinese architecture, after a time, began to take its place with Chinese gardens as a vindication of the new aesthetic creed. That it, too, could, to an aesthetically sensitive European, seem to reveal an essentially different and really superior kind of beauty—of which the secret was irregularity, concealment of formal design, and surprise—may be seen from a letter of a French Jesuit missionary who was also a painter, le

[40] *Memoirs of Mr. Gray*, Sec. V, Letter VIII; cited in notes to Mason's *Works*, I, 404.

frère Attiret. This letter, written in 1743 and published in vol. XXVII (1749) of the *Lettres édifiantes et curieuses*, was, for the later part of the century, one of the important media through which Chinese taste was interpreted. I therefore quote the most pertinent part of it.

My eyes and my taste, since I have been in China, have become a little Chinese. . . . It is because of the great variety which they give to their buildings that I admire the fertility of their minds. I am, indeed, somewhat inclined to think that we are impoverished and sterile, in comparison with them.

In their greater structures, public buildings, *etc.*, the Chinese, Attiret observes, demand " symétrie et bel ordre," but in their pleasure-houses there reigns almost everywhere *un beau désordre, une antisymêtrie.*

One would say that each palace is made after the ideas or the model of some foreign country, that everything is arranged separately and at random, that one part is not made for another. From the description of this one might suppose that it produces a disagreeable impression; but when one sees it, one thinks otherwise, and admires the art with which this irregularity is conducted. All is in good taste, and so well disposed that one does not see the whole beauty of it at a single view; it provides enjoyment for a long time and satisfies all one's curiosity.[41]

The entire letter, englished by Joseph Spence under the pseudonym of Sir Harry Beaumont, is included in Dodsley's *Fugitive Pieces* (1761), I, 61 ff.: *A Particular Account of the Emperor of China's Gardens, near Pekin: in a Letter from F. Attiret, a French Missionary, now employed by that Emperor to paint the Apartments in those Gardens, to his Friend at Paris.*

Of Attiret's letter the echo may still be heard in the last decade of the century; Bernardin de St. Pierre refers to it in a passage of his *Harmonies de la Nature* (written 1793, published 1814), complaining that architecture has usually imitated only what he calls the " fraternal harmonies " of Nature, which consist in symmetry and consonance, and neglected the *harmonies conjugales*, of which the essence is contrast, and which,

---

[41] The passage has been cited in Mlle Belevitch—Stankevitch's dissertation, *Le Goût Chinois en France au temps de Louis XIV*, 1910.

if introduced into this art, would above all " free it from the monotony which is its common fault." He adds:

On peut encore employer diverses beautés en architecture, d'après les autres harmonies de la nature. Les Chinois en savent là-dessus plus que nous, comme on peut s'en convaincre dans la lettre du frère Attiret, peintre, qui nous a donné une description très-intéressante de l'architecture de leurs palais.[42]

Returning to the middle of the century, we find Horace Walpole a zealous, though he was not to prove a faithful, convert. " I am," he writes to his friend Mann in 1750, " almost as fond of the Sharawadgi, or Chinese want of symmetry, in buildings as in grounds and gardens." And he consequently finds classical architecture unsatisfying: in Grecian buildings " the variety is little and admits of no charming irregularities." [43] Walpole's Gothicism of this period was closely related to his taste for *sharawadgi*; for it was apparently something of a commonplace of the time that " the Beauty of Gothick Architecture consists, like that of a Pindarick Ode, in the Boldness and Irregularity of its Members." [44]

Note how a defender of the classic tradition in 1755 couples the Chinese with the Gothic fashion and attacks them both in the name of simplicity and regularity:

[42] *Œuvres posthumes*, ed. Aimé-Martin, 1833, p. 330. In the preface to his *Arcadie* Bernardin says that he has composed his book *suivant les lois de la nature et à la manière des chinois*.

[43] *Letters*, ed. Toynbee, III, 4.

[44] Letter of John Ivory Talbot in *An Eighteenth Century Correspondence* edited by Lilian Dickins and Mary Stanton (1910), p. 303. The identity of the notions of Gothic and Chinese has been briefly noted by Mr. Hussey: " As Shaftesbury had seen no difference between the ' deformity' of Gothick and Chinese taste, so did the minds of the mid-century confound them." For the connection of the idea of the irregularity of the Pindaric ode with that of the Chinese style, cf. Robert Lloyd's *The Poet* (1762):

> And when the frisky wanton writes
> In Pindar's (what d'ye call 'em)—flights,
> Th' uneven measure, short and tall,
> Now rhyming *twice*, now *not at all*,
> In *curves* and *angles* twirls about,
> Like *Chinese railing*, in and out.

On the aesthetic ideas connected with eighteenth-century Gothicism, chiefly in England, and their relation to the *goût chinois*, cf. also " The First Gothic Revival and the Return to Nature," below.

The applause which is so fondly given to Chinese decorations or to the barbarous productions of a Gothic genius, . . . seems once more to threaten the ruin of that simplicity which distinguishes the Greek and Roman arts as eternally superior to those of every other nation. . . . The present vogue of Chinese and Gothic architecture has, besides its novelty, another cause of its good reception; which is, that there is no difficulty in being merely whimsical. A spirit capable of entering into all the beauties of antique simplicity is the portion of minds used to reflection, and the result of a corrected judgment; but here all men are equal. A manner confined to no rules cannot fail of having the crowd of imitators in its party, where novelty is the sole criterion of elegance. It is no objection that the very end of all building is forgot; that all reference to use and climate, all relation of one proportion to another, of the thing supporting to the thing supported, of the accessory to the principal, is often entirely subverted. . . . As this Chinese and Gothic spirit has begun to deform some of the finest streets in the capital, whenever an academy shall be founded for the promoting the arts of sculpture, painting, and architecture, some scheme should be thought of at the same time to discourage the encroachment of this pretended elegance; and an Anti-Chinese society will be a much more important institution in the world of arts, than an Anti-Gallican in that of politics.[45]

A satire against Chinese architecture and gardening inspired by somewhat different aesthetic predilections is to be seen in James Cawthorne's poem *Of Taste*, 1756. The poet evidently was no classicist; he laments that

> Half our churches, such the mode that reigns,
> Are Roman theatres or Grecian fanes;
> Where broad-arched windows to the eye convey
> The keen diffusion of too strong a day.

But he recognized in the Chinese mode an exaggerated revulsion against both classical models and the principles which they were supposed to embody:

> Of late, 'tis true, quite sick of Rome and Greece,
> We fetch our models from the wise Chinese;
> European artists are too cool and chaste,
> For Mand'rin is the only man of taste;
> Whose bolder genius, fondly wild to see

---

[45] *The World*, March 27, 1755.

His grove a forest, and his pond a sea,
Breaks out—and whimsically great, designs
Without the shackles or of rules or lines.[46]

A Chinese designer, as conceived by this poet of the mid-eighteenth century, was manifestly a very romantic fellow—in more than one sense of the term. The poem goes on to depict the effects of his influence in England:

Form'd on his plans our farms and seats begin
To match the boasted villas of Pekin.
On every hill a spire-crowned temple swells,
Hung round with serpents and a fringe of bells.
In Tartar huts our cows and horses lie,
Our hogs are fattened in an Indian stye;
On every shelf a Joss divinely stares,
Nymphs laid on chintzes sprawl upon our chairs;
While o'er our cabinets Confucius nods,
Midst porcelain elephants and china gods.

4

The chief enthusiast and propagandist for Chinese gardens in the second half of the eighteenth century is commonly said to have been Sir William Chambers; and though this is true, it is also true that he almost completely reversed the usual account of the aesthetic principles underlying Chinese gardening, and in doing so dealt its vogue in England a very heavy blow. Chambers had visited China in his youth, and in 1757 had published a volume of *Designs of Chinese buildings, furniture, dresses, machines and utensils, engraved by the best hands from the originals drawn in China by Mr. Chambers. . . . To which is annexed a description of their temples, houses, gardens, etc.* (London, 1757).[47] This magnificent folio can hardly have been widely accessible; but the section on gardening was re-

[46] *Of Taste, an Essay,* 1756. In Chalmers (1810), XV, 246. For a satire on the " improvement " in architecture " not merely by the adoption of what we call Chinese, nor by the restoration of what we call Gothic, but by a happy mixture of both," see *The World,* Feb. 20, 1754. Cf. also the prose *Essay on Taste* of the Aberdeen philosopher Alexander Gerard (1756, published 1759) in which the tendencies " to imitate the Chinese or revive the Gothic taste " are coupled as twin examples of a craving for novelty rather than " real beauty."

[47] There is a French version of the *Design,* Lond., Haberkorn, 1757.

printed in Percy's *Miscellaneous Pieces relating to the Chinese.*[48] Chambers's admiration for Chinese architecture was at this time moderate, to say the least:

Let it not be suggested that my intention is to promote a taste so much inferior to the antique, and so very unfit for our climate: but a particular so interesting as the architecture of one of the most extraordinary nations in the universe cannot be a matter of indifference to any true lover of the arts, and an architect should by no means be ignorant of so singular a stile of building. . . . Though, generally speaking, Chinese architecture does not suit European purposes; yet in extensive parks and gardens, where a great variety of scenes are required, or in immense palaces, containing a numerous series of apartments, I do not see the impropriety of finishing some of the inferior ones in the Chinese taste. Variety is always delightful; and novelty, attended with nothing inconsistent or disagreeable, sometimes takes the place of beauty. . . . The buildings of the Chinese are neither remarkable for magnitude or richness of materials; yet there is a singularity in their manner, a justness in their proportion, a simplicity, and sometimes even beauty, in their form, which recommend them to our notice. I look upon them as toys in architecture; and as toys are sometimes, on account of their oddity, prettyness, or neatness of workmanship, admitted into the cabinets of the curious, so may Chinese buildings be sometimes allowed a place among compositions of a nobler kind.[49]

But of the Chinese gardens he speaks much more highly, though still in the usual vein:

The Chinese excell in the art of laying out gardens. Their taste in that is good, and what we have for some time past been aiming at in England, though not always with success. . . . Nature is their pattern and their aim is to imitate her in all her beautiful irregularities. . . . As the Chinese are not fond of walking, we seldom meet with avenues or spacious walks, as in our European plantations: the whole ground is laid out in a variety of scenes and you are led, by winding passages cut in the groves, to the different points of view, each of which is marked by a seat, a building, or some other object. The perfection of their gardens consists in the number, beauty, and diversity of these scenes. The Chinese gardeners, like the European painters, collect from nature the most pleasing objects, which they

[48] Dodsley, Lond., 1762, vol. II.
[49] *Designs*, etc. 1757, preface.

endeavour to combine in such a manner, as not only to appear to the best advantage separately, but likewise to unite in forming an elegant and striking whole.[50]

Even in this early work of Chambers, it is true, features of the Chinese gardens were mentioned which could hardly be described as close imitations of nature. But this aspect of the Chinese taste—or of his account of it—comes out more clearly in his *Dissertation on Oriental Gardening*, 1772, which brought on a crisis in the history of the *goût chinois* and led to one of the most characteristic and celebrated of eighteenth-century literary rows.[51] The superiority of the Chinese to the English gardens was now proclaimed by Chambers in extravagant terms naturally annoying to British *amour propre*, and especially to the friends and admirers of Capability Brown, the reigning English practitioner, and Chambers's rival:

Amongst the Chinese, Gardening is held in much higher esteem, than it is in Europe; they rank a perfect work in that Art, with the greatest productions of the human understanding; and say, that its efficacy in moving the passions, yields to that of few other arts whatever. Their Gardeners are not only Botanists, but also Painters and Philosophers; having a thorough knowledge of the human mind, and of the arts by which its strongest feelings are excited.[52]

Not of such sort are the English " improvers."

In this island [the art] is abandoned to kitchen gardeners, well skilled in the cultivation of sallads, but little acquainted with the principles of ornamental gardening. It cannot be expected that men, uneducated and doomed by their condition to waste the vigour of life in hard labour, should ever go far in so refined, so difficult a pursuit.[53]

The gardens of Europe Chambers condemned almost without exception. His ridicule of the " antient style " still prevailing

[50] *Ibid.*

[51] There is also a French edition, *Dissertation sur le jardinage de l'Orient*, Lond., G. Griffin, 1772-3. A German translation by Ewald appeared in 1775. To the second English (1773) and the first French edition is annexed an *Explanatory Discourse* by " Tan Chet-qua of Quang-chew-fu, Gent.," a recent Chinese visitor to London. The *Discourse*, which is, of course, by Chambers, was his reply to Mason's *Heroic Epistle*.

[52] *Dissertation*, p. 13.

[53] *Dissertation*, preface.

on the Continent, where "not a twig is suffered to grow as
Nature directs, nor is a form admitted but what is scientific,
and determinable by rule and compass," merely repeated the
current fashions. What was, to his contemporaries, sensational
about the book was that it treated with even greater contempt
"the new manner . . . universally adopted in England," in
which "no appearance of art is tolerated."

Our gardens differ very little from common fields, so closely is vulgar
nature copied in most of them: there is generally so little variety, and
so much want of judgment in the choice of the objects, such a poverty
of imagination in the contrivance, and of art in the arrangement, that
these compositions rather appear the offspring of chance than design;
and a stranger is often at a loss to know whether he be walking in a
common meadow, or in a pleasure ground, made and kept at a very
considerable expence: he finds nothing to delight or amuse him; nothing to keep up his attention, or excite his curiosity, little to gratify the
senses, and less to touch the passions, or gratify the understanding.[54]

In short, "neither the artful nor the simple style of gardening is right, the one being too much refined and too extravagant a deviation from nature; the other, like a Dutch
picture, an affected adherence to her, without choice or judgment. One manner is absurd; the other is insipid and vulgar:
a judicious mixture of art and nature, an extract of what is good
in both manners, would certainly be more perfect than either."
It is, then, as the exemplar of this that the Chinese garden is at
first commended by Chambers to the study of his countrymen.
    Yet it presently appears that in a "judicious mixture" na-
ture and art are not present in equal parts, but that the second
is the more abundant ingredient:

Though the Chinese artists have nature for their general model, yet
are they not so attached to her as to exclude all appearance of art: on
the contrary, they think it, on many occasions, necessary to make an
ostentatious shew of their labour. Nature, they say, affords us but few
materials to work with; plants, ground and water, are her only productions: and though both the forms and arrangements of these may
be varied to an incredible degree, yet have they but few striking
varieties; the rest being of the nature of changes rung upon a bell,

[54] *Ibid.*, preface.

which, though in reality different, still produce the same uniform kind of jingling; the variation being too minute to be easily perceived.

Art must therefore supply the scantiness of nature; and not only be employed to produce variety, but also novelty and effect: for the simple arrangements of nature are met with in every common field, to a certain degree of perfection; and are therefore too familiar to excite any strong sensation in the mind of the beholder, or to produce any uncommon degree of pleasure.

After describing the Chinese fashion of scattering about their grounds " statues, busts, bas-reliefs, and every production of the chisel," and also " antient inscriptions, verses, and moral sentences," Chambers represents the Chinese artists as justifying their methods expressly on the ground that all improvements are deviations from the natural.

Our vestments, say they, are neither of leather, nor like our skins, but formed of rich silks and embroideries; our houses and palaces bear no resemblance to caverns in the rocks, which are the only natural habitations; nor is our music either like thunder, or the whistling of the northern wind, the harmony of nature. Nature produces nothing either boiled, roasted or stewed; and yet we do not eat raw meat: nor doth she supply us with any other tools for all our purposes, but teeth and hands; yet we have saws, hammers, axes, and a thousand other implements: in short, there is scarcely anything in which art is not apparent; and why should its appearance be excluded from gardening only? Poets and painters soar above the pitch of nature, when they would give energy to their compositions. The same privilege, therefore, should be allowed to gardeners: inanimate, simple nature is too insipid for our purposes: much is expected from us; and therefore, we have occasion for every aid that either art or nature can furnish. The scenery of a garden should differ as much from common nature, as an heroic poem [55] doth from a prose relation: and gardeners, like poets, should give a loose rein to their imagination; and even fly beyond the bounds of truth, whenever it is necessary to elevate, to embellish, to enliven, or to add novelty to their subject.[56]

This anti-naturalism is still more marked in the *Explanatory Discourse*. " Till my arrival in England," says Chambers's Chinese gentleman,

[55] This is, of course, the explanation of the title of Mason's satire.
[56] *Ibid.*, 20-21. *Cf.* Reichwein, *op. cit.*, 116.

I never doubted but the appearance of art was admissible, even necessary, to the essence of a splendid Garden: and I am more firmly of that opinion, after having seen your English Gardens; though the contrary is so violently maintained by your countrymen, in opposition to the rest of the world, to the practice of all other polished nations, all enlightened ages; and, as far as I am able to judge, in opposition to reason. . . . We admire Nature as much as you do; but being of a more phlegmatick disposition, our affections are somewhat better regulated: we consider how she may be employed, upon every occasion, to the most advantage; and do not always introduce her in the same garb; but show her in a variety of forms; sometimes naked, as you attempt to do; sometimes disguised; sometimes decorated, or assisted by art; scrupulously avoiding, in our most common dispositions, all resemblance to the common face of the country, with which the Garden is immediately surrounded; being convinced, that a removal from one field to another, of the same appearance, can never afford any particular pleasure, nor ever excite powerful sensations of any kind.[57]

Nor does Chambers limit his attack upon the program of imitating mere nature to the special case of gardens. The whole doctrine of imitation, and with it the theory that the source of aesthetic pleasure lies in the recognition of the resemblance of a work of art to its original, is repudiated. Nature is often deplorably *wanting* in wildness and in variety, and is consequently incapable of arousing strong feeling; in these cases her aesthetic deficiencies must be made good by art. Chambers's Chinese visitor observes:

Both your [English] artists and connoisseurs seem to lay too much stress on nature and simplicity; they are the constant cry of every half-witted dabbler, the burthen of every song, the tune by which you are insensibly lulled into dullness and insipidity. If resemblance to nature were the measure of perfection, the waxen figures in Fleet-street would be superior to all the works of the divine Buonarotti; the trouts and woodcocks of Elmer, preferable to the cartoons of Raphael: but, believe me, too much nature is often as bad as too little, as may be deduced from many examples, obvious to every man conversant in polite knowledge. Whatever is familiar is by no means calculated to excite the strongest feelings; and though a close resemblance to familiar objects may delight the ignorant, yet, to the skilful, it has but few charms, never any of the most elevated sort; and is sometimes

[57] Second ed., 144.

even disgusting: without a little assistance from art, nature is seldom tolerable; she may be compared to certain viands, either tasteless or unpleasant in themselves: which, nevertheless, with some seasoning become palatable; or, when properly prepared, compose a most delicious dish.[58]

One of the deficiencies of nature in the matter of landscape-design—at least in England—was that her scenes were often not sufficiently " horrid " and " romantic "; where this was the case, the " assistance of art " would consist, for example, in transforming ordinary hills into " stupendous rocks, by partial incrustations of stone, judiciously mixed with turf, fern, wild shrubs, and forest trees." In short, " there would be no deviation, however trifling, from the usual march of nature, but what would suggest, to a fruitful imagination, some extraordinary arrangement, *something to disguise her vulgarity*." [59]

Even " simplicity," sacred word alike of neo-classicism and aesthetic primitivism, receives little reverence from Chambers. It is manifestly even more against the primitivist than the classicist that the following passage is directed:

With respect to simplicity, wherever more is admitted than may be requisite to constitute grandeur, or necessary to facilitate conception, it is always a fault. To the human mind some exertion is always necessary: it must be occupied to be pleased; and is more satisfied with a treat than with a frugal repast: for though it doth not delight in intricacies, yet, without a certain, even a considerable, degree of complication, no grateful sensations can ever be excited. Excessive simplicity can only please the ignorant or weak, whose comprehensions are slow, and whose powers of combination are confined. Simplicity must therefore be used with discretion, and the dose be adapted to the constitution of the patients; amongst savages and Hottentots, where arts are unknown, refinements unheard of, an abundant portion may be necessary; but wherever civilization has improved the mental faculties, a little, with proper management, will go a very great way: need I prove what the music, poetry, language, arts, and manners of every nation demonstrate, beyond the possibility of a doubt? [60]

[58] *Ibid.*, 145-6.

[59] *Ibid.*, *Explanatory Discourse*, 132; my italics.

[60] *Ibid.*, 146-7. I have corrected an obvious error of punctuation in the original, which has a comma after " patients," and a semi-colon after " Hottentots."

It was much more the pleasure of surprise than the pleasure of recognition that Chinese designers, according to Chambers, endeavored to afford the beholder. The effects they sought were to be attained only through variety and novelty; and imitation, even of the best models, was no part of their program. " The artists of that country are so inventive, and so various in their combinations, that no two of their compositions are ever alike: they never copy or imitate each other; they do not even repeat their own productions; saying, that what once has been seen, operates feebly at a second inspection; and that whatever bears even a distant resemblance to a known object, seldom excites a new idea." [61] Originality, in short, was sought after by Chinese artists. But originality, except in the expression of the same standardized ideas, was inconsistent with neo-classical aesthetic theory; and it was scarcely less inconsistent with the ideal of imitating " natural " effects.

The Chinese gardeners, it will be seen, were, according to Chambers, practising aesthetic psychologists. They therefore classified their designs according to the psychological effect to be produced, and distinguished them " by the appellations of the pleasing, the terrible, and the surprizing." Of these, " the first are composed of the gayest and most perfect productions of the vegetable world; intermixed with rivers, lakes, cascades, fountains, and water-works of all sorts: being combined and disposed in all the picturesque forms that art or nature can suggest. Buildings, sculptures, and paintings are added to give splendor and variety to these compositions; and the rarest productions of the animal creation are collected to enliven them: nothing is forgot, that can either exhilerate the mind, gratify the senses, or give a spur to the imagination." The " pleasing scenes " were not, however, necessarily cheerful; under this appellation were included—one would gather from Chambers—the equivalents, in terms of Chinese gardening, of what in European poetry was called *le genre sombre*. For certain parts of their gardens were especially laid out for the purpose of evoking a mood of agreeable melancholy and a sense of the transitoriness of all natural beauty and human glory. It was

[61] *Ibid.*, 104.

thus that a Chinese gardener composed a Gray's *Elegy* in the language of horticulture:

The plantations of their autumnal scenes consist of many sorts of oak, beech, and other deciduous trees that are retentive of the leaf, and afford in their decline a rich variegated colouring; with which they blend some ever-greens, some fruit-trees, and the few shrubs and flowers which blossom late in the year,—placing amongst them decayed trees, pollards, and dead stumps, of picturesque forms, overspread with moss and ivy. The buildings with which these scenes are decorated, are generally such as indicate decay, being intended as mementos to the passenger. Some are hermitages and almshouses, where the faithful old servants of the family spend the remains of life in peace, amidst the tombs of their predecessors, who lie buried around them: others are ruins of castles, palaces, temples, and deserted religious houses; or half-buried triumphal arches and mausoleums, with mutilated inscriptions, that once commemorated the heroes of antient times: or they are sepulchres of their ancestors, catacombs and cemeteries of their favourite domestic animals; or whatever else may serve to indicate the debility, the disappointments, and the dissolution of humanity: which, by co-operating with the dreary aspect of autumnal nature, and the inclement temperature of the air, fill the mind with melancholy, and incline it to serious reflections.[62]

As for their " surprizing " or " supernatural " scenes, these are

of the romantic kind, and abound in the marvellous; being calculated to excite in the mind of the spectator quick successions of opposite and violent sensations. Sometimes the passenger is hurried by steep descending paths to subterraneous vaults, divided into stately apartments, where lamps, which yield a faint and glimmering light, discover the pale images of antient kings and heroes, reclining on beds of state; their heads are crowned with garlands of stars, and in their hands are tables of moral sentences: flutes, and soft harmonious organs impelled by subterraneous waters, interrupt, at stated intervals, the silence of the place, and fill the air with solemn melody.

Sometimes the traveller, after having wandered in the dusk of the forest, finds himself on the edge of precipices, in the glare of day-light, with cataracts falling from the mountains around, and torrents raging in the depths beneath him; or at the foot of impending rocks, in gloomy valleys, overhung with woods; or on the banks of dull moving rivers,

[62] *Dissertation*, second ed., 37-8.

whose shores are covered with sepulchral monuments, under the shade of willow, laurel, and other plants, sacred to Manchew, the Genius of sorrow.

His way now lies through dark passages cut in the rocks, on the sides of which are recesses, filled with Colossal figures of dragons, infernal furies, and other horrid forms, which hold, in their monstrous talons, mysterious cabalistic sentences, inscribed on tables of brass; with preparations that yield a constant flame; serving at once to guide and to astonish the passenger: from time to time he is surprized with repeated shocks of electrical impulse, with showers of artificial rain, or sudden violent gusts of wind, and instantaneous explosions of fire; the earth trembles under him, by the power of confined air; and his ears are successively struck with many different sounds, produced by the same means; some resembling the cries of men in torment; some the roaring of bulls, and howl of ferocious animals, with the yell of hounds, and the voices of hunters; others are like the mixed croaking of ravenous birds; and others imitate thunder, the raging of the sea, the explosion of cannon, the sound of trumpets, and all the noise of war.

His road lies through lofty woods, where serpents and lizards of many beautiful sorts crawl upon the ground, and where innumerable apes, cats and parrots, clamber upon the trees to imitate him as he passes; or through flowery thickets, where he is delighted with the singing of birds, the harmony of flutes, and all kinds of soft instrumental music: sometimes, in this romantic excursion, the passenger finds himself in spacious recesses, surrounded with arbors of jessamine, vine and roses; or in splendid pavilions, richly painted and illumined by the sun: here beautiful Tartarean damsels, in loose transparent robes, that flutter in the scented air, present him with rich wines or invigorating infusions of Ginseng and amber, in goblets of agate; mangostans, ananas, and fruits of Quangsi, in baskets of golden filagree; they crown him with garlands of flowers, and invite him to taste the sweets of retirement, on Persian carpets, and beds of camusathskin down.[63]

The " scenes of terror " described by Chambers can hardly have been wholly the work of art, or have been found within the confines even of the largest gardens; they seem rather to consist of stretches of desolate country-side, with their effects heightened by various artificial aids to horripilation. For we are told that they

[63] *Dissertation*, second ed., 42-4.

are composed of gloomy woods, deep vallies inaccessible to the sun, impending barren rocks, dark caverns, and impetuous cataracts rushing down from all parts. The trees are ill formed, forced out of their natural directions, and seemingly torn to pieces by the violence of tempests: some are thrown down and intercept the course of the torrents; others look as if blasted and shattered by the power of lightening: the buildings are in ruins; or half consumed by fire, or swept away by the fury of the waters: nothing remains entire but a few miserable huts dispersed in the mountains; which serve at once to indicate the existence and wretchedness of the inhabitants. Bats, owls, vultures, and every bird of prey flutter in the groves; wolves, tigers and jackalls howl in the forests; half-famished animals wander upon the plains; gibbets, crosses, wheels and the whole apparatus of torture, are seen from the roads; and in the most dismal recesses of the woods, where the ways are rugged and overgrown with poisonous weeds, and where every object bears the marks of depopulation, are temples dedicated to the king of vengeance, deep caverns in the rocks, and descents to gloomy subterraneous habitations, overgrown with brushwood and brambles; near which are inscribed, on pillars of stone, pathetic descriptions of tragical events, and many horrid acts of cruelty, perpetrated there by outlaws and robbers of former times: and to add both to the horror and sublimity of these scenes, they sometimes conceal in cavities, on the summits of the highest mountains, founderies, lime-kilns, and glass works; which send forth large volumes of flame, and continued clouds of thick smoke, that give to these mountains the appearance of volcanoes.[64]

Such scenes, the *Explanatory Discourse* points out, already exist in England in abundance; and it is neither practicable nor desirable to "beautify" out of existence the "commons and wilds, dreary, barren, and serving only to give an uncultivated appearance to the country." On the contrary, they may, with only the slightest additions from art, "easily be framed into scenes of terror, converted into noble pictures of the sublimest cast, and, by an artful contrast, serve to enforce the effect of gayer and more luxuriant prospects." For actual "gibbets with witches hanging *in terrorem* upon them"; "forges, collieries, mines, coal tracts, brick or lime kilns, glass-works, and dif-

[64] Second ed., 44-45. It was, above all, this passage that provided easy material for Mason's satire in *An Heroic Epistle to Sir William Chambers*. It sounds less like a design for a garden than for a landscape painting somewhat in the manner of Salvator Rosa.

ferent objects of the horrid kind"; half-famished animals, ragged cottagers, and their picturesquely dilapidated huts:—all these were already common features of the English scene, " particularly near the metropolis." All that was needed was that " a few uncouth struggling trees, some ruins, caverns, rocks, torrents, abandoned villages, in part consumed by fire," should be " artfully introduced and blended with gloomy plantations," in order to " compleat the aspect of desolation, and serve to fill the mind, where there was no possibility of gratifying the senses." [65]

That Chambers had in the *Dissertation* somewhat heightened his descriptions, and put into the mouths of Chinese gardeners aesthetic doctrines of his own, is half-admitted in the *Explanatory Discourse*: whether the gardens described have any existence " but in Chet-qua's brain . . . is immaterial; for the end of all that I have said, was rather as an Artist, to set before you a new style of gardening; than as a Traveller to relate what I have really seen." [66]

Chambers too, then, was seeking to introduce a kind of aesthetic " Romanticism " of which both the principles and the examples were attributed to the Chinese gardeners; but it was in the main a different kind from that initiated by Temple's formulation of the notion of *sharawadgi*. The two had, indeed, one or two elements in common: the repudiation of the ideals of " regularity," symmetry, simplicity, immediately obvious unity of design, and a tendency to seek " variety " in an artistic composition. But beyond this there were radical differences. For Chambers, " nature " was no longer a sacred word, and conscious and deliberate art, transcending the limitations and " vulgarity " of nature, was an essential in the practice of gardening or any other art. And the aim of the Chinese garden-designers, as he described it, was not to " imitate " anything; it was to produce horticultural lyric poems, to compose, out of a mixture of trees, shrubs, rocks, water, and artificial objects, separate scenes having quite diverse qualities and subtly devised for the purpose of expressing and evoking varying

[65] *Dissertation*, 130-131.   [66] *Op. cit.*, 159.

moods, " passions " and " powerful sensations." In this he was foreshadowing *another* variety of " Romanticism " which was to become conspicuous in literature and music in the following century.

But, as I have said, the effect in England of Chambers's intervention was, on the whole, highly unfavorable to the Chinese vogue. Few of his contemporaries were ready to give up " nature "—in *some* sense of the word—as the norm for art, and least of all in the art of gardening. If the Chinese gardens were not truly " natural," so much the worse for them. His attack upon the reigning fashion in garden design had also the curious result of converting the question of the merits of the Chinese style into a sort of party issue, on which Tories and Whigs, the court party and its opponents, were likely to take opposite sides. The outcome was the defection of some of the principal earlier enthusiasts for the *goût chinois* [67]—which, if there was any truth in what Chambers had written, could *not* be correctly designated as the *goût* anglo-*chinois*. Though Chambers was able to carry out to some extent his own conception of a Chinese garden—including the introduction of such highly artificial objects as pagodas into English landscapes—at Kew, his attempt to bring about the adoption of a radically " new " style, based upon fundamentally different aesthetic ideas, seems to have had little success; and when similar ideas later made their appearance in other arts, this was apparently not due to the influence of Chambers's *Dissertation*.

But the conception of a previously unrecognized kind of " beauty " timidly propounded by Temple a century earlier had better fortune and greater effects. The principal object of the present paper has been to show the large and the temporally primary part played by the Chinese influence, and especially by the conception of *sharawadgi* as an aesthetic quality, in the gradual conscious revolt against neo-classical standards which took place during the first three-quarters of the eighteenth century. Though this revolt had its beginning, on a considerable scale, in the arts of gardening and architecture, it speedily

[67] Walpole, for example, by the 1780's had concluded that " fantastic sharawadgis " are as remote from nature as " regular formality " (*Essay on Modern Gardening*, 1785).

extended to literature and all the arts; and its later and purely literary manifestations were at least greatly facilitated and accelerated by the introduction of a new canon of aesthetic excellence and by its repetition and elaboration by a succession of influential writers in the following decades. A turning-point in the history of modern taste was reached when the ideals of regularity, simplicity, uniformity, and easy logical intelligibility, were first openly impugned, when the assumption that true beauty is " geometrical " ceased to be one to which " all consented, as to a Law of Nature." And in England, at all events, the rejection of this assumption seems, throughout most of the eighteenth century, to have been commonly recognized as initially due to the influence and the example of Chinese art.

VIII. THE FIRST GOTHIC REVIVAL AND THE RETURN TO NATURE *

I T IS ONE of the commonplaces of the history of taste that in the late seventeenth and the early eighteenth century Gothic architecture was generally regarded by well-bred persons with contempt. Its very name was a term of disparagement; for the adjective "gothic" was a word which it was fashionable to apply to all manner of objects in a sense equivalent to "barbarous and tasteless." A typical virtuoso of the early seventeen-forties, just returned from the *grand tour*, is described as "perpetually railing at the climate and manners of his native country, and pronouncing the word Gothic fifty times an hour." [1] It performed much the same necessary function that, in certain circles, the adjective "Victorian" performs today. Tight-lacing was, to those who disapproved of it, a "gothic ligament"; [2] and duelling was denounced by Bishop Berkeley as a "Gothic crime." [3] A received opinion from which one dissented was a *préjugé gothique*.[4] The term also took on a certain political coloring; since it not only vaguely suggested "the old-fashioned" in general, but, more specifically, the political and social system of the Middle Ages, *i. e.*, feudalism, it sometimes served the progressives of the period as an unpleasant way of referring to anything the Tories approved—as in a couplet in Akenside's *Odes* (1745):

> And now that England spurns her Gothic chain,
> And equal laws and social science reign.[5]

In Thomas Warton's juvenile poem *The Triumph of Isis:*

> 'Twas theirs new plans of liberty to frame:
> And on the Gothic gloom of slavish sway
> To shed the dawn of intellectual day.

---

* First published in *Modern Language Notes*, XXVII (1932), 414-446.
[1] In the prose satire *Ranelagh House*, 1747. It is attributed by Halkett and Laing to "Joseph Wharton."
[2] Mason, *English Garden*, I, note 1. [4] Rousseau, *Dialogues*, I.
[3] *Alciphron*, V, 13. [5] Book II, Ode I.

At the very end of the century a French writer observed that
" encore aujourd'hui, par la force d'un long usage, le mot
gothique exprime tout ce qui dans les arts et dans les mœurs
rappelle les siècles d'ignorance." [6] Other examples of the
depreciative use of the term may be found in abundance in the
historical dictionaries and manuals of literary history.

While this general connotation of the word helped to give
the architectural style literally a bad name, to link it verbally
in the thought of many of the period with other things in
ill repute, it is necessary, in order to understand the more
significant motives, or ostensible motives, of the dislike of
Gothic buildings, to note what aesthetic qualities were supposed to be characteristic of such buildings. And to this end
we must first ask what edifices, or what specific style, eighteenth-
century writers had in mind when they applied the adjective
to architecture. The word had in fact—as has not, I believe,
been generally noted—three distinct denotations; and with each
of these different grounds of disapproval were associated. (1)
It frequently signifies any structure not in the classical style;
examples of this may be found in the Oxford Dictionary; *e. g.*,
1693, Dryden's translation of Dufresnoy: " All that is not
in the ancient gust is called a barbarous or Gothic manner ";
1742, Langley's *Ancient Architecture*, Diss. I.: " Every ancient
building which is not in the Grecian mode is called a Gothic
building." (Langley himself, however, thought the style, at
least in its English manifestations, should more properly be
called " Saxon "). In the *Encyclopédie* we are told that " cette
manière barbare a infesté les beaux arts depuis 611 jusqu'en
1450." But (2) in many cases it is clearly of the Romanesque
(in England the Saxon or the Norman) style that those who
write of " the Gothic " are thinking—a style which many supposed to have been actually introduced by the Goths or other
Northern barbarian invaders of the Roman empire. This
Nordic theory of the origin of Gothic goes back at least to
Vasari (1550), who refers to *una specie di lavori che si chia-
mano Tedeschi*, the style of which " was invented by the
Goths." [7] (3) In John Evelyn's *Account of Architects and*

---

[6] *Encycl. méthodique: Architecture:* II, 457.　　[7] *Vite*, 1807 ed., I, 254.

Architecture, 1697, we find a two-fold origin, and two incongruous aberrations, attributed to the " Gothic " style: [8]

It is the ancient *Greek* and *Roman Architecture* which is here intended, as most entirely answering all those Perfections required in a faultless and accomplished Building; such as for so many Ages were so renowned and reputed by the universal Suffrages of the civilized World, and would doubtless have still subsisted, and made good their Claim, and what is recorded of them, had not the *Goths*, *Vandals* and other barbarous Nations subverted and demolished them, together with that glorious Empire, where those stately and pompous Monuments stood; introducing in their stead, a certain fantastical and licentious Manner of Building, which we have since called *Modern* (or *Gothic* rather), Congestions of heavy, dark, melancholy and *Monkish Piles*, without any just Proportion, Use or Beauty, compared with the truly *Ancient*. So as when we meet with the greatest Industry, and expensive *Carving*, full of *fret* and lamentable *Imagery*, sparing neither of Pains nor Cost, a judicious Spectator is rather distracted and quite confounded, than touched with that Admiration which results from the true and just Symmetry, regular Proportion, Union and Disposition, great and noble Manner, which those *August* and *Glorious Fabricks* of the *Ancients* still produce.

It was after the Irruption and Swarms of those truculent People from the *North*, the *Moors* and *Arabs* from the *South* and *East*, over-running the Civilized World, that wherever they fixed themselves, they soon began to debauch this noble and useful Art; when, instead of those beautiful *Orders*, so majesticall and proper for their Stations, becoming Variety, and other ornamental Accessories, they set up those slender and misquine *Pillars*, or rather Bundles of *Staves*, and other incongruous Props to support incumbent Weights, and pondrous arched Roofs, without Entablature; and though not without great Industry, as M. D'Aviler well observes, nor altogether naked of gaudy *Sculpture*, trite and busy Carvings, it is such as rather gluts the Eye than gratifies and pleases it with any reasonable Satisfaction. [For example, let any Man of Judgement look] a while upon *King Henry* the Seventh's *Chappel* at Westminster, . . . on its sharp *Angles*, *Jetties*, narrow *Lights*, lame *Statues*, *Lace*, and other *Cut-work* and *Crinkle-Crankle*. . . . [In the *Modern Architecture*], the universal and unreasonable Thickness of the Walls, clumsy Buttresses, Towers, sharp-pointed Arches, Doors and other Apertures, without proportion; nonsensical Insertions of various Mar-

---

[8] Prefixed to his edition of Roland Fréart's *A Parallel of the Ancient Architecture with the Modern*. The passage is cited from the fourth edition, 1733, pp. 9 ff.

bles impertinently placed; Turrets and Pinnacles thick set with *Monkies* and *Chymaeras* (and abundance of busy Work and other Incongruities) dissipate and breake the Angles of the Sight, and so confound it, that one cannot consider it with any Steadiness, where to begin or end; taking off from that noble *Air* and *Grandure*, bold and graceful Manner, which the Ancients had so well and so judiciously established.

The confusion of architectural ideas here is manifest. Evelyn, while assuming that both the " Goths " and the " Arabs " were responsible for the introduction of the " fantastical and licentious manner of building," gives the same name to the productions of both, and speaks as if the qualities which he condemns with such breathless vehemence were to be found together in the same structures. But it was plain to any eye that they were not. It is hard to conceive how anyone who had ever seen such churches as Salisbury Cathedral, the choir of Lincoln, the Sainte Chapelle, St. Ouen in Rouen, or King's College Chapel could possibly call them " congestions of heavy, dark, melancholy, monkish piles "; while it was equally inappropriate to describe such Norman buildings as Durham Cathedral or St. Bartholomew's the Great as " supported on slender and misquine pillars or bundles of staves," or as full of " lace and other cut-work." The essential difference, not merely in technical details but in spirit, between (at least) early Romanesque and what we call Gothic was evident, and the need for a distinction in terminology to express this difference began to be felt. The term usually adopted was determined by another erroneous historical hypothesis concerning the origin of true Gothic (in our sense). Thus Wren wrote in 1713, with reference to Henry III's additions to Westminster Abbey, that what " we now call the Gothick manner of architecture . . . should with more reason be called the Saracen style." [9] Similarly the article " Architecture " in the *Encyclopédie* distinguishes " Gothic " style from that of the later Middle Ages. The former lasted only until the time of Charlemagne. Thereafter " France applied herself to the art with some success, . . . so that by degrees architecture, changing its aspect, fell into the opposite excess, by becoming too light (*légère*); the architects of this period made the beauties of the architecture consist in

[9] *Parentalia* (1750), 297.

a delicacy and a profusion of ornament hitherto unknown; an excess into which they doubtless fell through opposition to the Gothic which had preceded them, or through a taste which they had received from the Arabs and Moors, who had introduced this style into France from the Southern countries, as the Vandals and Goths had brought in from the Northern countries *le goût pesant et gothique.*" In the middle and late eighteenth century this distinction became familiar, and the style which we call Gothic was commonly designated " Saracenic," " Arabic," or " Arabesque." So in J. F. Sobry's *De l'architecture*, 1776 (p. 201):

> Les Arabes . . . nous apportèrent une nouvelle architecture. Cette architecture plus légère, plus ornée, plus simple, aussi solide et aussi facile à exécuter que la Gothique, fut reçue universellement; . . . et ces édifices, quoique rejettés aujourdhui par le plus grand nombre, trouvent encore des admirateurs.

As a much later historian of architecture, Quatremère de Quincy, in the *Encyclopédie méthodique*, 1800, put it, " it has seemed to some critics that the bizarre style of this architecture in its ornaments and in the employment of its diverse forms, would lead one to regard it as an emanation of those countries in which *le goût irrégulier* has at all times fixed its empire—I mean Asia." [10]

Nevertheless, the same writers who, on occasion, distinguish " the Gothic" from " the Saracenic," sometimes continue to apply the former adjective to the latter style also, with or without the qualification "modern." Wren says of a part of old St. Paul's that it " was apparently of a more modern Gothickstile, not with round (as in the old church) but sharp-headed arches," [11] and the same nomenclature appears in the *Encyclopédie* (Art. "Gothique," vol. VII): there is an " ancient" and a " modern Gothic"; the latter is exemplified by Westminster Abbey and " la cathédrale de Litchfreld" (*sic*). Fénelon had, however, called the style supposedly invented by the Arabs " l'architecture gothique" without qualification.

---

[10] *Op. cit., Architecture*, vol. II, 455 ff.

[11] *Parentalia*, 1750, p. 272. In France the same distinction of "ancient and modern Gothic" had been made by J. F. Félibien des Avaux, *Recueil historique* . . . , 1687, préf.

Let us, with these facts concerning the then current terminology in mind, try to determine the grounds on which Gothic was so generally condemned by the late seventeenth and eighteenth century taste. The faults found in the " Gothic " (or " ancient Gothic ") and the " Saracenic " (or " modern Gothic ") styles, were, it is already evident, in the main precisely opposite faults. The former was rude, ponderous, stiff, sombre, depressing: " Gothic gloom " was one of the conventional descriptive phrases for characterizing its effect upon the mind. The latter was condemned as wanting in solidity, as too " light " and too soaring, as " frivolous " and " fanciful " and over-refined, as overladen with ornament, as confusing the eye with an excessive multiplicity of separate parts and obtrusive details. Perhaps the most reiterated charge, obviously directed against the " modern " rather than the " ancient Gothic," was that of over-ornateness; the glorifiers of the classic mode never tired of referring to " le fade goût des ornements gothiques " (Molière: *La Gloire du Dôme du Val-de-Grâce*).[12] Fénelon writes in the *Lettre sur les occupations de l'Académie française* (chap. X):

Les inventeurs de l'architecture qu'on nomme *gothique*, et qui est, dit-on, celle des Arabes, crurent sans doute avoir surpassé les architectes grecs. Un édifice grec n'a aucun ornement qui ne serve qu'à orner l'ouvrage; . . . tout est simple, tout est mesuré, tout est borné à l'usage; on n'y voit ni hardiesse ni caprice qui impose aux yeux; les proportions sont si justes, que rien ne paraît fort grand, quoique tout le soit; tout est borné à contenter la vraie raison. Au contraire, l'architecte gothique élève sur des piliers très minces une voûte immense qui monte jusqu'aux nues; on croit que tout va tomber, mais tout dure pendant bien des siècles; tout est plein de fenêtres, de roses et de pointes; la pierre semble découpée comme du carton; tout est à jour, tout est en l'air. N'est-il pas naturel que les premiers architectes gothiques se soient flattés d'avoir surpassé, par leur raffinement, la simplicité grecque?

The passage was stolen bodily by the writer of the article " Gothique " in the *Encyclopédie*, who added that " the principal characteristic " of this style is that of being " chargé d'orne-

---

[12] Cf. Félibien des Avaux, *Recueil historique*, préf.: The " modern Gothic " architects " ont passé dans un aussi grand excès de délicatesse, ques les autres avoient fait dans une extrême pesanteur et grossièreté."

ments qui n'ont ni goût ni justesse." It is evident from these and other passages that the ill repute of Gothic (*i. e.*, " Saracenic ") in general was in part due to a valid aesthetic reaction against the excesses of the English Late Perpendicular and the French Flamboyant styles; but the attributes found in an extreme form in these were commonly ascribed to " modern Gothic " as a whole.

1. The gravest indictment in eighteenth century eyes was thus, apparently, that brought against the " modern Gothic " of the thirteenth to the fifteenth centuries. Its chief offenses, by classical standards, were those indicated in the passages just cited: its want of a rational " simplicity and plainness " and the introduction of ornament without use or structural necessity. The beauty of a Grecian temple, said Berkeley in *Alciphron* (I, 3), " ariseth from the appearance of use, or the imitation of natural things whose beauty is originally founded in the same principle. Which is, indeed, the grand distinction between Grecian and Gothic architecture: the latter being fantastical, and for the most part being founded neither in nature nor reason, neither necessity nor use." [13] It was, it is clear, the lack of an effect of simplicity, resulting from the multiplication of members, profusion of small details, absence of unbroken surfaces, that Addison had in mind when he spoke of the " meanness of manner " of a Gothic cathedral, in the passage in *Spectator*, No. 415, which seems, by our standards of taste, so astonishing:

Let anyone reflect on the disposition of mind in which he finds himself at his first entrance into the Pantheon at Rome . . . and consider how little in proportion he is affected with the inside of a Gothic Cathedral, though it be five times larger than the other; which can arise from nothing else but the Greatness of the Manner in the one and the Meanness of Manner in the other.

The psychological explanation of this he finds in " *Monsieur Fréart's* Parallel of the Ancient and Modern Architecture," [14] which explains how " the same quantity of superficies " may seem " great and magnificent " or " poor and trifling " — the

[13] *Alciphron*, Dialogue 3, § 9.

[14] Addison is, as his editors have noted, quoting from Evelyn's translation of Fréart's work.

former if "the Division of the Principal Members of the Order consist of but few Parts," but all of these "great, and of a bold and ample Relievo"; the latter if "there is a Redundancy of those smaller Ornaments, which divide and scatter the Angels of the sight into a multitude of Rays, so pressed together that the whole will appear but a confusion."

Partly the same, partly a different attempt to explain psycho- logically what in Gothic is displeasing is offered by Montesquieu in his *Essai sur le goût*. This writing manifests some of the elements of the dawning "romantic" taste; Montesquieu in- sists that—along with "order" and "symmetry"—"surprise," "variety," "contrast" are among the chief sources of aesthetic enjoyment. But he is unwilling to grant that Gothic really possesses these excellences:

Gothic architecture appears to be very full of variety, but the confusion of the ornaments fatigues us by reason of their smallness, which pre- vents us from distinguishing one from another, and by reason of their number, of which the effect is that there is none upon which the eye can come to rest. Thus this architecture is displeasing in the very fea- tures of it which were designed to render it agreeable. A building in the Gothic order is a sort of enigma for the eye that looks upon it; and the mind is embarrassed, as when one puts before it an obscure poem.

But aside from any psychological theories of the aesthetics of architecture, the relative lack of "simplicity" regarded— on the whole justly—as characteristic of Gothic was bound to be condemned by an early eighteenth-century classicist for another reason; it was in conflict with his most sacred catch- word. To want simplicity was to fail in "conformity to nature." This was, of course, the supreme criterion of excellence applied then, as in the two preceding centuries, to everything from re- ligion to the construction of cowsheds; and it was on the ground of its greater "naturalness" (in certain of the senses of that protean term) that classical architecture had been extolled by its orthodox eulogists. La Bruyère in *Les Caractères* ("Des Ouvrages de l'esprit") not only illustrates the identification of "classic" with "natural," but also argues that the archi- tects had first set the example which ought to be followed in literary style:

On a dû faire du style ce qu'on a fait de l'architecture: on a entière-
ment abandonné l'ordre gothique que la barbarie avait introduit pour
les palais et pour les temples; on a rappelé le dorique, l'ionique et le
corinthien, . . . Combien de siècles se sont écoulés avant que les hommes,
dans les sciences et les arts, aient pu revenir au goût des anciens et
reprendre enfin le simple et le naturel.

The same equation—natural = simple = classic—with the same
parallel between architectural and poetic style appears again in
Spectator, No. 62, where Addison likens Gothic designers to
poets who seek to manifest their "wit" by introducing conceits—elaborate and far-fetched metaphors—or other ingenuities and complexities, instead of making "a thought shine in
its own natural beauties. Poets who want this Strength of
Genius to give that majestick simplicity to Nature, which we so
much admire in the Works of the Ancients, are forced to hunt
after foreign Ornaments, and not to let any piece of Wit of
what kind soever escape them. I look upon these writers as
Goths in Poetry, who like those in Architecture, not being able
to come up to the beautiful Simplicity of the old Greeks and
Romans, have endeavored to supply its place with all the ex-
travagances of an irregular fancy." And having the support
of "so great an authority as Mr. Dryden," Addison "ventures
to observe, That the taste of most of our English poets, as well
as readers, is extremely Gothick." So, later in the century, in
some aesthetic observations of Shenstone's. We value things,
he says, because of their "natural production," or the appearance of it, and this is why we do not "view with pleasure the
labored carvings and futile diligence of Gothic artists. We view
with much more satisfaction some plain Grecian fabric, where
art, indeed, has been equally but less visibly industrious." [15]
William Whitehead in *The World*, 1753, damned the Gothic
on similar grounds. Writing satirically of "the reigning follies
of this various island" which have arisen "under the name of
our approaches to nature," he continues:

Taste in my opinion, ought to be applied to nothing but what has as
strict rules annexed to it, though perhaps imperceptible by the vulgar, as
Aristotle, among the critics, would require, or Domenichimo, among the
painters, would practise. People may have whims, freaks, caprices per-

[15] *Unconnected Thoughts on Gardening*, in *Works*, 1764, II, 143.

suasions, and even second-sights, if they please; but they can have no
taste which has not its foundation in nature, and which, consequently,
may be accounted for. From a thousand instances of our imitative incli-
nations I shall select one or two, which have been, and still are, notorious and general. A few years ago everything was Gothic; our houses,
our beds, our book-cases, and our couches were all copied from some
parts or other of our old cathedrals. The Grecian architecture, . . . that
architecture which was taught by nature and polished by the Graces,
was totally neglected. Tricks and conceits got possession everywhere.
Clumsy buttresses were to shock you with disproportion; or little pillars
were to support vast weights; ignorant people, who knew nothing of
gravity, were to tremble at their entrance to every building, lest the
roofs should fall upon their heads. This, however odd it might seem,
and however unworthy the name of Taste, was cultivated, was admired,
and still has its professors in different parts of England. There is something in it, they say, congenial to our old Gothic constitution; I should
rather think, to our modern idea of liberty, which allows everyone the
privilege of playing the fool, and of making himself ridiculous in whatever way he pleases.[16]

Thus the classicist revolt against Gothic architecture was
itself, as interpreted by eighteenth-century theorists, a "return
to Nature." The error of the Gothic architects was that they
had deviated too widely from "Nature's simple plan"; while,
in the words of the *Encyclopédie* (art. "Architecture"), the
architects of the Renaissance in France and Italy "applied
themselves to recapturing *la première simplicité, la beauté et
la proportion, de l'ancienne architecture.*"[17]

2. If the "modern Gothic" erred perhaps even more than
the "ancient" in its departure from the simplicity of Nature,
both styles stood indicted on another count: lack of symmetry.
And in this also they were held to fail to "imitate nature."
"Architecture," said D'Alembert in the *Discours préliminaire
de l'Encyclopédie*, "is limited to imitating, by the grouping
and combination of the different bodies which it employs, the
symmetrical arrangement which nature more or less sensibly

[16] *The World*, No. 12. The passage is of special interest, not only as testimony as to the currency of the new Gothic mode before 1753, but as illustrating the connection, in some minds, between "Gothic irregularity" and moral
individualism or political liberalism—the reverse of the association of ideas
earlier noted.
[17] This idea was attacked by Goethe in *Von deutscher Baukunst*, 1772.

observes in each individual, and which contrasts so well with the beautiful variety of every whole." It should be observed, however, that the term " symmetry" did not necessarily mean for eighteenth-century critics merely bilateral uniformity. It is defined by Montesquieu in the *Encyclopédie* (art. " Goût"), after Vitruvius, as " the relations, proportions and regularity of parts necessary to produce a beautiful whole"; and its nature, and a psychological theory as to why it is indispensable, are suggested in the same article. The " general rule" is laid down that " any object which we are to see *d'un coup d'oeil*" should have " symmetry," should be " simple and single and have all its parts related to the principal object." " Symmetry," in short, was a kind of simplicity; and the theory of it was that anything that militates against unity of effect, that produces upon the eye or the mind a distracting multiplicity of impressions which cannot be immediately recognized as forming a single well-defined pattern, is inconsistent with beauty and fails to give properly aesthetic pleasure. The demand for symmetry in architecture thus expressed the same fundamental psychological theory as the insistence upon the unities in the drama and the disapproval of the mixture of *genres.* Bilateral repetition of the same forms was merely one of the principal means of producing this singleness of effect, or immediately obvious unity of design.

Now " symmetry" in the ordinary sense was, of course, not really disregarded by the Gothic designers, especially of churches; and in interiors it was often actually manifest in a high degree.[18] That a lack of it seemed to eighteenth-century virtuosi and critics to be characteristic of the style was partly due to the historical accident that few great Gothic buildings were completed in accordance with the original designs. But this fact was little known or considered at the time. The conception of the style was derived from the actual visible aspect of many of its principal monuments; and thus the notions of asymmetry and irregularity came to be firmly associated with the term " Gothic" in its architectural use.

[18] This fact was recognized by Hutcheson, and he accordingly granted that Gothic has " real beauty," though not the highest—inasmuch as it has in a

3. For strict neo-classical theorists, however, "regularity" meant more than sensibly apparent symmetry and repetition of identical members; it implied the observance of uniform and exact mathematical rules of proportion, such as had been laid down by Vitruvius. Illustrations of this conception are abundant throughout the century. And here too the Gothic architects were found wanting; they were usually supposed to have designed by rule of thumb or spontaneous inspiration. Thus, Thomas Warton when in 1782, under the influence of Reynolds, he repented his former Gothicism, compared the Gothic

> builder's model, richly rude,
> By no Vitruvian symmetry subdued,

with

> the chaste design,
> The just proportion and the genuine line

of classic art.[19]

All of the foregoing grounds of disparagement of Gothic architecture are interestingly summed up in Goethe's account of the preconceptions with which he first approached the Cathedral of Strasbourg in 1770:

> Auf Hörensagen ehrte ich die Harmonie der Massen, die Reinheit der Formen, war ein abgesagter Feind der verworrnen Willkürlichkeiten gotischer Verzierungen. Unter die Rubrik Gotisch, gleich dem Artikel eines Wörterbuches, häufte ich alle synonymische Misverständnisse, die mir von Unbestimmtem, Ungeordnetem, Unnatürlichem, Zusammengestoppeltem, Aufgeflicktem, Überladenem jemals durch den Kopf gezogen waren.[20]

4. The neo-classic criterion of universal acceptability was sometimes invoked for the disparagement of the Gothic, as in the familiar lines addressed to Reynolds by Thomas Warton in the same poem:

limited degree the same attributes as the classical. (*Inquiry into the Original of our Ideas of Beauty and Virtue*, 1725, § 6; cited from third ed., 1729, p. 76.)

[19] *Verses on Sir Joshua Reynold's Painted Window at New College, Oxford*, 1782.

[20] *Werke*, Jubiläumsausgabe, Vol. 33, 7.

> Thy powerful hand has broke the Gothic chain,
> And brought my bosom back to truth again;
> To truth by no peculiar taste confined,
> Whose universal pattern strikes mankind.

The criterion was obviously, in this case, even more illogically applied than in the case of literature; for, by the eighteenth-century reckoning, all European mankind had preferred for some eight hundred years or more to build "Gothic" structures, while the Greek and Roman modes, so far as was known, had prevailed only a few centuries longer. There was thus no historical support for the supposition that the one was "universal" while the other was not. The notion expressed in Warton's lines was not, I think, one which had much part in producing the disapproval of Gothic architecture, or even in the "rationalization" of this attitude. There was a conventional association between the idea of "the classic" and the idea of that of which the validity and beauty is recognized by all men of all races and all types at all times; and since Gothic structures were *not* "classic"—in the sense of accordant with Greek or Roman models—it was, by a mere verbal confusion, assumed by Warton that they were less "classic" in the sense of "universally approved or enjoyed," than the creations of Palladio or his imitators.

Such were the four principal preconceptions which it was necessary to overcome before Gothic could gain the approval of those for whom the first rule of all art was that it should "imitate" or "conform to Nature."

A renewal of Gothic building had begun in England upon a considerable scale before the dogma of the inferiority of Gothic was seriously challenged. This was the consequence of a new sense on the part of architects of what "harmony" of style required. Many builders since the sixteenth century had without compunction plastered classical orders, pediments and arcades upon Gothic structures. But before the end of the seventeenth century it began to be felt by connoisseurs and designers that this was an impropriety. It was better that a building should be all in one style, even though that was a bad style, than that it should be a mixture of incongruous modes. Wren was an influential preacher of this principle. It is true that, in his proposals for restoring old St. Paul's before the Fire, he declared that " it will be as easy to perform it after a good Roman manner, as to follow the Gothic rudeness of the old design." He proposed to put over the cross of the transepts of this Gothic structure " a spacious *dome* or *rotundo*, with a *cupola* or hemispherical roof, and upon the *cupola* a *lantern* with a spring top." But in the Memorial giving his plan for restoring Westminster Abbey he wrote:

> I have made a design . . . still in the Gothic form, and of a style with the rest of the structure, which I would strictly adhere to, throughout the whole intention; to deviate from the old form would be to run into a disagreeable mixture, which no person of good taste could relish.[21]

When, therefore, his pupil and collaborator, Hawksmoor, and Kent, a designer immensely in the fashion in the time of the first two Georges, were called upon to complete or enlarge Gothic buildings, they commonly tried — seldom, it must be said, with much success — to adhere in some degree to the style of the original structure. We find Hawksmoor, for example, almost simultaneously building two college quadrangles at Oxford. At All Souls the old front quadrangle remained; and Hawksmoor designed (about 1720) for the new north court the dormitories with tall twin towers which latter-day critics have so much berated — the most conspicuous piece of eighteenth-century Gothic in Oxford. Hard by at Queen's, however, the college authorities were willing, and apparently preferred, to have their noble group of medieval buildings razed to the ground; and Hawksmoor showed in the present Italianate outer court and facade of that college what he inclined to do when given a free hand.

It is of this preliminary episode in the history of the Gothic revival that we get an amusing glimpse in the third book of Mason's *The English Garden* (1779). The hero of the tale had inherited a Gothic castle from his ancestors — a mansion whose "turrets, spires and windows"

> bespoke its birth
> Coëval with those rich Cathedral fanes
> (Gothic ill-named).

---

[21] *Parentalia*, 302.

But having a Gothic dwelling, he must also have a Gothic barn, cowyard, and dovecote, and an imitation ruined abbey to conceal the ice-house; [22]

> The fane conventual there is dimly seen,
> The mitred window, and the cloister pale,
> With many a wandering column; ivy soon
> Round the rude chinks her net of foliage spreads.

Yet even Mason's hero, with all his zeal for the Gothic, could not, it must be admitted, refrain from mixing the styles. Mason himself, in a prose passage, carried the argument farther, and suggested that "harmony" generally required Gothic buildings in England, since so much of the existing architecture, especially in country places, was in that style.

Occasional expressions of an actual admiration, or even preference, for Gothic appear in the 1720s and 1730s; but the movement for the actual building of new structures in what was supposed to be this style apparently takes its start in the early forties. Batty Langley's *Ancient Architecture Restored and Improved by a Great Variety of Usefull Designs, Entirely New, in the Gothick Mode, for the Ornamenting of Buildings and Gardens* appeared in 1742 and his *Gothick Architecture Improved by Rules and Proportions* in 1747. To the former work is prefixed a list of 114 "Encouragers to the Restoring of the Saxon Architecture" — presumably the subscribers to the volume — ranging from a large company of dukes and earls to smiths and carpenters. Langley did not hesitate to declare that "the best Gothic buildings in *Magnificence* and *Beauty* greatly exceed all that have been done by both Greeks and Romans." With all his errors of taste and understanding, Langley must be accorded a place of some consequence in the history of aesthetic fashions and in the preparation for the Romantic medievalism, as the first professional architect, and perhaps the first English writer of his age, who boldly proclaimed, not merely the respectability of Gothic, but its actual superiority to classical architecture both "ancient" and "modern," and zealously endeavored to persuade his contemporaries to build in the Gothic style.

[22] *The English Garden*, III (1779), 59 ff.

In this endeavor, however, he had a close second in Sanderson Miller. A country gentleman, a man of letters and an antiquarian, Miller was a person of some importance in his day, whose name became all but forgotten until his correspondence with a pleasant circle of friends was resurrected in 1910.[23] Having first, in 1744, remodelled his own ancestral seat of Radway Grange into what he conceived to be a more truly Gothic character, he was thereafter induced by many of the nobility and gentry to make similar improvements on their estates. Between 1745 and 1750 we find him designing numerous houses, church-towers, stables, *etc.*, in the new-old style; and he seems to have been especially in demand as a designer of ruins. One of his admirers, Lord Dacre, writes him:

> Your fame in Architecture grows greater and greater every day, and I hear of nothing else. . . . You'll soon eclipse Mr. Kent, especially in the Gothic way, in which to my mind he succeeds very ill.[24]

By the late seventeen-forties, then, a Gothic revival—marked, it is true, by more enthusiasm than discrimination—was in full swing; as early as 1753 we have found it spoken of as an old story.[25] It was in domestic structures rather than in churches that the new enthusiasm oftenest found expression; and it seems to have raged especially in the construction of small outbuildings, forming a part rather of the landscape than of the architectural design. On the grounds of Envil, for example, there was a "Gothic billiard-room," designed by Miller; and we even hear of a "Gothic cock-pit." This limitation in the scope afforded the new Gothic builders was doubtless mainly due to the fact that the great official appointments were still usually held by architects of the older school. That the supreme examples of the possibilities of Gothic were to be found in the medieval churches seems, however, to have been clearly enough recognized.

It is true that this neo-Gothicism of the middle of the century apparently did not persist in full vigor, and that some of its most celebrated adherents afterwards wholly or partially

[23] *An Eighteenth-Century Correspondence*, ed. by Lilian Dickins and Mary Stanton.

[24] *Op. cit.*, 275.

[25] Cf. also Walpole's *Letters*, III, 187.

abjured their early faith. Into the reasons for this I shall not here inquire. The fact remains that the break with the classical tradition in architecture had been made; and the reaction was destined to be but a temporary one.

The question which interests the student of the history of ideas concerns the reasons for this change of taste in architecture and kindred arts of design. All such changes, no doubt, owe much to the natural craving for variety and novelty, and to the need of feeling oneself superior in taste to one's immediate forebears, which has periodically characterized the passing generations of Occidental mankind. There is some truth, too, in the philosophy of the history of art which Professor Grierson has propounded — *viz.*, that the human mind inevitably goes through a recurrent alternation of "classical" and "romantic" phases (though I think this an unhappy use of the terms), the former being periods in which men for a time rest content— unquestioning, self-confident, and like-minded—in some established synthesis, while the latter are the periods in which it is discovered afresh that every "synthesis effected by the human mind involves exclusions and sacrifices," that "all balances in human life are precarious," and that an attempt to frame a new and more comprehensive synthesis has become imperative.[26] But (aside from other possible criticisms) no such general explanations help us to understand why *particular* innovating movements took the specific directions which they did, or occurred at the times at which they did occur. Even though it be assumed that in "the systole and diastole of the human heart" a revolutionary period in art was due to begin in the second quarter of the eighteenth century, why should this have had as one of its earliest manifestations a new appreciation of the qualities found in medieval architecture and a tendency to imitate (at first by no means successfully) medieval models.

What I suggest as a partial answer to this question is that this new appreciation of Gothic—not merely in England in the 1740s and 50s but in its later eighteenth-century manifestations also—was made possible by the supposed discovery that this

[26] H. J. C. Grierson: *Classical and Romantic*, 1923. Mr. Grierson has merely invented a new and confusing terminology for Comte's antithesis of "organic" and "transitional" periods.

style in architecture was really more "natural," more "in conformity with Nature," than the classical — in other words, by
certain changes in ideas which enabled the "Goths" to steal
the classicists' catchword. For the sacred though happily equivocal formula remained unchanged throughout; if it had not been
possible plausibly to regard Gothic as a true "imitation of
Nature" it could hardly have gained any wide acceptance in
the eighteenth century. What may be called the necessary
"naturalizing" of Gothic, however, took place chiefly in two
ways, one of minor consequence, the other of great importance
in the general history of aesthetic ideas and taste.

1. We find early in the century occasional suggestions that
a Gothic interior is a sort of indoor equivalent of a much admired feature of an English garden or of a natural landscape.
In his *Itinerarium Curiosum*, 1724, William Stukely, a pioneer
tourist, wrote, after visiting the cloisters of Gloucester Cathedral:

> Nothing could have made me so much in love with Gothic Archi-
> tecture (so-called), and I judge for a gallery, library, or the like, 'tis
> the best manner of building, because the idea of it is taken from a walk
> of trees, whose touching heads are curiously imitated by the roof.[27]

The idea was elaborated in a note to one of Pope's *Epistles* by
Bishop Warburton:

> When the Goths had conquered Spain, . . . they struck out a new
> species of architecture, unknown to Greece and Rome; upon original
> principles, and ideas much nobler than what had given birth to classical
> magnificence. For this northern people having been accustomed, dur-
> ing the gloom of Paganism, to worship the Deity in groves, . . . when
> their new religion required edifices they ingeniously projected to make
> them resemble groves as nearly as the distance of architcture would
> admit. . . . And with what skill and success they executed the project
> . . . appears from hence, that no attentive person ever viewed a regular
> avenue of well-grown trees, intermixing their branches overhead, but
> it presently put him in mind of the long vista through the Gothic
> cathedral. . . .

This became a widely accepted commonplace; Sobry writes (*op.
cit.*, 1776, p. 28):

[27] Cited in *An Eighteenth-Century Correspondence*, p. 262.

La colonne Arabesque, et le pilier de cette Ordonnance, représentent plusieurs arbres liés ensemble et élancés, dont les branchages forment les arrêtes des voûtes. . . . Les chambranles de cette ordre dérivent de la même idée. Ce sont les branchages qui accompagnent l'ouverture des portes et des fenêtres.

This idea that the Gothic style had actually originated in such a direct imitation of Nature was still among the hypotheses which Quatremère de Quincy thought it necessary to examine and refute in 1800. Some, he writes, "either repeating what Warburton said, or hitting upon the same idea themselves, have imagined Gothic architecture to be a fantastic system of imitation—i. e., of a forest or of an *allée de jardin*. These writers conceive that the Gothic architects propose l to themselves, in the interiors of their churches, *une aussi puérile singerie*." Such theorists had, of course, Quatremère points out, merely taken an accidental effect for a cause: "at all times and in all architures there are to be found resemblances with objects which never had served as their models." [28] Schelling, however, a few years later, elaborating upon the theme that "die Architektur hat vorzugweise den Pflanzenorganismus zum Vorbild," still held to the Warburtonian theory, declaring a Gothic building to be essentially a "huge tree or row of trees," and elaborating the parallel in even greater detail.[29] Partly for this reason, Schelling rejected "the now customary opinion that the Saracens brought this architectural style with them into the Occident," and claimed for it a native German origin:

Wenn Deutschland in den ältesten Zeiten mit Wäldern bedeckt war, so lässt sich denken dass auch beim ersten Anfang der Zivilisation in der Bauart, vorzüglich der Tempel, die Deutschen das alte Vorbild ihrer Wälder nachgeahmt haben, dass auf diese Weise die gotische Baukunst in Deutschland ursprünglich heimisch war, und von da aus sich vorzüglich nach Holland und England verpflanzte.

Thus "die gotische Baukunst ist ganz naturalistisch, roh, blosse unmittelbare Nachahmung der Natur." [30] Schelling did not himself, it is true, see in this a reason for preferring Gothic to

[28] *Encyclopédie méthodique: Architecture*, II, 459.
[29] *Philosophie der Kunst*, first delivered as lectures in 1802-3; in *Schellings Werke*, herausgegeben von O. Weiss, 1907, III, 232-3.
[30] *Ibid.*, 234.

classical architecture; for like most of the German Romanticists, he was not in the main a primitivist or a "naturalist" in matters of aesthetics — or of ethics.[31] The (supposedly) more highly developed forms of this art he regarded as superior to its crudely "natural" forms; "harmony," which is "the ruling part of architecture" depends upon "proportions or ratios"; and "the Ionic order has this attribute in the highest degree." [32] Nevertheless, in the passage cited he was expressing a conception of the nature and origin of Gothic still current in his time; and it was in this conception that some of his contemporaries and his eighteenth-century predecessors who *did* believe in the "unmittelbare Nachahmung der Natur" found an argument in justification of their enthusiasm for Gothic.

Another theory of the origin of Gothic (advanced by some of its admirers) which is mentioned by Quatremère brings it into accord with "Nature" by tracing it back to "the structure of the dwellings of primitive man." "From the fact that it is agreed with respect to certain architectures that they had, in a certain type of primitive construction and in the characteristics of the dwellings which necessity suggested in the infancy of societies, a sort of model or type which imitation perfected in succeeding ages, it has been maintained that the Gothic architecture must in like manner have had in Nature its model and the type which it imitated." This also Quatremère refutes at length, arriving at the opposite conclusion that *le gothique serait né non dans l'enfance mais dans la décrépitude de l'état social.*[33]

2. Much more significant, however, than these simple parallels between Gothic forms and actual natural objects or primitive dwellings was the transfer of the aesthetic *principle of irregularity*—as a newly discovered implication of the rule of "imitating Nature" — from the art in which it had first manifested itself on a great scale—that of laying out gardens— to architecture. This transition Burke expressly remarked in 1757; and he added the interesting suggestion that the prior vogue of the formal garden had been due to an improper in-

---

[31] On this *cf.* the essay "On the Discrimination of Romanticisms."
[32] *Op. cit.*, 242-3.
[33] *Encyclopédie méthodique: Architecture*, II, 459-460.

trusion of architectural ideas into the designing of landscapes—
that is to say, of man into nature. For the idea that beauty
results from certain proportions between the parts of objects,
he declared, was never drawn from a study of nature.

> I am the more fully convinced that the patrons of proportion have
> transferred their artificial ideas to nature, and not borrowed from thence
> the proportions they use in works of art; because in any discussion of
> this subject they always quit as soon as possible the open field of natural
> beauties, the animal and vegetable kingdoms, and fortify themselves
> within the artificial lines and angles of architecture. . . . But nature
> has at last escaped from their discipline and their fetters; and our
> gardens, if nothing else, declare, we begin to feel that mathematical
> ideas are not the true measure of beauty.[34]

But if aesthetic principles derived from architecture had previously invaded gardening, in Burke's time the reverse process
was going on; aesthetic ideas first developed and popularized
in the latter art were being carried back into architecture. And
in this, I suggest, lies a large part of the explanation of the
first Gothic revival in actual architectural design, and of the
new appreciation of England's glorious heritage of medieval
Gothic buildings. For the qualities which had long been regarded as the characteristic deformities of Gothic art were, in
great part, precisely those which it had now become the fashion
to deem the highest virtues in garden design. What everybody
was supposed to know was that Gothic architecture was characterized by a kind of wildness and irregularity. Horace Walpole
in the *Anecdotes of Painting*, in a passage in which his earlier
Gothic enthusiasm has diminished though by no means wholly
evaporated, writes that " it is difficult for the noblest Grecian
temple to convey half so many impressions to the mind as a
cathedral does of the best Gothic taste." This he sets down to
the credit not primarily of the architects but of the ecclesiastics,
who "exhausted their knowledge of the passions in composing
edifices whose pomp, mechanism, vaults, tombs, painted windows, gloom and perspectives, infused such sensations of romantic devotion; and they were happy in finding artists capable of
executing such machinery. One must have taste to be sensible

[34] *Sublime and Beautiful*, Pt. III, § 4.

of the beauties of Grecian architecture; one only wants passions to feel Gothic." In a later note Walpole explains that he had intended to ascribe "more address to the architects of Gothic churches than to those of St. Peter's, not as architects but as politicians. . . . Gothic churches infuse superstition—Grecian, admiration. . . . I certainly do not mean by this little contrast to make any comparison between the rational beauties of regular architecture, and the unrestrained licentiousness of that which is called Gothic." "Yet," he cannot refrain from adding, "I am clear that the persons who executed the latter had much more knowledge of their art, more taste, more genius, and more propriety than we choose to imagine." [35]

But in the art of the landscape-architect, we have seen, a kind of aesthetic licentiousness, a "lovely wildness" and irregularity had come to be a merit; and regularity, symmetry, proportion, passed for violations of the first and great commandment, to "follow Nature." And it seemed legitimate to assume that characteristics which are the supreme excellences of one art cannot be defects in another. It had, it is true, for a time been remarked that the principles of gardening and architecture are opposed. One of the earliest of English writers on architecture, Wotton, 1624, noted "a certain contrariety between buildings and gardening; for as fabrics should be regular, so gardens should be irregular, or at least cast into a very wild regularity." [36] This distinction was accepted by several eighteenth-century enthusiasts for the "natural garden." [37] But the cleavage between the two arts — however sound in principle — could not, in the actual movement of taste and opinion, be rigidly or lastingly maintained. Aesthetic ideas and, still more, aesthetic susceptibilities learned in one field inevitably passed over into the other. The transfusion might, of course, be in either direction: in which direction depended partly upon the relative position of the arts in the interest of theorists and connoisseurs, partly upon the natural sequence of stages in the working out of the implications of the aesthetic imperative *naturam sequere*. The influ-

[35] *Op. cit.*, 1849 ed., I, 117 f.

[36] *Reliquiae Wottonianae*, 4th ed., p. 64.

[37] E. g., by Mason (*English Garden*, I, 1. 395), his annotator Burgh, and Heely (*Beauties of Hagley*, I, 21).

ence in the seventeenth century, as we have seen, was from architecture to gardening — and hence unfavorable to Gothic. But when, through the example of the English garden and the enthusiastic preaching of its admirers, a whole generation had learned to find there a "beauty in irregularity," some were sure to better their instruction and seek for the same beauty elsewhere. Many, no doubt, had always in fact experienced pleasure in long-drawn aisles and fretted vaults and soaring pinnacles and broken sky-lines; but no man of taste could permit himself to give way to this. Now, however, it could be argued upon accepted aesthetic principles that the recognized attributes of Gothic were legitimate sources of enjoyment. The doctrine of what may be called the primacy of irregularity was no longer limited to the theory of landscape-design, but was explicitly generalized.

Regularity and exactness [says a writer of the 1740s] excite no pleasure in the imagination unless they are made use of to contrast with something of an opposite kind. . . . Thus a regular building perhaps gives us little pleasure; and yet a fine rock, beautifully set off in claro-obscuro, and garnished with flourishing bushes, ivy, and dead branches, may afford us a great deal; and a ragged ruin, with venerable old oaks, and pines nodding over it, may perhaps please the fancy yet more.[88]

Batty Langley, it is true—such errors are frequent with pioneers —had endeavored to commend Gothic by dwelling upon the "rules and proportions" to be found in some features of the style — i. e., by assimilating it so far as possible to the older standards. But this notion was unconvincing and apparently made little impression. The effective way to vindicate the style was to declare, as did Mason, that in it "harmony results From disunited parts." The merit of his hero's Gothic dwelling was that in it

No modern art
Had marred with misplaced symmetry the pile.

The true spirit of the Gothic enthusiast, in short, was that expressed by a friend of Sanderson Miller's who wrote in 1753 requesting a design for a new house:

[88] W. Gilpin: *A Dialogue upon the Gardens . . . at Stow in Buckinghampshire*, 1748.

I would by no means have my Front regular: . . . since the Beauty of Gothick Architecture (in my opinion) consists, like that of a Pindarick Ode, in the Boldness and Irregularity of its Members.[39]

The excellence of the so-called "Chinese sharawadgi"—the term being applied first to gardens but later to buildings also— as the eighteenth-century admirers of it held, was essentially the same; it was a beauty, or at least a pleasurable aesthetic quality, which did *not* depend upon the recognition, at all events at the first glance, of a single general scheme of arrangement in which the position of each part was "regular," *i. e.*, manifestly determined by the recognizable nature of the scheme as a whole. *Sharawadgi* was beauty without regularity and without immediately apparent design. It was for this reason that the Chinese and Gothic modes were so often associated in the eighteenth-century mind.

The customary parallel of architectural and poetic styles tended, as the revolt against the classical models grew, to promote the same identification of natural irregularity with aesthetic excellence in all the arts; and the three changes in taste which were developing at the same time gave one another mutual support. A taste for English or Chinese gardens, for Gothic buildings, and for Shakespeare, were often regarded as fundamentally the same taste; from the validity of any one a justification for either or both the others was sometimes deduced; and the ultimate theoretical ground for all three was the same assumption that art must have the attributes which distinguish the works of "Nature" and constitute a truly "natural" beauty — "Nature," however, being used, not in the classicist's sense but in the diametrically opposite sense. This is illustrated in the two most celebrated of English eighteenth-century characterizations of Shakespeare. Pope—who in theory though not in practice was something of a pioneer in all three of the new movements—begins his *Preface* (1725), it will be remembered, by a recital of the "characteristic excellencies for which (notwithstanding his defects) Shakespeare is justly and universally elevated above all other dramatic writers"; and the first and most fundamental of these is his closeness to nature:

[39] *An Eighteenth-Century Correspondence*, p. 303.

Homer himself drew not his art so immediately from the fountains of Nature . . . [Shakespeare] is not so much an imitator as an instrument of Nature; and it is not so just to say that he speaks from her as that she speaks through him.[40]

And the *Preface* ends with a parallel between a Shakespearean play and a Gothic building: both have the same merits and the same defects:

I will conclude by saying of Shakespeare, that with all his faults, and with all the irregularity of his drama, one may look upon his works, in comparison with those that are more finished and regular, as upon an ancient majestic piece of Gothic architecture compared with a neat modern building; the latter is more elegant and glaring, but the former is more strong and more solemn. It must be allowed, that in one of these there are materials enough to make many of the other. It has much the greater variety, and much the nobler apartments; though we are often conducted to them by dark, odd, and uncouth passages. Nor does the whole fail to strike us with greater reverence, though many of the parts are childish, ill-placed, and unequal to its grandeur.[41]

Forty years later Dr. Johnson in his *Preface to Shakespeare* condones and even extols Shakespeare's "irregularity" on the ground that Nature itself is irregular and "gratifies the mind with endless diversity," and is for just these reasons the more pleasing and the more sublime. In these passages the two most eminent English spokesmen of neo-classical aesthetic doctrine may be seen in the act of giving away the key to the classicists' position, by shifting the aesthetic connotation of "conformity to nature" from simplicity to complexity and from regularity to irregularity; and in doing so they at the same time admit, even though with reservations, the excellence, and even the superiority, of the recognized examples of the latter qualities in architecture, in landscape, and in the drama.

As the foregoing passages illustrate, the same reversal of valuation took place with respect to the attribute of "variety" as with respect to "irregularity." The classicists in architecture (examples have already been cited) had complained that there was too much variety in Gothic structures, that their ornament

---

[40] *Op. cit.*, in *Works*, Elwin and Courthope ed., X, 534-5. Addison had said much the same thing in *Spectator*, No. 592.
[41] *Ibid.*, 549.

was too diverse and profuse, their carvings full of "fret and lamentable imagery." But when so respectable an aesthetic authority as Addison had declared the great beauty of natural landscapes to consist in the fact that in them "the eye is fed with an infinite variety of images without any certain stint or measure," the architectural corollary was certain sooner or later to be drawn. Walpole complained in 1750 of Grecian architecture that "the variety is little and admits no charming irregularities." [42] When Goethe in 1770 found his anti-Gothic prejudices falling from him at his first acquaintance with a great Gothic church, he gave as one of the principal causes of the impression thus made upon him,

die grossen harmonischen Massen, *zu unzählig kleinen Teilen belebt, wie in Werken der ewigen Natur*, bis aufs geringste Käferchen, alles Gestalt, und alles zweckend zum Ganzen.[43]

But in his later, classicist phase, after his Italian journey, Goethe reverted to the sort of criticism of Gothic which we have seen in Fréart, Evelyn and Addison:

Leider suchten alle nordischen Kirchenverzierer ihre Grösse nur in der multiplizierten Kleinheit. Wenige verstanden, diesen kleinlichen Formen unter sich ein Verhältnis zu geben; und dadurch wurden solche Ungeheuer wie der Dom in Mailand, wo man einen ganzen Marmorberg mit ungeheuren Kosten versetzt und in die elendesten Formen gezwungen hat.[44]

These two aspects of Gothic — "variety," consisting largely in the multiplication of divisions and of minute and diverse ornaments, and "irregularity" — were well summed up later in the century by a notable contributor to the diffusion in his own time of the taste both for naturalness in gardens and for medieval architecture:

In Gothic buildings the outline of the summit presents such a variety of forms, some open, some fretted and variously enriched, that even

---

[42] *Letters*, ed. Toynbee, II, 433.

[43] *Werke*, Jubiläumsausgabe, vol. 33, p. 9; italics mine.

[44] *Werke, Jubiläumsausgabe*, vol. 33, p. 47. *Cf.* the *Einleitung zu den Propyläen*, 1798. "Dem deutschen Künstler, so wie überhaupt jedem neuern und nordischen, ist es schwer, ja beinahe unmöglich, von dem Formlosen zur Gestalt überzugehen" (*ibid.*, p. 115).

where there is an exact correspondence of parts, it is often disguised by an appearance of splendid confusion and irregularity. In the doors and windows of Gothic churches, the pointed arch has as much variety as any regular figure can well have, the eye is not so strongly conducted from the top of one to that of the other, as by the parallel lines of the Grecian; and every person must be struck with the extreme richness and intricacy of some of the principal windows of our cathedrals and ruined abbeys.[45]

"Richness and intricacy" were precisely the qualities which the architectural classicists had professed most to disapprove. The same attributes were declared by Friedrich Schlegel to be the very essence of Gothic and its supreme merit; it is an art which is true to Nature because it produces the same impression of "inexhaustible fullness" and diversity of forms that Nature itself does: "Das Wesen der gotischen Baukunst besteht in der natürlichen Fülle und Unendlichkeit der innern Gestaltung und äussern blumenreichen Verzierungen."[46]

Both these qualities were closely related to another attribute— the suggestion of infinity—which had likewise been much insisted upon by those who had set forth the theory of the English garden. This note also had been sounded by Addison; it was thus expanded by a later English writer, Gilpin:

There is nothing so distasteful to the eye as a confined prospect (where the reasonableness of it does not appear). . . . The eye naturally loves liberty, and when it is in quest of prospects will not rest content with the most beautiful dispositions of art, confined within a narrow compass, but (as soon as the novelty of the sight is over) will begin to grow dissatisfied, till the whole limits of the horizon be given it to range through.[47]

The Abbé Delille was apparently paraphrasing these passages when he observed that "the eye loves an air of liberty":

Laissez donc des jardins la limite indécise . . .
Où l'œil n'espère plus, le charme disparoît.[48]

---

[45] Uvedale Price: *An Essay on the Picturesque*, 1794, p. 51.
[46] *Grundzüge der gotischen Baukunst*, 1805, in *Sämmtl. Werke*, VI, 201.
[47] Gilpin, *On the Gardens at Stow*, 1748. It will have been noted that some of the admirers of the Chinese gardens praised them for their avoidance of unlimited prospects. Here the *goût chinois* and the Gothic parted company.
[48] *Des jardins*, 5th ed., p. 23.

The appreciation of this quality was strengthened by the vogue of Burke's Essay: "Nothing," he wrote, "can strike the mind with its greatness which does not make some sort of approach towards infinity; which nothing can do whilst we are able to perceive its bounds." [49] But it was observed—though not, perhaps, until somewhat later in the century — that in this, too, Gothic rather than classical architecture came nearer to producing the aesthetic impression given by English gardens and by "Nature" itself. It produced it partly by its variety and profusion of detail, but partly by a special peculiarity of Gothic design which Bernardin de St. Pierre, among others, pointed out. "L'architecture gothique de nos temples affectait le sentiment de l'infini":

Les voûtes élevées, supportées par des colonnes sveltes, présentaient, comme la cime des palmiers, une perspective aérienne et céleste qui nous remplit d'un sentiment religieux. L'architecture grecque, au contraire, malgré la régularité de ses ordres et la beauté de ses colonnes, offre souvent dans ses voûtes un aspect lourd et terrestre, parcequ'elles ne sont pas assez élevées par rapport à leur largeur.[50]

By the end of the century this had become one of the familiar themes of the enthusiasts for Gothic. "It is well known," wrote John Milner in 1800—quoting Burke as an authority— "that height and length are amongst the primary sources of the sublime . . . [Now in Gothic] the aspiring form of the pointed arches, the lofty pediments, the tapering pinnacles, the perspective of uniform columns, ribs and arches repeated at equal distances, produce an artificial infinite in the mind of the spectator, when the same extent of plain surface would perhaps hardly affect it at all." [51] This, it will be observed, precisely contradicts the theory of Fréart adopted by Addison about the psychological effect of multiplicity of detail and broken surfaces.

The late Professor W. P. Ker has observed that "the Middle Ages have influenced modern literature more strongly through their architecture than through their poems. Gothic churches

[49] Sublime and Beautiful, Pt. II, § 4.

[50] Harmonies de la Nature, written about 1793, published in 1814; in Oeuvres posthumes, 1833, p. 66.

[51] From Preface to Essays on Gothic Architecture by Warton, Bentham and Grose.

and old castles have exerted a medieval literary influence on many authors who have had no close acquaintance with old French and German poets and not much curiosity about their ideals or their style. . . . The thrill of mystery and wonder came much more from Gothic buildings than from the *Morte d' Arthur.*" [52]   The truth of this is doubtless now generally recognized. Less familiar is the fact for which I have here presented some of the evidence—that the revival of an appreciation of medieval architecture, with its manifold consequences, was itself in great part an aspect of the eighteenth-century " return to Nature." But this " return " was in truth, as we have seen, rather a substitution of one for another way of conceiving of " Nature " as the norm and model of art. The fundamental aesthetic formula of the neo-classicist was the fundamental formula of the gothicist; but the crucial word had reversed its meaning. This shift in the dominant connotation of " Nature " was partly, of course, the effect of a change in taste due to other causes; but it was also itself one of the apparent causes of that change, and it was pretty certainly a *conditio sine qua non.* Until very near the close of the century, hardly any reputable aesthetic theorist or connoisseur of the arts had the hardihood to blaspheme the sacred word; if the merits of Gothic were, in that age, to be vindicated, it must be by showing that type of art to be more faithful than its rival to the universally accepted standard. And the change in the conception of " naturalness " in art began, it is important to remember, before and independently of the beginning of medievalism in architecture. It began in the art in which it was most glaringly apparent that " conformity to Nature " is *not* consistent with formal and regular design, symmetry, simplicity, and the rest of the classical attributes. The earliest Gothic revival, that which took place in England, had for its herald and precursor the new fashion in the designing of artificial landscapes and the new liking for wildness, boldness, broken contours and boundless prospects in natural landscape. It was no accident that the principal early partisans of the *goût anglo-chinois* were among the principal

[52] *Cambridge History of English Literature,* X, p. 217.

early partisans of Gothic architecture. The one movement prepared the way for the other because it released the inhibitions which the neo-classic principles imposed, or were generally understood to impose, upon certain latent capacities for aesthetic enjoyment; and it did this the more effectively, because the more insidiously, by simply giving to the first and great commandment of the neo-classic code a profoundly different, yet a seemingly obvious and unavoidable, interpretation. Clad in the mantle of "Nature" the great art of the Middle Ages first regained aesthetic respectability; when it had done so, many other modes of medievalism followed in its train.

IX. HERDER AND THE ENLIGHTENMENT PHILOSOPHY OF HISTORY *

A SERIES OF eminent German writers between 1780 and 1796 published what may be called progressivist philosophies of history; and these were, of course, intrinsically adverse to most forms of primitivism, and implied the rejection of the assumption of the superiority of "nature" to "art." The most important of these writings are Lessing's *Erziehung des Menschengeschlechts*, 1780; Herder's *Ideen zu einer Philosophie der Geschichte der Menschheit*, 1784-91, and some parts of the *Briefe zu Beförderung der Humanität*, 3te Sammlung, 1794, especially Bk. VI; Kant's *Idee zu einer allgemeinen Geschichte in weltbürgerlicher Absicht* (1784) and *Muthmasslicher Anfang der Menschengeschichte*, 1786; Schiller's *Was heisst und zu welchem Ende studiert man Universalgeschichte* (1789) and *Briefe über die ästhetische Erziehung des Menschen* (1795). The present study will be concerned with Herder's rôle in this development, considered in the light of its contrast with older but still persistent conceptions of history and of the value—or non-value—of historical studies.[1]

* A previously unpublished fragment from a course of lectures on some of the major ideas of the Enlightenment. The discerning reader of the present volume will observe the relation between this essay and those numbered VI, II, III, VIII, X and XV. It outlines one important phase in the supersession of that general underlying scheme of ideas summarized in "The Parallel of Deism and Classicism"; it indicates an aspect of the transition from universalism and primitivism to the idea of *perfectibilité* different from those found in Rousseau and Monboddo; and it shows one of the antecedents of that program of an endlessly expansive and progressive art which was enunciated by the early German Romanticists. But between Herder's *Ideen* and this last there intervened in Germany a belated but brief phase of classicism, and consequently of "retrospectivism"; and the influence of Herder's work upon the Schlegels, the initiators of the new movement after 1796, though certainly not wholly inoperative, was less potent and decisive than that of Schiller's *Letters on the Aesthetic Education of Man* and, especially, of his essay *On Naïve and Sentimental Poetry*.

[1] On this general subject see an important article by Mr. H. S. V. Ogden, "The Rejection of the Antithesis of Nature and Art in Germany, 1780-1800," *Jour. of English and Germanic Philology*, XXXVIII, 1939.

It is true that in some of these writers the primitivistic tradition and the idea of progress, the apotheosis of "nature"
and the reverence for "art," are still incongruously combined,
or are struggling with one another for the mastery. This is
conspicuously true in the case of Herder, who in the *Ideen* and
elsewhere patently wavers between conflicting preconceptions.
At times he expatiates in a more than Rousseauistic vein, though
evidently under Rousseau's influence, on the evils of civilized
life. The *thätige freie Leben der Natur* is the happy patrimony
of "the so-called savages" (*Wilden*); their existence is health-
ful, independent, calm, peaceful; they have no unsatisfied desires, because simple pleasures and few belongings content
them; and one has but to read "the unembellished speeches of
those we call savages" to recognize in them, unmistakably,
"sound understanding and natural reasonableness (*natürliche
Billigkeit*)."[2] But "art and the overweening luxury of man"
have corrupted Nature.[3] Herder, moreover, influenced by the
Ossian craze, was one of the promoters of the idea that, because
primitive peoples are "nearer to nature," their poetry is necessarily better, and that it is difficult to write genuine poetry in a
highly civilized age; this appears especially in his *Spirit of
Hebrew Poetry* (1783), and in his enthusiasm for the collection of folk-poetry (*Volkslieder*, 1778-9). In "sensibility for
the beauty and greatness of nature" a child often surpasses
withered age, *und die einfachsten Nationen haben an Natur-
bildern und Naturempfindung die erhabenste, rührendste Dichtkunst.*[4] Upon this theme Macaulay was still dilating in his
first contribution to the *Edinburgh Review*, the essay on Milton,
in 1825.

But these vestigial survivals of primitivism were quite irreconcilable with what finally came to be the dominant ideas of
Herder's philosophy: the principle of plenitude and the related
idea of cultural progress. Professor Martin Schütze has distinguished four successive phases of Herder's attitude towards
"the myth of the Golden Age" and the ideal of the natural
man, but concludes that in the end, especially in the *Ideen*,

[2] *Ideen* in *Sämmtl. Werke*, ed. Suphan, XIII, 317.
[3] *Ibid.*, 323.
[4] *SW.*, XIII, 7-8.

"the genetic view held sway exclusively."[5] When Herder has reached this point, *vestigia nulla retrorsum* becomes for him the law of history; to turn back, not only to the original but to any earlier stage of culture in general, or in any one of man's activities, is not only impossible for him, but if it were possible, would be undesirable. Nature advances *von einfachen Gesetzen, so wie von groben Gestalten, ins Zusammengesetztere, Künstliche, Feine*;[6] and since Nature's ways are the model for man's, and since in any case he is subject to her laws and consequently *must* conform to this general law or trend, his life, thought and art will and should proceed from simpler and ruder phases to the complex, the refined, yes, and the artificial. Herder, like Shakespeare before him, while still looking upon nature as a norm, now has come to recognize that "art," in the sense indicated, the work of man's laboring thought, however subtle, can no longer be disparaged in the name of nature. "Let us," he exclaims, "thank the Creator that he has given our race intellect (*Verstand*) and to this has made art essential." *Im Fortgange der Zeiten liegt also ein Fortgang des Menschengeschlechts.*

This progressivist philosophy of history was inimical not only to aesthetic primitivism but to classicism, which in Herder's eyes was a kind of primitivism. He writes in the *Ideen* (Bk. V, ch. 4):

That this march of time (*Zeitenfortgang*) has had an influence upon the mode of though (*Denkart*) of our race is undeniable. Seek now, or attempt, an Iliad, try to write as Aeschylus, Sophocles and Plato did; it is impossible. The simple mind of the child (*Kindersinn*), the untroubled outlook upon the world, in short, *die griechische Jugendzeit*, is past. So is it with the Hebrews and the Romans; on the other hand, we know and understand a multitude of things of which both the Hebrews and the Romans were ignorant. The one had had a day's teaching, the other a century's. Tradition has been enriched, the Muse of the age, history itself, speaks with a hundred voices and sings with a hundred tones. Grant that, in the immense snowball which the movement of time has rolled up for us, there may be included as much folly and confusion as you please, nevertheless even this confusion is a child of the centuries, it could arise only out of the indefatigable ad-

[5] *Mod. Philol.*, XIX (1921-2), 376-7.   [6] *Ideen, SW.*, XIII, 49.

vance of one and the same being. Any return to the old times, even the famous Great Year of Plato, is, in accordance with the very concept of the world and of time, an impossibility. We are carried forward; the stream never returns to its source.

The progress even of the practical arts and sciences, lamented by Rousseau, must, says Herder, on the whole promote also progress in morals and in the fine arts. Technological inventions may for a time be misused, may become the instruments of a corrupting luxury, but in the end, "we cannot doubt, every right use of the human understanding necessarily must and will make for the advancement of humanity (*Humanität*) . . . Every conquest in the useful arts makes man's property more secure, lightens fatigue, enlarges the scope of his action, and thus lays the foundations for a broader culture and humanity."

There was associated with this progressivism a species of historical relativism which was clearly, in Herder's mind, a corollary of the principle of plenitude. When the notion of the Scale or Chain of Being was translated from its static to its temporalized version,[7] some of the related ideas inherent in the former passed over into the latter. There was implicit in the conception from the beginning a cosmic determinism, which in Spinoza had become fully explicit. Every grade in the scale or link in the chain had to be, and to be just what it was, because the scheme of things as a whole (which was assumed to be the only rational scheme of things) required it; and because each, in its own place in the pattern, was thus required by reason, it was also good. And, with the common tendency of determinists (*except* Spinoza) to convert "must" into "ought," to exhort men to be or do what, upon the premises of the argument, it should be impossible for them *not* to be or do, earlier eighteenth-century moralists were prone to discourse upon man's obligation to keep to his distinctive place in the scale, to endeavor neither to rise above it nor fall below it.[8] Now in Herder, at least in the later period of his thought, the fixed Chain of Beings has been, in the main, converted into a chain of cultural stages, a *Kette der Bildung*, a *sequence* instead of a *structure* realized all at once and immutably; but in this new

---

[7] Cf. *The Great Chain of Being*, chap. IX.
[8] See *The Great Chain of Being*, 200 ff., and Essay IV, above.

form of the idea the same two implications of the older form are assumed; every link in this temporal chain is necessary, it too could not be other than what it is; and so the static cosmological determinism latent in the older conception is converted into a historical determinism. Herder regards the necessity as a good, and also, with the same unconscious inconsistency as before, makes out of it an imperative: all the cultural characteristics of any age are what they ought to be, what the law of history demands at that point in the process, and therefore each in its own time and place has its own value and justification, and none is to be judged or condemned from the point of view of another. And the rule for the individual is: hold fast to your own place in the *Kette der Bildung*, be true to your own age, and do not try to imitate or return to any other. In this, again, was obviously implicit a condemnation of that moaning about the inferiority of the moderns, in art and taste and in other respects, which was to be so characteristic of the German classicists of the early 1790s. Let me quote, in justification of these remarks, some passages of Herder's. Already in his essay on Ossian (1773) he writes:

You laugh at my enthusiasm for the savages almost as Voltaire did at Rousseau. . . . But do not think that I therefore scorn our virtues of manners and morals. The human race is destined for a progress of scenes, of educations, of manners. Woe to the man who is displeased with the scene in which he is to appear, act, and live! But woe also to the philosopher who, in making theories on mankind and manners and morals, knows only his own scene, and judges the first scene always the worst. If *all* belong to the whole of the progressive drama, *each* must display a *new and notable side* of mankind. Take care, lest I visit on you presently a psychology drawn from Ossian's poems.[9]

In the essay *On the Cause of the Decline of Taste* (also of 1773): "What of Shakespeare? Had he no taste, no rules? More than anyone else; but they were the taste of *his* time, the rules for that which *he* could accomplish. Had he with his genius lived in the time of the ancients, does anyone believe he would have fought against taste?"[10] — *i. e.*, against the so-called classical taste.

[9] Tr. of M. Schütze, *Mod. Philol.*, 1921-2, p. 365.
[10] *SW.*, ed. Suphan, V, 653.

And from the *Ideen* (the passage perfectly expresses what I have called the temporalized version of the principle of plenitude): "The historian of mankind must, like the Creator of our race or like the genius of the earth, view without partiality and judge without passion. . . . Nature has given the whole earth to her human children and has permitted all to germinate upon it that, by virtue of its place and time and potency, could germinate. All that can be, is; all that can come to be, will be; if not today, then tomorrow." [11] "Nature's year is long; the blooms of her plants are as many as these growths themselves and as the elements that nourish them. In India, Egypt, China, that has come to pass which nowhere and never will again come to pass upon the earth; and so in Canaan, Greece, Rome, Carthage. The law of necessity and congruity (*Convenienz*), which is composed of potencies and place and time, everywhere brings forth different fruits." [12] And again: "In the kingdom of mankind that which *can* come to pass, under given circumstances of nationality, time and place, will come to pass: of this Greece affords the richest and finest example." In another passage of the *Ideen* Herder is speaking of the rise and fall of Rome:

Let us also consider this—like any other phenomenon of nature whose causes and consequences we seek freely to investigate—without foisting any set pattern upon it. The Romans were and became what they could become; everything declined or endured among them of which the decline or endurance was possible. Time rolls on and with it the child of Time, Humanity (*Menschheit*), in its many forms. Everything has come to bloom upon the earth which *could* do so, each in its own time and in its own *milieu*; it has faded away, and it will bloom again, when its time comes again.[13]

(Herder has in this last forgotten what he has elsewhere said about the impossibility of the recurrence of any phase which has once been passed through.)

Already apparent in Herder, then, were, *inter alia*, two norma-

---

[11] *Ideen*, Bk. XI, ch. 6; *SW*, XIV, 85-6. "Alles was seyn kann, ist; alles, was werden kann, wird; wo nicht heut, so morgen."

[12] *Ibid.*, 86. So also 227: "auf unsern Planeten . . . alles wird gebohren, was auf ihm gebohren werden kann."

[13] *Ideen*, Bk. XIV, ch. 6; *SW*, XIV, 203.

tive principles that were destined to find a place in the German " Romantic " ideology: (a) Towards all the elements of all cultures other than one's own—whether of some earlier period in history or of another race or region—one should cultivate a catholicity of appreciation and understanding, based upon the historical necessitarianism and historical optimism which has been outlined.

The significance of this relatively new way of evaluating past history and also the institutions, traditions and arts of foreign peoples, can be adequately recognized only if one has in mind the very different way of looking at history which had been customary—though not without important exceptions—in the Enlightenment; and to get this contrast-effect, let us recall what that had been.

Dominated by the assumption that rationality—or " nature " as " right reason "—implies that there is only one invariant valid standard for each mode of human activity—morals, politics, art—the typical *Aufklärer* tended to look upon the past course of human events as mainly a spectacle without rational meaning. For plainly no *one* norm had been realized in it: the civilizations of different ages and peoples had been endlessly various. That this should have been the case was, indeed, anomalous, from the point of view of which I am speaking, since it was a basic assumption that *fundamentally* human nature is everywhere the same. As a German writer, J. Freyer, in his *Geschichte der Geschichte der Philosophie* has well observed: [14]

To the scientific thought of the *Aufklärung* a problem of peculiar difficulty presented itself in *history*. . . . If, in all that happens, and has ever happened, what is at work is simply the mind of man, unvarying in its laws, how account for the changes of modes of action and forms of culture which history shows?

So far as this assumption of *actual* uniformity was uppermost in an eighteenth-century writer's mind, he was likely to argue that no changes of much consequence in human nature and human life *have* occurred. The things that outwardly distinguish one period of history from another are merely surface-

[14] *Op. cit.* (1902), 1 and 3.

appearances, of minor importance. A sentence from an eighteenth-century book—which is nevertheless a book of history—cited by Freyer in another writing will illustrate how definitely and consistently this presupposition was held: it is from Mascou's *Geschichte der Teutschen:*

The stage-setting [in different periods of history] is, indeed, altered, the actors change their garb and their appearance; but their inward motions arise from the same desires and passions of men, and produce their effects in the vicissitudes of kingdoms and peoples.[15]

In history so viewed there could, obviously, be no plot, no progress or general trend, not even any especially interesting differences between age and age.

The same way of thinking about history, expressed in a formal antithesis between "natural" and "historical" truths, is well illustrated—along with several other of the tendencies of the Enlightenment—in an extremely popular little book of the later eighteenth century, Bernardin de St. Pierre's *La Chaumière Indienne,* 1790. An English savant in India, member of an expedition sent out by the Royal Society to visit many countries and interrogate their wise men on a long series of questions, is compelled by a storm to take refuge in the cabin of a poor *pariah,* and finds in him the wisdom which he had sought in vain from the Brahmins and the pundits. The Englishman asks the *pariah* above all three questions: 1st. " By what means is one to find the truth?" "Our senses," the inquirer observes, "often deceive us, and our reason leads us astray still more. The reason differs with almost every man; it is at bottom, I believe, nothing but the particular interest of each individual; and this may account for its varying so much throughout the whole earth. There are not two religions, two nations, two tribes, two families—what do I say? there are not two men, who think in the same way. How then are we to proceed in the search for truth, if the intelligence cannot serve us therein?" "It appears to me," replied the *pariah,* "that it is to be done by means of a simple heart. The mind and the senses may err; but a simple heart, though it may be deceived, never deceives." "Your

[15] In Freyer's Leipzig dissertation, 1911, with the same title as his monograph above cited.

reply is profound," said the doctor. "Truth is to be sought first with the heart, not with the mind. *Les hommes sentent tous de la même manière, et ils raisonnent différemment*, because the principles of truth are in nature, while the consequences which men draw from them are founded in their own interests." But he goes on to his second question, which, he says, is more difficult: "*Where* is truth to be sought for? A simple heart depends on ourselves, but the truth depends on other men. Where, then, shall we find it, if those who surround us are seduced by their prejudices or corrupted by their interests, as for the most part they are? I have travelled among many peoples; I have examined their libraries, consulted their learned men; and nowhere have I found aught but contradictions, doubts, and opinions a thousand times more various than their languages. If then the truth is not to be found in the most famous repositories of human knowledge, where must one go to seek for it? Of what benefit is it to have a simple heart among men whose understandings are false and whose hearts are corrupted?" "I should be suspicious of the truth," said the *pariah*, "if it came to me only through the mediation of such men; it is not among them that we must seek for it, it is in nature. Nature is the source of all that exists; its language is not variable, as is that of men and their books. Men make books, but nature makes things . . . *Tout livre est l'art d'un homme, mais la nature est l'art de Dieu.*" — "You are right," said the Englishman; "nature is the source of *les vérités naturelles*; but what is the source of historical truths, if it is not in books? How else assure ourselves to-day concerning an event which happened two thousand years ago? . . . As you well say, a book is only the work of a man; we must needs therefore give up all historical truth, since it can come to us only by means of men, subject to error." — "Of what import to our happiness," said the Indian, "is the history of bygone things? The history of what is, is the history of what has been and of what shall be."

However, what was more frequently dwelt upon was the other side of the picture of past history and of the contemporary scene, here sketched by Bernardin. Fundamentally the same, human nature nevertheless *had* manifested itself in infinitely diverse ways. The constant in it, that which is given to every man, for Bernardin—as the arch-representative of the sentimentalist strain of Rousseauism—was "a simple heart"; it would more usually have been called "reason"—which was, however, a very different thing from "reasoning" and not essentially different from "a simple heart," since both signified a faculty, common to all, of knowing a few simple and fundamental truths, *vérités naturelles*, which were believed to be sufficient for man's guidance. But whatever you *called* it, it *was*, at any rate, uniform, and history was not uniform; some irrational passion or passions, "interest" or "vanity" or "self-esteem" or "prejudices," had, mysteriously, caused men to deviate widely—and in many divergent directions—from the way of nature. When you attended to this side of the matter, history presented the aspect, not of essential changelessness, but of countless changes which ought never to have occurred. It was the melancholy story of man's aberrations from the normal. It is an expression of this attitude towards history that Browning puts into the mouth of a figure chronologically not of the Enlightenment but of the Renaissance, in the speech of the dying Paracelsus:

> I saw no use in the past: only a scene
> Of degradation, ugliness and tears,
> The record of disgraces best forgotten,
> A sullen page in human chronicles,
> Fit to erase.

The contempt (inspired largely by this rationalistic uniformitarianism) of the Cartesians in the seventeenth century for historical studies was notorious,[16] and was attacked by the pioneer in the early development of the philosophy of history, Vico, in the *Scienza Nuova*, 1725. For a mid-eighteenth-century example, there is a remark of Bishop Warburton's about Thomas Hearne's great collection of chronicles and other sources for English history in some 60 volumes: "There is not one [of these writings] that is not a disgrace to letters, most of them are to common sense, and some even to human nature." As Mrs. Humphry Ward, who quoted this dictum in one of

[16] Bouillier: *Histoire de la philosophie cartésienne*, 1868, II, 536, 544.

her essays, observed, "the exquisite folly of this sentence is apparent enough to our age, which cannot have enough of documents, and would give a whole cartload of Warburton for another Pepys; but it expressed a very common eighteenth-century judgment."[17] "Think," Mrs. Ward exclaims, "of what the great word 'history' meant in relation to religion before 1789, and what it has come to mean since!"

In spite of the prevalence of this negative *philosophy* of history, historical curiosity would not down, historical writing was on the increase, and the antiquarians were busily collecting materials for it — Hearne (1678-1733) being a conspicuous example of the fact. And there was a motive for the study of history which, if not suggested by these preconceptions, could at least be plausibly supported by means of them. No man, it is true, could be supposed to know historical facts by the unaided light of nature; but you might at least reenforce the light of nature with historical facts. If you meant by the truths of "nature" (among other things) the permanent and unvarying laws of the relations of cause and effect between conduct—especially the conduct of governments—and the happiness of nations or the prosperity of states, then history could be regarded as a collection of edifying *illustrations* of these immutable truths. It was not the general course of history, the record of man's progress, the discrimination of the necessary sequence of differing stages of racial development, that was to be studied; the historian was to look for repeated exemplifications of fixed rules. These rules could, no doubt, be discovered apart from history; but they became more vivid and effective by being manifested, and manifested over and over again, in concrete instances. The study of history could thus be justified on the ground that it affords useful object-lessons in the eternal (or at least, empirically universal) truths of morals and politics[18] — and most of all on the ground that it is full of awful

---

[17] *New Forms of Christian Education*, 1898.

[18] The unconscious confusion of two senses of "nature"—*viz.*, "nature" as "right reason," a body of universal and intuitively known truths of morals and religion, and "nature" as the cosmical order and its "laws," which are in fact known only empirically—is an early and persistent phenomenon in the history of the normative use of this term; see the essay on Tertullian, below. Examples of it are extremely numerous in the eighteenth century.

warnings. For it was the negative side of its teaching that tended most to be emphasized. Even a record of what was chiefly human error and folly might profitably be studied as a reminder of man's proneness to certain follies and of the mischiefs which they cause.

These are, in the main, the conceptions set forth in Bolingbroke's *Letters on the Study and Use of History* (1735). The "true use of history," he observes loftily, "is not to gratify our idle curiosity about the past, not to feed our vanity by tales of the great exploits of our ancestors or fellow-countrymen, not to provide us with vicarious adventures." No: "history," says Bolingbroke—it is his most famous and oftenest quoted saying, except for those which Pope rewrote in verse in the *Essay on Man*—"history is philosophy teaching by example"; that is, it is a series of illustrations of fundamental general truths, as applicable to man's life in one age as in another:

The school of example is the world; and the masters of this school are history and experience.

And history, though it cannot absolutely take the place of personal experience, can do a good deal to provide us with the same teaching earlier in life, before we have taken our parts in the world of action, and it does so with less cost to ourselves; we learn from it at the expense of other men. Above all it teaches more fully and accurately:

The examples which history presents to us, both of men and events, are generally complete: the whole example is before us, and consequently the whole lesson, or sometimes the various lessons which philosophy proposes to teach us, by example. . . . We see men at their whole length in history, and we see them generally there through a medium less partial at least than that of experience.

This advantage belongs in the highest degree to the study of ancient history, says Bolingbroke; for while in modern history the examples may be incomplete, in ancient, "the beginning, the progression, and the end appear, not of particular reigns, much less of particular enterprises, or systems of policy alone, but of governments, of nations, of empires, and of all the various systems that have succeeded one another in the course of their duration." Bolingbroke is here, indeed, assuming that the general lessons which history has to teach, as to the social effects of specific causes, the results of differing systems of government, and the like, can best be learned from *large* slices of historical fact. But there is no suggestion that there is a significant succession of non-recurrent phases in the whole of history and, especially, no historical relativism, no recognition of the possibility that, for example, the conditions of life, and even human nature itself, may have so changed in time, or may so vary with race, that the political experiences of the Greeks and Romans may be inapplicable to the problems of a different age or people. We may see here, then, the underlying presupposition which largely explains the fondness of many seventeenth- and eighteenth-century political and other writers for examples and models in classical history. The "*great* use of history, properly so called, as distinguished from the writings of mere annalists and antiquaries," as Bolingbroke finally sums it up, is to illustrate, as it were, the eternal natures of things, to bring us nearer to the Platonic Ideas:

By comparing, in this study, the experience of other men and ages with our own, we improve both: we analyse, as it were, philosophy. We reduce all the abstract speculations of ethicks, and all the general rules of human policy, to their first principles. With these advantages every man may, though few men do, advance daily towards those ideas, those increated essences a Platonist would say, which no human creature can reach in practice, but in the nearest approaches to which the perfection of our nature consists.[19]

Naturally connected with these ideas was a moral which has, indeed, something in common with the historical catholicity of Herder, but is not really identical with it—an anti-nationalistic moral. Among the most important of the more concrete truths which history teaches, according to Bolingbroke, is the folly of national self-esteem and the absurdity of judging of things by the accidental standards of one's own community and time:

There is scarcely any folly or vice more epidemical among the sons of men than that ridiculous and hurtful vanity, by which the people of each country are apt to prefer themselves to those of every other; and

[19] *Works* (1809), III, 408.

to make their own customs, and manners, and opinions, the standards of right and wrong, true and false. . . . Nothing can contribute more to prevent us from being tainted with this vanity, than to accustom ourselves early to contemplate the different nations of the earth, in that vast map which history spreads before us, in their rise and their fall, their barbarous and their civilized states, in the likeness and unlikenesses of them all to one another, and of each to itself. . . . I might . . . bring several instances, wherein history serves to purge the mind of those national prejudices and partialities that we are apt to contract in our education, and that experience for the most part rather confirms than removes: because it is for the most part confined like our education.[20]

Historical study is thus for Bolingbroke one of the principal means of emancipation from what he calls "confined" points of view. But though there is here at least the suggestion of a universal tolerance of the idiosyncrasies of other ages and other peoples, Bolingbroke's more characteristic attitude is one of universal intolerance of idiosyncrasy *as* idiosyncrasy. To believe that one's own way of life, political system, or what not, so far as it is different from that of others, is superior, is absurd; but then all the others, insofar as they deviate from the one uniform standard of nature, are absurd, too; whereas Herder's implication is that none of them are absurd, but all necessary and right and "according to nature."

It ought to be added parenthetically—lest any be led to take these last-quoted observations of Bolingbroke's to mean that he was a pure cosmopolitan—that he in the end contrives to reconcile them with a eulogy of the emotion of patriotism:

Though an early and proper application to the study of history will contribute extremely to keep our minds free from a ridiculous partiality in favour of our own country, and a vicious prejudice against others; yet the same study will create in us a preference of affection to our own country.. . . . Surely, the love of our country is a lesson of reason, not an institution of nature. Education and habit, obligation and interest, attach us to it, not instinct. It is, however, so necessary to be cultivated, and the prosperity of all societies, as well as the grandeur of some, depends upon it so much; that orators by their eloquence, and poets by their enthusiasm, have endeavored to work up this precept of morality into a principle of passion.

[20] *Ibid.*, 332.

Here it is less Bolingbroke as philosopher of the Enlightenment who speaks, than Bolingbroke the experienced practical politician, who knew very well how indispensable it was, especially for those who sought to increase the "grandeur" of their own country, to cultivate in the multitude this passion which is not given us by "nature," and to make use of it in their statecraft.

A pretty similar conception of history, with the principal emphasis upon its exhibition of errors to be avoided, is expressed in Voltaire's *Dictionnaire philosophique*, art. "Histoire," [21] in the section *De l'utilité de l'histoire:* "Cet avantage consiste dans la comparaison qu'un homme d'état, un citoyen, peut faire des loix et des moeurs étrangères avec celles de son pays: c'est ce qui excite les nations modernes à enchérir les unes sur les autres dans les arts, dans le commerce, dans l'agriculture. Les grandes fautes passées servent beaucoup en tout genre. On ne sauroit trop remettre devant les yeux les crimes et les malheurs causés par des querelles absurdes. Il est certain qu'à force de renouveller la mémoires de ces querelles, on les empêche de renaître." The article adds (the remark, though irrelevant to our theme, is interesting) that the chief utility of *modern* history, and its advantage over ancient, is in teaching all potentates that since the fifteenth century any power which became too preponderant always found the others forming a coalition against it. This system of a balance of powers was unknown to the ancients.

At the very end of the century we find the Comte de Portalis still dilating upon the same conception of history as essentially a collection of awful warnings. "What men most easily forget is the imperfection of their nature. History ought to remind them of this incessantly." It is true, the author admits, that there are good deeds here and there, *bonnes actions isolées*, to serve as "impressive evidences that the breath of God has not wholly departed from men." Nevertheless, history is concerned chiefly to give us—not, indeed, merely a "recapitulation of crimes"—but *l'utile tableau des calamités qui les suivent*; . . . *les leçons du malheur ont un caractère de force et d'universalité qui leur est propre.*[22]

[21] *Oeuvres*, Beuchot ed., 1829, XXX, 207.
[22] Portalis [Joseph Marie], Comte de (1778-1858): *Du devoir de l'historien*

Against the contrasting background of these widely current attitudes towards history, the nature and historical importance of Herder's way of thinking about it stand out sharply.

But (b) the other implication of those ideas of his which were summarized at the beginning was a kind of particularism. Nature, having through the supposedly necessary and benign process of historical development, placed you in a particular situation, that situation is the best for you; you, as an individual, *are* what that process has made you; and you will be, as it were, out of your native element if you try to be anything different. A modern man should be modern, a German profoundly German, an Englishman distinctively English. But there was a latent incongruity between this preaching of the wisdom and duty of being content with the characteristics of your own age and national culture, and the idea of progress. In the static version of the principle of plenitude, the rule, as we have seen, worked both ways; don't rise above or fall below the place which Nature has assigned to you. But in this temporalized version, the rule was assumed to work only in one way; you are not to go back, but you must go forward; yet this presupposes a dissatisfaction with the situation in which the historic process has placed you, a sense that the time is out of joint and needs setting right. Herder was not, I think, very sensible of this incongruity—partly because he was little sensible of the relation of discontent to progress, or what is supposed to be progress. He does not emphasize the fact that historic change takes place in many cases through a series of revulsions, not to say revolutions, on the part of one generation against fashions of thought and taste previously dominant. He tends in the main to think of the process as running on smoothly and automatically, like the natural growth and branching of a plant, rather than as a spasmodic affair of fits and starts, a series of crises and interludes between crises. At all events, *both* themes are cherished by him: the inevitability and excellence of the conditions under which one finds oneself, and the glowing prospect of changes by which man will transcend those conditions. The *Ideen* concludes with a glorification of the existing

de bien considérer le caractère et le génie de chaque siècle en jugeant les grands hommes qui y ont vécu. Paris, 1800.

culture of Europe, to the production of which all past history has converged, and with a forecast of a future advance through the same forces that have brought about past progress: it will be a *Kultur durch Betriebsamkeit, Wissenschaften und Künste*. The traditional primitivistic preconceptions with which Herder set out have now been completely overcome.[23]

[23] Though Herder also believed in the late appearance of man upon the earth, after other animals had come into being in a progressive order in which the human type was gradually approximated, he did not accept the theory of the transformation of species, nor even Monboddo's thesis (which he discusses) of the identity of species of man and the orang-outang. The opinion that *Affe und Mensch Ein Geschlecht sei* is " an error which even the facts of anatomy contradict." See Lovejoy, " Some Eighteenth Century Evolutionists," *Popular Science Monthly*, 1904, pp. 327-336.

X. THE MEANING OF 'ROMANTIC' IN EARLY GERMAN ROMANTICISM *

IT IS GENERALLY agreed that the word "romantic"— which still "über die ganze Welt geht und so viel Streit und Spaltungen verursacht"[1]—was launched upon its tempestuous career through nineteenth-century criticism and philosophy by Friedrich Schlegel. It was in the second number of the *Athenaeum* (1798) that he first proclaimed the supremacy of "die romantische Poesie," and thus converted the adjective—already a *Modewort* in some of its older uses[2]—into the designation of an aesthetic ideal and the catchword of a philosophical movement. But why was "romantisch" the word chosen by "the new school" as the shibboleth of their sect? The question is of primary consequence for the general history of Romanticism. To understand the central ideas, the purpose and the program of the first of the many who have been called Romanticists, it is obviously needful to understand what there was in the meaning of this notoriously multivocal word that made it seem to them the most fitting to inscribe upon their banners.

The answer to this question which for nearly half a century has been the usual one was apparently first propounded by Haym. The key to the two Schlegels' use of the expression

---

* Published in *Modern Language Notes*, XXXI (1916).
[1] Goethe to Eckermann, March 21, 1830.

[2] Though instances of the use of the word in the seventeenth century can be cited, it came into fashion only after the middle of the eighteenth, chiefly, at least in its application to landscape, in consequence of the vogue of the translations of Thomson's *Seasons*. An interesting contribution to the earlier history of the word in Germany has been made by J. A. Walz, "Zum Sprachgebrauch des 18. Jahrhunderts," in *Zs. f. d. Wortforschung*, XII (1910), 194. More elaborate studies of the subject have appeared since the above essay was published: Richard Ullmann and Helene Gotthard, *Geschichte des Begriffes "Romantisch" in Deutschland*, Berlin, 1927: and Alfred Schlagdenhauffen, *Frédéric Schlegel et son Groupe*, Paris, 1934. The conclusions of both on the general question are largely in agreement with those of this essay, but neither traces the development of Fr. Schlegel's conception in the manner attempted in this and the essay following.

Haym sought in a correlation of the celebrated *Fragment*[3] in which "die romantische Poesie" is dithyrambically defined, with Friedrich's essay on *Wilhelm Meister* in the same number of the *Athenaeum*. The program of the aesthetic revolution which the young enthusiasts proposed to carry out was, Haym declares, inspired and shaped chiefly by their admiration for the models lately set by Goethe; and for Friedrich, Goethe's masterpiece was *Wilhelm Meisters Lehrjahre*. His first acquaintance with this novel was to him the revelation of a new poetic *genre*, comprehending and transcending all others. Consequently Schlegel, "immer bereit zu neuen Konstruktionen und neuen Formeln, schöpft aus dem Wilhelm Meister die Lehre, dass der echte Roman ein *non plus ultra*, eine Summe alles Poetischen sei, und er bezeichnet folgerecht dieses poetische Ideal mit dem Namen der 'romantischen' Dichtung."[4]

According to this explanation, therefore, "romantisch" was to Schlegel equivalent in meaning to "romanartig"; it at the same time involved a special reference to Goethe's novel as the archetype of all *Romane*; the adoption of it as the designation of the "poetisches Maximum" implied the thesis of the superiority of the *Roman* over all other *genres*; and it was from the characteristics of *Meister* that the general notion of "the Romantic," at least as an aesthetic category, was derived.[5]

This account of the matter has since 1870 been repeated by many writers, and appears still to be one of the commonplaces of the manuals of German literature, of the encyclopaedias, and even of monographs on Romanticism. Thus Thomas writes: "By a juggle of words *Romanpoesie* became *romantische Poesie*, and Schlegel proceeded to define 'romantic' as an ideal of perfection, having first abstracted it from the unromantic *Wilhelm Meister*."[6] Similarly Porterfield in his *German Romanticism* (1914, p. 44): Fr. Schlegel "went to Jena in 1796, where he worked out the theory of Romanticism from

---

[3] No. 116 in Minor's numbering: *Fr. Schlegel 1794-1802*, hereinafter referred to as *Jugendschriften*.

[4] Haym, *Die romantische Schule* (1870), 251.

[5] The other principal source of Romanticism Haym found in Fichte's philosophy; the movement he describes as essentially a combination of *Goethianismus* and *Fichtianismus*.

[6] *German Literature* (1909), 332.

Goethe's 'Wilhelm Meister.'" Other recent writers who apparently adopt Haym's view of the importance, in the genesis of Romanticism, of the conception *Roman* and of the model presented in *Meister* are Kircher,[7] Scholl,[8] and Schiele.[9] Marie Joachimi summarily rejects Haym's explanation of "romantic," but does not offer any examination of his arguments nor any inductive study of Fr. Schlegel's use of the term.[10] Walzel's admirable *Deutsche Romantik* (1908) does not discuss the question directly, though it would seem to be inferable from the general account of the origins of the Romantic ideas given in this volume and in the earlier introduction to *Goethe und die Romantik*,[11] that Walzel does not accept Haym's theory. The question of the origin and original sense of the term is likewise left undiscussed in Enders's recent work on Friedrich Schlegel (1913). It is pertinent to the theme of this paper to note also that the authors of at least two recent treatises on Romanticism expressly deny the supposition, prevalent before the publication of Haym's monumental work, that Fr. Schlegel's use of "romantisch" is to be understood in the light of the antithesis "classical-romantic." Thus Kircher: "Es ist der grosse Irrtum, die Antithese des Klassischen und Romantischen in den Mittelpunkt der Schlegelschen Theorie zu stellen. Nie und nirgends ist sie von Fr. Schlegel ausgesprochen worden." [12]

It is the purpose of the present study to attempt an *Auseinandersetzung* with the still prevalent account of the source and original meaning of the term "romantic" (in its use in the *Frühromantik*) and of the sources and content of the aesthetic and philosophical ideas for which the word stood. Incidentally, the tenability of the last-quoted negations will, I trust, have a good deal of light thrown upon it. What is, for the purpose

[7] *Phil. der Romantik* (1906), 163.
[8] "Fr. Schlegel and Goethe" in *PMLA.*, XXI (1906), 128-132.
[9] *Schleiermachers Monologen* (1914), xxvii.
[10] *Die Weltanschauung der Romantik* (1905), 118.
[11] Schüddekopf-Walzel in *Schriften der Goethe-Gesellschaft*, 13 (1898).
[12] *Phil. der Romantik*, 152. Ricarda Huch has expressed a similar view (*Blütezeit der Romantik*, 5th ed., 52). The section on the subject in Schlagdenhauffen's *Frédéric Schlegel et son Groupe*, 1934, though it recognizes that "romantic" meant for Schlegel much more than "novelistic," still makes too much of the connection of *romantisch* with *Roman*, and seems to me to miss the real process of the formation of the concept.

in hand, necessary first of all is a consideration of the two writings of Schlegel's upon which Haym chiefly based his interpretation.

The essay on *Wilhelm Meister*, by itself, has nothing whatever to say, expressly or by any clear implication,[13] concerning the meaning of the term "romantische Poesie." True it is that Schlegel therein speaks of Goethe's novel with ardent enthusiasm, that he finds in it many of the traits elsewhere enumerated among the characteristics of "romantic" poetry, that he sees in it the dawn of a new day in German, and even in European, literature. All this, however, falls far short of a proof of the equation: "romantische Poesie" = "Romanpoesie" = writings possessed of the qualities of *Wilhelm Meister*. But it can not be denied that *Fragment 116* — the one beginning: "die romantische Poesie ist eine progressive Universal-poesie" —reads as if it meant by "romantische Poesie" simply "der Roman" as a *genre*. For it speaks of that type of "poetry" which it defines, as a "Form" or "Dichtart," as distinct from other recognized *genres*. In the following sentence, in particular, the identification of "die romantische Poesie" with the novel seems almost explicit: "Es giebt keine Form, die so dazu gemacht wäre, den Geist des Autors vollständig auszudrücken: so dass manche Künstler, die nur auch einen Roman schreiben wollten, von ungefähr sich selbst dargestellt haben." There are also in other *Fragments* some indications of a disposition to assign an especially typical significance to the *Roman* in general, as a characteristically modern and a peculiarly adequate vehicle of self-expression; *e. g., Lyc.-Fgm.* 78:

Mancher der vortrefflichsten Romane ist ein Compendium, eine Encyclopädie des ganzen geistigen Lebens eines genialischen Individuums; Werke, die das sind, selbst in ganz andrer Form, wie Nathan, bekommen dadurch einen Anstrich vom Roman.

And in *Ath.-Fgm.* 146, Friedrich Schlegel remarks that all modern poetry "has a tinge" of the character of the *Roman*.

Yet if this be the derivation and original meaning, for the

[13] The adjective occurs three times in a colloquial but vague sense, without reference to any special type or tendency in the history of literature, and therefore without pertinency to the question dealt with in this paper.

Romantiker, of "romantische Poesie," one is confronted with an odd and incongruous fact: namely, that none of their subsequent explanations of the term betray any knowledge of this meaning, or are in the least reconcilable with it. Only two years later (1800) in the *Gespräch über die Poesie* contained in the third volume of the *Athenaeum*, Fr. Schlegel puts into the mouth of one of the interlocutors of his dialogue an entirely plain account of what the word meant for him, from what it was derived, and in what authors the qualities supposed to be connoted by it were supremely exemplified:

Ich habe ein bestimmtes Merkmahl des Gegensatzes zwischen dem Antiken und dem Romantischen aufgestellt.   Indessen bitte ich Sie doch, nun nicht sogleich anzunehmen, dass mir das Romantische und das Moderne völlig gleich gelte.

There are, that is, modern poems which are not romantic, *e. g.*, *Emilia Galotti*, which is " so unaussprechlich modern und doch im geringsten nicht romantisch." To know what is truly romantic one must turn to Shakespeare,

in den ich das eigentliche Centrum, den Kern der romantischen Fantasie setzen möchte.   Da suche und finde ich das Romantische, bei den ältern Modernen, bey Shakespeare, Cervantes, in der italiänischen Poesie, in jenem Zeitalter der Ritter, der Liebe und der Mährchen, *aus welchem die Sache und das Wort selbst herstammt. Dieses ist bis jetzt das einzige was einen Gegensatz zu den klassischen Dichtungen des Alterthums abgeben kann.*[14]

The dialogue also, it is true, "defines" a "Roman" (by which is meant, a *good* "Roman") as " ein romantisches Buch";

[14] *Athenaeum*, III, 122-3.   Cf. id., 121: " das Eigenthümliche der Tendenz der romantischen Dichtkunst im Gegensatz der antiken "; 79, " es gelang dem Guarini, im Pastorfido, den romantischen Geist und die classische Bildung zur schönsten Harmonie zu verschmelzen." There are, it should be added, half a dozen instances of " romantisch " in the dialogue in which the word refers, not to a class of literature, but to a quality or spirit supposed to be characteristic of that class. E. g., 83: " Spenser gab seinem (Shakespeare's) neuen romantischen Schwunge Nahrung "; " diese Ausbildung hauchte allen seinen Dramen den romantischen Geist ein, . . . und sie zu einer romantischen Grundlage des modernen Dramas constituirt, die dauerhaft genug ist für ewige Zeiten "; 107: " Jedes Gedicht soll eigentlich romantisch und jedes soll didaktisch seyn." This use is, of course, entirely in keeping with the definition cited above; the romantic spirit is a somewhat which is " eigentümlich modern."

but it by no means affirms the converse of this definition. On the contrary, "das Drama so gründlich und historisch wie es Shakespeare z. B. nimmt und behandelt, ist die wahre Grundlage des Romans." Nor is anything of the nature of a narration or "history" essential to a romantic work: "Ein Lied kann eben so gut romantisch sein als eine Geschichte." [15]

It is, indeed, true that one of the interlocutors in the dialogue reads an essay *Über den verschiedenen Styl in Goethe's früheren und späteren Werken*, in which *Wilhelm Meister* is even more highly praised than in Schlegel's essay of two years earlier. But the use of the word "romantisch" in this essay is significant. Goethe is *not* spoken of as the typical representative of romantic poetry; his greatness is regarded by the imaginary author of the essay as consisting rather in his having accomplished "the ultimate task of all poetry," namely, "die Harmonie des Classischen und des Romantischen." Everywhere in *Meister* "der antike Geist" is evident behind the modern envelope. "Die beyden künstlichsten und verstandvollsten Kunstwerke im ganzen Gebiet der romantischen Kunst" are Hamlet and Don Quixote; it is "they alone which admit of a comparison with Goethe's universality." Here Goethe seemingly outranks his great precursors; but he is at the same time placed outside the "Gebiet der romantischen Kunst." And it is important to remember that, in the course of the discussion, this enthusiastic glorification of Goethe is somewhat severely handled by the other interlocutors. Antonio complains that "die Urtheile darin etwas zu imperatorisch ausgedrückt sind. Es könnte doch seyn, dass noch Leute hinter dem Berge wohnten, die von einem und dem andern eine durchaus andre Ansicht hätten." [16] More-

---

[15] Schlegel's "Antonio" in his *Brief über den Roman* (*Ath.*, III, 123). In the version of the *Gespräch über die Poesie* which appears in the collected works of Schlegel, there is added, as a sort of conclusion of the whole matter, a long speech by another interlocutor, Lothario, which places the *genre* to which both the novel and the drama belong upon a lower plane than the epic, "das einer tieferen Naturquelle entspringt und . . . die Seele der Poesie ist," and ascribes the highest rank of all to lyrical poetry, especially the religious lyric (*Werke*, 1846, v, 240). Since this passage does not appear in the original *Athenaeum* text, it cannot be cited as evidence for the ideas of the early school.

[16] In the text of the dialogue in the *Collected Works* this comment reads: "Es könnte doch seyn, dass in andern, uns noch entfernten Regionen der

over, most of the participants in the dialogue point out that precisely that "unification of the ancient and the modern" for which Goethe had been chiefly eulogized, is a thing intrinsically impossible of achievement. Certainly in their metrical forms, urges one speaker, ancient and modern poetry remain forever opposed; there is no *tertium quid* in which the aesthetic values of the one form and of the other can be combined. Nor, adds another speaker, can the qualities of ancient and modern diction coexist. And, observes a third, in the all-important matter of the "Behandlung der Charaktere und Leidenschaften" the methods and aims of ancient and modern poetry are "absolutely different" and uncombinable. In the former, the characters are "idealisch gedacht, und plastisch ausgeführt, wie die alten Götterbilder"; in the moderns, on the contrary, "ist der Charakter entweder wirklich geschichtlich, oder doch so construirt, als ob er es wäre; die Ausführung hingegen ist mehr mahlerisch individuell, nach Art der sprechenden Aehnlichkeit im Porträt." Finally, Lothario plainly declares that no tragic poet can serve two masters, can be strictly classical and typically romantic at once. The reason why the subject-matter of "ancient" tragedies, or of modern imitations of them, must be mythological, not historical, is because we now demand in the case of a historical theme "die moderne Behandlungsart der Charaktere, welche dem Geist des Alterthums schlechthin widerspricht. Der Künstler würde da auf eine oder die andre Art, gegen die alte Tragödie oder gegen die romantische, den Kürzern ziehen müssen." [17]

Schlegel's explanations of the meaning of "romantisch," as an historico-critical term, in the *Gespräch über die Poesie* are, of course, duly noted by Haym, when in the course of his treatise he comes to deal with that writing. Their incompatibility with the earlier explanation based upon *Fragment* 116

unermesslichen Kunstwelt, diese neue Kunstonne, welche Sie uns aufgestellt haben, von jenen fernen Planetenbewohnern ganz anders angesehen würde, und ihnen in einem andern minder stark glänzenden Lichte erschiene" (V, 316).

[17] *Ath.*, III, 186-187. It is an odd commentary upon the supposed derivation of the idea of "romantische Poesie" from *Wilhelm Meister*, that early in 1799 we find Fr. Schlegel welcoming Tieck's *Sternbalds Wanderungen* (1798) as "der erste Roman seit Cervantes, der romantisch ist, und darin weit über Meister" (*Briefe an seinen Bruder*, 414).

in the first volume of the *Athenaeum* is recognized by him.[18] These explanations in 1800 Haym is compelled to regard as a revision of Fr. Schlegel's earlier conception of " romantische Poesie." " Formerly Schlegel had, it is true, derived this conception, at least in the main, from the *Roman*; now, while the same derivation is still fundamental, he emphasizes more strongly than before the historical relations of the conception." [19] And by the time of A. W. Schlegel's Berlin lectures (1801-1804) the change to a " new and more difficult conception of the Romantic has become entirely explicit (ganz herausgerückt)." [20]

What I wish to show is that this supposed later sense of " romantische Poesie " is in reality the primary one; that *Ath.-Fgm.* 116, in so far as it uses the term in the sense of " Romanpoesie " or merely " Roman," is a momentary and misleading aberration from an all but constant usage, before, during and after 1798; and that Haym's emphasis upon the *Roman* in general, and upon *Wilhelm Meister* in particular, as the source from which Schlegel drew the idea of " romantic poetry," throws the history of the genesis of Romanticism very seriously out of perspective.

Haym himself has noted that Schlegel occasionally, especially in his earliest publication, uses the word " romantisch " with

---

[18] Haym had, however, in his original presentation of this explanation quite unjustifiably claimed for it the sanction of Schlegel's usage in this dialogue: "Der Schlüssel zum Verständniss liegt in erster Linie darin, dass romantische Poesie einfach für Romanpoesie gesetzt ist.   Der gleiche Sprachgebrauch herrscht ganz unzweifelhaft in Schlegel's späterem ' Gespräch über die Poesie.' " (*Die rom. Schule*, 252.)

[19] *Die rom. Schule*, 688-9.

[20] *Op. cit.*, 813. The elder Schlegel's explanations of the term in these lectures are here duly summarized by Haym; but it is perhaps worth while to recall two of the most significant passages.   In the introduction to his third series Wilhelm Schlegel declares that he hopes speedily to remove any doubt "ob es denn wirklich eine romantische, d. h. eigenthümlich moderne, nicht nach den Mustern des Alterthums gebildete Poesie gebe."   And the employment of the adjective " romantisch " to express this idea is justified as follows: "Ich will hier bemerken, dass der Name *romantische* Poesie auch in dieser historischen Rücksicht treffend gewählt sey.   Denn Romanisch, *Romance*, nannte man die neuen aus der Vermischung des Lateinischen mit der Sprache der Eroberer entstandnen Dialekte; daher Romane, die darin geschriebenen Dichtungen, woher denn romantisch abgeleitet ist, und ist der Charakter dieser Poesie Verschmelzung des altdeutschen mit dem späteren, d. h. christlich gewordnen Römischen, so werden auch ihre Elemente schon durch den Namen angedeutet." (*Vorlesungen über schöne Litt. u. Kunst*, ed. by Minor, 1884, III, 7 and 17.)

reference to "das epische Rittergedicht," and also with the meaning of "medieval and early modern poetry in general."[21] Examples of these uses, however, are far more numerous in all periods than Haym indicates. Some additional examples are worth citing.

On February 27, 1794, Friedrich writes to his brother that the problem of the poetry of their age seems to him to be that of "die Vereinigung des Wesentlich-Modernen mit dem Wesentlich-Antiken," and adds by way of explanation:

Wenn Du den Geist des Dante, vielleicht auch des Shakespeare erforschest und lehrest, so wird es leichter seyn, dasjenige, was ich vorhin das *Wesentlich-Moderne* nannte, und was ich vorzüglich in diesen beyden Dichtern finde, kennen zu lernen. Wie viel würde dazu auch die Geschichte der romantischen Poesie beytragen, zu der du einmal den Plan fasstest?—Die Geschichte des neuern Dramas und des Romans wäre dann vielleicht nicht so schwer.[22]

With the problem which here preoccupies the younger brother we are not, for the moment, concerned. Suffice it here to note that a "history of romantic poetry" would apparently (though the language is not unequivocal) deal with Shakespeare and Dante, and clearly would *not* include the more recent drama and the novel; and that the conceptions of "romantic" poetry and of "the essentially modern" are already closely united in Schlegel's mind.

In the essay *Ueber das Studium der griechischen Poesie* (1794-5) the term "romantische Poesie" constantly occurs, sometimes as a designation for the romances of chivalry, sometimes with the broader meaning already noted, of "medieval and early modern literature." It is perhaps in the former sense that Schlegel uses the expression when, in justification of his assertion that Shakespeare is "the most complete and most characteristic representative of the spirit of modern poetry," he writes: "In ihm vereinigen sich die reizendsten Blüthen der Romantischen Phantasie, die gigantische Grösse der gothischen Heldenzeit, . . . mit den feinsten Zügen moderner

---

[21] Haym, 251 and note.
[22] Walzel, *Fr. Schlegels Briefe an seinen Bruder*, 170. This contemplated "History of Romantic Poetry" is again referred to in a letter of Dec. 7, 1794.

Geselligkeit," *usw.*[23] The broader sense, however, appears to be intended in the passage in which Schlegel, lamenting the literary degeneracy of later ages, asks: " Was ist die Poesie der spätern Zeit als ein Chaos aus dürftigen Fragmenten der Romantischen Poesie? . . . So flickten Barbaren aus schönen Fragmenten einer bessern Welt Gothische Gebäude zusammen." [24]

In February of 1798 — *i. e.*, almost at the moment of the composition of the essay on *Meister* and the *Fragmente* in the *Athenaeum*—Friedrich proposed to his brother that they should write jointly a series of " Letters on Shakespeare," which should include, among other things, " eine Charakteristik aller romantischen Komödien," " eine Theorie der romantischen Komödien, mit Vergleichung von Shakespeare's Nebenmännern, Gozzi, die Spanier, Guarini, etc."; and a " Charakteristik des romantischen Witzes, mit Rücksicht auf Ariost und Cervantes." Examples of a similar use in the *Gespräch über die Poesie* have already been cited. In the second volume of the *Athenaeum* (II, 324) Schlegel, speaking of the lack of a good German translation of Don Quixote, writes: " Ein Dichter und vertrauter Freund der alten romantischen Poesie, wie Tieck, muss es seyn, der diesen Mangel ersetzen will." Instances of the same general sense in writings of Fr. Schlegel after the *Athenaeum* period are frequent: *e. g.*, in the essay on Boccaccio, 1801, he speaks of " die ursprüngliche Fabel von Florio und Blanchefleure " as " eine romantische Dichtung," and comments on " die kindliche Einfalt des romantischen Mährchens." [25] In the edition of Schlegel's collected works prepared for publication by himself

---

[23] Minor, *Jugendschriften*, I, 107.

[24] Minor, *op. cit.*, p. 112. Other examples of " romantisch " in the same essay are " Die Phantasterey der romantischen Poesie "; " die modernen Ritter der romantischen Poesie "; Ariosto and " andre scherzhaft romantischen Dichter "; " der Fantasie-Zauber der romantischen Sage und Dichtung "; " die fantastischen Gestalten der romantischen Dichtkunst "; " jene seltsame Muse der romantischen Spiele und Rittermärchen "; " Wieland's romantische Gedichte "; " Tasso hat sich von der romantischen Manier nicht weit entfernt "; " Versuche, die romantische Fabel oder die christliche Legende in einen idealischen schönen Mythus zu metamorphosieren." Schlegel once speaks of " das Romantische Gedicht der Griechischen und Römischen Epopöe," in a passage in which he is bringing out the similarity between the Homeric epic and the romance of chivalry. Of " romantisch " in the sense " romanartig " there seems, besides *Ath.-Fgm.* 116, to be only one (probable) example: *Lyc.-Fgm.* 49.

[25] *Werke*, 1864, VIII, 13.

he brings together, under the designation of "Beyträge zur romantischen Dichtkunst," four essays, dealing with Boccaccio, with Camoens, and other early Portuguese and Spanish and Italian poets, with "Northern Poetry" (Ossian, the Edda, the Nibelungenlied, *etc.*), and with Shakespeare.

Thus the adjective "romantisch," as applied to classes or bodies of literature or to individual writings was in habitual use by Fr. Schlegel throughout the seventeen-nineties, and subsequently, as an ordinary historical epithet. When, therefore, he rhapsodized over "romantische Poesie" in the best known of the *Athenaeumsfragmente*, he was not coining a new term, nor even employing one unusual in his circle. If Haym's interpretation of this *Fragment* alone is correct, Schlegel was there using the word in a very unusual and paradoxical sense. *Romantische Poesie* as equivalent to *Romanpoesie*, or *der Roman*, is almost a ἅπαξ λεγόμενον, incongruous even with the senses of the word in other *Athenaeumsfragmente*. When Shakespeare's universality is said to be "der Mittelpunkt der romantischen Kunst," it is manifest that *romantisch* can not refer to a *genre* of which Shakespeare offers no examples. When it is declared that "aus dem romantischen Gesichtspunkt," the very *Abarten* of poetry, even the eccentric and the monstrous, have their value as aids to universality ("provided only they be original"), it seems improbable that nothing more than the "novelistic" point of view is meant.

It is, in any case, evident that in the *Athenaeum*, and thereafter, *romantisch*, as a term of literary criticism, no longer merely *denotes* either a certain class of writings or a certain period of the history of literature. The word is now all compact of aesthetic and philosophical connotations. There is now, as we have seen, not only a body of poetry which is called *romantisch*, but also *ein romantischer Gesichtspunkt*. The essential question, then, is: From what more concrete sense did this larger, philosophical meaning of the term *romantische Poesie* develop? Haym's interpretation implies that it was derived primarily from reflection upon the nature of the *Roman* as a *genre*, and above all from a generalization of the aesthetic qualities illustrated, and the aesthetic principles inculcated, in Goethe's *Roman*. This view will, in the second part of this study, be shown to be erroneous. I shall there endeavor to prove that the conception of Romantic art was virtually completely formulated by Fr. Schlegel *before* his acquaintance with *Wilhelm Meister*, and before his own conversion to the " romantic point of view"; that this conversion, moreover, was probably not due to the influence of Goethe, but partly to other external influences and partly to the immanent logic of his own earlier aesthetic principles; and that, therefore, the emphasis upon *Fgm.* 116 and upon the relation of the meaning of *romantisch* to the *Roman* and to *Meister* (for which Haym is chiefly responsible) tends to obscure the real origins both of the name, and (which is much more important) of the idea, of "the Romantic," in its aesthetic and philosophical signification.

II

The chief preoccupation of Friedrich Schlegel's mind during the half-dozen years preceding the earliest manifestoes of the Romantic School was the question of the nature, the relations, and the relative values, of " the ancient " and " the modern " in art. That there is some profound and significant unlikeness between the spirit, the informing idea, of classical and of modern art and taste—this was the assumption from which his earliest and most characteristic reflection upon aesthetic questions proceeded. The long essay *Über das Studium der Griechischen Poesie* (1794-5) is the outstanding illustration of the place which this antithesis had in his thought; but he could scarcely write upon any theme without giving evidence of his absorption in the problem.[26] There is, he declared in 1796, a sort of "civil war in the kingdom of culture"—a "Kampf des Alten und des Neuen "— and it is therefore indispensable to an understanding of the history of humanity that "the con-

---

[26] Cf. especially *Über die Grenzen des Schönen*, 1794; *Lyceum-Fragment* 84; and the following from A. W. Schlegel's Berlin lectures of 1801-4, à propos of ancient and modern poetry: " Der verschiedne Geist beyder, ja der zwischen ihnen obwaltende Gegensatz, und wie man deswegen bey ihrer Beurtheilung von anders modifizirten Prinzipien ausgehn müsse, um jede ohne Beeinträchtigung der andern anzuerkennen: diess ist einer von den Hauptpunkten den mein Bruder und ich in unsern kritischen Schriften von verschiednen Seiten her ins Licht zu setzen gesucht haben." (*Op. cit.*, III, 6, in *Deutsche Litteraturdenkmale* XIX, 6.)

cepts of the ancient and the modern be given a definite meaning (*fixirt*) and be deduced from human nature itself." [27]

Schlegel's interest in this question, however, was not the interest of a historian but of an aesthetician. "Ancient" and "modern" expressed less a chronological than a philosophical distinction. The tendencies for which either term stood might manifest themselves, and admittedly to some extent did manifest themselves, in the period customarily denoted by the other. Schlegel's conception of "das Wesentlich-Antike," in particular, was much more the product of aesthetic theorizing than of historical inquiry; though he sincerely believed that conception to express the predominant character of Greek art, his generalizations about the ancients were so hasty and, in some points, so palpably absurd as to lend themselves very easily to Schiller's satire in the *Xenien*. When, in accord with the prevailing fashion of the time, Schlegel in his first period (1793-96) glorified ancient and belabored modern poetry, he was really engaged in formulating two antithetic critical theories, and in vindicating one of them at the expense of the other.

The antithesis, stated in more descriptive terms, was that between *die schöne Poesie* and *die interessante Poesie*, the "poetry of beauty" and the "poetry of the interesting"; or between "objectivity" and "subjectivity" as governing principles in artistic creation and aesthetic appreciation. The doctrine which Schlegel at this time held was, in essence, a sort of aesthetic rationalism. It regarded "beauty" as an "objective" attribute, which works of art do or do not possess, irrespective of their relation to the feelings and the experience of the artist, if not wholly irrespective of their relation to the feelings of the reader, hearer or beholder. An aesthetic value, to be genuine, must be "of universal validity," neither expressive of, nor dependent for its effect upon, the subjective "interest" of this or that individual; and there is, or ought to be, an "allgemeingültige Wissenschaft des Geschmacks und der Kunst." The "pure [28] laws of beauty," therefore, are objective and universal principles, rigid and invariable. The end of art is the attain-

---

[27] In the review of Herder's *Briefe zur Beförderung der Humanität*, *Jugendschriften* II, 42.

[28] "Pure" probably in the Kantian sense, *i. e.*, *a priori*.

ment of this beauty through fidelity to these laws; its end is *not* to imitate or emulate sensible nature, nor yet to record the inner reactions of the artist upon nature and life. The foremost of its laws, therefore, is that of self-limitation, restriction of its themes and its modes of expression, by the exclusion both of the intrinsically ugly and of whatever is inconsistent with the rigorous unity, the clearness of outline and the singleness of total effect, of any individual work. There was in Schlegel's early aesthetic writings not a little of that smug talk about "good taste" and "technical correctness" (especially in the drama) which was later to become a favorite object of the Romanticists' ridicule.[29]

It is not, however, the purpose of this paper to offer any thorough exposition of the classicism of Fr. Schlegel's first period. Our concern is with his formulation of the opposite aesthetic ideal, which he at that time rejected, but with the definition of which, especially in the *Studium-Aufsatz*, he was scarcely less occupied. What I wish here to point out is that his conception of "das eigentümlich Moderne" was, in its essentials, completely formed long *before* the period of the *Athenaeum*, and did not materially alter when he passed from his *Gräkomanie* of 1793-5, through the transitional stage of 1796, to the Romanticism of 1797 and thereafter. The "romantische Poesie" of which we hear so much after 1798 was simply the "interessante Poesie" of the earlier period. What altered was only Schlegel's valuation of this type of poetry.

In the writings of 1793-5 the principal characteristics attributed to "the distinctively modern" are these: a disposition to imitate in art the "Fülle und Leben" which are the "Vorrecht der Natur," at the expense of the unity and coherency which are the "Vorrecht der Kunst";[30] a consequent inclina-

---

[29] For all this, v. *Über die Grenzen des Schönen* (1794), *Von den Schulen der griechischen Poesie* (1794), *Über die weiblichen Charaktere, usw.* (1794), and especially the *Studium-Aufsatz* (1796) *passim*, in Minor's edition of Schlegel's *Jugendschriften*; also the (supposed) earlier form of the last-mentioned essay in *DNL*, vol. 143. As Alt has noted (*Schiller u. die Brüder Schlegel*, 1904), W. von Humboldt had, in *Die Horen*, 1795 (IV, 31-33), drawn the same contrast between *das Schöne* and *das Interessante*, had denied to the latter any "purely aesthetic" value, and had found a weakness for it to be a characteristic fault of modern taste.

[30] *Über die Grenzen des Schönen* (1794); in Minor, *Jugendschriften* I, 23.

tion to over-ride all fixed laws and limits, "als wenn nicht alle Kunst beschränkt und alle Natur unendlich wäre"; [31] a tendency to produce, not, as does ancient art, that "Befriedigung wo die kleinste Unruhe aufgelöst wird, wo alle Sehnsucht schweigt," but rather an insatiable longing; [32] a relative indifference to "form," to pure "beauty," in comparison with expressiveness and richness of content, and, in particular, an eagerness to catch and express, not the universal and typical (which alone is consonant with "beauty"), so much as the differentness of things, the unique and the individual—"ein subjektives Interesse an einer bestimmten *Art* von Leben, an einem individuellen Stoff"; [33] an especial interest in individuals of exceptional originality or force; [34] a liking for the representation of the positively ugly or grotesque; [35] a constant confusion and intermixture of *genres*; [36] a fusion of philosophical with purely aesthetic interests, so that "die Philosophie poetisirt und die Poesie philosophirt"; [37] and a lack of aesthetic disin-

Observe how precisely Schlegel here defines, while damning, the characteristics which he later came to regard as the essence of the Romantic temper: "Das furchtbare und doch fruchtlose Verlangen sich ins Unendliche zu verbreiten, der heisse Durst das Einzelne zu durchdringen"—these two cravings, sprung from a common source, and characteristic of the modern spirit, he now holds to be the arch-enemies of both aesthetic and moral worth.

[31] *Ibid.*, I, 24.

[32] *Jugendschriften* I, 87, 89.

[33] *Jugendschriften* I, 91, lines 19-22; 80, ll. 34-40. For the thesis that the universal, *i. e.*, the generic, not the individual, is the object of true (and of ancient) art, *cf.* I, 38-9, 89, 135. This craving for the representation of "the individual" is what Schlegel means by the often mentioned *penchant* of the moderns for *das Charakteristische*. W. von Humboldt also identified a preference for "Charakter-Ausdruck" (*i. e.*, expressiveness in the representation of the individual person or situation) with that craving for the "interesting" which he lamented in modern taste, as inconsistent with a pure appreciation of *Grazie und Schönheit* (*Die Horen*, 1795, IV, 33).

[34] This is one of Schlegel's senses of "the interesting"; "Interessant nehmlich ist jedes originelle Individuum, welches ein grösseres Quantum von intellektuellem Gehalt oder ästhetischer Energie enthält" (*Jugendschriften* I, 109). Aesthetic condemnation is pronounced on this upon essentially Platonistic grounds: since such "interestingness" involves the idea of relative magnitude and "since all magnitudes are capable of addition *ad infinitum*," there can be no such thing as a "höchstes Interessantes," *i. e.*, no fixed and absolute standard with respect to this quality.

[35] *Jugendschriften* I, 88, l. 39.

[36] *Op. cit.*, I, 22, 89, 102-3, 122, 146, 150, 157.

[37] *Op. cit.*, I, 89.

terestedness and detachment on the part of the artist, a tendency to use all forms of poetic utterance as means for
expressing his personal attitude towards reality, instead of
devoting himself to the realization of pure, "objective" beauty
in the work of art which he produces.[38]

Describe these characteristics in rhapsodical, instead of cen-
sorious, language, and you have most of the elements of Fr.
Schlegel's later characterizations of Romantic poetry, and of
das Romantische in general: universality of interest and of
theme; insatiable progression and perpetual self-transcendence;
Streben nach dem Unendlichen; glorification of *Werden* above
Vollendung; supreme interest in the *Selbstdarstellung des
genialischen Individuums*; inclusion even of the abnormal and
"monstrous" in the province of art, as elements in "universality"; demand for the *Vereinigung aller getrennten Gattungen
der Poesie*; identification of philosophy with poetry; and insistence upon the unrestrained freedom of the creative artist,
"der kein Gesetz über sich leidet." And, in particular, you have
in the earlier and disapproving accounts of *das Wesentlich-
Moderne* most of the features emphasized in *Ath.-Fgm.* 116.
Though that fragment at first appears to be simply a eulogy
of the novel as a *genre*, the ground of the eulogy is that the
novel is peculiarly capable of attaining those qualities which
Schlegel had long since described as the distinguishing traits
of the "essentially modern."

Not only the characteristics, but also the principal historic
embodiment, of the modern ideal in poetry, are the same for
Schlegel before and after his adoption of that ideal as his own.
Shakespeare, we are told, in a passage already cited, is "among
all artists the one who shows most completely and most strikingly the spirit of modern poetry." But, to Schlegel in 1795,
this means that the English dramatist is, in spite of, or because
of, his genius, also the most striking example of the aesthetic
aberrations of modern art—of "das grosse Übergewicht des
Individuellen, Charakteristischen und Philosophischen in der
ganzen Masse der modernen Poesie." Shakespeare's "uner-
schöpfliche Fülle" Schlegel cordially recognizes; "his individuality is the most interesting thus far known." Yet any

[38] *Op. cit.*, 1, 81, ll. 1-23, and l. 76 to p. 82, l. 17.

critic who treats Shakespeare's poetry "als schöne Kunst" only falls "into the deeper contradictions, the greater his penetration and the more thorough his knowledge of the poet. . . . None of Shakepseare's dramas attains beauty in its *totality* (ist in *Masse* schön); never does the principle of beauty determine the construction of the play as a whole. And even the beauties to be found in the parts are, as in nature, seldom free from an admixture of the ugly. What is beautiful is not there for its own sake, but as a means to quite a different end — in the interest of the expression of character or of a philosophical idea. Shakespeare is often rough and unpolished when a finer rounding-off of his material would have been easy. He is so precisely for the sake of this superior interest. Not seldom his abundance means inextricable confusion, and the result of the whole is an endless conflict. It cannot even be said that he presents us truth in its purity. He gives us only a one-sided view of truth, even though it be the broadest and most comprehensive. His representation is never objective, but always personal,[39] an expression of his individuality."[40] Even the greatest plays of Shakespeare exhibit the characteristic faults of modern art. Thus, *e. g.*, *Romeo and Juliet* exemplifies the "unnatural mixture of the pure *genres* of poetry," for it belongs to the class of modern dramas which may be called "lyrical" — not in the sense that they contain lyrical passages, but in the more significant sense that the poems themselves, while dramatic in form, are in essence merely "die dramatische Aeusserung einer lyrischen Begeistrung." *Romeo and Juliet* is "but a romantic sigh over the transiency of the joy of youth." The very excellence of the execution merely makes the more evident the "monstrosity of the type."[41] Even *Hamlet*, "masterpiece of artistic sagacity" though it is, is yet only an unbeautiful picture of the complete disharmony of a human soul: "der Totaleindruck dieser Tragödie ist ein Maximum der Verzweiflung." It is thus the best example of a "philosophical tragedy," which is "the exact contrary to the aesthetic

[39] *Manierirt*: the word, as Schlegel's definition shows, has for him this sense.
[40] *Jugendschriften* I, 109; cf. also 107, l. 30.
[41] *Jugendschriften* I, 102-3.

tragedy." For the latter, which is " die Vollendung der schönen Poesie," has " for its final outcome the highest harmony." [42]

While Shakespeare in 1794-5 still represented for Schlegel the perversion of modern taste, even in a writer of the highest gifts, Goethe was then the object of the critic's supreme reverence and the ground of hope of a return to sound aesthetic principles and practice. But it was, be it noted, a Goethe who had not yet published *Wilhelm Meister*, and who was praised wholly for his "classical" qualities — for his "serenity," his "balance," his "objectivity," his "nearness to the Greeks," his freedom from the usual modern over-valuation of *das Interessante.* "Goethe's poetry is the dawn of genuine art and of pure beauty . . . His works are an irrefutable proof that the objective is actually possible." In the values that belong to *die charakteristische Poesie* he is perhaps surpassed by Shakespeare. But it is not at such inferior values that he aims: "das Schöne ist der wahre Massstab, seine liebenswürdige Dichtung zu würdigen." Thus the time is ripe for a general aesthetic revolution, which shall bring to an end " die Herrschaft des Interessanten, Charakteristischen und Manierirten," and renew the felicity already attained by Greek art, when — through a happy instinct, rather than by formulated principles — the laws of unity, balance, measure, of pure beauty, still ruled the practice of the artist.[43]

In 1798, when Schlegel has become a professed Romanticist, it is still Shakespeare who represents most fully the (now admired) characteristics of modern poetry. Thus in *Ath.-Fgm.* 247, he, Dante, and Goethe make up "der grosse Dreiklang der modernen Poesie"; and while Dante's "prophetic poem" is "the highest of its kind," and Goethe's "rein poetische Poesie ist die vollständigste Poesie der Poesie," it is Shakespeare's "universality" which is "wie der Mittelpunkt der romantischen Kunst." It is not even true that (as Haym implies) in the essay on *Wilhelm Meister* Goethe figures as the sole or the supreme representative of the critic's new ideal of

---

[42] *Jugendschriften* I, 106-108. Alt (*Schiller u. die Brüder Schlegel*, p. 18) strangely refers to this passage as evidence that Schlegel at this period was "far removed from a disparagement of modern poetry." For Schlegel's later recantation of precisely these strictures upon Shakespeare, see *Ath.-Fgm.* 247-252.

[43] *Jugendschriften* I, 114-116.

poetic excellence. When—remarks Schlegel—Goethe reaches
the climax of his *Bildungsroman*, the point at which both his
hero and his readers are to be enabled "das Höchste und das
Tiefste zu fassen," he finds in Shakespeare the "great model"
which he needs for this purpose; "for what poet could better
serve for this, than he who preëminently deserves to be called
the Infinite?" [44] No language quite so exalted is used of Goethe
in the essay. His place here, relatively to Shakespeare, is the
same as that which had already been indicated in the first
number of the *Athenaeum* by A. W. Schlegel—whose *Beiträge
zur Kritik der neuesten Litteratur*, in that number, constituted,
it must be remembered, the initial manifesto of "the new
school." For Shakespeare, we there are told, Goethe has become "ein neues Medium der Erkenntniss; so dass *von beyden
gemeinschaftlich* eine Dichterschule ausgehn kann." It is in
having given to the new age a sense of Shakespeare's true meaning and value that a great part, if not the chief part, of Goethe's
epoch-making significance is represented as consisting. In 1800,
again, we have found the younger Schlegel describing Shakespeare as "das eigentliche Centrum, der Kern der romantischen
Fantasie" — in the passage which constitutes the principal
formal definition of "romantisch," the word here being expressly declared to be a synonym of "modern, in contrast with
the classical poetry of antiquity." [45]

Thus Friedrich Schlegel had the conception of "the Romantic"
in art before him from the first, both in abstract formulation

[44] The reference is, of course, to Goethe's interpretations of Hamlet.

[45] *Athenaeum*, III, 122; *Jugendschriften* II, 372. As a further illustration
of the supremacy of Shakespeare in the poetic hierarchy recognized by the early
Romanticists, and also as evidence upon their general conception of "Romantic"
poetry, it is worth while to cite Tieck's prospectus of his *Poetisches Journal*, at
the end of the original edition of his *Romantische Dichtungen* (1799-1800):
"Mein Hauptzweck wird sein, meine Gedanken über Kunst und Poesie . . .
zu entwickeln. Sie werden sich daher vornehmlich an die Werke der anerkannt
grössten Dichter der Neuern anknüpfen, von denen meine Betrachtungen immer
ausgehn. So werden z. B. Briefe über Shakespeare einen stehenden Artikel in
jedem Stücke ausmachen, . . . worin ich . . . mich in historische und kritische
Untersuchungen einlassen werde, die über die Werke dieses unerschöpflichen
und immer noch nicht genug verstandenen Geistes Licht verbreiten können.
Ähnliche Aufsätze über die ältere Englische und Deutsche und die glänzenden
Perioden der Spanischen und Italiänischen Litteratur sollen damit in Verbindung
gesetzt werden und nach und nach ein Gemählde der ächten modernen Poesie
(nicht dessen was so oft dafür ausgegeben worden ist) darstellen."

and in its concrete embodiment in Shakespeare. The heart of his earlier aesthetic doctrine lies in a phrase already cited: *alle Kunst ist beschränkt*. But over against this "classical" ideal he had already clearly conceived of an art to which the limitations of the supposed unchanging "laws of objective aesthetic validity" were intolerable: an art more enamored of life than of beauty; content to take nothing less than everything for its province; resolved to possess and to express the entire range of human experience; more interested in the individual variant than in the generic type; sensible that the abundance and infinite interconnectedness of Nature are incompatible with any sharp cleavage of things from one another, and not more afraid of "confusion" than Nature is; aware that the distinctiveness, the idiosyncrasy, of the individual artist's vision is one of the elements in this abundance of Nature, and ought therefore not to be suppressed in art; and mindful that the task which it thus sets before itself is endless, and that no stage reached in the progress of it can be definitive.[46]

The genesis of Romanticism, then, is very seriously misconceived, when it is supposed (as by Haym and many others after him) that the conception of "Romantic poetry" was formed by Schlegel only about 1796 or later; that he "abstracted it from *Wilhelm Meister*"; that it implied a sort of apotheosis of the novel among the literary *genres*; and that Schlegel's

---

[46] This conception—the original Schlegelian conception—of Romantic poetry, as reproducing the *Fülle des Lebens*, and consequently as characterized above all by universality and expressiveness was shared by Novalis: "Der Romantiker studirt das Leben, wie der Maler, Musiker und Mechaniker Farbe, Ton und Kraft. Sorgfältiges Studium des Lebens macht den Romantiker, wie sorgfältiges Studium von Farbe, Gestaltung, Ton und Kraft, den Maler, Musiker und Mechaniker." "Je persönlicher, localer, temporeller, eigenthümlicher ein Gedicht ist, desto näher steht es dem Centro der Poesie" (*Schriften*, 1837, II, 224-5). The program of such a Romanticism, which aims at the portrayal of what Schlegel called *das Charakteristische*, has manifestly much in common with realism, but is differentiated by the place which it, with some inconsistency, gives to the "subjectivity" of the poet. Novalis, however, was chiefly responsible for introducing a very different conception of "the Romantic"—due partly to the influence of certain older, popular senses of the word—whereby it signifies the remote, the strange, the ill-defined: "in der Entfernung wird alles romantisch" (*ibid.*, p. 221; cf. also p. 236). The common element in the two conceptions was the notion of "the infinite" as the object of art—this notion coming, through a confused association of ideas, to be taken in two highly antithetic senses. On this see the following essay.

first elucidation of it was in the *Athenaeum* in 1798. The theory of Romanticism was, so to say, a by-product of the prevalent classicism of the early seventeen-nineties. Desiring to define more clearly what they conceived to be the spirit and the ruling principles of the ancient art which they revered, several philosophical aestheticians of the period were led to define at the same time, with equal fullness, the spirit and ruling principles of the opposite of that art, to elaborate a theory of *das eigentümlich Moderne*. The result was that some of them — Fr. Schlegel notably, but not he only—presently transferred their allegiance to that which they had at first studied chiefly in order that they might the better condemn it. Grown accustomed to its dreadful face, they ended by embracing it. By 1798 Fr. Schlegel had for nearly five years been discussing Romantic poetry. And he can not have derived from *Wilhelm Meister* a conception with which he was entirely familiar before he had read that romance.[47] What befell in 1796 was neither the discovery, nor the invention, of the Romantic doctrine of art by Fr. Schlegel, but merely his conversion to it.

Who, or what, was the means of grace chiefly instrumental to that conversion? With this question I shall deal more fully in another essay; for the present I must be content to say, without argument, that in the case of one famous writing published in 1795-6 there is conclusive evidence of its immediate and powerful effect in the alteration of Schlegel's aesthetic opinions; and that this writing was not *Wilhelm Meister* but Schiller's essay *Über naïve und sentimentalische Dichtung*.[48] Schiller here offered a vindication of the moderns upon principles peculiarly

[47] The essay *Über die Grenzen des Schönen* was finished by April, 1795; that *Über das Studium usw.* was begun in the spring of 1794, finished by December, 1795, but not published until 1797. The footnote referring to *Wilhelm Meister* (*Jugendschriften* I, 106) is evidently a later addition. The earlier form of this essay (*Vom Wert des Studiums der Griechen u. Römer*, first printed in *DNL*, 143) was completed by July, 1794; I am not, however, certain that the *DNL* text is identical with the original. *Wilhelm Meister* appeared in parts, 1795-6. The first mention of it in Friedrich's letters to his brother is under date of June 16, 1795; the elder brother had not then seen the book.

[48] Especially the first two parts, published in the *Horen* at the end of 1795. The decisive importance of this essay in Schlegel's philosophical development has already been emphasized by Enders (*Friedrich Schlegel*, 1913, pp. 259-263) and Walzel (*Deutsche Romantik*, 1908, pp. 29-31; cf. also his "Schiller als Romantiker" in *Vom Geistesleben des 18. u. 19. Jahrhunderts*).

adapted to impress Fr. Schlegel—principles which, in fact, became the basis of his subsequent conviction of the superiority of "Romantic" art. But Schlegel's aesthetic theory had from the first been in a state of unstable equilibrium; only a slight impulsion was needed to turn it upside down. The limitations of "classicism" were uncongenial to his temperament; and it is frequently manifest — especially in the passages on Shakespeare — that the youthful critic secretly admired much that he felt obliged by the rigor of his creed to condemn. Not only was his nature thus out of harmony with his doctrine; his doctrine was also out of harmony with itself. It contained from the beginning explicit theses or definite admissions — derived largely from Kant — which were, though he was not yet aware of the fact, incongruous with the sort of aesthetic gospel that he was then so ardently preaching.

It remains only, in conclusion, to bring all this to bear upon the semasiological question propounded at the beginning of this study. We have seen that the Romantic aesthetics was formulated, I will not say altogether clearly, but about as clearly as it ever was, before the word "romantic" was definitely chosen as its designation, and also before the doctrine itself was adopted by its formulator. What Schlegel meant by the "romantische Poesie" which he extolled after 1797 was, as has been shown, in all essentials the same thing as he had meant by "interessante Poesie" in 1794-6, viz., the qualities and tendencies which he conceived to be distinctive of modern literature. It can not, therefore, be held (in spite of the apparent testimony of Ath.-Fgm. 116 in favor of Haym's view), that the term "romantische Poesie" primarily signified either "Romanpoesie" or "romanartige Poesie," or that it contained an implicit reference to Wilhelm Meister as the typical romantic book. It signified from the first, as both Schlegels in their eventual explanations of it testified, "eine eigentümlich moderne, nicht nach den Mustern des Altertums gebildete Poesie," together with the ideals and aesthetic values which they believed to be alien to the spirit of ancient art.[49]

[49] Note also the language of A. W. Schlegel when, in 1809, he offered a retrospective summary of the original aims of the Romantic School. He has been speaking of the barrenness of the so-called "classical" period of modern

But it may still be asked: given this as the meaning to be expressed, why should "romantisch" have been the word chosen to express it? The answer is not difficult. *Modern* would not do, because it suggested a merely chronological distinction, whereas, as we have seen, much more than a chronological distinction was intended. The earlier antithesis *schön vs. interessant* would hardly serve, after Schlegel's change of view, since to most ears it would imply a depreciation of precisely the kind of poetry which he now regarded as the higher. In 1796, in a typically transitional writing, we find him formally urging the adoption of the words "objectiv" and "interessant" as "new technical terms" to distinguish the Sophoclean from the Shakespearean type of tragedy.[50] This proposal soon fell to the ground. Even *interessant*, one may conjecture, was open to two objections. While *modern* had too exclusively chronological a connotation, *interessant* had no chronological connotation at all; and it had acquired, through its use by Schlegel himself and by W. von Humboldt, a distinctly dyslogistic coloring. Meanwhile, there lay ready at hand a word, as it seemed, ideally adapted to convey the conception present to Fr. Schlegel's mind. "Romantisch" had hitherto chiefly meant for the Schlegels (as has been shown) not, indeed, "modern" in general, but "post-classical," including specifically both the medieval and the early modern. It thus, even in its purely historical or chronological sense, was better fitted than *modern* to express one side of the aesthetic antithesis now in question; for it was in the Middle Ages and in the earlier modern period that the qualities which Schlegel had defined as antithetic to the classical were best represented, while the later modern centuries had been characterized by pseudo-classical revivals and other deviations from type. In particular, *romantisch* was from the first associated in Fr. Schlegel's mind with Dante, Cervantes and Shakespeare; and as we have seen, it was these,

---

literature; and continues: "So ungefähr standen die Sachen immerfort, bis vor nicht langer Zeit, einige, besonders Deutsche Denker, versuchten . . . zugleich die Alten nach Gebühr zu ehren, und dennoch die davon gänzlich abweichende Eigenthümlichkeit der Neueren anzuerkennen. . . . Diese haben für den eigenthümlichen Geist der modernen Kunst den Namen 'romantisch' erfunden" (*SW.*, 1846, V, p. 9).

[50] In the *Vorrede* to *Die Griechen u. Römer; Jugendschriften* I, 83.

especially the last, who, both before and after Schlegel's change of view, were to him the typical representatives of *die interessante Poesie*, of *das Wesentlich-Moderne*. Above all, *romantisch* had a less fixedly chronological import than *modern*, and was therefore more capable of connoting certain aesthetic characteristics, the exclusively modern origin of which was a significant but not the essential fact. Thus no other single word could, from the point of view of Schlegel's own usage, express so well as *romantisch* precisely what he wished to convey. In view of these considerations, we have every reason for regarding, not only the meaning given to *romantisch* by the Schlegels in 1799 and thereafter as the original meaning, but also the grounds then assigned for their selection of the word as the original grounds. Haym's long-current explanation of the signification and origin of the term, as well as the usual account of the genesis of the idea, must accordingly be rejected. Only—one must add, in order to make Haym's error intelligible —it is true that the adjective continued to have at times, for Schlegel, some obscure association with the noun *Roman*, in a sense of the latter which included the novel as well as the medieval romances; and that in the characterization of *die romantische Poesie* in *Ath.-Fgm.* 116, this association of ideas —either through confusion or, as one suspects, through a desire to mystify his readers—is made conspicuous. But even in this passage, as we have already seen, Schlegel is only secondarily expatiating upon the possibilities of the *Roman* as a *genre*; he is primarily setting forth, as he had often before set forth, the aesthetic aims and temper which to him differentiated truly modern from classical art.

XI. SCHILLER AND THE GENESIS OF
GERMAN ROMANTICISM *

1.

IN THE preceding paper I have shown that the conception of "Romantic" poetry was developed by Friedrich Schlegel as a consequence of his preoccupation during his first period (1793-6) with the problem of formulating the distinguishing characteristics of classical, or ancient, and of modern art. The aesthetic qualities which, after he had learned to admire them, Schlegel named "Romantic," were simply the qualities which he had earlier defined, and condemned, as the attributes of *das eigentümlich Moderne*. During his period of classicism Schlegel, as I have also pointed out, adhered to an aesthetic theory in which the (suppposed) example of Greek practice, and abstract principles derived by analogy from the Kantian epistemology, were curiously interwoven. Art must aim at "objective" beauty, must conform to aesthetic laws which are based upon the essential constitution of the human mind as such, and are therefore the same for all peoples and in all ages. Modern poetry, in its typical manifestations, is degenerate because it is "interessante Poesie," that is, because it appeals to the varying subjective "interest" of individuals or of special types of mind; because it takes for its theme "das Charakteristische," that is, the individual person or unique situation, rather than the generic type; and because, in its endeavor to represent the fullness and variety of life, it forgets the fundamental truth that "all art consists in limitation," by austere adherence to which Greek poetry had been able to achieve aesthetic perfection.

All this is close akin to Schiller's aesthetics of the same period. Schiller at this time, as Walzel has remarked, fully shared the *Gräkomanie* for which he afterwards ridiculed Schlegel; and it was in its "objectivity" that, for him too, the

* First published in *Modern Language Notes*, XXXV, 1920.

superiority of ancient art lay.[1] "Objective" beauty, though it
depends upon an appeal to the senses and requires a sensible
medium, is "independent of all *empirical* conditions of sensibility, and remains the same even when the subjective condition
(*Privatbeschaffenheit*) of the individual is altered. . . . It is
pleasing, not to the individual merely, but to the species."
Like the valid judgment in the Kantian logic, the work of art
must attain "necessity and universality." "Das Gebiet der
eigentlich schönen Kunst kann sich nur so weit erstrecken, als
sich in der Verknüpfung der Erscheinungen Notwendigkeit
entdecken lässt." But nothing is "necessary" in the constitution of any individual mind except its "generic character."
The poet, therefore, must address himself exclusively to those
feelings which are uniform and common to the race; and in
order to do this, he must, at least for the moment, strip himself of all that is peculiar and distinctive in his own personality.
"Nur alsdann, wenn er nicht als der oder der bestimmte
Mensch (in welchem die Gattung immer beschränkt sein
würde), sondern wenn er als Mensch überhaupt empfindet, ist
er gewiss, dass die ganze Gattung ihm nachempfinden werde."[2]
Schiller's rage against the unique, the individual as such, goes
so far, in this "classical" period of his aesthetic opinions, that
he does not shrink from asserting the singular paradox that
"every individual man is the less man, by so much as he is
individual."[3] And in "objective" art the thing portrayed, as
well as the mind of the artist, must be generalized, purged of
all that is specific or idiosyncratic: "in einem Gedicht darf
nichts wirkliche (historische) Natur sein, denn alle Wirk-
lichkeit ist mehr oder weniger Beschränkung jener allgemeinen
Naturwahrheit."[4]

In the *Briefe über die ästhetische Erziehung des Menschen*
(published in *Die Horen* in the beginning of 1795) Schiller's
position is in some respects a transitional one. But he still
insists upon the "objectivity," "universal validity," and immutability of aesthetic standards; regards the quieting of the

---

[1] *Zerstreute Betrachtungen, usw.* 1793.
[2] From the review of Friedrich Matthisson's *Gedichte*, 1794.
[3] *Ibid.*
[4] *Ibid.*

passions as a criterion of beauty; reiterates the already familiar
thesis of the "disinterestedness" of aesthetic enjoyment; denies
aesthetic value to "didactic" or "philosophical" poetry; defines the creation or perception of beauty as at once complete
freedom and rigorous subjection to law; characterizes art as a
kind of "play"; and assigns to the Greeks the rank of "supreme
masters" in art. In making the "aesthetic" result from the
interaction of two antithetic elements or impulsions in the
human mind, the *sinnlicher Trieb* or *Stofftrieb* and the *Formtrieb*, Schiller again was merely devising a terminology of his
own to express an antithesis which was prominent in Schlegel's
early aesthetic essays. The *Stofftrieb* has "life in the widest
sense for its object" and causes the artist to seek "the most
many-sided contact with the world."[5] The *Formtrieb* "seeks
unity and permanence" rather than fullness and variety of
content; it "imposes harmony upon the diversity of the
manifestations of man's nature"; it gives laws which are not
subject to change, and is the source of all "necessity and
universality" in our judgments of whatever sort. Just so did
Schlegel contrast the craving for *Stoff*, which he conceived to
be the weakness of modern taste, with the predominance of
the sense of form in Greek art: "Im Grunde völlig gleichgültig
gegen alle Form, und nur voll unersättlichen Durstes nach
Stoff, verlangt auch das feinere Publikum von dem Künstler
nichts als interessante Individualität."[6]

Schiller, it is true, already regarded both these "impulsions"
as necessary in any valid operation of the mind, whether it be
a logical judgment or an act of aesthetic creation or appreciation. Arguing as he did from the analogy of Kant's theory of
knowledge, he was, of course, pre-committed to this view.
There are, he observes, two extremes in aesthetic theory, both
faulty in their one-sidedness. There are those who "fear to
rob beauty of its freedom by a too severe analysis"; but these
fail to reflect "that the freedom in which they are entirely
right in placing the essence of beauty is not lawlessness, but a
harmony of laws, not caprice, but the highest internal necessity."

[5] Letter 13.
[6] *Über das Studium usw.*; Minor, *Jugendschriften*, I, 91.

There are, on the other hand, those who "fear lest through a too bold inclusiveness, the distinctness of the concept of beauty may be destroyed"; these forget that "this distinctness of beauty which they are equally right in demanding, consists, not in the exclusion of certain realities, but in the absolute *in*clusion of all; so that it is not limitation (*Begrenzung*) but infinitude." [7] This seems a negation of the maxim in which Schlegel summed up the essence of classicism: *alle Kunst ist beschränkt.* But for Schiller, too, in point of fact, "form" is still the paramount consideration in art: "nur von der Form ist wahre ästhetische Freiheit zu erwarten. Darin also besteht das eigentliche Kunstgeheimnis des Meisters, dass er den Stoff durch die Form vertilgt." [8]

Thus throughout the first half of the seventeen-nineties Schiller and Friedrich Schlegel, in spite of minor differences, employed the same general categories in their reflection upon aesthetic questions and adhered to the same type of aesthetic doctrine — to a doctrine characterized by an insistence upon "objective" aesthetic standards, by a conviction of the priority of "form" over "content," of unity over expressiveness, in art, and by a belief in the superiority of ancient art, as the most adequate realization of these standards. Meanwhile there were at work in Fr. Schlegel's thought from the first two forces which became powerful predisposing causes of his eventual conversion from the "classical" to the Romantic ideal. The first of these was the influence upon him of the very philosophy from which he and Schiller had derived the principal theoretical justification for their classicism. That justification, as I have said, consisted largely in a transfer to the field of aesthetics of certain conceptions and categories which they had found in Kant's epistemology. But there was a curious duality about the Kantian influence; it tended in two quite opposite directions. An aesthetics constructed out of analogies taken from the theoretical philosophy of Kant, and from one portion of his moral philosophy, would, indeed, seek to confine art within the strait-jacket of "laws of universal validity," uniform for all peoples and all times, and to attain this uniformity by the avoidance of

[7] Letter 18.   [8] Letter 22.

all themes and moods which are "characteristic," *i. e.*, individual or local or peculiar to a special historical situation. But there was another part of Kant's ethics which suggested, by analogy, a very different standard of aesthetic values. In its final formulation, the categorical imperative is represented by Kant as an ideal capable, not of actual realization, but only of an endlessly progressive approximation:

> The object of a will that is capable of being determined by the moral law is the production in the world of the highest good. Now, the supreme condition of the highest good is the perfect harmony of the disposition with the moral law . . . — a perfection of which no rational being existing in the world of sense is capable at any moment of his life. . . . Since, nevertheless, such a harmony is morally required of us, . . . the pure practical reason forces us to assume a practical progress towards it, *in infinitum*, as the real object of our will. . . . A finite rational being is capable only of an infinite progress from lower to higher stages of moral perfection.[9]

Fichte had, by 1794, converted this Kantian conception of the moral ideal as an endless pursuit of a forever unattainable goal into a metaphysical principle, and had represented the very nature of all existence as an infinite and insatiable striving of the Absolute Ego, whereby it first sets up the external world as an obstacle to its own activity, and then gradually but endlessly triumphs over this obstacle. The notion of infinity thus took precedence in philosophy over that of the finite and determinate, the category of Becoming over that of Being, the ideal of activity over that of achieved completion, the mood of endless longing over that of quietude and collectedness of mind.

Now *this* Kantian principle, when transferred from ethics to aesthetics, was obviously irreconcilable with those critical standards which were of the essence of the young Schlegel's "classicism"; it implied that the "laws of beauty" are relative and variable from age to age, and that art is subject to a continuous evolution. What, therefore, we find in his aesthetic writings from the beginning is a conflict between the two tendencies, both alike chiefly Kantian in their origin—a conflict

[9] *Kritik der praktischen Vernuft*, A, 219-221.

in which the ideal of classical "objectivity" at first has on the whole the upper hand, but only precariously and by means of palpable inconsistencies. In what is probably the earliest of Schlegel's attempts to define the essence of classical and of modern culture (*Vom Wert des Studiums der Griechen und Römer*, 1794) we already find him attempting to "*explain* ancient history by means of a theory based upon the most recent philosophy," i. e., upon the Kantian. There are, he observes, two possible ways of conceiving the general course of history— as a movement which returns upon itself in repeated cycles, or as an endless and unceasing progression. The first of these conceptions, the *System des Kreislaufes*, satisfies the better the demands of what Kant called the theoretical reason; it does so, Schlegel apparently means, because it alone enables us to conceive of the content of history, in Kantian terms, as a "completed synthesis," as a genuine unity. But "the only way of representing history which would satisfy the *practical* reason," with its necessity for seeking a perpetually nearer approach to an unattainable perfection, is the *System der unendlichen Fortschreitung*. Thus, upon Kantian principles, "it is manifest *a priori* that there must exist two types of culture, according as the *representative* faculty or the *conative* faculty (*das vorstellende oder das strebende Vermögen*) is primary and preponderant: a natural and an artificial culture; that the former must come first in time, and is a necessary antecedent to the latter; and that the *System des Kreislaufes* is possible only in the natural type of culture, the *System der unendlichen Fortschreitung* only in the artificial type." [10]

Thus the culture of the ancients is based upon the former, modern culture upon the latter, conception of the historic process. The underlying common factor in the civilization of the Greeks and Romans, the thing which gives unity to their history, is the manifold influence upon their thought and life of the *System des Kreislaufes*, in other words, of the assumption that no continuous forward movement, in any province of

---

[10] I accept Walzel's identification of the version of this essay printed by him in DNL, 143, with the original text, though the possibility that this version may represent one of the two later revisions does not seem to me to be absolutely excluded. The internal evidence, however, is on the whole in favor of the earlier date.

human activity, is to be expected or desired. This, "more or less definitely expressed, was not only the view of the greatest Greek and Roman historians, but was also the universal mode of thought of the people—which erred only in this, that it regarded the outcome of their own history as having universal validity, as if it were the outcome of the history of all mankind." The circularity of ancient civilization is shown, among other ways, by its inevitable decline. Having a finite goal, it was able to attain that goal completely; but after it had done so, it could change only for the worse.

Since modern civilization is, on the other hand, informed by a wholly different conception of history, its art and all the other manifestations of its distinctive spirit cannot and should not be mere attempts to reproduce the alien excellence attained by the ancients. We moderns "must learn that it is not our vocation to live *wie Bettler von den Almosen der Vorwelt.*" Every age, like every individual, is an end in itself, and has "an inalienable right to *be* itself." "Through the satisfaction of the demands of the practical reason, which alone determines the direction of modern culture, the power and perfection of ancient culture gains its highest worth; and if *our* history must remain ever uncompleted, our goal unattained, our striving unsatisfied, yet is our goal infinitely great." This has the air not only of a declaration of independence of "classical" standards, but even of a bold proclamation of the superiority of the aesthetic and moral ideals of the modern world. Yet the greater part of the essay is rather a glorification of the ancients. "The study of the Greeks and Romans is a school of the great, the good, the noble, the beautiful, of *humanity*; from it we may regain free abundance, living power, unity, balance, harmony, completeness, which the still crude art of modern culture has belittled, mutilated, confused, deranged, dismembered and destroyed." "The most eminent Greeks and Romans of the best period are a sort of supermen (*wie Wesen übermenschlicher Art*), men in the highest style." [11] Here, manifestly, is a doctrine imperfectly at

[11] Cf. also the following (*op. cit.*, p. 263): "In der Geschichte der Griechen und Römer sind die Stufen der Bildung ganz bestimmt, die reinen Arten entschieden und vollkommen, das Einzelne so kühn und vollendet dass es das Ideal seiner Art, der Grieche der Mensch κατ' ἐξοχήν ist, die Gründe einfach, die

unity with itself, a *Gräkomanie* which is trying to keep house with its own negation. If modern art has a fundamentally different meaning and ideal, it was an obvious inconsistency to demand that the modern artist should gain his inspiration from ancient models; and if the modern ideal of *unendliche Vervollkommnung* is the higher, not even the best embodiments of a distinctively "classical" culture could properly be regarded as exemplifying the full possibilities of human nature.

The same unstable equilibrium in Schlegel's standards is illustrated in another of his essays, of about the same date, which deals more specifically with aesthetic questions (*Über die Grenzen des Schönen*).[12] While, here too, the superiority of the poetry of the ancients is emphatically asserted, and while the classical ideal, with its insistence upon form, measure, restraint, the Delphic μηδὲν ἄγαν, both in art and conduct, is extolled, it is nevertheless also remarked that classical art, since its excellence was rather the result of instinct than of reflective insight, was not merely incapable of progress, but was predestined to aberration and degeneration. The very defects of modern art, on the other hand, are the ground of hope, *unsere Mängel sind unsere Hoffnungen*; for those defects arise from the predominance in it of man's self-conscious intelligence (*Verstand*), "dessen zwar langsame Vervollkommnung gar keine Schranken kennt." And when this faculty "has accomplished its task of assuring to mankind a permanent basis and giving to it an unchangeable *direction*, there will then be no more occasion to doubt whether man's history is forever to return upon itself like a circle, or is endlessly to progress from better to better." The whole essay leaves a singularly confused impression upon the reader; for the author appears unable to decide between the two aesthetic ideals which alternately present themselves to his mind. He craves, in fact, *both* achieved perfection and the potentiality of progress, both inner harmony and unappeasable self-dissatisfaction; and since modern art by

Ordnung fliessend, die Massen gross und einfach, das Ganze vollständig. Sie ist der Kommentar der Philosophie, der ewige Kodex des menschlichen Gemüts, eine *Naturgeschichte des sittlichen und geistigen Menschen*."

[12] First published in *Der neue Teutsche Merkur*, May, 1795; Minor, *Jugendschriften*, I, pp. 21-27.

its very essence, as he conceives it, lacks the one type of excellence, and ancient art lacks the other, he seems unable to pronounce in favor of either.

What, amid these waverings and inconsistencies, it is, for our present purpose, important to note in the early writings of Fr. Schlegel is that they contain ideas (along with their opposites) which closely approximate certain of the characteristic conceptions of Schiller's later essay *Über naive und sentimentalische Dichtung*. In them already we find the following antitheses, each pair being parallel to, or correlative with, all of the others: [18]

> *Klassische Kunst—moderne Kunst;*
> *Natürliche Bildung—künstliche Bildung;*
> *Vorstellendes Vermögen—strebendes Vermögen;*
> *System des Kreislaufes—System der unendlichen Fortschreitung.*[14]

The second force which drove Schlegel towards his later, or Romantic, position need only be mentioned here, as I have already called attention to it. It was the influence of a quality of his own natural taste and temperament. However much, under compulsion of the theory to which he was committed, he might deplore the modern world's craving for "content," for "the interesting," for "the characteristic" and individuated, and its relative indifference to the laws of pure form, it was none the less true that in his nature what Schiller had called the *Stofftrieb* was exceedingly powerful, not to say preponderant. His curiosity about life and human nature was far too keen to make it likely that he would be permanently content with a theory of art which required the poet to portray only generalized types, and forbade him to let any disclosure of his own personality or his own mood slip into his compositions. One example, among many which might be cited, of this inner incongruity between the temper of Friedrich Schlegel's mind and his early aesthetic theory, may be seen in his essay "On the

[18] *Jugendschriften*, I, 22.

[14] It is also to be remarked that Schlegel already saw in the introduction of Christianity the prime cause of that change of ideals and of conceptions of the historic process which differentiates modern from classical art. But this is a subject that calls for separate treatment. Cf. *Vom Wert des Studiums der Griechen und Römer*, in DNL, 143, p. 261, and *Jugendschriften*, I, 99; II, 42.

Female Characters in Greek Poetry." While insisting that the Greek poets were true to the principles of fine art in refraining from the attempt to paint with portrait-like detail "interesting men and women as individuals," Schlegel cannot forbear to lament that no such individualized and realistic portraits of Greek character have come down to us.[15]

Schlegel's Romantic doctrine of art, then, was already implicit in these two characteristics of his first period: (a) in the implication of the analogy from the Kantian ethics to aesthetics, *viz.*, that art should be characterized by a constant enlargement of its boundaries and an endless progression towards an unattainably remote ideal, rather than by any definitive perfection of form attainable by adhering to immutable laws and narrow limitations of aim; and (b) in his temperamental admiration for such a poet as Shakespeare and his strong though suppressed desire for a poetry which, imitating Shakespeare, should take all of life for its province, and make the abundance and fidelity of its expression of life the sole criterion of artistic success. Yet Schlegel, until 1796, never wholly yielded to this temperamental inclination and never recognized the full consequences of the Kantian analogy or its inconsistency with his classicism and his standards of *objektive Schönheit*. On the contrary, in his long disquisition "On the Study of Greek Poetry," completed in 1795, his *Objektivitätswut*, his rage against the aberrations of the moderns, his reverence for "the *a priori* laws of pure beauty," his conviction that poetry can be true to its vocation only by the most rigorous limitation of the range of its themes and of its methods—all these seem stronger than ever. Some impulsion from without was necessary to enable him to take the one step farther which was required by the concessions he had already made, and so to pass definitely to the position to which he was to give the name "Romantic."

I now shall present the evidence which shows conclusively that this impulsion came from Schiller's essay *Über naive und sentimentalische Dichtung*, especially the second part of it, published in *Die Horen* in December, 1795. But I shall at the same time attempt to make clear the precise logical relation

[15] *Jugendschriften*, I, 39.

between Schiller's conception of "sentimentalische Dichtung" and Schlegel's ideal of "romantische Poesie"—a relation in which there is even more of difference than of similarity.

2.

Friedrich Schlegel himself bore clear and emphatic testimony to the decisive impression produced upon him by his first reading of the second instalment of Schiller's *Über naive und sentimentalische Dichtung*. In a letter to A. W. Schlegel, January 15, 1796, he writes:

> Dann hat mich Schiller's Theorie des Sentimentalen so beschäftigt, dass ich einige Tage nichts andres gethan habe, als sie lesen und Anmerkungen schreiben. . . . *Schiller hat mir wirklich Aufschlüsse gegeben.* Wenn mir innerlich so etwas kocht, so bin ich unfähig etwas andres ruhig vorzunehmen. Der Entschluss, noch diesen Winter eine Skizze meiner Poetik für den Druck auszuarbeiten, ist nun fest genommen.[16]

The effect of this reading was apparent in the preface which Friedrich soon after wrote for the collection of his essays on Greek poetry, then in press. His indebtedness to Schiller's essay is now publicly acknowledged; it has given him "a broader insight into the nature of *die interessante Poesie* and thrown a new light upon the limitations of the scope of classical poetry."[17] If he had read it earlier, his account of the origin and character of modern poetry, in his present book, would have been "incomparably less incomplete." He adopts, in fact, in his preface an unmistakably apologetic tone with respect to the (earlier-written) essays which the volume contains. He begs his readers not to take his strictures upon the moderns as his

---

[16] *Briefe an seinen Bruder*, 253; italics mine. A little later (Feb., 1796) Schlegel writes that, in essentials, he is also fully in agreement with Schiller's "Erklärung und Herleitung des elegischen Dichters"—i. e., with the fourth part of the essay (*ibid.*, 263).

[17] Schlegel here adopts *sentimental* as antithetic to *objektive Poesie*, and as equivalent to an important part, though not the whole, of what he had hitherto signified by *interessant*. His definition of the first of these terms is: "eine poetische Aeusserung des Strebens nach dem Unendlichen, die mit einer Reflexion über das Verhältnis des Idealen und des Realen verknüpft ist." (*Jugendschriften*, I, 81.) It should be noted that Schlegel expressly uses "sentimental" as interchangeable with Schiller's "sentimentalisch."

final judgment on the subject. He would now, he suggests, have his arguments construed merely as hypothetical. *If* the " pure laws of beauty and of art " are to determine our aesthetic standards, *if* " objectivity" is a requisite to aesthetic value, *then* modern poetry must be condemned, since it does not even aim at conformity to these standards, but finds its ideal in " das Interessante d. h. subjektive aesthetische Kraft." But if there are other criteria of genuine aesthetic worth, then, precisely by pointing out this characteristic of modern poetry, Schiller has—as Schlegel significantly intimates—prepared the way for nothing less than " eine sehr glänzende Rechtfertigung der Modernen."

He is not, indeed, even yet willing to repudiate completely his former idols. It is only a " provisional validity" that he can concede to " das Interessante in der Poesie." Doubtless the perfection of form of ancient poetry was due to the limitations of its content; doubtless it is the destiny of modern poetry to transcend these limitations, and in doing so to pass through many stages in which " pure beauty" is subordinated to the progressive enrichment of the content and material of the art. Thus, during all these stages, it must be admitted " dass das Interessante, als die nothwendige Vorbereitung zur unendlichen Perfektibilität der ästhetischen Anlage, ästhetisch erlaubt sei." But the goal is still a complete conformity to " the laws of an objective theory" of the beautiful and to " the example of classical poetry." Yet, as Enders has remarked,[18] this reservation is rather nominal than real; for since the goal is confessedly unattainable, capable only of being endlessly approached, and the *Interessante* is meanwhile to be the standard of poetic excellence, it is with the latter alone that either poet or critic can ever be actually concerned.

It is precisely the transitional character of this preface of 1797, and the express acknowledgment which it contains that the transition then in process in Schlegel's opinions was due to Schiller, which constitute the most decisive evidence that the essay *On Naïve and Sentimental Poetry* was the chief instrument of the conversion of Schlegel to his new—that is, to his

[18] *Friedrich Schlegel*, 1913, 263.

Romantic—aesthetic faith. A little later, in the *Lyceumsfragmente* (1797), we find the transition completed. Schlegel now unsparingly ridicules his own earlier *Objektivitätswut*, affirms the superiority of "the modern" on grounds similar to those which had been set forth by Schiller,[19] and promulgates some of the most characteristic articles of the Romantic creed.

It is not difficult to see what it was in Schiller's essay that produced so great an effect upon the younger man's mind, and furnished him at once with new "solutions." For the essay—especially the second part — was, in the first place, addressed directly to the problem which had been Schlegel's absorbing preoccupation from the beginning of his career as critic and aesthetic theorist; it was an attempt to define the immanent *ideas* of ancient and of modern poetry, to formulate the *moralische Bedeutung* (in Schiller's phrase) of both. And some of the essentials of the formulation were the same as those which Schlegel had already reached through his own reflection. That the modern man is no longer "in unity with Nature"; that the modern poet, in contrast with the ancient, is characteristically "subjective," disposed to be interested rather "in the impression which objects make upon him than in the objects themselves"; that the "ancient poet moves us through Nature, through the truth of sense, through a present and living reality, while the modern poet moves us through ideas"; that, most characteristically of all, modern art is a *Kunst des Unendlichen* while ancient art is a *Kunst der Begrenzung*—these were themes upon which Schlegel himself had copiously discoursed. What gave Schiller's essay its revolutionary significance for him was that it found in these traits of modern art the evidence, not of degeneracy, but of "an infinite superiority in kind" to the spirit and aims of ancient art; that it recognized the "path followed by modern poets" as one necessarily followed by mankind everywhere, in the case both of the race and of the

---

[19] *Fgm.* 93: "In den Alten sieht man den vollendeten Buchstaben der ganzen Poesie: in den Neuern ahnet man den werdenden Geist"; 91: "Die Alten sind nicht ein willkührlich auserwähltes Kunstvolk Gottes; noch haben sie den alleinseligmachenden Schönheitsglauben." Cf. also 107. — The typically 'Romantic' of the *Lyceumsfragmente* are, besides these, Nos. 7, 16, 20, 34, 42, 48, 60, 64, 82, 87, 95, 104, 108, 115. No. 84 perhaps represents rather the transitional position of the above-mentioned *Vorrede*.

individual—in other words, as a normal stage in the evolution
of art; that it roundly condemned the practice (so characteristic
of Schlegel's earlier aesthetic writings) of "first drawing a
one-sided conception of the generic nature of poetry from the
ancients and then depreciating the moderns by contrasting them
with this conception"; and that it clearly implied that there
could be no "objective" aesthetic principles, in one of the
senses in which the term had been hitherto used by both Schlegel
and Schiller—no standards and no models which could be set
up as complete, final, "necessary," immutable, and of "universal validity"—since the attempt to limit the artist by such
standards would be an attempt to arrest that ceaseless "progression" which is the distinctive vocation and the glory of
modern art.

What Schiller did for Schlegel, it will be seen, was not so
much to suggest to him new arguments as to give him, by example, the courage to follow through, even to a revolutionary
conclusion, an argument which had already been suggested to
him by an analogy from the ethics of Kant and the metaphysics
of Fichte. That conclusion consisted in the thesis which may
be defined as the generating and generic element in the Romantic doctrine—the thesis, namely of the intrinsic superiority of a
Kunst des Unendlichen over a *Kunst der Begrenzung*, and of
the consequently higher rank of modern, i. e., of "progressive"
and "subjective," art, in comparison with the static and more
purely "objective" art of classical antiquity, with its cramping
perfection of form and its rigorous self-limitation. In the sense
that he brought Fr. Schlegel to this fundamental Romantic
conviction, Schiller may be described as the spiritual grandfather
of German Romanticism.

Schlegel's later formal definitions of "the Romantic" show
abundantly that that notion had the same generic (though not
the same specific) essence as Schiller's conception of "sentimental poetry," of an "art of infinity" which is the true expression of the modern spirit. Thus Schlegel writes in 1800:
"Nach meiner Ansicht und meinem Sprachgebrauch ist eben
das romantisch, was uns einen sentimentalen Stoff in einer fantastischen Form darstellt." He goes on to explain that he uses
the word "sentimental," not in its vulgar sense, but to desig-

nate that which is characterized by the "spirit of love"; and that by "love," in turn, he means more than an emotional interest in individuals, which is but a "Hindeutung auf das Höhere, Unendliche, Hieroglyphe der unendlichen Liebe und der heiligen Lebensfülle der bildenden Natur." So, elsewhere in the same writing, Schlegel speaks of "that broader sense of the word romantic" in which it signifies "die Tendenz nach einem tiefen unendlichen Sinn." [20] Yet it would be profoundly false to represent Schiller's conception of "sentimentalische Dichtung" as equivalent to Schlegel's idea of "romantische Poesie." So far from identical are they, that in certain respects the Romantic poet à la Schlegel corresponds rather to Schiller's "natural (*naive*) poet." This fact is at once apparent from the examples given by Schiller. Homer, indeed, is for him a "natural" poet; but so are certain great moderns—Shakespeare, Molière, Goethe. For Schlegel, on the other hand, as I have already pointed out, Shakespeare was "the very centre and core of romantic poetry." So conspicuous a difference in the classification of individual poets points to some significant divergence between the two notions "sentimentalisch" and "romantisch."

The point of divergence can be fairly precisely determined. The two writers agree in regarding the excellence of modern poetry as consisting in the "infinity" of its "content" (*Gehalt*), in its dedication to the quest of a never fully realizable ideal, in its unceasing *Annäherung zu einer unendlichen Grösse*. But it is not chiefly of the *same* "infinity" that Schiller and Schlegel are thinking; and the "endless progression" which one of them desiderates is a progression in a different respect, and in a different direction, from that to which the other would have modern art aspire. For the vague and ambiguous notion of a "striving after an infinite content," in art or in life, which, as I have said, was common to Schiller and to the Romanticists in general, was capable of at least five distinct, though not in all cases mutually exclusive, interpretations. It might be taken in an ethical, or in a quasi-mystical, or in a hedonic sense, or

[20] *Jugendschriften*, II, 370-372, 364. *Cf.* the passage in which Novalis in January, 1798, predicts the coming of a "höhere," an "erweiterte Poesie, die man könnte *die Poesie des Unendlichen* nennen." Here, too, the formula is Schiller's; but it is also the formula for "the Romantic."

(there seems to be no adjective for this) in the sense of striving for striving's sake, or in what may be called a realistic sense, that of an endeavor after richness and variety in the representation of reality. In other words, the poet might (1) find the inspiration of his art in some moral ideal, or moral passion, too lofty or too many-sided or too exacting ever to be fully realized or worthily expressed; or (2) his art might manifest a *Streben nach dem Unendlichen* in the sense of a preference for the mysterious or the vague or the remote, or of a yearning after some consummation of which the allurement lay in its indefinability and its transcendence of all ordinary experience; or (3) he might be temperamentally characterized by an insatiable craving for ever new emotions or enjoyments or possessions (like Carlyle's "infinite bootblack") and might devote his art to the exhibition of this peculiarity of his own; or (4) he might set up *insatiability* as such as a conscious ideal, and make the glorification of this ideal the theme of his art (as in *Faust*); or (5) he might conceive it to be the function of art to express with ever increasing but never complete adequacy the infinite variety and inexhaustible interestingness of "life" — *i. e.*, of the aspects of nature and the phases of human experience, especially of inner experience. This equivocality of its fundamental notion of "infinity" is the principal reason why the Romantic doctrine developed into such various and incongruous forms, and why the term "Romantic" has come to have so confusing a diversity of connotations.

Now, the "infinite striving" of Schiller's "sentimental poet" was chiefly of the first of these five sorts; it was a striving for the fuller realization or the more adequate and worthy expression of a moral ideal. His dissatisfaction arising from the "contrast between the ideal and reality," for example, is not a mere sense of the failure of the world to satisfy our desires; it is "ein tiefes Gefühl moralischer Widersprüche, ein glühender Unwillen gegen moralische Verkehrtheit." [21] The poet who expresses the true ideal of modern art will not care to portray "*actual* human nature" but only "*true* human nature," i. e.,

[21] Schiller's reference here is specifically to the satiric poet, who is (when he conforms to these requirements) one of the two principal species of "sentimental" poet.

humanity in which the higher and distinctively human faculty of the self-active Reason is dominant.[22] True, the satiric poet must necessarily put before us the imperfections or absurdities of humanity; but he does so in order the better to express the ideal through contrast, and through the scorn or the indignation which he must always feel, and make his reader feel, for the baseness or pettiness or irrationality, in individual character or social customs, which he describes. The poet's aim must always be to elevate as well as entertain his reader, *Veredlung* as well as *Erholung*. In short, the aesthetic doctrine of the essay *Über naive und sentimentalische Dichtung* is of a highly moralistic sort.[23]

Quite other was Fr. Schlegel's interpretation of the "infinite striving" which he too looked upon as the characteristic of modern art. In the author whose own first contribution to Romantic literature was to be *Lucinde*, that striving by no means aimed at the "infinity" of an ideal of moral perfection too sublime and austere for human nature to attain; it aimed rather at the infinity of actual life—good and bad alike—as the subject-matter of the poetic art. Schlegel took the general conception, in short, chiefly in the last of the five special senses which I have above distinguished. He had long since, in the days of his Graecomania, set down, among the characteristics of modern art and taste which he then so severely reprehended, a desire to reproduce in literature the "Fülle und Leben" which are the "Vorrecht der Natur," a "frightful and yet fruitless yearning to spread out to the infinite and a burning eagerness to penetrate to the very heart of the individual"; and he now incorporates in his new doctrine, as aesthetic

---

[22] "Wirkliche Natur ist jeder noch so gemeine Ausbruch der Leidenschaft, er mag auch wahre Natur sein, aber eine wahre *menschliche* ist er nicht: denn diese erfordert einen Antheil des selbstständigen Vermögens an jeder Aeusserung, dessen Ausdruck jedesmal Würde ist." *Über naive usw.*, Pt. 5.

[23] This is true at least of the main drift and emphasis of Schiller's argument. He occasionally, however, lapses into a somewhat different conception of "sentimentalisch," apparently without being himself aware of the difference. When, for example, he speaks of Werther—not the novel, but the character which Goethe chose in that novel to portray—as an illustration of the exaggeration of the "sentimental" type, he must be supposed to have forgotten some of his own distinctions. For it was scarcely from an excessive zeal in the pursuit of a moral ideal that Werther suffered.

desiderata, all the elements of his former damnatory definition of the modern spirit.[24] It was, then, this ambition for "Reichtum des Stoffes," this aspiration to match in art the abundance and diversity and complexity of Nature, that for Schlegel constituted the "infinity" of the Romantic ideal.

The contrast becomes the more striking in a passage in which Schlegel reads into Schiller's term his own meaning. There is, he wrote in 1800, one particular element "in der Bedeutung des Sentimentalen, was gerade das Eigenthümliche der Tendenz der romantischen Poesie im Gegensatz der antiken begreift" — *viz.,* its interest in actual life, and its consequent predilection "für den eigentlich historischen Stoff." "Romantic poetry rests wholly upon historical grounds." Autobiographies, "confessions," such as Rousseau's (which, Schlegel adds, are a far better *Roman* than his *Héloise*), literary "arabesques," such as the novels of Jean Paul—these are "die einzigen romantischen Naturprodukte unsers Zeitalters." "All so-called *Romane*" should be valued "in proportion to the amount of direct personal observation (*eigne Anschauung*) and of the representation of life which they contain; and from this point of view, even the successors of Richardson, however much they may have wandered from the right path, are welcome. We can at least learn from Cecilia Beverley how people were bored in London, when to be bored was the fashion, and how a British lady came to grief through excess of delicacy and ended by destroying herself. The oaths, the Squires, and the like, in Fielding, are, as it were, stolen from life itself, and the *Vicar of Wakefield* gives us a deep insight into the way the world looked to a country parson. . . . But how sparingly and in driblets do these books mete out to us the little portion of reality (*das wenige Reelle*) which they contain! And how much better a *Roman* than the best of these is almost any book of travels or collection of letters or autobiography, to one who reads them in a romantic spirit!"[25] But in Schiller, this pre-

[24] Cf. the preceding essay.

[25] From the "Brief über den Roman" in the *Gespräch über die Poesie,* 1800; *Jugendschriften,* II, 372, 374-5. It is true that the same writing contains also a dithyrambic passage, already quoted in part, in which we are told that sentimental poetry, being concerned with "ein unendliches Wesen," does not "fix its interest

occupation with *das Reelle* is not the mark of the "sentimental" but of the "natural" poet. "Natural poetry has a dependence upon experience of which the sentimental knows nothing." "Die sentimentalische Dichtung ist die Geburt der Abgezogenheit und Stille, und dazu ladet sie auch ein; die naive ist das Kind des Lebens, und in das Leben führt sie auch zurück." [26] One passage of Schiller's especially sharply manifests the contrast between his "sentimentalisch" and Schlegel's "romantisch." There are, he remarks, two ways in which poetry may have "einen unendlichen Gehalt"; and in one of these ways, even the "natural" poet may be said to aim at "infinity"—when, namely, "he represents an object *with all its limits*, when he individualizes it." What Schiller seems to mean here is that the complete representation even of a single object, with all of its concrete determinations and relations—of an object *perfectly* individualized—would be an infinite task. But not this sort of infinity, he goes on, is the task of the sentimental poet; he raises the object of his art to the infinite rather by "*removing* all its limitations, by idealizing it." Thus it is precisely the sort of "infinity" which is here exemplified for Schiller by "naive Dichtung" that is exemplified for Schlegel by Romantic poetry.

Thus it was that Schiller could classify Shakespeare as a "natural," while Schlegel classified him as a Romantic poet. The Shakespeare of the plays—and of the Shakespeare of the *Sonnets* Schiller, at least, appeared oblivious—does not unlock his heart; he does not, for the most part, represent idealized, but highly individualized, characters, "mit allen ihren Grenzen"; he does not appear to be much interested in the expression of an unattainable moral ideal; nor is he noticeably concerned about the *Veredlung* of his hearers or readers. But—as it seemed to Schlegel—he surpasses all other poets in the "uni-

---

only upon persons, events, situations and individual desires," but sees these only as symbols of a "higher and infinite love," *etc.* Schlegel, in other words, though he mainly takes the Romantic "infinite" in what I have called the realistic sense, lapses at rhetorical moments into the language more appropriate to the quasi-mystical sense. Yet even in the passage in question, he indicates that the "unendliche Wesen" that he has in mind is neither a supersensible reality nor a moral ideal; it is "die heilige Lebensfülle der bildenden Natur."

[26] *Über naïve usw.*; Schiller's *Werke*, 1847, XI, 233, 232.

versality" of his representation of life; and it is for this reason that he is the supreme representative of Romantic art.[27]

We may, finally, observe both the similarity and the contrast between "sentimentalisch" and "romantisch" by recalling the terms in which Schlegel defined the latter in the celebrated *Fragment 116* in the *Athenaeum* (1798) in which the adjective received, so to say, its first official definition. "Romantic poetry" is, first of all, a "progressive Poesie." It is "still in Becoming; indeed, this is its very essence, so that forever it can only *become*, and never *be*." In this, obviously, it resembles Schiller's "sentimental poetry." But Romantic poetry is also "Universalpoesie" — universal, be it noted, not in the sense of universality of appeal, but in the sense of totality, or all-inclusiveness of content, an all-inclusiveness which it can ever more nearly approximate but never attain. It must not only unite in itself the several forms and *genres* of poetry, but it must also "fill and cram every art-form with every sort of solid *Bildungsstoff* and animate the whole with the play of humor. It embraces everything whatsoever that is poetic, from the greatest system of art containing within itself other systems, to the sigh, the kiss, which the child breathes forth as it improvises an artless song . . . . It alone can become a mirror of the whole surrounding world, a picture of the age." And yet it also, more than any other, can express the reflection of the poet upon the objects which he represents. "It alone is infinite, because it alone is free; and it accepts this as its first law, that the freedom (*Willkühr*) of the poet shall suffer no law to be imposed upon it." "From the romantic standpoint," adds Schlegel in a later *Fragment*, "even the degenerate types of poetry — the eccentric and the monstrous — have their value as materials for and essays towards universality, if only there is really something in them, if they are original." [28]

---

[27] The notion of "subjectivity," which is included (though through different connections of ideas) both in the conception of "sentimental" and in that of "Romantic" poetry, introduces a confusing sort of cross-cleavage here, in the thought of both Schiller and Schlegel. To analyze the relation of this notion to the other elements of the two definitions, and thereby to clear up that confusion, would unduly lengthen this paper.

[28] *Fragment 139. Cf.* also, as a foreshadowing of later realism, *Fgm.* 124: "Wenn man aus Psychologie Romane schreibt . . . so ist es sehr inkonsequent

Such was the earliest aesthetic program of Romanticism. Its characteristic feature, the demand for totality in the representation of life, had both a subjective and an objective application. On the one hand, it was a demand for adequacy, and therefore for freedom, of *self*-expression on the part of the poet; hence the Romantic *étalage du Moi*. On the other hand, it was—and, with the first of the Romanticists, it was much more largely and emphatically—a demand for truth and completeness in the representation of the realities of human character and experience, in all their endless diversity; and in this aspect, the original Romantic program was the program of a genuine realism. Between these two applications of what seemed but a single idea, Schlegel does not appear to have very sharply distinguished; but there was a latent incongruity between the two which eventually became evident enough. In either of its interpretations, but especially in the second, the Romantic ideal of universality was manifestly foreign to Schiller's conception of " sentimental poetry," with its obsession with " the contrast between the real and the ideal," its lack of interest in " actual human nature," its insistence upon idealization. Nevertheless it was Schiller, as we have seen, who was chiefly, or, at all events, finally and decisively, instrumental in leading Friedrich Schlegel to adopt the Romantic ideal.[29]

---

und klein, auch die langsamste und ausführlichste Zergliederung unnatürlicher Lüste, grässlicher Marter, empörender Infamie, ekelhafter sinnlicher oder geistiger Impotenz scheuen zu wollen."

[29] For the English sequel to all this — the taking-over of these Schlegelian antitheses and aesthetic theorems by English " Romanticists," especially Coleridge and Hazlitt—see the following articles which have appeared since the above was published: W. Houghton Taylor, " ' Particular Character ': An Early Phase of a Literary Revolution," in *Publications of the Modern Language Association of America*, LX (1945), 161 ff.; and Stephen A. Larrabee, " Hazlitt's Criticism and Greek Sculpture," in *Journal of the History of Ideas*, II (1941), 77 ff.

XII. ON THE DISCRIMINATION OF ROMANTICISMS[1]

I

WE APPROACH a centenary not, perhaps, wholly undeserving of notice on the part of this learned company. It was apparently in 1824 that those respected citizens of La-Ferté-sous-Jouarre, MM. Dupuis and Cotonet, began an enterprise which was to cause them, as is recorded, "twelve years of suffering," and to end in disillusionment—the enterprise of discovering what Romanticism is, by collecting definitions and characterizations of it given by eminent authorities. I conjecture, therefore, that one of the purposes of the Committee in inviting me to speak on this subject was perhaps to promote a Dupuis and Cotonet Centennial Exhibition, in which the later varieties of definitions of Romanticism, the fruit of a hundred years' industry on the part of literary critics and professors of modern literature, might be at least in part displayed. Certainly there is no lack of material; the contemporary collector of such articles, while paying tribute to the assiduity and the sufferings of those worthy pioneers of a century ago, will chiefly feel an envious sense of the relative simplicity of their task. He will find, also, that the apparent incongruity of the senses in which the term is employed has fairly kept pace with their increase in number; and that the singular potency which the subject has from the first possessed to excite controversy and breed divisions has in no degree diminished with the lapse of years.

For if some Dupuis of to-day were to gather, first, merely a few of the more recent accounts of the origin and age of Romanticism, he would learn from M. Lassere[2] and many others that

---

[1] An address delivered at the fortieth Annual Meeting of the Modern Language Association of America, December 27, 1923; published in *PMLA*, vol. **XXXIX** (1924), 229-253. The reference in the first paragraph is to Alfred de Musset's *Lettres de Dupuis et Cotonet*, 1836. In reprinting the address a few later definitions or characterizations of "Romanticism" have been added.

[2] *Le Romantisme français* (1919), 141 and *passim*.

Rousseau was the father of it; from Mr. Russell [3] and Mr. Santayana [4] that the honor of paternity might plausibly be claimed by Immanuel Kant; from M. Seillière that its grandparents were Fénelon and Madame Guyon; [5] from Professor Babbitt that its earliest well-identified forebear was Francis Bacon; [6] from Mr. Gosse that it originated in the bosom of the Reverend Joseph Warton; [7] from the late Professor Ker that it had "its beginnings in the seventeenth-century" or a little earlier, in such books as "the *Arcadia* or the *Grand Cyrus*"; [8] from Mr. J. E. G. de Montmorency that it "was born in the eleventh century, and sprang from that sense of aspiration which runs through the Anglo-French, or rather, the Anglo-Norman Renaissance"; [9] from Professor Grierson that St. Paul's "irruption into Greek religious thought and Greek prose" was an essential example of "a romantic movement," though the "first great romantic" was Plato; [10] and from Mr. Charles Whibley that the Odyssey is romantic in its "very texture and essence," but that, with its rival, Romanticism was "born in the Garden of Eden" and that "the Serpent was the first romantic." [11] The inquirer would, at the same time, find that many of these originators of Romanticism—including both the first and last mentioned, whom, indeed, some contemporaries are unable to distinguish—figure on other lists as initiators or representatives of tendencies of precisely the contrary sort.

These differing versions of the age and lineage of Romanticism are matched by a corresponding diversity in the descriptions offered by those of our time who have given special care to the observation of it. For Professor Ker Romanticism was "the fairy way of writing," [12] and for Mr. Gosse it is inconsistent

[3] *Jour. of Philosophy*, XIX (1922), 645.
[4] *Egotism in German Philosophy*, 11-20, 54-64.
[5] *Mme Guyon et Fénelon précurseurs de Rousseau*, 1918.
[6] "Schiller and Romanticism"; *Mod. Lang. Notes*, XXXVII, 267 (1922), n. 28.
[7] *Proc. Brit. Acad.*, 1915-16, 146-7.
[8] *The Art of Poetry* (1923), 79-80.
[9] *Contemporary Review*, April, 1919, p. 473.
[10] *Classical and Romantic* (1923), 32, 31.
[11] Editor's Introduction to *Essays in Romantic Literature* by George Wyndham, (1919), p. xxxiii.
[12] *The Art of Poetry*, 79.

with " keeping to the facts "; [13] but for Mr. F. Y. Eccles [14] (following M. Pellissier) " the romantic system of ideas " is the direct source of " the realistic error," of the tendency to conceive of psychology as " the dry notation of purely physio-logical phenomena" and consequently to reduce the novel and the drama to the description of " the automaton-like gestures of *la bête humaine.*" To Professor Ker, again, " romantic " implies " reminiscence ": " the romantic schools have always depended more or less on the past." [15] Similarly Mr. Geoffrey Scott finds " its most typical form " to be " the cult of the extinct." [16] But Professor Schelling tells us that " the classic temper studies the past, the romantic temper neglects it; . . . it leads us forward and creates new precedents "; [17] while for some of the French "Romantic" critics of the 1820s and 1830s, the slogan of the movement was *il faut être de son temps.*[18] Mr. Paul Elmer More defines Romanticism as " the illusion of beholding the infinite within the stream of nature itself, instead of apart from that stream " — in short, as an apotheosis of the cosmic flux; [19] but a special student of German Romanticism cites as typical Romantic utterances Friedrich Schlegel's " alles Sichtbare hat nur die Wahrheit einer Allegorie," and Goethe's " alles Vergängliche ist nur ein Gleichnis "; [20] and for a recent German author the deepest thing in Romanticism is " eine Religion die dieses Leben hasst . . . Romantik will die gerade Verbindung des Menschlichen mit dem Überirdischen." [21] Among those for whom the word implies, *inter alia,* a social and political ideology and temper, one writer, typical of many, tells us that " Romanticism spells anarchy in every domain . . . a systematic hostility to everyone invested with any particle of social authority—husband or *pater-familias,* policeman or

---

[13] *Aspects and Impressions* (1922), 5.
[14] *La Liquidation du Romantisme* (1919), 14 f.
[15] *The Art of Poetry,* 50.
[16] *The Architecture of Humanism* (1914), 39.
[17] *P. M. L. A.,* XIII, 222.
[18] Cf. George Boas in *Journal of Aesthetics,* I (1941), 52-65.
[19] *The Drift of Romanticism* (1913), xiii, 247.
[20] Marie Joachimi, *Die Weltanschauung der Romantik* (1905), 52.
[21] Julius Bab, *Fortinbras, oder der Kampf des 19. Jahrhunderts mit dem Geiste der Romantik.*

magistrate, priest or Cabinet minister ";[22] but Professor Goetz Briefs finds "the climax of political and economic thought within the Romantic movement" in the doctrine of Adam Müller, which sought to vindicate the sanctity of established social authority embodied in the family and the state; "by an inescapable logic the Romanticist ideology was drawn into the camp of reaction."[23] From M. Seillière's most celebrated work it appears that the Romantic mind tends to be affected with an inferiority-complex, "une impression d'incomplètude, de solitude morale, et presque d'angoisse";[24] from other passages of the same writer we learn that Romanticism is the "imperialistic" mood, whether in individuals or nations—a too confident assertion of the will-to-power, arising from "the mystic feeling that one's activities have the advantages of a celestial alliance."[25] The function of the human mind which is to be regarded as peculiarly "romantic" is for some "the heart as opposed to the head,"[26] for others, "the Imagination, as contrasted with Reason and the Sense of Fact"[27]—which I take to be ways of expressing a by no means synonymous pair of psychological antitheses. Typical manifestations of the spiritual essence of Romanticism have been variously conceived to be a passion for moonlight, for red waistcoats, for Gothic churches, for futurist paintings;[28] for talking exclusively about oneself, for hero-worship, for losing oneself in an ecstatic contemplation of nature.

The offspring with which Romanticism is credited are as strangely assorted as its attributes and its ancestors. It is by different historians—sometimes by the same historians—supposed to have begotten the French Revolution and the Oxford Movement; the Return to Rome and the Return to the State of Nature; the philosophy of Hegel, the philosophy of Schopenhauer, and the philosophy of Nietzsche—than which few other

[22] G. Chatterton-Hill, Contemporary Rev. (1942), 720.
[23] Journal of the History of Ideas, II (1941), 279 ff.
[24] Le mal romantique, 1908, vii.
[25] Cf. R. Gillouin, Une nouvelle philosophie de l'histoire moderne et française, 1921, 6 ff.; Seillière, Le péril mystique, etc., 2-6.
[26] Wernaer, Romanticism and the Romantic School in Germany, p. 3.
[27] Neilson, Essentials of Poetry, 1912, ch. III.
[28] For the last mentioned, cf. Gosse in Proc. Brit. Acad., 1915-16, 151.

three philosophies more nearly exhaust the rich possibilities of philosophic disagreement; the revival of neo-Platonic mysticism in a Coleridge or an Alcott, the Emersonian transcendentalism, and scientific materialism; Wordsworth and Wilde; Newman and Huxley; the Waverley novels, the *Comédie Humaine*, and *Les Rougon-Macquart*. M. Seillière and Professor Babbitt have been especially active in tracing the progeny of Romanticism in the past century; the extraordinary number and still more extraordinary diversity of the descendants of it discovered by their researches are known to all here, and it therefore suffices to refer to their works for further examples.

All this is a mere hint, a suggestion by means of random samples, of the richness of the collection which might be brought together for our Centennial Exposition. The result is a confusion of terms, and of ideas, beside which that of a hundred years ago — mind-shaking though it was to the honest inquirers of La-Ferté-sous-Jouarre — seems pure lucidity. The word "romantic" has come to mean so many things that, by itself, it means nothing. It has ceased to perform the function of a verbal sign. When a man is asked, as I have had the honor of being asked, to discuss Romanticism, it is impossible to know what ideas or tendencies he is to talk about, when they are supposed to have flourished, or in whom they are supposed to be chiefly exemplified. Perhaps there are some who think the rich ambiguity of the word not regrettable. In 1824, as Victor Hugo then testified, there were those who preferred to leave *à ce mot de romantique un certain vague fantastique et indéfinissable qui en redouble l'horreur*, and it may be that the taste is not extinct. But for one of the philosopher's trade, at least, the situation is embarrassing and exasperating; for philosophers, in spite of a popular belief to the contrary, are persons who suffer from a morbid solicitude to know what they are talking about.

Least of all does it seem possible, while the present uncertainty concerning the nature and *locus* of Romanticism prevails, to take sides in the controversy which still goes on so briskly with respect to its merits, the character of its general influence upon art and life. To do so would be too much like consenting to sit on a jury to try a criminal not yet identified, for a series of apparently incompatible crimes, before a bench of learned judges engaged in accusing one another of being accessories to whatever mischief has been done. It is to be observed, for example, that Messrs. Lasserre, Seillière, Babbitt and More (to mention no others) are engaged in arguing that something called Romanticism is the chief cause of the spiritual evils from which the nineteenth century and our own have suffered; but that they represent at least three different opinions as to what these evils are and how they are to be remedied. M. Lasserre, identifying Romanticism with the essential spirit of the French Revolution, finds the chief cause of our woes in that movement's breach with the past, in its discarding of the ancient traditions of European civilization; and he consequently seeks the cure in a return to an older faith and an older political and social order, and in an abandonment of the optimistic fatalism generated by the idea of progress. M. Seillière, however, holds that "the spirit of the Revolution in that in which it is rational, Stoic, Cartesian, classical . . . is justified, enduring, assured of making its way in the world more and more";[29] and that, consequently, the ill name of Romanticism should be applied to the revolutionary movement only where it has deviated from its true course, in "the social mysticism, the communistic socialism of the present time." He therefore intimates that the school of opinion which M. Lasserre ably represents is itself a variety of Romanticism.[30] But it is equally certain that M. Seillière's own philosophy is one of the varieties of Romanticism defined by Mr. Babbitt and Mr. More; while Mr. Babbitt, in turn, has been declared by more than one of the critics of his last brilliant book, and would necessarily be held by M. Seillière, to set forth therein an essentially Romantic philosophy. Thus Professor Herford says of it (justly or otherwise) that its "temper is not that of a 'positivist' of any school, but of a mystic," and that "it is as foreign to Homer and Sophocles, the exemplars of true classicism if any are, as it is to Aristotle."[31]

[29] Le mal romantique, xli.

[30] "Il y a même beaucoup de romantique dans la façon dont le combattent certains traditionalistes imprudents, dont M. Lasserre paraît avoir quelquefois écouté les suggestions dangereuses" (loc. cit.).

[31] Essays and Studies by Members of the English Association, VIII (1923),

What, then, can be done to clear up, or to diminish, this confusion of terminology and of thought which has for a century been the scandal of literary history and criticism, and is still, as it would not be difficult to show, copiously productive of historical errors and of dangerously undiscriminating diagnoses of the moral and aesthetic maladies of our age? The one really radical remedy—namely, that we should all cease talking about Romanticism—is, I fear, certain not to be adopted. It would probably be equally futile to attempt to prevail upon scholars and critics to restrict their use of the term to a single and reasonably well-defined sense. Such a proposal would only be the starting-point of a new controversy. Men, and especially philologists, will doubtless go on using words as they like, however much annoyance they cause philosophers by this unchartered freedom. There are, however, two possible historical inquiries which, if carried out more thoroughly and carefully than has yet been done, would, I think, do much to rectify the present muddle, and would at the same time promote a clearer understanding of the general movement of ideas, the logical and psychological relations between the chief episodes and transitions, in modern thought and taste.

One of these measures would be somewhat analogous to the procedure of contemporary psychopathologists in the treatment of certain types of disorder. It has, we are told, been found that some mental disturbances can be cured or alleviated by making the patient explicitly aware of the genesis of his troublesome "complex," i. e., by enabling him to reconstruct those processes of association of ideas through which it was formed. Similarly in the present case, I think, it would be useful to trace the associative processes through which the word "romantic" has attained its present amazing diversity, and consequent uncertainty, of connotation and denotation; in other words, to carry out an adequate semasiological study of the term. For one of the few things certain about Romanticism is that the name of it offers one of the most complicated, fascinating, and instructive of all problems in semantics. It is, in short, a part of the task of the historian of ideas, when he applies himself

113. Cf. also the present writer's review of Mr. Babbitt's *Rousseau and Romanticism*, *Mod. Lang. Notes* (1920).

to the study of the thing or things called Romanticism, to render it, if possible, psychologically intelligible how such manifold and discrepant phenomena have all come to receive one name. Such an analysis would, I am convinced, show us a large mass of purely verbal confusions operative as actual factors in the movement of thought in the past century and a quarter; and it would, by making these confusions explicit, make it easier to avoid them.

But this inquiry would in practice, for the most part, be inseparable from a second, which is the remedy that I wish, on this occasion, especially to recommend. The first step in this second mode of treatment of the disorder is that we should learn to use the word "Romanticism" in the plural. This, of course, is already the practice of the more cautious and observant literary historians, in so far as they recognize that the "Romanticism" of one country may have little in common with that of another, and at all events ought to be defined in distinctive terms. But the discrimination of the Romanticisms which I have in mind is not solely or chiefly a division upon lines of nationality or language. What is needed is that any study of the subject should begin with a recognition of a *prima-facie* plurality of Romanticisms, of possibly quite distinct thought-complexes, a number of which may appear in one country. There is no hope of clear thinking on the part of the student of modern literature, if—as, alas! has been repeatedly done by eminent writers—he vaguely hypostatizes the term, and starts with the presumption that "Romanticism" is the heaven-appointed designation of some single real entity, or type of entities, to be found in nature. He must set out from the simple and obvious fact that there are various historic episodes or movements to which different historians of our own or other periods have, for one reason or another, given the name. There is a movement which began in Germany in the seventeen-nineties — the only one which has an indisputable title to be called Romanticism, since it invented the term for its own use. There is another movement which began pretty definitely in England in the seventeen-forties. There is a movement which began in France in 1801. There is another movement which began in France in the second decade of the century, is linked with the German movement, and took over the German name. There is the rich and incongruous collection of ideas to be found in Rousseau. There are numerous other things called Romanticism by various writers whom I cited at the outset. The fact that the same name has been given by different scholars to all of these episodes is no evidence, and scarcely even establishes a presumption, that they are identical in essentials. There may be some common denominator of them all; but if so, it has never yet been clearly exhibited, and its presence is not to be assumed *a priori*. In any case, each of these so-called Romanticisms was a highly complex and usually an exceedingly unstable intellectual compound; each, in other words, was made up of various unit-ideas linked together, for the most part, not by any indissoluble bonds of logical necessity, but by alogical associative processes, greatly facilitated and partly caused, in the case of the Romanticisms which grew up after the appellation "Romantic" was invented, by the congenital and acquired ambiguities of the word. And when certain of these Romanticisms have in truth significant elements in common, they are not necessarily the same elements in any two cases. Romanticism A may have one characteristic presupposition or impulse, X, which it shares with Romanticism B, another characteristic, Y, which it shares with Romanticism C, to which X is wholly foreign. In the case, moreover, of those movements or schools to which the label was applied in their own time, the contents under the label sometimes changed radically and rapidly. At the end of a decade or two you had the same men and the same party appellation, but profoundly different ideas. As everyone knows, this is precisely what happened in the case of what is called French Romanticism. It may or may not be true that, as M. A. Viatte has sought to show,[32] at the beginning of this process of transformation some subtle leaven was already at work which made the final outcome inevitable; the fact remains that in most of its practically significant sympathies and affiliations of a literary, ethical, political, and religious sort, the French "Romanticism" of the eighteen-thirties was the antithesis of that of the beginning of the century.

[32] *Le Catholicisme chez les Romantiques*, 1922.

But the essential of the second remedy is that each of these Romanticisms—after they are first thus roughly discriminated with respect to their representatives or their dates—should be resolved, by a more thorough and discerning analysis than is yet customary, into its elements — into the several ideas and aesthetic susceptibilities of which it is composed. Only after these fundamental thought-factors or emotive strains in it are clearly discriminated and fairly exhaustively enumerated, shall we be in a position to judge of the degree of its affinity with other complexes to which the same name has been applied, to see precisely what tacit preconceptions or controlling motives or explicit contentions were common to any two or more of them, and wherein they manifested distinct and divergent tendencies.

II

Of the needfulness of such analytic comparison and discrimination of the Romanticisms let me attempt three illustrations.

1. In an interesting lecture before the British Academy a few years since, Mr. Edmund Gosse described Joseph Warton's youthful poem, *The Enthusiast*, written in 1740, as the first clear manifestation of "the great romantic movement, such as it has enlarged and dwindled down to our day. . . . Here for the first time we find unwaveringly emphasized and repeated what was entirely new in literature, the essence of romantic hysteria. *The Enthusiast* is the earliest expression of complete revolt against the classical attitude which had been sovereign in all European literature for nearly a century. So completely is this expressed by Joseph Warton that it is extremely difficult to realize that he could not have come under the fascination of Rousseau, . . . who was not to write anything characteristic until ten years later." [33] Let us, then, compare the ideas distinctive of this poem with the conception of *romantische Poesie* formulated by Friedrich Schlegel and his fellow-Romanticists in Germany after 1796. The two have plainly certain common elements. Both are forms of revolt against the neo-classical aesthetics; both are partly inspired by an ardent admiration for

[33] " Two Pioneers of Romanticism," *Proc. Brit. Acad.*, 1915, pp. 146-8.

Shakespeare; both proclaim the creative artist's independence of "rules." It might at first appear, therefore, that these two Romanticisms, in spite of natural differences of phraseology, are identical in essence—are separate outcroppings of the same vein of metal, precious or base, according to your taste.

But a more careful scrutiny shows a contrast between them not less important—indeed, as it seems to me, more important— than their resemblance. The general theme of Joseph Warton's poem (of which, it will be remembered, the sub-title is "The Lover of Nature") is one which had been a commonplace for many centuries: the superiority of "nature" to "art." It is a theme which goes back to Rabelais's contrast of Physis and Antiphysie. It had been the inspiration of some of the most famous passages of Montaigne. It had been attacked by Shakespeare. Pope's *Essay on Man* had been full of it. The "natural" in contrast with the artificial meant, first of all, that which is not man-made; and within man's life, it was supposed to consist in those expressions of human nature which are most spontaneous, unpremeditated, untouched by reflection or design, and free from the bondage of social convention. "Ce n'est pas raison," cried Montaigne, "que l'art gagne le point d'honneur sur notre grande et puissante mère Nature. Nous avons tant rechargé la beauté et richesse de ses ouvrages par nos inventions, que nous l'avons tout à fait étouffée." There follows the *locus classicus* of primitivism in modern literature, the famous passage on the superiority of wild fruits and savage men over those that have been "bastardized" by art.[34]

Warton, then, presents this ancient theme in various aspects. He prefers to all the beauties of the gardens of Versailles

> Some pine-topt precipice
> Abrupt and shaggy.

He rhetorically inquires:

> Can Kent design like Nature?

---

[34] *Essais*, I, 31. There is a certain irony in the fact that the sort of naturalism here expressed by Montaigne was to be the basis of a Shakespeare-revival in the eighteenth century. For Shakespeare's own extreme antipathy to the passage is shown by the fact that he wrote two replies to it — a humorous one in *The Tempest*, a serious and profound one in *The Winter's Tale*.

He laments
> That luxury and pomp . . .
> Should proudly banish Nature's simple charms.

He inquires why "mistaken man" should deem it nobler
> To dwell in palaces and high-roof'd halls
> Than in God's forests, architect supreme?

All this, if I may be permitted the expression, was old stuff. The principal thing that was original and significant in the poem was that Warton boldly applied the doctrine of the superiority of "nature" over conscious art to the theory of poetry:
> What are the lays of artful Addison,
> Coldly correct, to Shakespeare's warblings wild?

That Nature herself was wild, untamed, was notorious, almost tautological; and it was Shakespeare's supposed "wildness," his non-conformity to the conventional rules, the spontaneous freedom of his imagination and his expression, that proved him Nature's true pupil.

Now this aesthetic inference had not, during the neo-classical period, ordinarily been drawn from the current assumption of the superiority of nature to art. The principle of "following nature" had in aesthetics usually been taken in another, or in more than one other, of the several dozen senses of the sacred word.[35] Yet in other provinces of thought an analogous inference had long since and repeatedly been suggested. From the first the fashion of conceiving of "nature" (in the sense in which it was antithetic to "art") as norm had made for antinomianism, in some degree or other—for a depreciation of restraint, for the ideal of "letting yourself go." There seems to be an idea current that an antinomian temper was, at some time in the eighteenth century, introduced into aesthetic theory and artistic practise by some Romanticist, and that it thence speedily spread to moral feeling and social conduct.[36] The his-

---

[35] This is not rhetorical exaggeration; more than sixty different senses or applications of the notion of "nature" can be clearly distinguished.

[36] So apparently Mr. Gosse: "When the history of the [Romantic] school comes to be written, there will be a piquancy in tracing an antinomianism down

toric sequence is precisely the opposite. It was Montaigne again
—not usually classified as a Romanticist—who wrote:

> J'ai pris bien simplement et crûment ce précepte ancien: ' que nous
> ne saurions faillir à suivre Nature' . . . Je n'ai pas corrigé, comme
> Socrate, par la force de la raison, mes complexions naturelles, je n'ai
> aucunement troublé, par art, mon inclination; je me laisse aller comme
> je suis venu; je ne combats rien.[37]

It was Pope who asked:

> Can that offend great Nature's God
> Which Nature's self inspires?

and who spoke of

> Wild Nature's vigor working at the root

as the source of the passions in which all the original and vital
energies of men are contained.

Aside from a certain heightening of the emotional tone, then,
the chief novelty of Warton's poem lay in its suggesting the
application of these ideas to a field from which they had usually
been curiously and inconsistently excluded, in its introduction
of antinomianism, of a rather mild sort, into the conception of
poetic excellence.[38] But this extension was obviously implicit
from the outset in the logic of that protean "naturalism"
which had been the most characteristic and potent force in
modern thought since the late Renaissance; it was bound to be
made by somebody sooner or later. Nor was Warton's the
first aesthetic application of the principle; it had already been
applied to an art in the theory and practice of which eighteenth-
century Englishmen were keenly interested — the art of landscape design. The first great revolt against the neo-classical
aesthetics was not in literature at all, but in gardening; the

from the blameless Warton to the hedonist essays of Oscar Wilde and the frenzied
anarchism of the futurists" (op. cit., 15).

[34] Essais, III. 12.

[38] The title of the poem and some elements of its thought and feeling —
especially its note of religious "enthusiasm" for "Nature" in the sense of
the visible universe — are akin to, and probably derivative from, Shaftesbury's
Moralists. But in Shaftesbury there is no opposition of "nature" to "art"
and no antinomian strain, either ethical or aesthetic; "decorum," "order,"
"balance," and "proportion" are among his favorite words.

second, I think, was in architectural taste; and all three were inspired by the same ideas.[39] Since, the "artful Addison" had observed, "artificial works receive a greater advantage from their resemblance of such as are natural," and since Nature is distinguished by her "rough, careless strokes," the layer-out of gardens should aim at "an artificial rudeness much more charming than that neatness and elegancy usually met with."[40] This horticultural Romanticism had been preached likewise by Sir William Temple, Pope, Horace Walpole, Batty Langley, and others, and ostensibly exemplified in the work of Kent, Brown, and Bridgman. Warton in the poem in question describes Kent as at least doing his best to imitate in his gardens the wildness of Nature:

> He, by rules unfettered, boldly scorns
> Formality and method; round and square
> Disdaining, plans irregularly great.

It was no far cry from this to the rejection of the rules in the drama, to a revulsion against the strait-laced regularity and symmetry of the heroic couplet, to a general turning from convention, formality, method, artifice, in all the arts.

There had, however, from the first been a curious duality of meaning in the antithesis of "nature" and "art"—one of the most pregnant of the long succession of confusions of ideas which make up much of the history of human thought. While the "natural" was, on the one hand, conceived as the wild and spontaneous and "irregular," it was also conceived as the simple, the naïve, the unsophisticated. No two words were more fixedly associated in the mind of the sixteenth, seventeenth, and early eighteenth centuries than "Nature" and "simple." Consequently the idea of preferring nature to custom and to art usually carried with it the suggestion of a program of simplification, of reform by elimination; in other words, it implied primitivism. The "natural" was a thing you reached by going back and by leaving out. And this association of ideas—already obvious in Montaigne, in Pope, and scores of other extollers of "Nature"—is still conspicuous in Warton's poem.

[39] Cf. the essay on "The First Gothic Revival," etc., above.
[40] Spectator, No. 144.

It was the "bards of old" who were "fair Nature's friends."
The poet envies

> The first of men, ere yet confined
> In smoky cities.

He yearns to dwell in some

> Isles of innocence from mortal view
> Deeply retired beneath a plantane's shade,
> Where Happiness and Quiet sit enthroned,
> With simple Indian swains.

For one term of the comparison, then, I limit myself, for
brevity's sake, to this poem to which Mr. Gosse has assigned
so important a place in literary history. There were, of course,
even in the writings of the elder Warton, and still more in
other phenomena frequently called "Romantic," between the
1740's and the 1790's, further elements which cannot be considered here. There is observable, for example, in what it has
become the fashion to classify as the early phases of English
Romanticism, the emergence of what may be called gothicism,
and the curious fact of its partial and temporary fusion with
naturalism. It is one of the interesting problems of the analytic
history of ideas to see just how and why naturalism and gothicism became allied in the eighteenth century in England, though
little, if at all, in France. But for the present purpose it suffices
to take *The Enthusiast* as typical, in one especially important
way, of a great deal of the so-called Romanticism before the
seventeen-nineties — a Romanticism, namely, which, whatever
further characteristics it may have had, was based upon naturalism (in the sense of the word which I have indicated) and was
associated with primitivism of some mode or degree.

2. For in this fundamental point this earlier "Romanticism"
differed essentially from that of the German aesthetic theorists
and poets who chose the term "Romantic poetry" as the most
suitable designation for their own literary ideals and program.
The latter "Romanticism" is in its very essence a denial of the
older naturalistic presuppositions, which Warton's poem had
manifested in a special and somewhat novel way. The German
movement, as I have elsewhere shown, received its immediate

and decisive impetus from Schiller's essay *On Naïve and Senti-mental Poetry*; and what it derived from that confused work was the conviction that "harmony with nature," in any sense which implied an opposition to "culture," to "art," to reflection and self-conscious effort, was neither possible nor desirable for the modern man or the modern artist. The *Frühromantiker* learned from Schiller, and partly from Herder, the idea of an art which should look back no more to the primitive than to the classical — the notions of which, incidentally, Schiller had curiously fused — for its models and ideals; which should be the appropriate expression, not of a *natürliche* but of a *künst-liche Bildung*; which, so far from desiring simplification, so far from aiming at the sort of harmony in art and life which is to be attained by the method of leaving out, should seek first fullness of content, should have for its program the adequate expression of the entire range of human experience and the entire reach of the human imagination. For man, the artificial, Friedrich Schlegel observed, *is* "natural." "Die Abstraktion ist ein künstlicher Zustand. Dies ist kein Grund gegen sie, denn es ist dem Menschen gewiss natürlich, sich dann und wann auch in künstliche Zustände zu versetzen." And again: "Eine nur im Gegensatz der Kunst und Bildung natürliche Denkart soll es gar nicht geben." To be unsophisticated, to revert to the mental state of "simple Indian swains," was the least of the ambitions of a German Romantic — though, since the unsophisticated is one type of human character, his art was not, at least in theory, indifferent even to that. The Shakespeare whom he admired was no gifted child of nature addicted to "warblings wild." Shakespeare, said A. W. Schlegel, is not "eine blindes wildlaufendes Genie"; he had "a system in his artistic practise and an astonishingly profound and deeply meditated one." The same critic seems to be consciously attacking either Joseph Warton's or Gray's famous lines about Shakespeare when he writes: "Those poets whom it is customary to represent as carefree nurslings of nature, without art and without schooling, if they produce works of genuine excellence, give evidence of exceptional cultivation (*Kultur*) of their mental powers, of practised art, of ripely pondered and just designs." The greatness of Shakespeare, in the eyes of *these*

Romantics, lay in his *Universalität*, his sophisticated insight into human nature and the many-sidedness of his portrayal of character; it was this, as Friedrich Schlegel said, that made him "wie der Mittelpunkt der romantischen Kunst." It may be added that another trait of the Romanticism found by Mr. Gosse in Joseph Warton, namely, the feeling that didactic poetry is not poetic, was also repudiated by early German Romanticism: "How," asked F. Schlegel again, "can it be said that ethics (*die Moral*) belongs merely to philosophy, when the greatest part of poetry relates to the art of living and to the knowledge of human nature?"[41]

The difference, then, I suggest, is more significant, more pregnant, than the likeness between these two Romanticisms. Between the assertion of the superiority of "nature" over conscious "art" and that of the superiority of conscious art over mere "nature"; between a way of thinking of which primitivism is of the essence and one of which the idea of perpetual self-transcendence is of the essence; between a fundamental preference for simplicity—even though a "wild" simplicity—and a fundamental preference for diversity and complexity; between the sort of ingenuous naïveté characteristic of *The Enthusiast* and the sophisticated subtlety of the conception of romantic irony: between these the antithesis is one of the most radical that modern thought and taste have to show. I don't deny anyone's right to call both these things Romanticism, if he likes; but I cannot but observe that the fashion of giving both the same name has led to a good deal of unconscious falsification of the history of ideas. The elements of the one Romanticism tend to be read into the other; the nature and profundity of the oppositions between them tend to be overlooked; and the relative importance of the different changes of preconceptions in modern thought, and of susceptibilities in modern taste, tends to be wrongly estimated. I shall not attempt to cite here what seem to me examples of such historical errors; but the sum of them is, I think, far from negligible.

Between the "Romanticism" which is but a special and

[41] Quotations in this paragraph from F. Schlegel are from *Athenaeum*, II, 1, p. 29; III, 1, p. 12; I, 2, p. 68; III, 1, p. 19. Those from A. W. Schlegel have already been cited by Marie Joachimi, *Weltanschauung der Romantik*, 179-183.

belated manifestation of the naturalism that had flourished since the Renaissance (and before it) and the "Romanticism" which began at the end of the eighteenth century in Germany (as well as that which appeared a little later in France) there is another difference not less significant. This is due to the identification of the meaning of "Romantic" in the later movement with "Christian"—and mainly with the medieval implications of that term. This was not the central idea in the original notion of "Romantic poetry" as conceived by Friedrich Schlegel. Primarily, as I have elsewhere tried to show,[42] the adjective meant for him and the entire school "das eigentümlich Moderne" in contrast with "das eigentümlich Antike." But it early occurred to him that the principal historic cause of the supposed radical differentiation of modern from classical art could lie only in the influence of Christianity. He wrote in 1796, before his own conversion to what he had already defined as the "Romantic," *i. e.,* modern, point of view:

So lächerlich und geschmacklos sich dieses Trachten nach dem Reich Gottes in der christlichen Poesie offenbaren möchte; so wird es dem Geschichtsforscher doch eine sehr merkwürdige Erscheinung, wenn er gewahr wird, dass eben dieses Streben, das absolut Vollkommene und Unendliche zu realisiren, eine unter dem unaufhörlichen Wechsel der Zeiten und bei der grössten Verschiedenheit der Völker bleibende Eigenschaft dessen ist, was man mit dem besten Rechte modern nennen darf.[43]

When, after reading Schiller's essay, Schlegel himself became a devotee of those aesthetic ideals which he had previously denounced, he wrote (1797):

Nachdem die vollendete natürliche Bildung der Alten entschieden gesunken, und ohne Rettung ausgeartet war, ward durch den Verlust der endlichen Realität und die Zerrüttung vollendeter Form ein Streben nach unendlicher Realität veranlasst, welches bald allgemeiner Ton des Zeitalters wurde.[44]

"Romantic" art thus came to mean—for one thing—an art inspired by or expressive of some idea or some ethical temper

[42] Cf. the essay on "The Meaning of Romantic," etc.
[43] Review of Herder's *Humanitätsbriefe*; in Minor, *Fr. Schlegel, 1794-1802.*
[44] Vorrede, *Die Griechen und Römer*, in Minor, *op. cit.*, I, 82.

supposed to be essential in Christianity. "Ursprung und Charakter der ganzen neuern Poesie lässt sich so leicht aus dem Christentume ableiten, dass man die romantische eben so gut die christliche nennen könnte," [45] said Richter in 1804, repeating what had by that time become a commonplace. But the nature of the essentially Christian, and therefore essentially Romantic, spirit was variously conceived. Upon one characteristic of it there was, indeed, rather general agreement among the German Romanticists: the habit of mind introduced by Christianity was distinguished by a certain insatiability; it aimed at infinite objectives and was incapable of lasting satisfaction with any goods actually reached. It became a favorite platitude to say that the Greeks and Romans set themselves limited ends to attain, were able to attain them, and were thus capable of self-satisfaction and finality; and that modern or "romantic" art differed from this most fundamentally, by reason of its Christian origin, in being, as Schiller had said, a *Kunst des Unendlichen*. "Absolute Abstraktion, Vernichtung des Jetzigen, Apotheose der Zukunft, dieser eigentlich bessern Welt!; dies ist der Kern des Geheisses des Christentums," declared Novalis. In its application to artistic practice this "apotheosis of the future" meant the ideal of endless progress, of "eine progressive Universalpoesie" in the words of Fr. Schlegel's familiar definition; it implied the demand that art shall always go on bringing new provinces of life within its domain and achieving ever fresh and original effects. But anything which was, or was supposed to be, especially characteristic of the Christian *Weltanschauung* tended to become a part of the current connotation of "Romantic," and also a part of the actual ideals of the school. Preoccupation with supersensible realities and a feeling of the illusoriness of ordinary existence was thus often held to be a distinctive trait of Romantic art, on the ground that Christianity is an otherworldly religion: "in der christlichen Ansicht," said A. W. Schlegel, "die Anschauung des Unendlichen hat das Endliche vernichtet; das Leben ist zur Schattenwelt und zur Nacht geworden." [46] Another recognized characteristic of Chris-

[45] *Vorschule der Aesthetik*, I, Programm V, § 23.
[46] *Vorlesungen über dramatische Kunst und Literatur*, 1809-11, in *Werke*, 1846, V, 16. Cf. also Novalis's *Hymnen an die Nacht*.

tianity, and therefore of the "Romantic," was ethical dualism, a conviction that there are in man's constitution two natures ceaselessly at war. The Greek ideal, in the elder Schlegel's words, was "volkommene Eintracht und Ebenmass aller Kräfte, natürliche Harmonie. Die Neueren hingegen sind zum Bewusstsein der inneren Entzweiung gekommen, welche ein solches Ideal unmöglich macht." [47] Directly related to this, it was perceived, was the "inwardness" of Christianity, its preoccupation with "the heart" as distinguished from the outward act, its tendency to introspection; and hence, as Mme de Stael and others observed, "modern" or "Romantic" art has discovered, and has for its peculiar province, the inexhaustible realm of the inner life of man:

Les anciens avaient, pour ainsi dire, une âme corporelle, dont tous les mouvements étaient forts, directs, et conséquents; il n'en est pas de même du coeur humain développé par le christianisme: les modernes ont puisé dans le repentir chrétien l'habitude de se replier continuellement sur eux-mêmes. Mais, pour manifester cette existence tout intérieure, il faut qu'une grande variété dans les faits présente sous toutes les formes les nuances infinies de ce qui se passe dans l'âme. [48]

It is one of the many paradoxes of the history of the word, and of the controversies centering about it, that several eminent literary historians and critics of our time have conceived the moral essence of Romanticism as consisting in a kind of "this-worldliness" and a negation of what one of them has termed "the Christian and classical dualism." Its most deplorable and dangerous error, in the judgment of these critics, is its deficient realization of the "civil war in the cave" of man's soul, its belief in the "natural goodness" of man. They thus define "Romanticism" in terms precisely opposite to those in which it was often defined by the writers who first called their own ideals "Romantic"; and this fashion, I cannot but think, has done a good deal to obscure the palpable and important historical fact that the one "Romanticism" which (as I have said) has an indisputable title to the name was conceived by those writers as a rediscovery and revival, for better or worse, of characteristically Christian modes of thought and

[47] Op. cit., V, 17.   [48] De l'Allemagne, Pt. II, chap. XI.

feeling, of a mystical and otherworldly type of religion, and a sense of the inner moral struggle as the distinctive fact in human experience—such as had been for a century alien to the dominant tendencies in 'polite' literature. The new movement was, almost from the first, a revolt against what was conceived to be paganism in religion and ethics as definitely as against classicism in art. The earliest important formulation of its implications for religious philosophy was Schleiermacher's famous *Reden* (1799) addressed "to the cultivated contemners of religion," a work profoundly—sometimes, indeed, morbidly —dualistic in its ethical temper. Christianity, declares Schleiermacher, is *durch und durch polemisch*; it knows no truce in the warfare of the spiritual with the natural man, it finds no end in the task of inner self-discipline.[49] And the *Reden*, it must be remembered, were (in the words of a German literary historian) "greeted by the votaries of Romanticism as a gospel."[50]

Now it is not untrue to describe the ethical tendency of the "Romanticism" which had its roots in naturalism—that is, in the assumption of the sole excellence of what in man is native, primitive, "wild," attainable without other struggle than that required for emancipation from social conventions and artificialities — as anti-dualistic and essentially non-moral. This aspect of it can be seen even in the poem of the "blameless

---

[49] Cf. *Fünfte Rede:* "Nirgends is die Religion so vollkommen idealisiert als im Christentum und durch die ursprüngliche Voraussetzung desselben; und eben damit ist immerwährendes Streiten gegen alles Wirkliche in der Religion als eine Aufgabe hingestellt, der nie völlig Genüge geleistet werden kann. Eben weil überall das Ungöttliche ist und wirkt, und weil alles Wirkliche zugleich als unheilig erscheint, ist eine unendliche Heiligkeit das Ziel des Christentums. Nie zufrieden mit dem Erlangten, sucht es auch in seinen reinsten Erzeugnissen, auch in seinen heiligsten Gefühlen noch die Spuren des Irreligiösen und der der Einheit des Ganzen entgegengesetzten und die von ihm abgewandten Tendenz alles Endlichen."

[50] Typical is the review of the book in the *Athenaeum*, II, 299: " Für mich ist das Christentum und die Art wie es eingeleitet und das, was ewig bleiben soll in ihm, gesetzt wird, mit das Grösste im ganzen Werk." Cf. also Schlegel's defense of Fichte against the charge of having "attacked religion": "Wenn das Interesse am Uebersinnlichen das Wesen der Religion ist, so ist seine ganze Lehre Religion in Form der Philosophie." There are, undeniably, also occasional manifestations of a conflicting strain in the *Frühromantiker*, especially in Novalis; but these are not the usual, dominant, innovating and characteristic things in the body of ideas of the school; they are rather vestigial structures, such as are to be found remaining in all new developments.

Warton," when he describes the life of the state of nature for which he yearns. But as a consequence of the prevalent neglect to discriminate the Romanticisms, the very movement which was the beginning of a deliberate and vigorous insurrection against the naturalistic assumptions that had been potent, and usually dominant, in modern thought for more than three centuries, is actually treated as if it were a continuation of that tendency. Thesis and antithesis have, partly through accidents of language and partly through a lack of careful observation on the part of historians of literature, been called by the same name, and consequently have frequently been assumed to be the same thing. An ideal of ceaseless striving towards goals too vast or too exacting ever to be wholly attained has been confused with a nostalgia for the untroubled, because unaspiring, indolent, and unselfconscious life of the man of nature. Thus one of the widest and deepest-reaching lines of cleavage in modern thought has been more or less effectually concealed by a word.

3. This cleavage between naturalistic and anti-naturalistic "Romanticism" crosses national lines; and it manifestly cuts, so to say, directly through the person of one great writer commonly classed among the initiators of the Romantic movement in France. The author of the *Essai sur les révolutions* and of the earlier-written parts of *Atala* may perhaps properly be called a Romantic; the author of the later-written parts of the latter work and of the *Génie du Christianisme* may perhaps properly be called a Romantic; but it is obvious that the word has, in most important respects, not merely different but antithetic senses in these two applications of it to the same person. Chateaubriand before 1799 represented in some sort the culmination of the naturalistic and primitivistic Romanticism of which Mr. Gosse sees the beginning in Joseph Warton; [51] he

[51] There are, for example, passages in the penultimate section of the *Essai sur les révolutions* which present a close parallel to some in *The Enthusiast*; e. g.: "O homme de la nature, c'est toi seul qui me fait me glorifier d'être homme! Ton coeur ne connaît point la dépendance; tu ne sais ce que de ramper dans une cour ou de caresser un tigre populaire. Que t'importent nos arts, notre luxe, nos villes? As-tu besoin de spectacle, tu te rends au temple de la nature, à la religieuse forêt . . . Mais il n'y a donc point de gouvernement, point de liberté?

had not only felt intensely but had even gratified the yearning to live " with simple Indian swains." That the Chateaubriand of 1801 represents just as clearly a revolt against this entire tendency is sufficiently evident from the repudiation of primitivism in the first preface to *Atala:*

> Je ne suis point, comme M. Rousseau, un enthousiaste des sauvages; . . . je ne crois point que la *pure nature* soit la plus belle chose du monde. Je l'ai toujours trouvée fort laide partout où j'ai eu occasion de la voir . . . Avec ce mot de nature on a tout perdu.[52]

Thus the magic word upon which the whole scheme of ideas of the earlier writing had depended is now plainly characterized as the fruitful source of error and confusion that it was. And in his views about the drama the Chateaubriand of 1801 was opposed *both* to the movement represented by *The Enthusiast* and to the German Romanticism of his own time. Shakespeare was (though mainly, as we have seen, for differing reasons) the idol of both; but Chateaubriand in his *Essai sur la littérature anglaise*[53] writes of Shakespeare in the vein, and partly in the words, of Voltaire and Pope. In point of natural genius, he grants, the English dramatist was without a peer in his own age, and perhaps in any age: " je ne sais si jamais homme a jeté des regards plus profonds sur la nature humaine." But Shakespeare knew almost nothing of the requirements of the drama as an art:

> Il faut se persuader d'abord qu' écrire est un art; que cet art a nécessairement ses genres, et que chaque genre a ses règles. Et qu'on ne dise pas que les genres et les règles sont arbitraires; ils sont nés de la nature même; l'art a seulement séparé ce que la nature a confondu . . . On peut dire que Racine, dans toute l'excellence de son art, est plus naturel que Shakespeare.

Chateaubriand here, to be sure, still finds the standard of art in " nature "; but it is " nature " in the sense of the neo-classical

De liberté? si: une délicieuse, une céleste, celle de la nature. Et quelle est-elle, cette liberté? . . . Qu'on vienne passer une nuit avec moi chez les sauvages du Canada, peut-être alors parviendrai-je à donner quelque idée de cette espèce de liberté."

[52] On the two strains in *Atala,* cf. Chinard, *L'Exotisme américain dans l'oeuvre de Chateaubriand,* 1918, ch. ix.

[53] The section on Shakespeare was published in April, 1801 (*Mélanges politiques et littéraires,* 1854, pp. 390 ff.).

critics, a sense in which it is not opposed, but equivalent, to an art that rigorously conforms to fixed rules. And the "great literary paradox of the partisans of Shakespeare," he observes, is that their arguments imply that "there are *no* rules of the drama," which is equivalent to asserting "that an art is not an art." Voltaire rightly felt that "by banishing all rules and returning to *pure nature*, nothing was easier than to equal the *chefs-d'oeuvre* of the English stage"; and he was well advised in recanting his earlier too enthusiastic utterances about Shakespeare, since he saw that "en relevant les beautés des barbares, il avait séduit des hommes qui, comme lui, ne sauraient séparer l'alliage de l'or." Chateaubriand regrets that "the *Cato* of Addison is no longer played" and that consequently "on ne se délasse au théâtre anglais des monstruosités de Shakespeare que par les horreurs d'Otway." "Comment," he exclaims, "ne pas gémir de voir une nation éclairée, et qui compte parmi ses critiques les Pope et les Addison, de la voir s'extasier sur le portrait de l'apothicaire dans *Roméo et Juliette*. C'est le burlesque le plus hideux et le plus dégoûtant." The entire passage might almost have been written with Warton's poem in mind, so completely and methodically does this later "Romanticist" controvert the aesthetic principles and deride the enthusiasm of the English "Romanticist" of 1740. It is worth noting, also, that Chateaubriand at this time thinks almost as ill of Gothic architecture as of Shakespeare and of *la pure nature:*

> Une beauté dans Shakespeare n'excuse pas ses innombrables défauts: un monument gothique peut plaire par son obscurité et la difformité même de ses proportions, mais personne ne songe á bâtir un palais sur son modèle.[54]

We have, then, observed and compared—very far from exhaustively, of course, yet in some of their most fundamental and determinative ideas — three "Romanticisms." In the first and second we have found certain common elements, but still more significant oppositions; in the second and third we have found certain other common elements, but likewise significant

---

[54] It is somewhat difficult to reconcile this with the eloquent passage on the Gothic church in the *Génie du Christianisme* (V, Ch. 8); yet even there, while ascribing to the Gothic style "une beauté qui lui est particulière," Chateaubriand also refers to its "proportions barbares."

oppositions. But between the first and third the common elements are very scanty; such as there are, it could, I think, be shown, are not the same as those subsisting between either the first and second or the second and third; and in their ethical preconceptions and implications and the crucial articles of their literary creeds, the opposition between them is almost absolute.

All three of these historic episodes, it is true, are far more complex than I have time to show. I am attempting only to illustrate the nature of a certain procedure in the study of what is called Romanticism, to suggest its importance, and to present one or two specific results of the use of it. A complete analysis would qualify, without invalidating, these results, in several ways. It would (for one thing) bring out certain important connections between the revolt against the neo-classical aesthetics (common to two of the episodes mentioned) and other aspects of eighteenth-century thought. It would, again, exhibit fully certain *internal* oppositions in at least two of the Romanticisms considered. For example, in German Romanticism between 1797 and 1800 there grew up, and mainly from a single root, *both* an "apotheosis of the future" and a tendency to retrospection — a retrospection directed, not, indeed, towards classical antiquity or towards the primitive, but towards the medieval. A belief in progress and a spirit of reaction were, paradoxically, joint offspring of the same idea, and were nurtured for a time in the same minds. But it is just these internal incongruities which make it most of all evident, as it seems to me, that any attempt at a *general* appraisal even of a single chronologically determinate Romanticism — still more, of "Romanticism" as a whole—is a fatuity. When a Romanticism has been analyzed into the distinct "strains" or ideas which compose it, the true philosophic affinities and the eventual practical influence in life and art of these several strains will usually be found to be exceedingly diverse and often conflicting. It will, no doubt, remain abstractly possible to raise the question whether the preponderant effect, moral or aesthetic, of one or another large movement which has been called by the name was good or bad. But that ambitious inquiry cannot even be legitimately begun until a prior task of analysis and detailed comparison—of the sort that I have attempted here to indicate

— has been accomplished. And when this has been done, I doubt whether the larger question will seem to have much importance or meaning. What will then appear historically significant and philosophically instructive will be the way in which *each* of these distinguishable strains has worked itself out, what its elective affinities for other ideas, and its historic consequences, have shown themselves to be. The categories which it has become customary to use in distinguishing and classifying "movements" in literature or philosophy and in describing the nature of the significant transitions which have taken place in taste and in opinion, are far too rough, crude, undiscriminating — and none of them so hopelessly so as the category "Romantic." It is not any large *complexes* of ideas, such as that term has almost always been employed to designate, but rather certain simpler, diversely combinable, intellectual and emotional components of such complexes, that are the true elemental and dynamic factors in the history of thought and of art; and it is with the genesis, the vicissitudes, the manifold and often dramatic interactions of these, that it is the task of the historian of ideas in literature to become acquainted.

XIII. COLERIDGE AND KANT'S TWO WORLDS[1]

THE *LIAISON* between literary and philosophical studies, upon the need for which the writer of this paper, among others, has elsewhere dilated, is, no doubt, regarded by some students of literature and its history as a *liaison dangereuse*. But in the case of Coleridge, at least, it is patently inevitable. Coleridge's metaphysical speculations were, on the whole, the most characteristic manifestation of his mind, his persistently recurrent preoccupation, and often the tacit premises in what he says when he is not apparently talking metaphysics. They were, no doubt—precisely because they were so deeply rooted in the man himself — usually the expression of needs of the emotions and of the imagination arising out of his native temperament and of its reactions upon his personal experiences. But it is only through these expressions that many of the underlying affective factors in his personality and his literary activity can be fully understood. To *know* Coleridge as man or as writer it is necessary to understand (if possible) the nature and interrelations of those philosophic ideas — abstract, often confused, usually sketchily expressed in any single passage, frequently conflicting with one another—which nevertheless were to him among the most vital things in his existence.

Nearly all of his final philosophy, as is evident to any reader of it, was related to, and could be subsumed under, that distinction between two methods of thought—or so-called "faculties" of knowledge—the Reason and the Understanding, which, in the form in which he held it, he had learned partly from Kant but more from Jacobi and Schelling. The recognition of the superiority of the former faculty as a source of philosophical insight carried with it for him many and very diverse consequences; but the most important use to which the distinction could be put was, in his view, that of vindicating philosophically man's moral freedom and accountability, and consequently the

[1] First published in *ELH, A Journal of English Literary History,* VII, 1940.

reality of genuinely moral evil—evil for which the individual himself is absolutely and alone responsible. That the abandonment of necessitarianism was the turning-point in his mental history has been often pointed out by others. In the *Confessio fidei* (1816)—of which the first part contains what Coleridge calls "the table of natural religion, i. e., the religion of all finite rational beings"—the first article is:

I believe that I am a free agent, inasmuch as, and so far as, I have a will, which renders me justly responsible for my actions, omissive as well as commissive.[2]

In *Aids to Reflection* (1825) it is above all because the Reason justifies the belief in human freedom that he assures the "youthful readers" of that work that

The main chance of their reflecting aright, and of their attaining to a contemplation of spiritual truths at all, rests on their insight into the nature of this disparity,[3]

i. e., between Understanding and Reason. I shall not multiply familiar quotations; it is impossible to read Coleridge's more connected expositions of his moral and religious philosophy without recognizing his engrossing concern to establish the freedom of the will. The purpose of this paper is to inquire into the precise nature and source of Coleridge's ideas on this matter, and to consider whether it was, in fact, "freedom" or its opposite that his reasonings, if accepted, established. It is this part of his thought which seems to me to have been least adequately expounded and insufficiently emphasized in the three most recent attempts at a comprehensive account of his philosophy and of its relation to Kant's.[4]

It has been supposed by some interpreters of Coleridge that his conversion from the necessitarianism which he had accepted under the influence of Hartley was due to (or found its ration-

---

[2] *Works*, ed. Shedd, 5 (1884), 15.

[3] *Ibid.*, 1, 246; for the argument as a whole, cf. *id.*,, pp. 152, 154, 232, 267, 271-275.

[4] Muirhead, *Coleridge as Philosopher*, 1930; R. Wellek, *Immanuel Kant in England*, 1931; E. Winkelmann, *Coleridge und die kantische Philosophie*, 1933. Lawrence Hanson's admirable *Life* of Coleridge (Vol. I) has not reached the period of the poet's final conversion from necessitarianism.

alization in) the arguments by which Kant in the *Kritik der reinen Vernunft* sought to show that the mind is "active" in the determination of the character of its own experience, and not merely a passive *tabula rasa* upon which sensations coming from without—and coming from a material world itself subject to mechanical laws—write their impressions. Three questions are to be distinguished here. (1) Is there in fact, in the Kantian thesis of the so-called "activity of the mind," any logical implication of the "freedom of the will"? The answer is that there obviously is not. The Kantian theory of the way in which our experience comes to be what in fact it is, is that two factors are combined in it: (a) a "manifold of sense," consisting of the diverse qualitative elements of our perceptual content — color, sound, and the like—in the reception of which the mind is wholly passive, and (b) the "forms" — time, space, and the categories — imposed upon this otherwise amorphous material by virtue of the fact that the mind has a constitution of its own, a set of frames or pigeon-holes into which the data of sense must be fitted in order that we may have anything that can properly be called "experience" at all. In so far as the fitting of the sensory material into these frames may be described as an act of the mind, "activity" may, in a sense, be attributed to that organ; but it is an "activity" without freedom. The forms are invariant for all minds, in accordance with the supposed universal and unalterable constitution of the Understanding as such. (2) Did Kant himself, nevertheless, regard the doctrine of the "activity of mind," in this epistemological sense, as implying the freedom of the will? Again the obvious answer is in the negative. What, in the constructive part of the *Kritik der reinen Vernunft*, he was chiefly concerned to show was that all the temporal events of our conscious life are completely predetermined. So far from regarding the sensationalist's assumption of the passivity of the mind as too deterministic, his objection to it was that it was not deterministic enough. If the theorems of mathematics and the laws of physics are merely statements about the habits of a world wholly independent of the mind, we have, Kant felt, no assurance that that alien world's habits are uniform and dependable; in technical terms, we could in that case make no "synthetic judgments *a priori*," could never generalize and predict with confidence. But if we can know how the mind, as the subject of experience, is itself constituted, we can know in advance (Kant assumed) that any experiences which we can ever have will conform to that constitution, will be subject to certain antecedently formulable general rules of concomitance and succession. And this necessity applies not only to the sequences of our sensations but also to our motives. "It matters not that these are internal, . . . that they have a psychological and not a mechanical causality, *i. e.*, that they produce actions by means of ideas and not by bodily movements; they are still *determining principles* of the causality of a being whose existence is determinable in time and consequently are subject to necessitating conditions in past time, which, therefore, when the subject has to act, *are no longer in his power*." [5] Thus the effect of the Kantian arguments for the "activity of the mind" should have been to confirm Coleridge in his necessitarianism—by providing him with a new and better proof of it than could be got from Hartley or Priestley. (3) Did Coleridge himself, however, (erroneously) suppose that the Kantian doctrine of "the activity of the mind" in giving form to its own experience *did* somehow imply indeterminism? The belief that he did appears to rest mainly upon two of his letters to Thomas Poole, of March, 1801. The first of these has been regarded by most of Coleridge's biographers as marking the point of his intellectual conversion from Hartleian necessitarianism—though not, doubtless, of his earliest emotional revulsion against it. The passage therefore demands somewhat careful scrutiny.

Coleridge begins by saying that the interval since his last letter to Poole "has been filled up in the most intense study"; and what follows is obviously a summary report of the results of that study. The letter concludes with the expression of an intention (one of his innumerable unrealized projects) to write and publish forthwith a work which will "prove that I have not formed an opinion without an attentive perusal of the works of my predecessors, from Aristotle to Kant." By this time, then, Coleridge evidently believed himself to have completed a sufficiently "attentive perusal" of Kant to be

[5] *Kr. d. pr. V.*, A, 172-3; italics in original.

qualified to expound the essentials of his doctrine; and it is a probable inference that this perusal had been at least a part, and the culminating part, of the "intense study" to which Coleridge refers. What, then, was the briefly indicated outcome of that study? "If I do not greatly deceive myself," Coleridge writes, "I have not only (a) *completely extricated the notions of time and space*, but have (b) overthrown the doctrine of association, as taught by Hartley, and with it all the irreligious metaphysics of modern infidels—especially (c) the doctrine of necessity."[6] Now (a) what did Coleridge mean by "extricating the notions of time and space?" The answer is not certain; but he must have meant one or the other of two things. *i.* The reference may have been to the Kantian separation of time and space from the properties of objective reality; the words sound, indeed, rather like a syncopated echo of a phrase of Kant's own, in concluding the exposition of his argument for "freedom": *Von so grosser Wichtigkeit ist . . . die Absonderung der Zeit (so wie des Raums) von der Existenz der Dinge an sich selbst.*[7] This was the essence of the supposed Kantian refutation of necessitarianism, to which we shall return. *ii.* It is, however, perhaps more probable that Coleridge meant "mutually extricated," *i. e.*, that he had completely distinguished the notions of time and space from one another. So construed, the point of the sentence is to be gathered from a passage of *Biographia Literaria* in which he discriminates "time *per se* . . . from our *notion* of time; for this is always blended with the idea of space, which, as the *contrary* of time, is therefore its measure."[8] This distinction, then, which sounds like an anticipation of Bergson but is in fact probably an echo of Schelling, may have been the first of the metaphysical discoveries which Coleridge believed himself to have made in the spring of 1801. The complete despatializing of "time *per se*" presumably implied that it is not "extended," that the "moments" of it are not, as are the points or regions of space, mutually external and exclusive, but rather compresent or inter-

[6] *Letters* (1895 ed.), 1. 348; italics in original. The letters in parentheses have been added for convenience in reference.
[7] *Kritik der pr. V.*, A, 184.
[8] *Biogr. Lit.*, ed. Shawcross, 1. 187.

penetrating. And this, in turn, is fairly evidently connected (though Coleridge himself characteristically does not make the connection explicit) with the idea of the true "self" of the individual as simultaneously apprehending or possessing all the experiences which *seem* separated as past and present; if it were not for the material body, Coleridge tells us, it is "probable" that "every human soul" would "have the collective experience of its whole past existence . . . Yea, in the very nature of a living spirit, it may be more possible that heaven and earth should pass away, than that a single act, a single thought, should be loosened or lost from that living chain of causes, to all whose links, conscious or unconscious, the free will, our only absolute *self*, is co-extensive and co-present." [9] Here — though in a way which thus far remains obscure, — "the free will" is identified with a self somehow transcending time (in the ordinary, spatialized notion of time). Whichever of these two interpretations of Coleridge's "extrication of the notions of space and time" be the right one, in neither case is the doctrine of freedom based upon, or confused with, the Kantian thesis of the "activity" of the Understanding in giving *a priori* form to its perceptual content.

But (b) the "doctrine of association" might, nevertheless, be naturally held by one who, like Coleridge, had formerly accepted it, to have been definitely "overthrown" by Kant's first *Critique*; for the thesis of *a priori* forms of perception and thought, if established, invalidated the supposed explanation of all thought-processes by quasi-mechanical, empirical associations of ideas. Did this, however, entail (c)—the overthrow of the "doctrine of necessity"? Coleridge's language ("with it") doubtless seems to suggest that he thought it did; and there *was* some logical connection between the two, of which Coleridge may well have been thinking. In so far as associationism implied determinism, a refutation of the former removed one of the *premises* of the latter—for a former associationist, the principal premise. But the fact that the particular Kantian reasoning by which associationism was "overthrown" was as deterministic in its implications as the Hartleian doctrine itself

[9] *Op. cit.*, 80. How much of Bergson's philosophy, especially of *Matière et Mémoire*, is implicit here, need not be pointed out.

can scarcely have been unknown to Coleridge at any time after he had gained even a superficial acquaintance with Kant; in many later passages he clearly recognized the fact and insisted upon it. It is, then, probable that it was the Kantian exclusion of space and time (at least of "spatialized" time) from the real, or non-phenomenal, world, that was the logical instrument of Coleridge's final and complete conversion from necessitarianism; and it is, we shall see, certain that, in his published writings, it was this that provided the usual philosophical basis of his own doctrine of freedom and of his most cherished religious and moral convictions.[10]

Before showing this, I digress to consider a supposed evidence of the influence of Kant upon Coleridge's poetry in the same period—namely, in "Dejection, an Ode," of which the first of several versions was published in 1802.[11] This poem, Professor Gingerich has said, "gives the fullest expression to be found in [Coleridge's] poetry of the transcendental principle." The generalization expressed in the lines

> O Lady! we receive but what we give,
> And in our life alone does Nature live . . .

this "is as radical transcendentalism as some of the poet's earlier conceptions were radical necessitarianism. The mind now is not an automaton, but an original creative force; nature becomes a mirror, not a mere mechanical instrument, in which man's mind can reflect itself."[12] Similarly, Frl. Winkelmann

---

[10] Shawcross in his edition of the Biographia Literaria (Introd., xxx), denies that "Coleridge's final abandonment of Hartley's system" is to be "attributed to the influence of Kant," and even thinks that "this letter forbids such a conclusion." This view, for reasons indicated in the text, and others, appears to me unconvincing. In the other letter usually cited in this connection (March 23, 1801, in Letters, 1. 352), Coleridge argues for the doctrine of the creative activity of the mind, and declares that "there is ground for suspicion that any system built on the passiveness of the mind must be false." But this is not connected with the issue concerning the freedom of the will; and, as already shown, if the reference is to Kant's disproof of "the passiveness of the mind" in the first Critique, there is no good reason to suppose that Coleridge so grossly misunderstood Kant as to find in that reasoning an argument for such freedom.

[11] Into the differences between these versions it is not necessary, for the purpose of this paper, to enter. They are fully dealt with by E. de Selincourt, Coleridge's 'Dejection,'" Essays and Studies by Members of the English Association, 22 (1936), where the text of the original ms. may be found.

[12] Essays in the Romantic Poets, 45-6.

declares that it is in these lines that there first appears quite clearly "*die kritisch-idealistische Geisteshaltung seiner ' philosophischen' Epoche*"; i. e., they too are expressions of the doctrine of the "activity of mind" in shaping its own experience; and another writer refers to the poem as "ces vers que l'on peut considérer comme une interprétation métaphysique de l'apriorisme kantien."[13] This reading of Kantian epistemology and metaphysics into the Ode seems to me to rest upon a pure confusion of ideas. Coleridge is not expressing the thesis of 'transcendental' idealism that the mind gives form to the world of óbjects that it perceives; he is expressing, out of a painful personal experience, the psychological fact that the power of natural beauty to give us pleasure is conditioned by our subjective states. What we must give to nature in order to receive it back is the aesthetic transfiguration:

> A light, a glory, a fair luminous cloud
> Enveloping the earth.

We must, in short, bring "joy" to the contemplation of the external world in order to receive joy from it; for

> Joy is the sweet voice, Joy the luminous cloud—
> We in ourselves rejoice!
> And thence flows all that charms or ear or sight . . .

Without this inner glow which we project into nature, it remains an "inanimate cold world." But this "beautiful and beauty-making power" the poet finds that he cannot command at will. In a mood of deep depression — arising, as we now know, in part from ill health and the effects of opiates taken to relieve it, in part from domestic unhappiness, in part from a feeling of moral weakness — he discovers that the delight he once found in the sunset, the stars, the crescent moon, is gone.

> I see them all, so excellently fair,
> I see, not feel, how beautiful they are.

This inability to respond emotionally to the spectacle of nature was, obviously, not the consequence of a reading of the *Kritik*

---

[13] B. Munteano, review of Wellek's *Kant in England*, in *Rev. de litt. comparée*, 13 (1933). 562; cf. J. W. Beach, *The Concept of Nature* . . . , p. 123.

der reinen Vernunft; the generalization which Coleridge bases upon this experience was not to be found in that work, which has nothing to say about the fact of empirical psychology that is dwelt upon in the poem; "joy" was *not* one of the *a priori* categories of Kant; and there is not even a formal parallel between Coleridge's psychological observation and Kant's metaphysical theorem, since "the mind" which Kant makes the source of the *a priori* percepts (space and time) and the categories is the generic mind, identical in all men and unmodified by circumstances, while Coleridge is insisting upon the *differences* between the aesthetic reactions of individual minds — and specifically, of his own mind (at the moment) and Wordsworth's—and even of the same mind in different moods.

There is in the Ode, it is true, the poetic intimation of an aesthetic theory; and this is in accord with the Kantian aesthetics in so far as it admits that there may be an intellectual recognition that an object is abstractly "beautiful," without emotion: "I see, not feel, how beautiful they are." But Kant had scornfully (and characteristically) declared that any "taste that requires an added element of *emotion* and *charm* for its delight, not to speak of adopting this as the measure of its approval, has not yet emerged from barbarism"; [14] whereas the burden of Coleridge's poem is the emptiness of this unemotionalized judgment, the indispensability, for any genuine aesthetic experience, of the non-intellectual and non-universal element which Kant had so loftily dismissed. There is also, in the original version of the poem, a delicate, perhaps a scarcely intended, hint of a criticism of Wordsworth, in the guise of a compliment — the suggestion that that "simple spirit," more serene and equable in temperament than Coleridge, and more fortunate in the circumstances of his life, "rais'd from anxious dread and busy care," was not wholly aware that he gave *to* nature the "life" and "joy" that he found in it, and that his power to do so was due to his temperament and circumstances. [15]

[14] *Kritik der Urteilskraft*, 223; Meredith tr., 64-65. The relation to the Kantian aesthetic doctrine of Coleridge's *Principles of Genial Criticism* (1814) and other later writings on the subject, there is not here space to consider.

[15] "That this contrast with Wordsworth was the root idea of 'Dejection,'" writes de Selincourt (*op. cit.*, p. 15), "becomes doubly clear when we relate the

This has been a divagation from my principal theme, due to a feeling that it is worth while to make an attempt—probably futile—to prevent certain current misreadings of "Dejection" from becoming stock annotations in future textbooks. It is more pertinent to the present subject to point out that, if that poem has any relevance to the question of the freedom of the will, it is not as a vindication of freedom. For what it records is the powerlessness of the poet's will to control even his moods. He would recapture his accustomed joy in nature, he would feel as Wordsworth feels, but he cannot; and his inability to alter his inner state is caused by external circumstances not of his own choice. It should be added, however, that, as artist, he finds a certain triumph in defeat; for he is able to derive, and to impart, aesthetic pleasure from the very emotion aroused by his inability to experience aesthetic pleasure—or at all events, from the poetic utterance of that emotion. The Ode is a paradox among poems in that it not merely—like many other poems—makes melancholy enjoyable, but achieves beauty by the description of the loss of the feeling for beauty. If Coleridge himself had considered this aspect of his poem, he would have gained from it a further pleasure; for he would doubtless have seen in it a welcome example of the "reconciliation of opposites," another striking illustration of the truth of the proverb he loved best: "Extremes meet."

Let us return to the examination of the actual Kantian source of Coleridge's ideas about the moral freedom of the individual. Kant's doctrine on the subject is, of course, familiar to all philosophical readers; but for the purposes of this paper it is necessary to summarize it briefly. It was connected with a characteristic of Kant's philosophy which is not always sufficiently recognized. Kant, not less than Plato, was a philosopher who believed in two worlds, or realms of being, corresponding to the two "faculties" of knowledge, the Understanding and the

facts of Coleridge's life . . . with those of Wordsworth's during the same period." Wordsworth, however, was not unmindful of the truth expressed in Coleridge's poem; e. g., in the familiar lines of *Yarrow Revisited* (1834):

> Yea, what were mighty Nature's self?
> Her features, could they win us,
> Unhelped by the poetic voice
> That hourly speaks within us?

Reason. There is "this" world, the world of existents and events in time and space, and another, a "supersensible" or "noumenal" or "intelligible" world, consisting of entities which are neither in time nor in space, for which there is no 'before' or 'after' and no 'here' or 'there.' But the realities belonging to this other world of Kant's, at least the ones in which he was chiefly interested, were not Platonic Ideas — hypostatized universals; they were supratemporal individuals, and the class of them pertinent to our subject were selves or egos. The human individual belongs to both orders; he has an "empirical" and a "noumenal" ego. The empirical ego is the concrete personality, the self that consists in or experiences the totality of sensations, thoughts, feelings, desires, impulses, that vary from moment to moment; and this ego, being in time and subject to change, is subject also to the complete causal determination which governs all changes in time. In short, the empirical ego is a part of "nature," a "phenomenon" (in the sense of that term in which it is the antithesis of "noumenon"); [16] it is an object of the Understanding, and must conform to the laws of the Understanding, which exclude freedom. In Kant's own words:

If we would attribute freedom to a being whose existence is determined in time, we cannot except him from the law of necessity as to all events in his existence, and consequently as to his actions also; for that would be to hand him over to blind chance. . . . It follows that if this were the mode in which we had also to conceive the *existence of these things in themselves*, freedom would have to be rejected as a vain and impossible conception.[17]

But the Practical Reason, *i. e.*, the moral consciousness, seemed to Kant, as to Coleridge, not merely to demand but logically to imply "freedom"; [18] without it, he declares, "no moral law

[16] A definition of the distinction of *phenomenon* and *noumenon* by Coleridge occurs in the British Museum *ms.*, Egerton fol. pp. 96-97 printed by Winkelmann, *op. cit.*, pp. 181 f. It is, however, somewhat inadequate as an explication of either Kant's or Coleridge's actual use of the term.

[17] *Kr. d. pr. V*, A, 170. Cf. the whole passage, *ibid.*, 167-185; in Abbott's English translation (*Kant's Theory of Ethics*, 1889), 187-197.

[18] It is often forgotten that Kant gave to the belief in freedom a different and superior logical status to that assigned to the "postulates" of God and immor-

and no moral imputation are possible." Freedom, then, must
be "saved"; and "no other way remains to do so but to attribute it" to the noumenal ego. It is true that Kant speaks of
the two egos as "the same being"; and if they were really
conceived by him as the same, his double doctrine would also
be an expressly self-contradictory doctrine. But two subjects
of discourse are not — and, properly speaking, are not conceived as — "the same" when defined by mutually exclusive
attributes; and a self which is in time and subject to change is
obviously not defined in the same terms as a self to which all
temporal predicates are inapplicable, and which is therefore
incapable of change. There must, it is also true, be—for Kant's
purposes — a connection between them; his two worlds, like
Plato's, must after all be somehow linked together. How Kant
conceives them to be connected we shall presently see; for the
moment it suffices to recognize that the freedom which he
asserts is that of a different *kind* of being from the self which
is not free, and that it is precisely for this reason that the joint
assertion of freedom and necessity is, in Kant's words, only an
"apparent contradiction."

It is in these passages of Kant, then, that we may recognize
the probable means—or at all events, one of the means—of
Coleridge's conversion—or his justification of his conversion—
from his earlier deterministic, pantheistic and optimistic views
(expressed best in the poems *Religious Musings* and *The
Destiny of Nations*) to his final creed. The most important
thing—by Coleridge's own standards of importance, which are
not necessarily those of the historian of nineteenth-century
thought—which he gained from his acquaintance with German
philosophy, was a feeling—or the confirmation of a feeling to
which he was already predisposed—of the moral indispensability of the belief in individual freedom, and—what was to

tality; cf. *Kr. d. Urt.*, A, 431-432: The possible objects of belief (*Fürwahr-
halten*) are divisible into three classes: matters of opinion (*Meinungssachen*),
matters of fact (*Thatsachen*), and matters of faith (*Glaubenssachen*). The Ideas
of God and immortality belong to the third class; but "it is very noteworthy
that *one* of the Ideas of the Reason is to be found among the matters of fact ...,
namely, the Idea of Freedom"; for this, "through the practical laws of the Pure
Reason, can be manifested in actual deeds" — and therefore, in experience. It
must, however, be added that — as the discerning reader will note — this last is
inconsistent with other parts of Kant's doctrine.

him equally indispensable—a means of logically justifying that belief, this means consisting in the Kantian scheme of the two worlds, and of man as a being belonging to both. It is true that more than one conception, explicit or implicit, of what "freedom" consists in may be discerned in the vast range of Coleridge's writings; on this, as on most philosophical questions, no single, clear-cut, and invariant way of thinking is to be found in him. But the source of the main and most persistent strain in his reflection on this, to him, all-important issue is unmistakable. The problem of the freedom of the will, he observes (in a relatively late writing) was not clearly understood by "Luther, Erasmus or Saavedra." In fact, "till the appearance of Kant's *Kritiques* [sic] of the pure and of the practical reason, the problem had never been accurately or adequately stated, much less solved." [19] The nature of this solution, as Coleridge understood it, is most fully expressed in several unfortunately separated passages in *Aids to Reflection*, which are here brought together:

Nature is the term in which we comprehend all things that are representable in the forms of Time and Space, and subjected to the relations of Cause and Effect; and the cause of the existence of which, therefore, is to be sought for perpetually in something antecedent. . . . It follows, therefore, that whatever originates its own acts, or in any sense contains in itself the cause of its own state, must be *spiritual*, and consequently *supernatural*; yet not on that account necessarily *miraculous*. And such must the responsible Will in us be, if it is to be at all. . . . No natural thing or act can be called originant. . . . The moment we assume an origin in nature, a true Beginning, and actual First—that moment we rise above nature. . . . [But] a moral evil is an evil that has its origin in the Will. . . . [To conceive of such evil as possible], let the evil be supposed such as to imply the impossibility of an individual's referring to any particular time at which it might be conceived to have commenced. . . . Let it be supposed, in short, that the subject stands in no relation whatever to Time, can neither be called in Time, nor out of Time; but that all relations of Time are alien . . . and heterogeneous in this question.[20]

[19] *Works*, 5. 280-1.
[20] *Works*, 1. 263, 273, 286-7; cf. *id.*, 265: "All the sophistry of the Predestinarians rests on the false notion of eternity as a sort of time antecedent to time. It is timeless, present with and in all times."

And again:

I still find myself dissatisfied with the argument against Freedom derived from the influence of motives, *Vorstellungen*, etc., . . . All that
we want to prove is the possibility of Free Will, or, what is really the
same, a Will. Now this Kant had unanswerably proved by showing
the distinction between *phenomena* and *noumena*, and by demonstrating
that Time and Space are relevant to the former only . . . and irrelevant
to the latter, to which class the Will must belong.

The "Will" here is—or belongs to—the noumenal ego; the
empirical ego which acts in time is not—or has not—a Will,
precisely because, as Coleridge holds, in full agreement with
Kant, it is in no concrete choice or act ever free, but completely
predetermined. It follows from this that Coleridge cannot be
said ever to have abandoned the form of necessitarianism which
he held in his Hartleian period; for that related solely to nature
and to man's temporal existence. Coleridge merely supplemented this determinism with respect to the *homo phenomenon*
by finding (as he thought) another kind of freedom in another
kind of world.

It should perhaps be added that in *Biographia Literaria*
(1817) the freedom or "activity" which Coleridge defends (in
chapters 5-8) against the Hartleian associationism is *not* the
Kantian kind of freedom; it is a property not of the noumenal
but of the phenomenal ego. What Coleridge here is chiefly
concerned to show, in his long meandering approach to his
doctrine about the poetic Imagination, is that "the will, the
reason, the judgment, and the understanding," and also "the
affections and the passions," are "determining causes of asso
ciation," and not, as Hartley's theory would make them, "its
creatures and among its mechanical effects." Upon that theory
"our whole life would be divided between the despotism of
outward impressions, and that of senseless and passive memory."
It is, thus, implied by the Hartleian system that "we only fancy
that we act from rational resolves, or prudent motives, or from
impulses of anger, love or generosity," while in reality all our
acts are determined by past involuntary conjunctions of sensations, themselves determined by merely mechanical laws of the
motion of material particles. But Coleridge finds it to be a

plain fact of experience that both emotive impulses and (what is most of all important) rational reflection on the value of future ends to be attained (the operation of "final causes"), do affect our thought-processes and thereby our action — are, indeed, "distinct powers, whose function it is to controul, determine and modify the phantasmal chaos of association" itself.[21] The vindication of a sort of freedom in this sense is for Coleridge a necessary preliminary to his account of the nature and working of the Imagination; it is as such a preliminary that it is introduced, and for that purpose it is sufficient. But in all this, obviously, Coleridge is dealing solely with concrete temporal processes of consciousness, and is asserting, against Hartley, the potency of certain kinds of causes—reasoning and purposive thought, spontaneous impulses of anger, love, etc.— for which associationism seemed to him to find no place. But such mental "powers" were still causes; nor does Coleridge clearly maintain that they are themselves uncaused, that their actual operation in time is wholly unrelated to any kind of antecedent events or conditions—which, indeed, he could not do, in consistency with his general philosophy. The refutation of Hartley, then, in *Biographia Literaria* is irrelevant to Coleridge's Kantian doctrine of the exclusively "noumenal" freedom of the individual.

The same Kantian dualism of the phenomenal and noumenal worlds is of the essence of Coleridge's doctrine of "Original Sin," for him the central truth of Christianity and, indeed, of ethics: "Wherever the Science of Ethics is acknowledged and taught, there the Article of Original Sin will be an Axiom of Faith in all classes." It is "no tenet first introduced and imposed by Christianity, and which, should a man see reason to disclaim the authority of the Gospel, would no longer have any claim on his attention, . . . no perplexity which has no existence for a philosophic Deist," but a "fact acknowledged in all ages, and recognized, but not originating, in the Christian Scriptures." [22] But the Coleridgean "Original Sin" was by no means that of Augustine or of orthodox theology in general — the

---

[21] *Biogr. Lit.*, I, 80, 81.
[22] *Aids to Reflection*; *Works*, 1. 284, 287; cf. *id.*, pp. 195-6, and *Table Talk*, 6. 418.

hereditary transmission to all the descendants of Adam of the taint arising from the sin of our first parents,

> The sad bequest of sire to son.

The traditional doctrine seemed to Coleridge superficial, mechanical, and, above all, immoral; since *we* are not Adam, it is not his sin, nor even its supposed consequence—the *non posse non peccare*—for which *our* wills are responsible.[23] *My* sinfulness must be inherent in me, not determined by my heredity, any more than by anything else external to my separate self; if it were I should not be free, and therefore no guilt would be imputable to me. There can be no sin which is *not* " original," *i. e.*, intrinsic and independent of any *prius*.[24] But no act of the temporal ego is thus original and free; and therefore, if man's being were simply temporal, the very notion of sin would be meaningless. The *locus*, then, of sin, as of freedom, can be only in the noumenal world, beyond time and the succession of causes and effects. Thus the portion of Coleridge's *Confessio fidei* which contains " the creed of revealed religion " begins:

> I believe, and hold it as the fundamental article of Christianity, that I am a fallen creature; that I am of myself capable of moral evil, but not of myself capable of moral good, and that an evil ground existed in my will, previously to any given act, or assignable moment of time, in my consciousness. I am born a child of wrath.

All the noumenal egos, in short, are *bad* egos. So, again, in one of Coleridge's marginalia on Kant:

> An ineffable act of Will choosing evil which is underneath or within the consciousness, . . . must be conceived as taking place in the *Homo Noumenon*, not the *Homo Phaenomenon*.[25]

And again in " Notes on *The Pilgrim's Progress* ":

> It is one thing to perceive this or that particular deed to be sinful, . . . and another thing to feel sin within us independent of particular

---

[23] For Coleridge's attack upon the traditional doctrine, see *Aids to Reflection, Works*, 1. 275-283.

[24] *Works*, 5. 16.

[25] Marginal note in Kant's *Metaphysik der Sitten*; ed. by H. Nidecker in *Rev. de Litt. Comp.*, 7 (1927), 337.

actions, except as the particular ground of them. And it is this latter without which no man can become a Christian.[26]

Coleridge's zeal to establish man's freedom was chiefly due to this desire to show that man is a sinner—a real and intrinsic sinner, not an unfortunate victim of circumstances.

But in what sense can freedom be intelligibly predicated of a noumenal or supratemporal ego? No doubt, if the reality of such an entity be admitted, its character is "uncaused," in the temporal sense of cause; as it is not in time, there was nothing prior to it which made it what it is. But the question remains whether it is *determined* by any non-temporal ground not itself —either, e. g., by an eternal logical necessity, as in Spinoza, or by an "eternal decree" of the Divine Will, as in Calvinism. The only answer to this which would leave the noumenal ego really free would be the negative answer: that its "intelligible character"—and therefore, its timeless sinfulness—is a blank, unrelated fact, which nothing else in the entire universe, not even God, in any degree explains. The eternal ego would need to be eternally isolated from everything else. What it is, it just timelessly happened to be, and there an end of the matter. This was a solution which neither Kant nor Coleridge could consistently and unequivocally adopt, for it implied that the noumenal order is a realm of utter unintelligibility, of pure chance, in which no sufficient reason, no reason of any kind, exists for anything; and it was, moreover, irreconcilable with the Christian doctrine of creation, which, even when philosophically construed as referring to a "timeless" act, all the more implied that the finite eternal selves owe their being— and their being what they are—to God. Kant had expressly insisted upon this:

If existence *in time* is merely a sensible mode of representation on the part of thinking beings in the world, and consequently does not apply to them as things-in-themselves, then the creation of these beings is a creation of things-in-themselves, since the notion of a creation does not belong to the sensible mode of existence and of causality, but can have reference only to noumena . . . God, as universal first cause, is also *the cause of the existence of substance* [*i. e.*, of things-in-themselves,

---

[26] *Works*, 5. 258.

not of " appearances "], a proposition which can never be given up without at the same time giving up the conception of God as the Being of all beings, and therewith denying his all-sufficiency, on which everything in theology depends.[27]

And Coleridge was as little disposed as Kant to deny the *Allgenugsamkeit* of deity; along with his desire to believe in the freedom of the will, he had an equally, or all but equally, strong inclination to think of God as the only *vera causa*,[28] and, indeed, as the all-comprehensive reality. Thus, *ca.* 1814,—in commenting on the dictum of the seventeenth-century divine, Richard Field, that " in the highest degree freedom of the will is proper to God only, and in this sense Calvin and Luther rightly deny that the will of any creature is or ever was free " — Coleridge adds: " except as in God, and God in us. Now the latter alone is will; for it alone is *ens super ens*. And here lies the mystery, which I dare not openly and promiscuously reveal." [29] To the philosophic reader Coleridge in this " reveals " enough to indicate that, at least when writing this comment, he conceived human freedom to mean only that God is free, and that, inasmuch as every creature's nature and action is determined by the will of God acting in him, he in a sense participates in that freedom. This, however, is a denial of individual freedom; it is essentially Calvinism, with a vaguely pantheistic coloring. Coleridge, however, at this time, evidently regarded this as a doctrine dangerous, though true. He also, as others have shown, had a strong inclination to the conception—akin to the Hegelian

---

[27] *Kr. d. pr. V.*, 187, 180. Kant, however, adds that " the circumstance that the acting beings are creatures cannot make the slightest difference," with respect to their freedom, " since creation concerns their supersensible existence, and therefore cannot be regarded as the determining ground of the appearances " (*ibid.*, p. 184). Yet, as will appear, Kant declared that the noumenal ego *is* the " determining ground," of those appearances which are the individual's temporal acts; so that the Creator is the cause of the latter at one remove.

[28] In " Religious Musings " Coleridge had spoken of the deity as the " sole operant." In a letter to Cottle of 1807, he writes that this expression " is indeed far too bold; may be misconstrued into Spinozism; and, therefore, though it is susceptible of pious and justifiable interpretation, I should by no means now use such a phrase " (*Biogr. Epistolaris*, 2. 10). What the " pious and justifiable interpretation " is Coleridge, unhappily, does not tell us; but to the conception expressed by the phrase his mind persistently tended to revert.

[29] *Works*, 5 (1884). 68.

—of the universe as an organic whole in which everything implies and is implied by everything else—in which, in other words, there is a complete mutual determination of things, and nothing is thinkable, except inadequately and falsely, in isolation. "The groundwork . . . of all pure speculation is the full apprehension of the difference between the contemplation of reason, namely, that intuition of things which arises when we possess ourselves as one with the whole, . . . and that which presents itself when, transferring reality to the negations of reality, . . . we think of ourselves as separated beings." The latter, " the abstract knowledge which belongs to us as finite beings, . . . leads to a science of delusion." [30]   But to think of our noumenal egos as " free," in the sense required by the Coleridgean notions of imputability and of Original Sin, is to think of them as "separate beings." Thus three potent motives in Coleridge's thought—his acceptance of the orthodox doctrine of creation (translated into Kantian terms), his strong religious feeling of the pervasiveness of a divine presence and power—the conviction that "God is All and in all"—and the quasi-Hegelian strain in his metaphysics, all were hopelessly at variance with his doctrine of individual freedom, and of an evil which originates solely in the individual.[31] Since he never abandoned the former, he cannot be said—nor can Kant—to have shown, or even consistently to have asserted, that the eternal or "intelligible character" of the individual ego is not necessitated by some reality other than itself.

[30] *The Friend*; *Works*, 2. 469-472.

[31] In a passage of the Huntington Library *ms.* which has been printed by Muirhead (*Coleridge as Philosopher*, 278-279, cf. also pp. 236-242) Coleridge faces the difficulty and makes an earnest and ingenious effort to reconcile the theses: (a) that "a particular will" has "no true being except as a form of the universal, and one with the universal Will," (b) that, in so far as morally bad, a "particular will makes a self that is not God, and hence by its own act becomes alien from God." The "solution" is that this separate (and therefore evil) will can not, after all, be *actually* separate, because "in God all actual reality is contained." No reconciliation, in short, is achieved; the reader is left with the choice between a simple contradiction in terms, or a denial of the independence (and therefore the responsibility) of the "particular will." None the less, this curious and largely verbal piece of reasoning evidently gave its author the *feeling* of having reconciled these opposite beliefs, both so needful for his peace of mind. For another passage in which Coleridge struggles with the same difficulty, see *Aids to Reflection*, in *Works*, 1. 274 n.

They did, however, expressly declare that this noumenal self—however *it* came to have the precise degree of inherent goodness or badness characteristic of it—is responsible for the behavior, good or bad, of the concrete individual. For, says Kant, in a man's noumenal existence,

nothing is antecedent to the determination of his will, but every action [i. e., in time,], and in general every modification of his existence, . . . even the whole series of his existence as a sensible being, is, in the consciousness of his supersensible existence, nothing but the *result* . . . of his causality as a noumenon.[32]

This, taken in conjunction with the doctrine about causality of the *Kritik der reinen Vernunft*, means that all human acts have a curious sort of two-fold causation: as natural phenomena, they are caused by antecedent natural phenomena, and are not free; they are also completely determined by the nature of the particular noumenal self whose acts they are— though it never acts in time.[33] We have similarly seen Coleridge asserting that the sinful I which is "independent of particular actions" is nevertheless "the particular ground of them," while also asserting that everything that belongs to "nature" and is "representable under the form of Time"—as all "particular actions" are — is determined by antecedent temporal causes. Whether these two conceptions are logically reconcilable I shall not here discuss; I point out only that if the noumenal ego's "intelligible character" is not—as for Coleridge it could not be —an isolated and arbitrary fact, to say that it is "responsible" for the temporal character and acts of the individual is another way of saying that *they* are not free. Thus the Coleridgean doctrine of Original Sin—of which also the germ may be found in Kant—represents all concrete moral evil, all the particular sins of individuals, as necessitated from all eternity by the in-

[32] *Kr. d. pr. V.*, A, 175; Abbott's tr., p. 191.
[33] It would appear, however, that Coleridge sometimes (as in the passage of *Biogr. Lit.* above cited, Shawcross 1. 80) conceived of the "absolute self" of the individual as simultaneously experiencing all of the moments of its temporal, phenomenal experience, as both "coextensive" and "co-present" with all "that living chain of causes." Though Coleridge finds "free-will" in this, there is nothing in this variation upon the notion of the noumenal ego and its relation to the temporal that invalidates the observation in the text above.

herently sinful nature of the immutable noumenal self of each of those individuals, this nature, in turn, being the result of no act of conscious choice on the part of any one of them, but simply an inexplicable eternal property of theirs—inexplicable unless, as in the passage cited above, it was conceived to be attributable to the (in itself "mysterious") will of God. This, it seems probable, was, in one phase of his philosophizing, Coleridge's real, but esoteric, view of the matter. If so, let it be repeated, man's freedom still more manifestly disappeared altogether—though of this consequence Coleridge was apparently imperfectly, or only intermittently, aware.

What was the relation of Coleridge's persistent quest of a vindication of the freedom of the will and of the doctrine of original sin to his individual psychology? Why did he *want*— as he manifestly did—to believe these things, and resort to such desperate metaphysical expedients to justify his beliefs? The answer is not simple; but one part of it may be suggested. I suppose that a literary psychologist in the current fashion would be likely to say that this strain in Coleridge's thought was a species of systematization and rationalization of an inferiority-complex; in Coleridge's time they would have called it by the pleasanter, and in his case the juster, name of humility — a humility not inconsistent with a consciousness of superior intellectual powers. After his youthful self-confidence and optimism were broken by a series of tragic experiences and disappointments — above all, disappointments with himself — he manifestly was often accompanied by a feeling of self-reproach, a sense of great gifts never put to commensurate use, and of inner inadequacy to situations which confronted him: a

> Sense of past youth, and manhood come in vain,
> And genius given, and knowledge won in vain.[34]

He was, in short, deeply conscious of guilt for, at least, a long succession of "omissive" sins. One way in which such a feeling may find both expression and relief is through those modes of religious experience called evangelical — the relief arising partly from the propitiatory attitude of humility itself, chiefly

[34] From "To William Wordsworth," written in 1807; *Poems*, ed. E. H. Coleridge, 407.

from an assurance of the possibility of redemption through an agency other than one's own works and merits.[35] Coleridge, at the same time, was an intensely ratiocinative mind, and needed to have an apparently philosophical basis for his religious emotions; and it was this that he found in part in the Kantian reasoning which has been outlined. From the premise—supposed to have been justified by Kant — of man's imputable iniquity, *plus* the assumption that this iniquity is universally and necessarily inherent in men's "noumenal" constitution, he deduced the necessity for a supernatural means of grace and of salvation.[36] Thus Kant opened for him the gate back into the emotionally congenial fields of evangelical faith and piety.

I conclude with a remark concerning the bearing of all this upon the nature of what is termed "Romanticism," and its effects upon religious and moral ideas. Coleridge is commonly described as one of the great English Romanticists and as the principal introducer of German Romanticism into the English-speaking world. But here—as in the most representative German Romantic writers—we see that one characteristic thing in the so-called Romantic influence was a revolt against naturalism, an ethical and metaphysical dualism, a philosophy of two worlds. I mention this because some eminent literary critics and historians have represented the whole Romantic influence as of quite the opposite character. There could scarcely be a greater historical error. Again, Mr. Muirhead has suggested that Coleridge's revulsion against the "necessitarian philoso-

---

[35] This supernatural redemptive action is also, in at least one passage, assigned to the noumenal world: the "influence of the Spirit of God" acts "directly on the *homo noumenon*" and through this upon "the *homo phenomenon* by the prearrangement of outward or bodily circumstances—what are commonly called, in pious language, providences." (Note on Kant's *Religion innerhalb der Grenzen der blossen Vernunft*, cited in Muirhead, p. 249.)

It should seem that a bad eternal ego should be eternally bad; but this implication, also, of his Kantian metaphysics Coleridge appears to have happily overlooked.

[36] Coleridge quotes with the symbol of "assent" the dictum of Thomas Adam that "the design of the Christian religion is to change men's views, lives and tempers, . . . by convincing men of their wretched guilt, blindness and impotence; by inculcating the necessity of remission, supernatural light and assistance; and actually promising and conveying these blessings." Cf. also his approval of Adam's reference to "the corruption of human nature" (*Critical Annotations of Samuel Taylor Coleridge*, ed. Taylor [1889], 6).

phy" of his early period is broadly explicable by the fact that such a philosophy "was in essence antagonistic to the romantic spirit of freedom that was the deepest strain in Coleridge's own being." Since "freedom" is one of the most equivocal of terms, I am uncertain what the "romantic spirit of freedom" is to be understood to be; and I am not wholly certain what the "deepest strain," among the many and conflicting strains, in Coleridge's being was. But if the foregoing analysis is at all correct, one of the deepest strains in it, and the one which gave rise to his belief in the freedom of the individual will, was a sense of sin—his own and other men's; and if anything distinctive of Coleridge's thought and feeling, after he turned away, under German influences, from the *Aufklärungsphilosophie* of his youth, is to be called "romantic," then a renascence of the sense of sin and of the doctrine of human depravity is one of the most evident of the "Romanticisms."

XIV. MILTON AND THE PARADOX OF
THE FORTUNATE FALL *

TO MANY READERS of *Paradise Lost* in all periods the most surprising lines in the poem must have been those in the Twelfth Book in which Adam expresses a serious doubt whether his primal sin—the intrinsic enormity and ruinous consequences of which had elsewhere been so copiously dilated upon —was not, after all, rather a ground for self-congratulation. The Archangel Michael, it will be remembered, has been giving Adam a prophetic relation of the history of mankind after the Fall. This, though for the greater part a most unhappy story, concludes with a prediction of the Second Coming and the Final Judgment, when Christ shall reward

> (462)   His faithful and receive them into bliss,
> Whether in Heav'n or Earth, for then the Earth
> Shall all be Paradise, far happier place
> Than this of Eden, and far happier days.
>   So spake the Archangel Michael; and then paused,
> As at the world's great period, and our Sire
> Replete with joy and wonder thus replied:
> "O Goodness infinite, Goodness immense,
> That all this good of evil shall produce,
> And evil turn to good—more wonderful
> Than that which by creation first brought forth
> (473)   Light out of darkness! Full of doubt I stand,
> Whether I should repent me now of sin
> By me done or occasioned, or rejoice
> Much more that much more good thereof shall spring—
> To God more glory, more good will to men
> (478)   From God—and over wrath grace shall abound."

The last six lines are Milton's expression of what may be called the Paradox of the Fortunate Fall. It is a paradox which has at least the look of a formal antinomy. From the doctrinal

---

* First published in *ELH, A Journal of English Literary History*, IV, 1937.

premises accepted by Milton and implicit in the poem, the two conclusions between which Adam is represented as hesitating were equally inevitable; yet they were mutually repugnant. The Fall could never be sufficiently condemned and lamented; and likewise, when all its consequences were considered, it could never be sufficiently rejoiced over. Adam's eating of the forbidden fruit, many theologians had observed, contained in itself all other sins;[1] as the violation by a rational creature of a command imposed by infinite wisdom, and as the frustration of the divine purpose in the creation of the earth, its sinfulness was infinite; and by it the entire race became corrupted and estranged from God. Yet if it had never occurred, the Incarnation and Redemption could never have occurred. These sublime mysteries would have had no occasion and no meaning; and therefore the plenitude of the divine goodness and power could neither have been exercised nor have become known to men. No devout believer could hold that it would have been better if the moving drama of man's salvation had never taken place; and consequently, no such believer could consistently hold that the first act of that drama, the event from which all the rest of it sprang, was really to be regretted. Moreover, the final state of the redeemed, the consummation of human history, would far surpass in felicity and in moral excellence the pristine happiness and innocence of the first pair in Eden—that state in which, but for the Fall, man would presumably have remained.[2] Thus Adam's sin—and also, indeed, the sins of his posterity which it "occasioned"—were the *conditio sine qua non* both of a greater manifestation of the glory of God and of immeasurably greater

---

[1] So Milton himself in *De doctrina chr.* 1, ch. 11 in *Milton's Prose Wks.*, Bohn ed., 4, p. 258: "What sin can be named, which was not included in this one act? It comprehended at once distrust in the divine veracity, and a proportionate credulity in the assurances of Satan; unbelief; ingratitude; disobedience; gluttony; in the man excessive uxoriousness, in the woman a want of proper regard for her husband, in both an insensibility to the welfare of their offspring, and that offspring the whole human race; parricide; theft, invasion of the rights of others, sacrilege, deceit, presumption in aspiring to divine attributes, fraud in the means employed to attain the object, pride and arrogance."

[2] On this last point, however, there were, in the early Fathers and later theologians, differing opinions; the view that the primeval state was not that in which man was intended to remain, but merely a phase of immaturity to be transcended, had ancient and respectable supporters. Into the history of this view I shall not enter here.

benefits for man than could conceivably have been otherwise obtained.

Necessary—upon the premises of orthodox Christian theology —though this conclusion was, its inevitability has certainly not been always, nor, it may be suspected, usually, apparent to those who accepted those premises; it was a disturbing thought upon which many even of those who were aware of it (as all the subtler theologians must have been) were naturally reluctant to dwell; and the number of theological writers and religious poets who have given it entirely explicit and pointed expression has apparently not been great. Nevertheless it had its own emotional appeal to many religious minds—partly, no doubt, because its very paradoxicality, its transcendence of the simple logic of common thought, gave it a kind of mystical sublimity; between logical contradiction (or seeming contradiction) and certain forms of religious feeling there is a close relation, of which the historic manifestations have never been sufficiently studied. And for writers whose purpose, like Milton's, was a religious interpretation of the entire history of man, the paradox served, even better than the simple belief in a future millennium or celestial bliss, to give to that history as a whole the character, not of tragedy, but of a divine comedy.[3] Not only should the drama have (for the elect — and about the unredeemed the elect were not wont to be greatly concerned) a happy ending, but the happy ending had been implicit in the beginning and been made possible by it. The Paradox of the Fortunate Fall has consequently found recurrent expression in the history of Christian religious thought; the idea was no invention, or discovery, of Milton's. In the present paper I shall note a few earlier phrasings of the same idea, which it is of interest to compare with Milton's. They may or may not be "sources" of P. L. 12. 469-478; they are in any case illustrations of a long tradition lying behind that passage.

1

To Milton-specialists the occurrence of a similar passage in Du Bartas is, of course, well known; but to facilitate com-

---

[3] This application of the phrase is borrowed from Professor C. A. Moore, PMLA 12 (1921). 11.

parison it seems worth while to cite the lines here. In the section of the *Seconde Semaine* entitled "The Imposture," after the Creator has pronounced sentence upon Adam, the poet interrupts his narrative to introduce a disquisition of his own, designed to answer the usual complaints against the justice of God in his dealings with Adam and his descendants:

> Here I conceive that flesh and blood will brangle,
> And murmuring reason with th'almighty wrangle.[4]

The ensuing essay in theodicy is apparently addressed primarily to mankind in general, though the poet sometimes rather confusedly seems, when he uses the second personal pronoun, to be thinking of those whose errors he is refuting, sometimes of Adam, sometimes of departed saints in general, sometimes of all the elect. The lines which concern us are the following:

> For thou complainest of God's grace, whose Still
> Extracts from dross of thine audacious ill,
> Three unexpected goods: praise for His name;
> Bliss for thyself; for Satan endless shame.
> Sith, but for sin, Justice and Mercy were
> But idle names; and but that thou didst erre,
> Christ had not come to conquer and to quell
> Upon the Cross, Sin, Satan, Death, and Hell,
> Making thee blessed more since thine offence
> Than in thy primer happy innocence . . .
> In earth thou liv'dst then; now in heaven thou beest:
> Then thou didst hear God's word; it now thou seest.
> Then pleasant fruits; now Christ is thy repast;
> Then might'st thou fall, but now thou standest fast.[5]

---

[4] Sylvester's tr., 1611 ed., p. 249.

[5] *The Complete Works of Joshua Sylvester*, ed. Grosart (1880), p. 111; in 1611 ed., p. 249. The original in Du Bartas, whom Sylvester here follows closely, is as follows:

> . . . sa grace
> Dont l'alambic extrait de ta rebelle audace
> Trois biens non esperez: scavoir, gloire pour soy,
> Vergongne pour Sathan, felicité pour toy.
> Veu que sans le peché sa Clemence et Justice
> Ne seroyent que vains noms; et que sans ta malice
> Christ ne fut descendu, qui d'un mortel effort
> A vaincu les Enfers, les Pechez, et la Mort,

Since, as we shall see, the thought was not original with Du Bartas, the passage in *P. L.* 12 is not one of those which can confidently be cited among the evidences of Milton's utilization of *La Semaine.* There is, however, a similarity in one detail which perhaps lends a slight probability to the supposition of a conscious or unconscious reminiscence by Milton of the corresponding passage in the French poet: the fact that both specify three "greater goods" which sprang from the evil inherent in the Fall.[6] Of these, two are identical in both passages—greater "glory" to God, greater benefits conferred by God upon man. The third is different; for the defeat and humiliation of Satan Milton substitutes, as the last happy consequence, the manifestation of the predominance of God's grace over his wrath— religiously a more moving and edifying conception, though less apposite to the plot of Milton's epic of the war between God and the rebel angels.[7] There are two other differences worth noting: (a) Milton gains greater dramatic effect by putting the paradox into the mouth of Adam himself—a ground for this being laid in the device of the preceding recital of the future history of man by the Archangel.[8] (b) In Milton, however,

---

Et te rend plus heureux mesme apres ton offence,
Qu'en Eden tu n'estois pendant ton innocence . . .
Tu viuois icy-bas, or tu vis sur le Pole.
Dieu parloit avec toy: or tu vois sa Parole.
Tu vivois de doux fruicts: Christ ore est ton repas
Tu pouvois trebucher: mais or tu ne peux pas.

(*La Seconde Semaine,* Rouen, 1592, p. 53.) It is to be remembered that not only were the poem of Du Bartas, and Sylvester's English version of it, famous and familiar in the 17th century, but also Simon Goulart's prose *Commentaires et Annotations sur la Sepmaine* . . . (1582, 1584) and Thomas Lodge's translation of Goulart: *A learned Summarie of the famous Poeme of William of Saluste, Lord of Bartas, wherein are discovered all the excellent Secrets in Metaphysicall, Physicall, Morall and Historicall Knowledge* . . . , 2 vols., 1637. The 1584 ed. of Goulart in the Harvard University Library does not contain the commentary on *The Second Week,* but the passage corresponding to Du Bartas's lines may be found in Lodge, *ed. cit.,* 2. 69-70: " The Poet expresseth this in the Verse 509, saying. That without sinne the Mercy and Justice of God had not so much been manifested," *etc.*

[6] This detail is not found in other expressions of the paradox known to me.

[7] This eventual consequence of the Incarnation and Resurrection had, however, been dwelt upon by Milton in *P. L.* 3. 250-8. If in writing the passage in Bk. 12, Milton was recasting that of Du Bartas, the change of the third " good " may be attributable to a desire to avoid repetition.

[8] Du Bartas employs the same device of a prophetic recital of subsequent history

the paradox is not so sharply expressed. Du Bartas puts quite categorically the point that but for the Fall there *could* have been no Incarnation and Redemption and that, "but for sin, Justice and Mercy were but idle names"; Milton's Adam is made to express merely a doubt whether he should repent his sin or "rejoice much more" over its consequences. Yet the logic of the paradox remains clear enough in Milton's lines; Adam could have had no reason for his doubt except upon the assumption that the sin was truly prerequisite to the "much more good" that was to follow—was, in Milton's own significant term, to "spring" from it—and an intelligent reader could hardly have failed to conclude that the doubt was to be resolved in favor of the second alternative.

Du Bartas, however, was not the only poetic precursor of Milton in the use of the paradox. It was peculiarly adapted both to the theme and the style of Giles Fletcher in his most ambitious poem, *The Triumph of Christ*. It naturally occurred to a devout but reflective mind when it dwelt rapturously upon that theme; the more intense the feeling of the sublimity of the redemptive act and the magnitude of the good both inherent in it and resultant from it, the more apparent the impossibility of regarding as merely evil the sin which had evoked it. And to a writer whose poetic method consisted chiefly in the multiplication of conceits and rhetorical antitheses, even when dealing with the gravest articles of his faith, such a paradox naturally had a special attraction. Consequently in *Christ's Triumph over Death* (1610) Fletcher, descanting upon the Passion of Christ in a series of what may be called antithetic parallels between the Fall and the Redemption—the two trees (i. e., the forbidden tree and the cross), the two gardens (Eden and Gethsemane), etc.—introduces the paradox—and converts it into a play upon words.

(*Seconde Semaine*, 1611 ed., p. 293) ; but here the prophet is Adam himself, who tells the story of things to come to Seth, and his prediction abruptly ends with the Deluge. If we were sure that Milton was, in Books 11-12, consciously recasting Du Bartas, the comparison between his and the earlier poet's use of the same group of themes would significantly illuminate the working of Milton's mind in the construction of his poem.

> Such joy we gained by our parentalls,
> That good or bad, whether I cannot wiss,
> To call it a mishap, or happy miss,
> That fell from Eden and to heav'n did rise.[9]

Fletcher, however, while raising the question clearly, is, like Milton's Adam, ostensibly non-committal about the answer to it; yet it is so put that the reader could hardly remain in doubt about the answer. A fall from Eden which made the greater joys of heaven possible was plainly no " mishap." [10]

The last act of Andreini's *L'Adamo* (1613) has a good deal in common with the last book of *Paradise Lost*, including a long speech by Michael in which, after reproachfully reminding Eve of her guilt—

> Tu cagionera a l'huomo
> E di doglia et di pianto— [11]

he proceeds to a prophecy of the final triumph of grace and of the future bliss to be enjoyed by the first pair and their progeny, both on earth, which will then be like Paradise, and in heaven.[12] In their response to this archangelic discourse, Andreini's Adam and Eve, like Milton's Adam, expand with gratitude and wonder over the benignant power which can so " unite " good with evil:

[9] *Op. cit.*, stanza 12; in *Giles and Phineas Fletcher: Poetical Works*, ed. F. S. Boas (1908) 1, 61.

[10] The second stanza following might be construed as a more affirmative expression of the paradox:

> Sweet Eden was the arbour of delight,
> Yet in his honey flowres our poyson blew,
> Sad Gethseman the bowre of baleful night
> Whear Christ a health of poyson for us drew;
> Yet all our honey in that poyson grewe.

If the " poyson " in the last two lines is that referred to in the second—i. e., the forbidden fruit, or the consequences of eating it—the final line is a figurative way of asserting once more the dependence of the Redemption upon the Fall. But it is possible that the " poyson " in the penultimate line signifies the Agony in the Garden and that the last line is merely a repetition of this.

[11] *Op. cit.*, tercentenary ed. E. Allodoli (1913). Act 5, Sc. 9, p. 140, ll. 4122-3; cf. " cagionera " with Milton's " occasioned " in 12. 475, apparently his only use of the word as a verb.

[12] *Ibid.*, p. 143, ll. 4235 ff.: " per la gioia D'esser rapito l'uomo A l'artiglio infernale il tutto gode, E pel diletto sembra il Cielo in terra e'n Paradiso il Mondo ": cf. *P. L.* 12. 462-5. The supreme good, however, Andreini, unlike Milton, expressly says, will be the beatific vision: " di Dio . . . il sacrosanto viso, . . . il sommo bel del Paradiso."

> Con la morte la vita,
> Con la guerra la pace,
> Col perder la Vittoria,
> Con l'error la salute
> E con l'Inferno il cielo
> Insieme unir, non è poter umano,
> Ma de l'eterno mano
> Omnipotenza summa. Ondè, Signore,
> Ch' Eva trafitta è sana,
> E perdendo trionfa, et vinta hà gloria.[13]

There is in these lines, especially in "perdendo trionfa," an evident adumbration of the paradox, but they hardly give it unequivocal expression.[14]

2

Some of Milton's precursors, then, in the century preceding *Paradise Lost*, had dwelt upon the idea that the Fall had not only been over-ruled for good by the divine beneficence, but had been the indispensable means to the attainment of far greater good for man and—if it may be so put—for God than

---

[13] *Ibid.*, p. 141, ll. 4157 ff.

[14] The later scenes of the fifth act of della Salandra's *Adamo Caduto* (1647), especially in a dialogue between two personified divine attributes, Omnipotence and Mercy, dwell upon the happy ending which was to follow the disaster of the Fall; the Incarnation and Atonement are foretold, and, as in Milton, there are devout ejaculations over *la gran Bontade* which is to be made manifest through this outcome; and it is remarked that other attributes of deity — Infinity and Charity — would thereby obtain wider scope for their exercise:

> L'Infinitade
> In compartirsi sin fra Creature.
> Applaudira la Caritade, mentre
> Verrà più dilatato il suo bel Regno.

But the essence of the paradox—the dependence of the possibility of all this upon the Fall—is not emphasized. In the equally cheerful outlook upon the future with which Vondel's *Lucifer* (1645) concludes, there is no hint of the paradox. That poems about the Fall should be given a happy ending by the introduction, through one device or another, of a prevision of the coming of Christ and the future bliss of the redeemed, may be said to have been a convention of this *genre*; and, as Professor C. A. Moore has pointed out in *PMLA* 12 (1921). 463 ff. the accepted dogma itself made it virtually incumbent upon the author of such a poem to foreshadow the "far happier place, far happier days," which the elect should know. To end upon a tragic note was to depart from both literary and theological orthodoxy. But a recognition of the Paradox of the Fortunate Fall was not a necessary or invariable part of a happy ending.

would have been possible without it. Milton's eighteenth-century annotators and editors soon began to point out—though with a characteristic and exasperating neglect to give definite references — that the idea had already been expressed in the patristic period. The earliest suggestion of such a source seems to have been given in J. Richardson's *Explanatory Notes and Remarks on Milton* (1734), in which line 473 is annotated: "*O felix culpa, quae talem ac tantum meruit habere Redemptorem!* 'tis an exclamation of St. Gregory." [15] Newton and other annotators in the same century were, prudently, still more vague in citation: "He seems to remember the rant of one of the Fathers, *O felix culpa, etc.*" [16] So far as I have observed, no modern editor has given any more precise reference for this yet more striking phrasing of the Paradox of the Fall. An extensive, though not exhaustive, search of the writings of St. Gregory [17] fails to disclose it. But it is to be found in a probably earlier, more noteworthy, and, at least to non-Protestants, more widely familiar source—a passage in the Roman Liturgy. [18] In the service for Easter Even (Holy Saturday) there is a hymn, sung by the deacon in the rite of blessing the paschal candle, which bears the title of *Praeconium* but is better known, from the word with which it opens, as the *Exultet* (*exultet iam angelica turba caelorum*); in it, a Catholic writer has remarked, "the language of the liturgy rises into heights to which it is hard to find a parallel in Christian literature." [19] In this rapturous exultation over the mystery of the Redemption the sentence already cited is preceded by another expressing the same paradox yet more pointedly: "*O certe necessarium Adae peccatum, quod Christi morte deletum est! O felix culpa, quae talem ac tantum meruit habere redemptorem!*" Adam's sin was not only a "happy fault" but "certainly necessary" —

[15] *Op. cit.*, 521.

[16] Fourth ed. (1757) of Thomas Newton's ed. of *P. L.*, 2, 429 (note). The parallel is not indicated in the earliest important commentary, Patrick Hume's *Annotations on Paradise Lost* (1695).

[17] Richardson's "St. Gregory" presumably refers to Gregory the Great (d. 604), since the citation is in Latin.

[18] For my knowledge of this fact, and for other valued assistance in this section, I am indebted to Professor G. La Piana of Harvard University.

[19] C. B. Walker, in *Catholic Encycl.*, art. "*Exultet.*"

necessary to the very possibility of the redemptive act, which, it may be supposed, was by the author of the hymn conceived as itself a necessary, and the central, event in the divine plan of terrestrial history.

The date of composition of the *Exultet* and that of its incorporation in the service of Easter Even can be determined only approximately.[20] It was originally no part of the Roman Liturgy, but appears first in the Gallican, which, as some liturgiologists hold, was probably in existence by the beginning of the fifth century;[21] but the earliest manuscript of this liturgy which includes the hymn in question is of the seventh century.[22] Certain conjectures concerning its authorship have been made, but none is supported by any substantial evidence;[23] in the words of the most careful modern study of the subject, "in the present state of the sources, one must give up the attempt to determine the authorship and even the place of origin of this famous hymn."[24] All that can be said, then, on the question of date, is that the passage which some of Milton's editors have regarded as the probable source of *P. L.* 12. 473 ff. was in liturgical use as early

[20] For the text of the hymn (in its oldest known form) see Duchesne, *Christian Worship*, 5th ed. (1923), p. 254; Migne, *Patr. Lat.*, 72, col. 269 f. For its history cf. Duchesne, *loc. cit.*: A. Franz, *Die kirchliche Benediktionen im Mittelalter* (1909) 1. 519-553; V. Thalhofer and L. Eisenhofer, *Handbuch der katholischen Liturgik* (1912) 1. 643 ff.; A. Gastoué, *Les vigiles nocturnes* (1908), p. 18; C. B. Walker, *loc. cit.*; J. Braun, *Liturgisches Handlexikon* (1922), art. "Praeconium paschale." An English version of the entire hymn may be found in I. Schuster, *The Sacramentary* (1925), 2. 293-5.

[21] Duchesne, *op. cit.*, p. 86, thinks the hymn may be as early as the middle of the fourth century.

[22] Cf. the liturgiological authorities cited.

[23] Some ancient manuscripts credit it to St. Augustine "when he was deacon," a highly improbable ascription (cf. Thalhofer and Eisenhofer, p. 644; Franz, 1. 534). It is probably due to the fact that Augustine, as he himself records (*De civ. Dei*, 15, 22), once wrote a short *laus cerei* in verse; but this was not the *Exultet*. It appears to have been originally the custom for the deacon to compose his own *praeconium* for the rite of blessing the Easter candle (Braun, *loc. cit.*), a practice of which the *locus* in Augustine gives probable evidence. One of Migne's editors (H. Menard in *Pat. Lat.*, 78, col. 335) suggests that the hymn may have been written by St. Ambrose, which is perhaps possible, but incapable of proof. Gastoué's suggestion of St. Ennodius of Pavia (d. 521) as the author appears to be due to a confusion of the *Exultet* with two quite different formulas of benediction composed by that Father (v. *Corp. script. lat. eccles.* 6. 415-419).

[24] Franz, *op. cit.*, 1. 534.

as the seventh and possibly as early as the fourth century, in the churches employing the Gallican sacramentary. It is, however, certain that the popularity of the hymn was so great that it presently drove out, even in the Roman Liturgy — apparently after some hesitancies on the part of the Popes — all rival formulas in the rite of blessing the Easter candle. It evidently " owed its triumph," as a Catholic historian of the liturgy has said, "to the fact that it was far superior to all these rivals both in expression and content." [25] In certain medieval missals there are some interesting variations in the wording of the two sentences relevant to the theme of this paper; [26] and it is of interest to note that these sentences were considered by some ecclesiastical authorities as dangerous, and were omitted from the hymn—rather generally in German and not infrequently in French and Italian sacramentaries.[27] But with the establishment of liturgical uniformity since the late sixteenth century, both sentences found an accepted and permanent place in the Missal of the Roman Church.

3

That the Protestant religious poets of the sixteenth and seventeenth centuries who gave expression to the Paradox of the Fortunate Fall had heard or read the part of the Catholic liturgy containing the *Exultet* is, of course, possible; but there is no need to suppose them to have done so. It is rather more likely that they—or at all events the earliest of them, Du Bartas— became acquainted with the idea through the reading of one of the Fathers, whose writings still had among Protestant theologians much authority. St. Ambrose, for example (4th c.), had flatly asserted that Adam's sin "has brought more benefit to us than harm" (*amplius nobis profuit culpa quam nocuit*),[28] and had even permitted himself the more generalized and

---

[25] Thalhofer and Eisenhofer, *op. cit.*, 644.

[26] E. g., in the Missal of Westminster Abbey (ed. Lagg, 1893, 2, 581) the words *et nostrum* follow *Adae peccatum*.

[27] See Franz, 1. 540 f., for examples, of which I cite only one: Hugo, Abbot of Cluny (d. 1109), commanded that these sentences should be "deleted and no longer read, *cum aliquando non bene haberetur ' O felix culpa,' et quod peccatum Adae necessarium esset.*"

[28] *De institutione virginis*, ch. 17. 104 (*MPL*, 16. 331).

hazardous apophthegm that "sin is more fruitful than innocence" (*fructuosior culpa quam innocentia*).[29] God "knew
that Adam would fall, *in order that* he might be redeemed by
Christ (*ut redimeretur a Christo*). *Felix ruina, quae reparatur
in melius!*"[30] The identity of the thought and the approximation of the phrasing here to those of the two sentences quoted
from the *Exultet* are evident; and it is probable that these
Ambrosian passages are the primary source of the expressions
of the paradox, alike in that hymn and in Du Bartas, Fletcher
and Milton. To the last two the idea may or may not have
been transmitted through Du Bartas;[31] or to any of them it is
possible that the medium of transmission may have been some
later patristic repetition or amplification of the theme. In the
century after Ambrose his enunciation of it was echoed, with
some weakening, by one of the greatest of the Popes, Leo I,
in his *First Sermon on the Lord's Ascension:*

Today we [in contrast with the first of our race] are not only confirmed in the possession of Paradise, but have even penetrated to the
higher things of Christ; we have gained more by the ineffable grace of
Christ than we had lost by the envy of the Devil.[32]

And in the next century Gregory the Great expressed the
paradox with all possible explicitness:[33]

What greater fault than that by which we all die? And what greater
goodness than that by which we are freed from death? And certainly,
unless Adam had sinned, it would not have behooved our Redeemer
to take on our flesh. Almighty God saw beforehand that from that evil
because of which men were to die, He would bring about a good which

---

[29] *De Jacob*, 6. 21.

[30] *In Ps. XXXIX*, 20 (*MPL*, 14. 1065).

[31] That Du Bartas "used Ambrose's *Hexaemeron*" is said by U. T. Holmes
and his associates to be a certainty (*The Works of Du Bartas* (1935), 1. 128);
it is improbable that Du Bartas's reading in Ambrose was confined to this writing.
Cf. Thibaut de Maisières, *Les poèmes inspirés du début de la Genèse* (1931),
p. 26. Milton, however, was acquainted with Ambrose at first hand; cf. *Tetra-
chordon* in *Prose Works*, Bohn ed. (1848), 3. 418.

[32] *MPL*, 54. 396: ampliora adepti per ineffabilem Christi gratiam quam per
diaboli amiseramus invidiam.

[33] Richardson, therefore, was perhaps not wholly wrong in indicating Gregory
as a source of the passage in *P. L.*, though in error in attributing the *O felix
culpa* to that saint.

would overcome that evil. How wonderfully the good surpasses the evil, what faithful believer can fail to see? Great, indeed, are the evils we deservedly suffer in consequence of the first sin; but who of the elect would not willingly endure still worse evils, rather than not have so great a Redeemer? [34]

4

In the foregoing examples, the writers who enunciated the paradox, it is evident, usually had chiefly in mind the relation of causal dependence between specific historical events, the Fall and the Redemption; and the argument was that the latter, or consequent, being preponderatingly a good, the former, as its necessary (though not sufficient) cause, must have been preponderatingly a good. Yet the Fall none the less remained, upon orthodox principles, a moral evil. These considerations, taken together, tended to suggest two larger and awkward questions. Was it true in general that the existence of moral evils is, from another and more comprehensive point of view, a good? And if, from such a point of view, the Fall was preponderatingly a good, was it not necessary to assume that its occurrence must after all have been in accordance with God's will? These questions, implicit in the notion of the *felix culpa*, were fairly explicitly raised and considered by Augustine; and his answers to both were, at least sometimes, in the affirmative; in other words, he not only accepted the paradox but gave it a more generalized form:

Although those things that are evil, in so far as they are evil, are not good; nevertheless, it is good that there should be not only goods but evils as well. For unless this—namely, that there be also evils—were

---

[34] *In Primum Regum Expositiones*, 4. 7; *MPL*, 7, 222: " Quae maior culpa, quam illa, qua omnes morimur? Et quae maior bonitas, quam illa, per quam a morte liberamur? Et quidem nisi Adam peccaret, Redemptorem nostrum carnem suscipere nostram non oporteret. Ex illo malo, quo morituri erant, bonum quod malum illum vinceret, omnipotens Deus sese facturum providerat. Cuius profecto boni magnitudo, quis fidelis non videat quam mirabiliter excellat? Magna quippe sunt mala, quae per primae culpae meritum patimur, sed quis electus nollet peiora mala perpeti, quam tantum Redemptorem non habere? " The echo of the last clause in the *Exultet* suggests that the author of the hymn may have been remembering *both* this passage of Gregory and those of Ambrose; in which case a seventh century date for the hymn, or at least for the part of it which here concerns us, would be indicated. But it is, of course, possible, that Gregory was echoing the *Exultet*.

a good, men would under no circumstances fall away from the omnipotent Good.[35]

i. e., neither Adam nor any man would ever have sinned. And again:

The works of God are so wisely and exquisitely contrived that, when an angelic and human creature sins, that is, does, not what God wished it to do, but what itself wishes, yet by that very will of the creature whereby it does what the Creator did not will, it fulfills what he willed — God, as supremely good, putting even evils to good use, for the damnation of those whom he has justly predestined to punishment and for the salvation of those whom he has benignantly predestined to grace.[36]

The greatest of the Latin Fathers was here manifestly skating on rather thin ice. It was always difficult for an acute-minded theologian with a strong sense of the divine sovereignty to admit that Adam's sin had really frustrated the will of God, and had compelled the deity to perform, unwillingly, acts which he would not otherwise have performed; it was, therefore, not easy, when dealing with these matters, always to avoid the thought that the Fall itself, with its consequences—so happy for the elect—was but a part of the eternal and ineluctable divine purpose for mankind. These passages of Augustine's thus reveal more clearly some of the moral difficulties and metaphysical pitfalls which lay behind the conception of the *felix culpa*—difficulties and pitfalls which Augustine himself cannot be said to have wholly escaped.[37]

---

[35] Ch. 96 (*MPL*, 40. 276): Quamvis ergo ea quae mala, in quantum mala sunt, non sint bona; tamen ut non solum bona, sed etiam sint et mala, bonum est. Nam nisi esset hoc bonum, ut essent et mala, nullo modo sinerentur ab omnipotente bono.

[36] *Ibid.*, ch. 100 (*MPL*, 40. 279): Opera domini [sunt] . . . tam sapienter exquisita, ut cum angelica et humana creatura peccasset, id est, non quod ille, sed quod voluit ipsa fecisset, etiam per eamdem creaturae voluntatem, qua factum est quod Creator noluit, impleret ipse quod voluit; bene utens et malis, tamquam summe bonus, ad eorum damnationem quos iuste praedestinavit ad poenam, et ad eorum salutem quos benigne praedestinavit ad gratiam.

[37] Donne in one of his sermons bases upon the authority of Augustine as well as of Scripture a similar remark that matters have been so ordered that sin in general—not specifically the sin of Adam—is made conducive to moral good: " If I cannot find a foundation for my comfort in this subtility of the Schoole, that sin is nothing, . . . yet I can raise a second step for my consolation in this,

The familiarity of the idea in the fourteenth century is shown by its occurrence both in *The Vision of Piers the Plowman,* *ca.* 1378, and in Wyclif's *Sermons.* In the former it is put into the mouth of Repentance, after the Seven Deadly Sins have made their confessions: God created man " most like to himself, and afterwards suffered him to sin,"

> And al for the best, as I bileve · what euer the boke telleth,
>   O *felix culpa*! *o necessarium peccatum ade*! *etc.*
> For thourgh that synne thi sone · sent was to this erthe,
> And bicam man of a mayde · mankind to save.[38]

Wyclif in a Christmas sermon preached, perhaps, to his rustic flock at Lutterworth in the early 1380s, did not shrink from the paradox, but on the contrary joined with it a still more sweeping optimism, of very dubious orthodoxy: all things, including sin, are for the best in the best of possible worlds, since all happens in accordance with God's will:

And so, as many men seien, alle thingis comen for the beste; for alle comen for Goddis ordenance, and so thei comen for God himsilf; and so alle thingis that comen fallen for the beste thing that mai be. Moreover to another witt men seien, that this world is betterid bi everything that fallith therinne, where that it be good or yvel . . . and herfore seith Gregori, that it was a blesful synne that Adam synnede and his kynde, for bi this the world is beterid; but the ground of this goodnesse stondith in grace of Jesus Christ.[39]

---

that be sin what it will in the nature thereof, yet my sin shall conduce and cooperate to my good. So *Ioseph* saies to his Brethren, *You thought evill against me, but God meant it unto good:* which is not onely good to *Ioseph,* who was not partaker in the evill, but good even to them who meant nothing but evill." What Donne has in mind here at least in part, however, is the more special idea that, after many little sins, a good round sin may be a means of grace, by bringing the sinner to a realization of his own state. " Though it be strangely said, yet I say it, That God's anger is good; so saies S. Augustine, *Audeo dicere,* Though it be boldly said yet must I say it, *Utile est cadere in aliquid manifestum peccatum,* Many sinners would not have been saved if they had not committed some greater sin at last, then before; for, the punishment of that sin, hath brought them to a remorse of all their other sins formerly neglected " (*LXXX Sermons* (1640), p. 171).

[38] B. Ms., *Passus V,* 489 ff., in Skeat, *The Vision of William Concerning Piers the Plowman* (1869), 60.

[39] *Select English Works of John Wyclif,* ed. Thomas Arnold (1869), Sermon XC, 1. 320-321. There is no corresponding passage in the Latin sermon from the same text and for the same festival: *Ioannis Wyclif Sermones,* ed. Loserth

An interesting late-medieval lyrical poem gives to the paradox a turn not found in any of the other examples here cited;
it is presented in its relation to the cult of the Virgin. Since
there would have been no Incarnation without the Fall, all that
phase of Catholic piety and religious emotion which centers
about the figure of the Virgin Mother manifestly owed its possibility to Adam's eating the forbidden fruit. There is also in
the poem, if I am not mistaken, a touch of sly humor; the
anonymous author hints that poor Adam, to whom not only
mankind in general but the Queen of Heaven herself are so
deeply indebted, has been rather badly treated. This further
inference from the idea of the *felix culpa* would, one may
suspect, hardly have been approved by St. Ambrose and St.
Gregory. Adam, the poet recalls, lay bound for four thousand
winters:

> And all was for an appil,
>   An appil that he tok . . .
> Ne hadde the appil takė ben,
>   The appil taken ben,
> Ne haddė never our lady
>   A bene hevenė quene.
> Blessed be the time
>   That appil takė was.
> Therefore we moun singen
>   ' *Deo gracias.*' [40]

A sixteenth century illustration of the vogue of the concept
of the *felix culpa* is to be found in the widely used Latin
Commentary on Genesis of the Jesuit Benito Pereira (Pererius).
The commentator is dilating, *à propos* of Genesis 1, 31, upon
the manner in which God transmutes evils—even moral evils
(*mala culpae*)—into good.

A signal proof and example of this is exhibited to us in the sin of
Adam. How grave this sin was, how far and wide it spread poison

---

(1888) 2. 1 ff. Wyclif also apparently confused in his memory the *Exultet* and
the passage of Gregory above cited, or else believed Gregory to have composed
the hymn.

[40] Professor Douglas Bush has kindly brought this poem to my notice. It is
printed in Chambers and Sidgwick's *Early English Lyrics* (1907), 102, and is
believed to have been written in the early fifteenth century.

and destruction, how severely it was punished, is acknowledged by all men. Yet this so great sin, such is the goodness and power of God, has been wonderfully converted into the greatest good and the most glorious of God's works, namely, the incarnation, passion and death of the Son of God. So that Gregory not unadvisedly or rashly somewhere exclaims, *O felix culpa, quae talem ac tantum meruit habere Redemptorem.*" [41]

Upon the crucial point of the paradox however—that God could not have performed this *praeclarissimum opus* if Adam had remained innocent—Pereira does not dwell.

5

For a final example, which will bring us back to Milton's century, I will cite one of the most famous and widely read of Catholic devotional works, the *Traité de l'amour de Dieu* of St. Francis de Sales (1616) [42]

The mercy of God [he writes] has been more salutary for the redemption of the race of men than the wretchedness of Adam has been poisonous for its destruction. And so far is it from being true that the sin of Adam has overcome the benevolence (*debonnaireté*) of God, that on the contrary it has served to excite and provoke it: so that, by a gentle and most loving antiperistasis [43] and opposition, that benevo-

---

[41] *Benedicti Pererii Valentini commentariorum et disputationum in Genesim tomus primus* (Leyden, 1594), 168. Pereira, like Wyclif, it will be observed, either attributes the *Exultet* to St. Gregory or has confused the phrase from the hymn with the dictum of Gregory above cited. The passage is a highly probable source of Richardson's similar error previously noted; and it is a conceivable source of the *locus* in Milton. On the importance of this and similar Renaissance commentaries on Genesis for the background of *P. L.*, see the article of Arnold Williams in *Studies in Philology*, April, 1937, pp. 191-208. But it is to be borne in mind that Pereira's work and the others mentioned by Williams were later than Du Bartas's poem.

[42] The passage is therefore of later date than those cited from Du Bartas and Giles Fletcher.

[43] A technical term of the physics of the period, signifying a process by which a quality or force in a substance is increased or intensified by the action of an opposing quality or force. Milton expresses the same idea in the hymn of the celestial choirs, 7. 613 ff.

> Who seeks
> To lessen thee, against his purpose serves
> To manifest the more thy might: his evil
> Thou usest, and from thence creat'st more good.

The " more good " here, however, is the creation of " this new-made world "

lence has been re-invigorated by the presence of its adversary: and, so to say, gathering together its forces in order to win the victory, it has caused grace 'to abound more exceedingly where sin abounded.' [44] Therefore the Church, in a holy excess of admiration, exclaims on the Eve of Easter: 'O sin of Adam, truly necessary' etc. [quotes the two sentences from the *Exultet*]. Of a truth, we can say with that man of ancient times: 'We should be lost (*perdus*) if we had not been lost'; [45] that is to say, our loss has been our gain, since human nature has received more gifts of grace (*plus de graces*) from its redemption by its Savior than it would ever have received from the innocence of Adam, if he had persevered in it. . . . The redemption of our Lord, touching our miseries, renders them more useful and amiable than the original innocence would ever have been. The Angels, the Savior tells us, " have more joy over one sinner that repenteth than over ninety-and-nine just persons that need no repentance "; and in the same way, the state of redemption is one hundred times greater in value than the state of innocence. [46]

Here the strangest aspect of the paradox is even more pointedly brought out than by Du Bartas or Milton: not only did the Fall make possible more good for man, but God himself *needed* a fallen race to evoke fully the divine attributes and powers.

6

It is unlikely that the pre-Miltonic expressions of the Paradox of the Fortunate Fall which I have noted are the only ones to be found in Christian literature from the fourth to the seventeenth centuries, but they pretty certainly include the most important; all but one of them could have been known to Milton at first hand; and they are sufficient to place in its proper historical perspective the passage of the Twelfth Book of *Paradise Lost* cited at the beginning. In that perspective, the passage ceases to be surprising, or indicative of any originality or of any great boldness in Milton's thought. A paradox which had

and of man, to " repair that detriment " resulting from the defection of the rebel angels—not the Redemption and its consequences.

[44] *Romans* 5. 20. The Pauline text gave a seeming biblical sanction to the paradox, though it does not in fact express the essential point of it.

[45] The reference is to a saying of Themistocles in Plutarch's *Life of Themistocles*, 39.

[46] *Op. cit.*, Bk. 2, ch. 5.

been embraced by Ambrose, Leo the Great, Gregory the Great, Francis de Sales, and Du Bartas; had for at least ten centuries had a place in many missals, and had finally been officially adopted by the Roman Church, was, obviously, sufficiently orthodox; and it had been put more sharply and boldly by at least two of the Doctors of the Church, by the composer of the *Exultet*, by the French mystic, and by the author of *La Semaine*, than by Milton. Though the hint of antinomianism latent in it had made many writers to whom it was probably familiar avoid expressing it, it had nevertheless a recognized and natural place in the treatment of the topic in Christian theology—that of the culmination of the redemptive process in human history—which was also for Milton the culminating theme in his poem. Yet it undeniably placed the story of the Fall, which was the subject of the poem announced at the outset, in a somewhat ambiguous light; when it was borne in mind, man's first disobedience could not seem the deplorable thing which, for the purposes of the poet—and of the theologian—it was important to make it appear. The only solution was to keep the two themes separate. In the part of the narrative dealing primarily with the Fall, the thought that it was after all a *felix culpa* must not be permitted explicitly to intrude; that was to be reserved for the conclusion, where it could heighten the happy final consummation by making the earlier and unhappy episodes in the story appear as instrumental to that consummation, and, indeed, as its necessary conditions.

XV. THE COMMUNISM OF ST. AMBROSE[1]

IN NO PATRISTIC writer is the persistent force of the classical tradition of primitivistic communism more evident than in St. Ambrose.[2] Though there is obviously no suggestion in the story in Genesis that, but for the Fall, private property would have remained unknown, Ambrose, by interpreting the story in the light of pagan conceptions of the Golden Age, confidently draws that inference—which, however, he seeks to support by suitable glosses upon scriptural texts. All things were made by the Creator to be held in common, and private ownership is contrary to nature; and when the mind of Ambrose is occupied with this theme he inclines to suggest that man's undoing was due to an initial act of cupidity, *prima avaritia*;[3] our first parents wanted to appropriate what did not belong to them. Thus he writes, *à propos* of the work of the fifth day of creation:

---

[1] This is a section from an uncompleted and unpublished second volume of *A Documentary History of Primitivism and Related Ideas* by A. O. Lovejoy and George Boas; the first volume, *Primitivism and Related Ideas in Antiquity* (1935) is hereafter referred to as *PA*. The present essay was first published in the *Journal of the History of Ideas*, III (1942), 458-468. Translations are for the most part based upon the texts in Migne's *Patrologia Latina*, XIV-XVI, 1880. The communistic strain is, of course, apparent in other fourth-century, and earlier, patristic writers, notably in St. Basil, by whom Ambrose was greatly influenced; but none appears to have carried it so far as Ambrose, except in relation to the special case of the monastic societies.

[2] For modern accounts of St. Ambrose's views on property, see P. Ewald, *Einfluss der stoisch-ciceronianischen Moral auf die . . . Ethik bei Ambrosius*, 1881; O. Schilling: *Reichtum u. Eigentum in der altkirchlichen Literatur*, 1908, pp. 134 ff.; R. W. and A. J. Carlyle, *A History of Mediaeval Political Theory in the West*, 1903, I, pp. 136 ff.; J.-R. Palanque, *Saint Ambroise et l'Empire Romain*, 1933, pp. 336 ff.; P. H. Dudden, *Life and Times of St. Ambrose*, II, 545-550; R. Thamin, *St. Ambroise et la morale chrétienne*, 1895, pp. 278-292.

[3] More usually, however, Ambrose hesitated between two other opinions concerning the psychological cause of the Fall, which is by implication the chief permanent source of evil in man. Sometimes he conceives Adam's disobedience to have been due to ὕβρις (*superbia* or *insolentia*), e. g., *Epist.* 73, 5; *Expos. Ps.* 118, 7. 9. In other passages he adheres to the view that the first sin was the desire for sensual pleasure, *appetentia voluptatis*, e. g., *Epist.* 63, 14.

Hexaemeron, V, 1, 2 (*MPL*, XIV, 220):

Alas! Before man was, that seductive thing, abundance of wealth, which is the mother of our luxury, began to be; before man was, there were means of voluptuous enjoyment. Therefore that which was to tempt men was created before nature was. But nature is nowise at fault; she provided our nourishment, she did not prescribe our vices. She gave these things as common possessions, so that you might not claim any of them as your private property.

Presenting in the *De officiis ministrorum* a Christian revision of the ethics of Cicero, Ambrose presses home, as Cicero had not had the consistency to do, that philosopher's famous declaration that " there is nothing that is private property by nature " and that " in human society community of rights to all things which nature has produced for the common use of all men is to be maintained." [4] Having enunciated this sweeping principle, Cicero had at once proceeded to hedge on it. Ambrose has no patience with such weakness; he finds it evident that private property originated simply through " usurpation." This great Doctor of the Church had thus virtually anticipated the dictum of the nineteenth-century French revolutionary: *la propriété c'est le vol.*

De officiis ministrorum, I, XXVIII, 132, 137 (*MPL*, XVI, 67):

132. Some [philosophers] have thought the idea (*forma*) of justice to be that each should hold common, that is public, things as public, private things as his own.[5] But not even this is according to nature; for nature has poured forth all things to be held in common by all. For God commanded all things to be produced so that sustenance should be common to all, and that the earth should be a sort of common possession of all men. Nature therefore created a common right [to these things], usurpation created private right. . . .[6] 137. Who would not wish to hold fast to this supreme virtue,[7] if it were not that

[4] *De officiis*, I, vii, 21 and I, xvi, 51. See *PA*, p. 258.

[5] The specific reference is evidently to the passage above cited (*De officiis*, I, xvi, 51); and in what follows Ambrose is directly attacking Cicero for drawing back, in the sequel, from the conclusion required by his premise.

[6] In the terminology of Roman law *usurpatio* could designate a lawful way of acquiring property; but it is clear from the context, and from Ambrose's general position, that he is here using the term in its bad sense. The expression is repeated in *De Nabuthe*, XII, 53: *quod commune est in omnium usum datum, tu solus usurpas.*

[7] I. e., justice, in the sense defined by Ambrose above.

the original avarice weakened and deflected the force of so great a virtue? For so long as we eagerly strive to increase our riches, to accumulate money, to occupy lands as our possessions, to be distinguished for our wealth, we put away from us the essential nature of justice and lose the spirit of common beneficence. For how can a man be just who seeks to snatch from another what the other needs for himself? [8]

But to assert that "by nature," or in the state in which man was originally created and was meant to remain, all things were to have been possessed in common, did not, for a Christian theologian, necessarily imply that private ownership is not an inevitable accompaniment of man's present depraved condition. Some interpreters of Ambrose have accordingly represented his radically communistic account of the ideal state of nature as not intended by him to have any practical application to the society of his own time.[9] Though it is certainly true that he regarded that state as not recoverable in its entirety in this world, it is not true that the idea of it did not continue to inspire him to attacks upon the existing economic inequalities and to a persistent and violent denunciation of "the rich" — denunciation which was combined with pity, since cupidity, Ambrose constantly insists, while it robs the poor of necessities, brings only unhappiness to the wealthy. The following passage is from a treatise—perhaps originally written in the form of sermons— on the story of Naboth's vineyard.[10]

[8] Ambrose repeats the substance of this in his *Exposition of Ps.* 118, 8, 22: " cum Dominus Deus noster hanc terram possessionem omnium hominum voluerit esse communem, et fructibus omnibus ministrare; sed avaritia possessionum iura distribuit ": "Since the Lord our God wished this earth to be the common possession of all men and to furnish fruits for all; but avarice brought about a division of the rights of ownership " (*MPL*, XV, 1372). Ambrose even deduces a similar moral from the very name of man (in Latin!); for he supposes that the word *homo* comes from *humus*, the soil, "which deprives no one of anything but gives all things bounteously to all and pours forth her various fruits for the use of all living things. Therefore the special and household virtue of man is called humanity, which consists in sharing with one's fellows " (*De off. min.*, III, iii, 16; *MPL*, XVI, 158).
[9] So O. Schilling, *op. cit.*, p. 146: " Somit begegnet uns hier die Auffassung: Wie nun einmal die menschliche Natur, seitdem die *prima avaritia* hervortrat, beschaffen ist, muss Privateigenthum bestehen als weniger ideale Institution gegenüber jener goldenen Zeit."
[10] I *Kings* xxi.

De Nabuthe Jezraelita, Ch. I, 2, Ch. II, 4, Ch. III, 11, Ch. V, 20 (*MPL*,
   XIV, 767-772) :

How far, ye rich, will you carry your insane cupidity? . . . Why do
you reject nature's partnership of goods, and claim possession of nature
for yourselves? The earth was established to be in common for all,
rich and poor; why do ye rich alone arrogate it to yourselves as your
rightful property? Nature knows no rich, since she brings forth all
men poor. For we are born without clothes and are brought forth
without silver or gold. Naked she brings us to the light of day, and
in want of food and covering and drink; and naked the earth receives
back what she has brought forth, nor can she stretch men's tombs to
cover their possessions. A narrow mound of turf is enough for rich
and poor alike; and a bit of land of which the rich man when alive
took no heed now takes in the whole of him. Nature makes no distinctions among us at our birth, and none at our death. All alike she
creates us, all alike she seals us in the tomb. Who can tell the dead
apart? Open up the graves, and, if you can, tell which was a rich
man. . . .

But why do you think that, even while you live, you have abundance
of all things? Rich man, you know not how poor you are, how destitute
you would seem even to yourself, who call yourself wealthy. The more
you have, the more you want; and whatever you may acquire, you
nevertheless remain as needy as before. Avarice is inflamed by gain,
not diminished by it. . . .

You crave possessions not so much for their utility to yourself, as
because you want to exclude others from them. You are more concerned
with despoiling the poor than with your own advantage. You think
yourself injured if a poor man possesses anything which you consider
a suitable belonging for a rich man; whatever belongs to others you
look upon as something of which you are deprived. Why do you delight
in what to nature are losses? The world, which you few rich men try
to keep for yourselves, was created for all men. For not alone the soil,
but the very heaven, the air, the sea, are claimed for the use of the few
rich. . . . Do the angels in heaven, think you, have their separate
regions of space, as you divide up the earth by fixed boundaries? . . .

How many men are killed to procure the means of your enjoyment!
A deadly thing is your greed, and deadly your luxury. One man falls
to death from a roof, in order that you may have your big granaries.
Another tumbles from the top of a high tree while seeking for certain
kinds of grapes, so that you may have the right sort of wine for your
banquet. Another is drowned in the sea while making sure that fish or
oysters shall not be lacking on your table. Another is frozen to death

while tracking hares or trying to catch birds with traps. Another is beaten to death before your eyes, if he chances to have displeased you, and your very viands are bespattered with his blood. . . . [11]

Such utterances—in another age and from another mouth—would fairly certainly have been described by prosperous conservatives as " incendiary "—as would, still more certainly, the following from the same writing.

De Nabuthe, XIII, 56 (*MPL*, XIV, 784) :

Do you think your great halls (*atria*) exalt you—when they ought rather to cause you remorse because, though they are big enough to take in multitudes, they shut out the voice of the poor? Though, indeed, nothing is gained by your hearing their voice if, when you hear it, you do nothing about it. In fine, does not your very dwelling-place admonish you of your shame, in that in building it you wished to show that your riches surpass [those of others] — and yet you do not succeed? You cover walls, but you leave men bare. Naked they cry out before your house, and you heed them not: a naked man cries out, but you are busy considering what sort of marbles you will have to cover your floors. A poor man asks for money, and does not get it; a human being begs for bread, and your horse champs a golden bit. You gratify yourself with costly ornaments, while other men go without food. How great a judgment, O rich man, do you draw down upon yourself! The people go hungry, and you close your granaries; the people weep, and you turn your finger-ring about. Unhappy man, who have the power but not the will to save so many souls from death: the cost of the jewel in your ring would have sufficed to save the lives of a whole people.

Some of the prosperous class in Ambrose's day, as in some later times, seem to have piously argued that the poor must, after all, be to blame for their own indigence, since God permits it, and that it would therefore be contrary to the divine will to share one's goods with them. To this Ambrose replies with warm indignation.

De Nabuthe, VIII, 40 (*MPL*, XIV, 778) :

Perhaps you will say, as you are commonly accustomed to say: We ought not to give to a man upon whom God has wished the curse of poverty to rest. But the poor are not cursed when it is written:

---

[11] This theme of the cost of luxury in human labor, suffering, and even death, had been a favorite one of the Cynic moralists; cf., e. g., *PA*, pp. 142-143.

"Blessed are the poor in spirit, for theirs is the kingdom of heaven."
It is not of the poor man but of the rich that the Scripture says: "He
that withholdeth corn shall be cursed." Moreover, you are not to ask
what each man's deserts are. Mercy is not ordinarily held to consist in
pronouncing judgment on another man's deserts, but in relieving his
necessities; in giving aid to the poor, not in inquiring how good they
are. For it is written: "Blessed is he that understandeth concerning
the poor and needy." [12] Who is it that understands concerning them?
He who has compassion on them, who bears in mind that sharing is the
way of nature (*consortem esse naturae*), who remembers that God made
both the poor man and the rich, who knows that he sanctifies his own
produce who gives some portion of it to the poor.

What is still more noteworthy in Ambrose is that he anticipated one of the principal economic criticisms directed by
modern Socialists against the competitive system of production
and distribution. His explicit reference, it is true, is to "the
acquisitive man" (*avarus*) rather than to the acquisitive society,
but his attack upon the former is in effect a condemnation of
the latter; and it is based upon the distinction between "production for profit" and "production for use" and upon the
assumption that the profit-motive tends to restriction of the total
product. The seller's interest, he observes, lies in high prices;
these presuppose limitation of the supply of goods offered for
sale and, if possible, monopoly of the market. But the interest
of the community as a whole requires that as much be produced
as can be consumed. Hence the profit-seeker's interest, Ambrose
argues, is directly opposed to the public interest—which is to
say that it is opposed to the purpose of God. The argument is,
of course, the stronger for Ambrose because he is thinking of
the profiteering speculator in grain, oil, and other necessaries,
and of the great landowner, the exploiter of the natural resources of the soil, which was created by God. Though the
factory-system had flourished on a considerable scale in some
industries in the first century and must have still existed on a
reduced scale in the fourth, Ambrose can not be said to have
been much aware of either the economic or the moral problems
pertinent to manufacturing industry. He is unacquainted with
the modern concept of capital in the sense of artificial instru-

[12] *Ps.* xli, 1: *Beatus qui intelligit super egenum et pauperem.*

ments of production which might be held to be the product of
the savings or the labor of the owner; and he has little to say
about the equities of the employer-employee relationship.
Though there is a brief conventional injunction (*Epist.* XIX, 3)
against defrauding the hired laborer (*mercenarius*) of his
merces debita, there is no suggestion as to how a "due wage"
is to be determined. Ambrose's chief concern, in short, is for
the "poor man" simply as consumer, not as laborer or partici-
pant in the productive process; and it is with this preoccupation
that he attacks the profit-motive and the system of production
which is controlled by it.[13]

De Nabuthe, VII, 35, 37 (*MPL*, XIV, 776-777):

35. The avaricious man is always the loser by abundant harvests,
since low prices of food-stuffs beat down [his gains].[13a] To mankind
in general it is fertility that is advantageous; only to the avaricious
man is sterility profitable. He is better pleased with high prices than
with abundant commodities; and he prefers to have something of which
he is the sole vendor, rather than something which he must sell along
with [i. e., in competition with] all the other vendors. Look at him! —
fearful lest a surplus of grain should accumulate and the excess which
the storehouses cannot hold should be handed over to the needy, and
the poor thus get a chance of some benefit. The rich man claims the
products of the earth for his own not because he wants to use them
himself but in order that he may deny them to others.[14] . . .

[13] Lending money at interest, however, as well as profit-seeking, falls under
Ambrose's condemnation; almost the whole of the *De Tobia* is devoted to this
theme. (Ed. with translation and commentary by Lois M. Zucker, Catholic
University of America, Patristic Series, Washington, 1933.)

[13a] The text of the majority of the *mss.* here—*vilitatem alimoniae calculatur*—
is manifestly corrupt. The translation is based on the reading *vilitate alimoniae
calcatur,* which is found in some *mss.*

[14] The idea here may have already been something of a commonplace. It had
been fairly clearly expressed in Diocletian's edict of 301 A. D., fixing a ceiling
for prices and wages. So long as prices are not regulated, says Diocletian, the
injurious effects of "the unbridled lust for plunder . . . are not mitigated even
by abundant stocks or plentiful harvests," for "the men who are engaged in
this sort of business . . . reckon it a loss to themselves when abundance comes
through the moderation of the weather." Such men are "constantly scheming
to confine even the gifts of the gods to their own profit, and to restrict the
prosperity of the public." Though "individually possessing riches so great and
overflowing that they would suffice for whole peoples, they seek to acquire other
men's property also, and hunt after ruinous rates" (the reference is clearly to
rates of profit rather than of interest). The purpose of his edict, Diocletian

37. What, again, will you do if your product still further increases next year? You should then destroy again the warehouses which you are now preparing to build, and build bigger. For the reason why God has given you fruitful harvests is that He might thereby either overcome your avarice or condemn it; wherefore you can have no excuse. But you keep for yourself what He wished to be produced through you for the benefit of many—nay, rather, you rob even yourself of it, since you would better preserve it for yourself if you distributed it to others.

It is sufficiently evident from these texts that St. Ambrose was no merely conventional preacher of the virtue of almsgiving, exhorting the rich to give to the poor as a way of laying up treasure in heaven. The otherworldly motive, though never long absent from his thought, was not decisive, when he dealt with these matters. He was zealous to bring about a better distribution of this world's goods; and his invectives against the rich were based less upon the ground that they lacked Christian charity than upon the ground that a social order marked by so great inequalities of economic condition was contrary to "natural" justice and an aberration from the normal order established at the beginning of human history. When a rich man gives to the poor he is not being generous; he is performing an act of restitution, returning to another what rightfully belongs to him (*de suo reddis*).[15] It is, however, also true that Ambrose apparently conceived of no other way of bringing about a return to what he considered the ideal order—in so far as any return to it could be hoped for at all—than by the voluntary action of individuals in "sharing" their unrightfully acquired wealth with their fellows, and by the extirpation, through moral suasion, of the acquisitive motive (*avaritia*), the lust to possess more than others, from men's bosoms. His invectives, it would appear, were intended to arouse the consciences of the

declares, is to put an end to the avarice of such men. (Text ed. by Elsa R. Graser in Tenney Frank's *Economic Survey of Ancient Rome*, V, p. 313; see also Frank F. Abbott, *The Common People of Ancient Rome*, pp. 145-178). This attempt to fix maximum prices by law, it will be remembered, proved a disastrous failure, according to Lactantius, writing less than 15 years later: " The scarcity grew much worse, until . . . the law was repealed from mere necessity " (cf. Abbott, *op. cit.*, p. 177).

[15] *De Nabuthe*, VII, 53; *MPL*, XIV, 783: Non de tuo largiris pauperi, sed de suo reddis . . . Omnium est terra, non divitum . . . Debitum igitur reddis, non largiris indebitum.

rich but not to excite insurgency among the poor. Thus, though he saw in communism not only the ideal which would have been realized in Eden if men had remained in their original innocence, but also (and for that reason) the ideal which ought to be realized in the Roman Empire of the fourth century, he proposed no coercive program for its realization. The approach to it in practice he apparently conceived to lie in the exercise of the influence of the Church, and especially of its preachers, in persuading the affluent to give away the excess of their possessions to the needy. Concretely, then, the only means to a more equitable distribution suggested by Ambrose was, after all, almsgiving—but almsgiving on a grand scale, and as an obligatory act of justice, not of pity or self-complacent benevolence.[16]

As has been intimated, Ambrose combines, and in some degree confuses, with his denunciation of inequality of wealth the familiar thesis of cultural, and especially of Cynic, primitivism, that wealth is in itself an evil to its possessor. "Belongings," beyond the bare necessaries of life, are nothing but a burden; the man who has them really belongs to them, and not they to him. "The Prophet rightly speaks of men of wealth and not of the wealth of men,[17] in order to show that such men are not the possessors of wealth but are possessed by it. For a possession ought to belong to its possessor, and not the possessor

---

[16] So in the sequel of the passage already cited from *In Ps*. 118 *Expos*., 8, 22: "Justum est igitur ut si aliquid tibi privatum vindicas, quod generi humano, immo omnibus animantibus in commune collatum est, saltem aliquid inde pauperibus aspergas: ut quibus iuris tui consortium debes, his alimenta non deneges": "It is therefore just that, if you claim something as your private property, which was conferred in common upon the human race, nay, upon all living beings, you should distribute at least some of it to the poor; so that you may not deny sustenance to those to whom you owe a share in your right" (*MPL*, XV, 1372). Commenting on the story of Zacchaeus (*Luke* xix, 1-11) Ambrose admits that "criminality is not inherent in the possession of means (*facultates*), but in not knowing how to use them. . . . To good men they may be aids to virtue." But they become such only by being given away. "The rich Zacchaeus," as the Gospel itself declared, "was undoubtedly saved (*electus a Christo*), but by giving half his goods to the poor and restoring fourfold whatever he had wrongfully (*fraude*) taken from any man" (*Expos. Evang. sec. Luc.*, VIII, 85; *MPL*, XV, 1791). Cf. also *De Nabuthe*, XIII, 13. 55: Doubtless the Scripture asserts that a rich man *may* be *sine macula* (*Ecclesiasticus* xxxi, 8), provided he "does not go astray after gold nor place his hope in treasures of money"; but such a one, Ambrose implies, is a great rarity.

[17] *Omnes viri divitiarum*; *Ps*. 75, 6.

to the possession. Whoever, therefore, does not use his patrimony as a possession, who fails to give to the poor, is the slave and not the master of his property." [18]

Ambrose does not, meanwhile, fail to warn the poor of the moral dangers peculiar to their condition; but even when he starts upon this topic he soon passes to that of the danger of having too much, denies that wealth is any ground for pride, and suggests, in the spirit of moderate primitivism, that the best society would be one in which all possessed a sufficiency and none superfluity.

Hexaemeron, VI, 53 (*MPL*, XIV, 280):

53. Take heed, then, ye poor, take heed, ye rich, that there are temptations in both poverty and riches. It is for this reason that the Wise Man says: "Give me neither poverty nor riches." [19] And the reason why he made this his prayer the same passage tells us; for it is enough for a man to have what is sufficient for him. But riches, just as they overload the belly with viands, overload the mind with cares and anxieties. Therefore he asks only that there be granted to him what is needful and sufficient; "lest I be full and become a liar, and say, Who seeth me; or lest I be poor and become a thief, and swear falsely in the name of the Lord." [20] We must, then, avoid and flee from the temptations of the world, so that the poor man may not become desperate nor the rich man insolent. For it is written: "When thou shalt have driven out the nations and shalt begin to enjoy their lands, thou shalt not say: My power and the might of my hand have gotten me this wealth." [21] So is he who ascribes his riches to his own merit, and therefore, like a man who fancies himself to have already passed his test, knows not his own error, and drags sin after him by a long rope. For if a man will believe that making money is only a matter either of luck or of low cunning, he will have no occasion for self-glorification; for where one of these is concerned [i. e., luck] there exists no need for labor and no ground for praise; and where the other [i. e., cunning] is concerned, there exists merely avarice unashamed, which does not understand where to set bounds to the quest of pleasure.

Primitivistic considerations, manifestly drawn from Cynic and

[18] *De Nabuthe*, XV, 63.

[19] *Proverbs* xxx, 8.

[20] *Ibid.*, xxx, 9; the Latin version used by Ambrose here differs considerably from the A. and R. V.

[21] *Deuteronomy* viii, 17; the beginning of the quotation is not exact.

Stoic sources, once more serve Ambrose's purpose when his concern is not to improve the lot of the poor but to console them and to inculcate patience. After all, he points out, the man who has small possessions lives more nearly the natural life which the philosophers had extolled; and the best gifts of the Creator are incapable of appropriation by the rich. These considerations are, however, supplemented by reminders of biblical teachings concerning the equality of all men before God, the extreme difficulty, approaching impossibility, of the salvation of the rich, and the compensations in another world which will redress the inequalities of this. The two somewhat incongruous strains are curiously interwoven in the following passage:

Hexaemeron, VI, 8, 52 (*MPL*, XIV, 279-280):

Take heed, O poor man, that if your flesh is mortal, your soul is precious and everlasting. If you lack money, you do not lack grace; and if you have no spacious house nor wide acres, the heavens spread above you, the earth is free. The elements are given to all in common, and the things that adorn the world lie open equally to rich and poor. Are the gilded ceilings of the costliest houses more beautiful than the face of heaven studded with glittering stars? Are the estates of rich men wider than the open spaces of the earth? Wherefore it is said to those who join house to house and field to field: "Will you dwell alone in the midst of the land?" [22] You, O poor man, have a greater house, in which you cry out and shall be heard: "O Israel," says the prophet, "how great is the house of God and how vast is the place of his possession. It is great and hath no end; it is high and immense." [23] The house of God is common to rich and poor; yet it is hard for a rich man to enter the kingdom of heaven. But you [poor man], perhaps, take it ill that you have no gold-plated lamps to give you light; yet the moon spreads abroad for you a far more resplendent illumination. You complain, it may be, of the cold, because not for you are there any sweating-chambers filled with steam from roaring fires; but you have the heat of the sun, which warms the whole earth for you and in the winter protects you from the cold. Do you think those happy who are attended by troops of obsequious servitors? But those who have need of other men's feet do not know how to use their own. . . . You consider it a luxury to lie on ivory beds, and do not consider how much greater a luxury is the earth, that spreads for the poor man beds of

[22] *Isaiah* v, 8.   [23] *Baruch* iii, 24, 25.

grass whereon there is sweet repose and gentle slumber, which he who stretches himself out in a golden bedstead seeks the whole night through and does not find. Oh how much happier does he think you, sleeping while he lies wakeful! I pass over what is much more important—that the righteous man who endures poverty here will enjoy abundance there, and that he who has been heavy-burdened with toil here will have his recompense there, whereas he who has received his good things here cannot hope to have them restored to him there. For poverty saves up its wages for the future, wealth consumes them in the present.[24]

In the end, of course, for Ambrose as for any consistent adherent of his faith, all earthly goods are overshadowed by otherworldly values; and when this side of his doctrine is dominant in his thought, material things and natural pleasures become not only worthless, but impediments to the soul in its progress towards its true felicity. "Nothing is useful, except that which is of service towards the life eternal; not that which serves for delectation in the present life. We recognize no advantages in wealth and possessions, but consider them disadvantages, unless they are rejected, and are reckoned rather as a burden when they come than as a loss when they are surrendered."[25] In Ambrose himself, however, this ultimate otherworldly strain appears never to have quenched the passion for what seemed to him distributive justice in terrestrial society.

The most significant fact concerning this side of the teaching of St. Ambrose is that so little came of it. The most powerful and most popular figure in the Latin Church through two critical decades, he played a large part in determining the direction which it was to take in theology, in its ecclesiastical polity, its liturgy, and its relations to the secular authority. But his preaching of a virtually equalitarian and communistic ideal of a Christian society had no effect commensurate with its earnestness and eloquence. To the reflective historian, this negative fact calls for an attempt at explanation; but such an attempt would require a long discussion upon which I shall not enter here.

[24] I. e., in this present world. Echoes of Seneca's *Epist.* XC are recognizable throughout the passage (cf. *PA*, pp. 264-274, and especially pp. 271 and 273-4. For the same strain in Cynicism, cf. *PA*, pp. 143-5).

[25] *De off. min.*, I, IX, 28, adopting at the end the reading: *eaque oneri cum veniunt magis existimantur quam dispendio cum erogantur.*

XVI. "NATURE" AS NORM IN TERTULLIAN *

WELL VERSED in the writings of Cicero and the Stoics and, (as Eusebius records) "accurately acquainted with the Roman law," [1] Tertullian carried over from these pagan sources into his teaching as Christian apologist and theologian a settled presumption that in "nature," in some sense or senses of the term, are to be found valid norms of belief and conduct.[2] What, then, did the word signify for him, and what consequences followed from this presumption?

I

Among the senses most conspicuous in his usage are three—evidently, in his thought, closely related and, indeed, mutually implicative—in which *natura* has a primarily epistemological reference. It designates, namely: (a) that which is known universally and without special revelation, *i. e.*, is attested by the *sensus communis* and the *consensus gentium*; (b) that, therefore, which was known (and, indeed, more clearly known) in the primitive age (*in primordio*, a favorite expression of Tertullian's); (c) that which is uncomplicated, easily intelligible, evident to the untutored, more or less dimmed to the learned and sophisticated, mind. *Natura*, in short, denotes the three marks, if not of truth as such, at least of those moral and religious truths which are fundamental and essential: univer-

---

* This essay, like the preceding, is a section from a proposed second volume of *A Documentary History of Primitivism and Related Ideas*, of which the first volume, *Primitivism and Related Ideas in Antiquity*, by George Boas and the present writer, apppeared in 1935. Other fragments from it are included in Professor Boas's forthcoming *Essays on Primitivism and Related Ideas in the Middle Ages*.

[1] *Historia ecclesiastica* II, 2.

[2] On the influence of Roman juristic conceptions on Tertullian's theology, cf. Alexander Beck, *Römisches Recht bei Tertullian und Cyprian*, in *Schriften der Königsberger Gelehrten Gesellschaft, Geisteswissenschaftliche Klasse*, 7 Jahr, 1930, Heft 2, 1930. On the ideas of *lex dei* and *lex naturae*, id., 59-64; Fuetscher, "Die natürliche Gotteserkenntnis bei Tertullianus," *Ztschr. für kath. Theologie*, Bd. 51, 1927.

sality, primevality, simplicity. The term *anima*, moreover, as used by Tertullian, frequently designates a noetic organ or function; it is the faculty through which these "natural" truths are apprehended, that which makes man "a rational animal, in the highest degree capable of thought and knowledge." [3] To accept the *arbitrium animae* is synonymous with *credere naturae*.[4]

It is, accordingly, a characteristic method of Tertullian's apologetic, especially in his earlier, or "Catholic," period, to invoke the testimony of the *anima naturaliter christiana*,[5] a "testimony better known than all literature, more widely current than all doctrine, more public than all publications." [6]

De testimonio animae 1.

6. But I do not invoke thee [the soul] as when, formed in schools, exercised in libraries, thou belchest forth wisdom gained by feeding in Athenian Academies and Porticoes; I call upon thee, simple and rude and unrefined and untaught, as they have thee who have thee only— a thing to be met with in its completeness on the road, at the streetcorner, in the workshop. I have need of thine inexperience, since in thy experience, so little as it is, no one has confidence. I ask of thee the things which thou bringest with thee to man, which thou knowest either of thyself or from thine author, whoever he may be.

De testimonio animae 5.

These testimonies of the soul are simple in proportion as they are true, they are known to plain folk in proportion as they are simple, they are universal in proportion as they are thus known, they are natural in proportion as they are universal, they are divine in proportion as they are natural. No one, I think, can regard them as trivial or ridiculous if he reflects upon the majesty of Nature, from which the

---

[3] *De testimonio animae* 1.

[4] *Ibid.*, 6.

[5] *Apologeticus* 17. This famous phrase is often somewhat misapplied in quotation; as used by Tertullian it refers, not to exceptional individual souls, *schöne Seelen*, which are "naturally Christian," but to the generic mind of man, and its meaning is close to that of the formula in which, in the eighteenth century, Matthew Tindal expressed an essential thesis of the deists: "Christianity as Old as the Creation." The phrase is, however, retracted in other passages, *e. g.*, *op. cit.* 18 and *De testimonio animae: non es [anima], quod sciam, Christiana. Fieri enim, non nasci solet, Christiana.*

[6] *De test. an.* 1.

authority of the soul is derived. Whatever [authority] you grant to the school-mistress you will allow also to the pupil; but Nature is the school-mistress, the soul the pupil; and whatever the one has taught or the other learned has come from God — the Teacher of the teacher. What the soul may learn from the teaching of its first instructor, thou canst judge from that which is within thee. . . . Is it strange if [the soul], being given by God, makes known the same truths which God has given it to his own to know? . . . Surely the soul existed before letters, and thought before books, and speech before pens, and man himself before the philosopher or the poet. Is it therefore to be believed that before literature and its publication men lived without uttering any such thoughts as these? Did no one speak of God and his goodness, no one of death, no one of the shades? Speech went a-begging, I suppose; nay, rather, it could not have existed at all, if those things which today are so obvious, so constantly present, so near at hand, being as it were born on our very lips, had no being in former times, before letters had begun to grow up in the world—before Mercury was born, I suppose.

Adversus Marcionem I, 10.

The soul is older than prophecy. For the soul's knowledge of truth is the gift of God from the beginning of things; it is one and the same in Egypt and in Syria and in Pontus. When men speak of 'the God of the Jews,' it is of the God of the soul that they speak. . . . God never will be hidden, never will be wanting; always will be understood, always be heard, always be seen, in such manner as he wishes. God has as his witness all that we are and all that in which we are.

"Nature," in this sense, is synonymous with "reason." "It is the rational element [in man] which we must believe to have been innate in the soul from its beginning, as the work of an Author who is himself rational"; the non-rational element is not properly called "natural." [7]

Thus there are two revelations—that originally implanted in the soul of the first man, never wholly lost by any rational being, as accessible to pagans as to Jews and Christians; and that later and supernaturally imparted, and recorded in the sacred writings. And in the *De testimonio animae* Tertullian hesitates to attribute to the latter any content or authority lacking in the former: *non multum refert, a deo formata sit animae*

[7] *De anima* 16.

conscientia an a litteris dei; "it makes no great difference whether the soul's knowledge was formed in it by God directly or by his book."[8]

Upon the universality and uniformity of the revelation of "nature" Tertullian is unwearied in his insistence. "Thy thinking is vain if thou supposest this to be given only in our language and in the Greek, so that thou dost deny the universality of nature" (*universitas naturae*). *Non Latinis nec Argivis solis anima de caelo cadit. Omnium gentium unus homo, varium nomen est, unus spiritus, varius sonus, propria cuique genti loquela, sed loquelae materia communis*; "the soul did not descend from heaven upon Latins and Greeks alone. Among all peoples, man is one though his names are various, the soul is one though its language is various. Every people has its own speech; but the matter of all speech is common to all" (*De test. an.* 6).

While what I have called primevality often seems, as in some passages already cited, to be conceived merely as an aspect or implicate of that universality which is the primary mark of Nature's teachings, it also often carries for Tertullian an evidential force of its own; thus, in a passage doubtless echoing Cicero, he employs the epistemology of chronological primitivism to aid his Christian apologetic. The very age of the Scriptures — he is apparently thinking of the Pentateuch — strengthens their authority.

Apologeticus 47.

Truth, if I mistake not, is the oldest of all things, and the antiquity (which has been already established) of the sacred writings helps me here, by making it the more easily credible that they were the treasury from which all later wisdom was drawn.

---

[8] *De test. an.* 5. In the later *De anima* (1), Tertullian declares that religious truth cannot be known with full certainty apart from the Christian revelation. Socrates did not know the immortality of the soul "with the assurance of verified [or exact] truth," *compertae veritatis*; "for to whom is truth verified without God? to whom is God known without Christ? in whom is belief in Christ established without the Holy Spirit? to whom is the Holy Spirit imparted without the sacrament of faith?" Yet even here Tertullian adds that "many truths are supplied by nature, as by the general sense (*publico sensu*) with which God has deigned to endow the soul"; and the fault of the pagan philosophy is that it is not truly in accord with nature (*naturalis*) (*ibid.* 2).

A curious piece of reasoning in *Adversus Hermogenem* and elsewhere asks: How is the question at issue between Tertullian and his theological opponents to be decided? Answer: first of all by the test of temporal priority; "Authority belongs to that which shall be found to be the more ancient, and it is assumed in advance that corruption [of the truth] is to be ascribed to the doctrine which is found to be later in date. For inasmuch as the false is a corruption of the true, the true must necessarily precede the false." All novelties in doctrine are therefore *eo ipso* heretical: "in so far as the rule of truth is prior in time, so far must all later doctrines be judged heresies." ⁹ Tertullian is, of course, in this last arguing for the sufficiency and authority of the beliefs of the primitive church, not of primitive man. A later age was to apply the test of priority more rigorously and consistently, and thereby rule out of court Christian dogma itself, in so far as it contained any additions to what was supposed to be the truly primeval creed of mankind.

In spite of his acceptance of what I have termed epistemological primitivism, Tertullian was no cultural primitivist of the sort exemplified by so many classical writers. He was no admirer of contemporary savages. In his treatise *Against Marcion*, the worst terms of abuse which he can find to direct against that theological adversary are: "fouler than any Scythian, more unstable than the Sarmatians who live in wagons, more uncivilized (*inhumanior*) than the Massagetae, more audacious than an Amazon." But these peoples were among the typical "noble savages" of classical primitivism. Both the character of the Black Sea country which most of these nomadic tribes inhabited, and their manners and customs, are painted by Tertullian in the most lurid and repellent colors. Fortunately, this land "is separated from our more civilized seas, as if it were somehow ashamed of its barbarity." ¹⁰

⁹ *Adv. Hermogenem* 1. The doctrine of Hermogenes, Tertullian charges, has this sort of novelty, and is therefore false. So in *De praescriptione* 31 and 34 Tertullian contrasts the "subsequentness of falsehood" with the "priority of truth."

¹⁰ *Adv. Marcionem* I, 1. The passage is given in full in *Primitivism in Antiquity* 342-3. The particular point of Tertullian's reference here to the region of the Euxine and to its inhabitants lies in the fact that Marcion was a native of that region. In one coming from such a country and such a breed, Tertullian

The content of the body of primevally and universally known truths consists, for Tertullian, in the first place of the moral law, *lex naturalis, lex primordialis.*

Adversus Judaeos 2.

Why should God, the Founder of the universe, the Governor of the whole world, the Moulder of man, the Planter of all nations, be supposed to have given through Moses a law to one people only, and not be said to have imparted it to all peoples? . . . But, as is congruous with the goodness of God and his justice, as the Moulder of the human race, he gave the same law to all peoples, which also at definite and stated times he bade them observe, when he willed, and through whom he willed, and as he willed. For in the beginning of the world he gave to Adam himself and to Eve a law, that they should not eat of the tree planted in the midst of the garden, but that if they did eat of it, they should die. Which law would have sufficed for them if it had been observed.

For, Tertullian goes on to declare, "the law given to Adam" contained implicitly all the content of the Mosaic law and of the two great commandments in which these were summed up by Christ.

Adversus Judaeos 2.

The primeval law was given to Adam and Eve in Paradise as the matrix of all the commandments of God. . . . Therefore in this general and primeval law of God, which he required to be observed with respect to the fruit of the tree, we recognize to have been implicit all the subsequent commandments specially laid down which became explicit at their own proper times. . . . In fine, I contend that before the law written by Moses on tables of stone, there was an unwritten law which was known naturally and was habitually kept by the fathers. For on what ground was Noah "found righteous," if the righteousness of the law of nature did not exist before he did? And on what ground was Abraham accounted a "friend of God," if not by reason of [his observance of] the justice and righteousness of the law of nature? . . . [11]

intimates, heresies so abominable as Marcion's are not surprising. Such were the amenities of theological controversy among early Christians.

[11] Cf. also *De corona* 6: "If you are looking for the law of God, you have it in that common one prevailing throughout the world, inscribed on the tables of nature (*in naturalibus tabulis*), to which the Apostle was wont to apppeal, as when, speaking of the veiling of women, he says, ' does not nature teach you? '

The hold which the conception of the *lex naturalis* had upon Tertullian's mind is the better shown by the very difficulties in which he was involved in attempting to reconcile it with the biblical story. His deduction of the ten commandments and the entire moral law from the original prohibition in Genesis 2 owes its plausibility to its circularity; and if, as he in the main assumes, the moral law of nature is known by the light of nature which shines in every man, the original and uncorrupted man should have had no need of a special spoken revelation to acquaint him with the divine will; and again, if the *lex primordialis* contained, at least implicitly, all the essentials of morals and was, also, "habitually kept by the patriarchs," it became somewhat difficult to understand why it was necessary that a law should subsequently be revealed through Moses which appeared, after all, to contain prescriptions *not* known to Adam or the patriarchs and not discoverable by the natural reason. In so far as this last difficulty arises from the ceremonial requirements of the Jewish law (*e. g.*, circumcision, sabbath-observance) Tertullian disposes of it by arguing that these requirements were not a part of the permanent moral law, but were special temporary rules designed for particular historical situations, and destined to be rescinded; the eternal law was the original one. If circumcision had been needful for man, God would have circumcised Adam, but in fact, *in paradisum constituens eum incircumcisum colonum paradisi praefecit*, "in settling him in Paradise, he appointed a man uncircumcised to be the occupant of Paradise"; the argument manifestly is that since circumcision was not required of the first man, it is not a part of that law which is of universal validity. So also even the most righteous of the patriarchs, such as Enoch, Melchizedek, Lot, were *incircumcisi nec sabbatizantes*; once more, then, these observances must have been of merely transitory and local obligation. Tertullian thus seeks to use the Aristotelian,[12] Stoic and juristic distinction between the law of nature

and as when, in the Epistle to the Romans, declaring that the Gentiles do by nature those things which the law requires, he suggests both a *lex naturalis* and a *natura legalis*—a law of nature and a nature that is a law." *Ibid.* 7: *naturae auctoritas* is equivalent to *communis sapientia.*

[12] See *Primitivism in Antiquity*, 109 f.

and "particular" or positive laws to justify, against Jewish adversaries of Christianity, the Pauline doctrine of the supersession of the law of the Old Covenant by that of the New.

The anti-intellectualism of Tertullian and his hostility to the Greek philosophic systems have become so notorious as to overshadow the fact that, in a whole series of passages such as have been cited, he appears less an Early Father of the Latin Church than an Early Father of the deism of the 17th-18th centuries, a precursor of Herbert of Cherbury, Toland, Tindal and Voltaire; certainly these could have found in him a rich store of texts suitable to be prefixed to their own writings. To make known the fundamental religious and moral truths, he too insists — the existence of God as Creator, his goodness, man's duty, and his immortality — no special revelation was necessary; and he has the deist's scorn for the notion that this universally needful knowledge was imparted "in a little corner of the world" to a chosen people. It "was not born with the Pentateuch"; "the pen of Moses did not introduce the knowledge of the Creator, but only repeated what must be dated back, not to Egypt and Moses, but to the beginning of things, to Adam and Paradise." Moreover, "the great majority of the human race have never so much as heard the name of Moses"; nevertheless all peoples "know the God of Moses." [13]

Tertullian's kinship—on one side of his thought—with the modern deists is further to be seen in his inclusion of the right of individual freedom in matters of religion among the dictates of the law of nature; though it must be recognized that such a thesis has throughout history been common among religious and other minority groups seeking to obtain liberty for themselves, and rare among the same groups after they have attained a position enabling them to deny it to others.

Ad scapulam 2.

It is one of the rights of man and privileges of nature that everyone should worship according to his own convictions. One man's religion neither harms nor helps another's. It is no part of religion to compel religion, which should rest upon free choice and not upon force—since even sacrificial victims are required to be of a willing mind.[14]

[13] *Adv. Marcionem* I, 10.
[14] This passage was known to and used by at least one of the champions of

Yet Tertullian's final position is, of course, remote from that of the deist. In the first place, he is careful to maintain that there may still be revelations of special and temporary laws not known to men of all ages by the natural reason: *nec adimamus hanc dei potestatem pro temporum condicione legis praecepta reformantem in hominis salutem*; [15] "let us not set aside this power of God to modify the precepts of the law in accordance with the circumstances of particular times, for man's salvation." And beyond this, the Christian creed, *the regula fidei*, which is *immobilis et irreformabilis*,[16] assuredly contains articles which not only can not be known by the natural reason but are, from its point of view, absurdities. *Stulta mundi elegit deus, ut confundat sapientiam*, and this is especially evident in the doctrine of the Incarnation: a God who literally became flesh, existed as an embryo in a womb, was born as a helpless infant, was circumcised, suffered physical pains and weaknesses, died by crucifixion. Thus Tertullian swings to the other extreme, and falls into his too famous defiance of reason: *mortuus est dei filius; prorsus credibile est, quia ineptum. Et sepultus resurrexit; certum est, quia impossibile est.*[17]

I have called this outburst "too famous" because its fame has tended to obscure the other side of Tertullian's doctrine: the possession by every man of a rational faculty, with the invariant deliverances of which it is clearly implied that all other legitimate beliefs must conform. In his polemic against Marcion he persistently attacks that theologian on the ground that his teachings are contrary to reason. He writes, for example, that anyone's belief as to the number of Gods (*numerus divinitatis*) "ought to be consistent with the highest reason (*summa*

religious freedom in the seventeenth century. It is quoted in full by Roger Williams in support of the thesis that "it agreeth both with humane reason and natural equity, that every man worship God uncompelled, and believe what he will" (*The Bloudy Tenent of Persecution for Cause of Conscience*, 1644, in *Narragansett Club Publications*, III, 1867, p. 35). I am indebted for the reference to Mr. Irwin Goldman, *ms.* dissertation on "The Beginnings of Theories of Natural Ethics and Theology in Seventeenth Century America," University of Michigan, 1936. It is a little surprising that Milton, who quotes Tertullian more than a score of times, did not make use of this passage.

[15] *Adv. Judaeos* 2.
[16] *De virginibus velandis* 1.
[17] *De carne Christi* 5.

ratione); otherwise the worship of divinity would be subject to wavering opinions"; *i. e.*, reason is the ultimate court of appeal, by whose decision alone can the discordant multiplicity of men's notions in matters of religion be adjudicated. Marcion. however, (according to Tertullian) believed that there are " two Gods "; this, Tertullian argues, is absurd, because it contradicts the very concept, or definition, of God; there cannot be two Supreme Beings. The premise here is precisely the reverse of *certum est quia impossibile.* In his anti-rationalistic mood, however, Tertullian is a partial precursor of Kierkegaard, who (in the words of a competent expositor of his philosophy) " brought to the fore the *paradoxical* quality of Christian truth, and the fact that, so far from appearing true to the human intellect, it constitutes an ' offense ' to our intellectual faculty as such." The same expositor adds—presumably having Tertullian in mind, among others—that " the early Christians knew that their faith was not intellectually respectable, and they believed against the understanding; the modern Christian is tempted to believe because his understanding assents to what is presented. But to believe because the understanding assents is in reality not to believe." [18] But in Tertullian, at least in his earlier phase, revolt against the understanding was neither a constant nor a usual attitude; his apologetic, with rare exceptions, is patently addressed to the intellect of the reader.

It is, nevertheless, true that the acceptance of "nature" as the norm of truth in the three interrelated senses already indicated, in which it stands for the organ or the content of a universal, intuitive and infallible knowledge, involves Tertullian in difficulties when he turns to the defense, not only of so paradoxical a doctrine as that of the Incarnation, but of other dogmas, such as the resurrection of the body, which manifestly are not intuitively apprehended nor supported by the *consensus gentium.* In dealing with these he is driven virtually to reverse his religious epistemology; the deeper truths are *not* simple and universally known, but hidden and obscure, and the " divine reason " and the natural may conflict.

[18] Robert Bretall, Introduction to *Kierkegaard Anthology*, 1946, xxiii.

De resurrectione carnis 3.

That which recommends the opinions commonly accepted is their very simplicity and their familiarity, and the agreement concerning them of many men's judgments; they are deemed the more faithful [to the truth] because they are plain and open and known to everyone. But the divine reason, on the contrary, lies in the marrow and inmost part of things, not on the surface, and is often at variance with the things that are immediately manifest.

Nevertheless, even the resurrection of the body is, in another sense, taught — and has from the beginning been taught — by "Nature," namely, by the analogies of natural processes. Everywhere death is followed by renewal; day succeeds night, spring winter; everything returns to its original state: *omnia in statum redeunt cum abscesserint, . . . nihil deperit nisi in salutem.* Thus God made known the resurrection of the dead *operibus antequam litteris.* "He sent nature to you as your first teacher, purposing to send also prophecy afterwards, so that, having been nature's disciple, you may the more readily believe prophecy" (*ibid.*, 12).

II

When, however, Tertullian passed from his preoccupation with "natural" truths, in the foregoing senses, to the vindication of a supernatural revelation supplementary to these, he was also led to conceive of religion as progressive. For, in the first place, the Judeo-Christian revelation in the past had plainly been gradual and cumulative. To Adam and the patriarchs were imparted only the rudiments of the knowledge needful for man's salvation; to these additions were made from time to time; "for what is there strange if he who initiates a process of instruction (*disciplina*) extends it, if he who begins it carries it farther?"[19] In the second place, revelation was not closed even with the teaching of Christ; for he himself promised the coming of the Holy Spirit who should lead believers "into all truth." And finally, the work of the Spirit cannot be assumed to be yet completed.

This way of thinking in Tertullian is best illustrated in the opening chapter of a treatise of his semi-Montanist period of

[19] *Adv. Judaeos* 2.

which the principal object was to prove that virgins should always remain veiled in public. Here was a rule which could not claim the sanction of remote antiquity—it had certainly not been observed in Eden! — nor of universal custom; hence, to establish his case, Tertullian, after first dwelling once more upon the immutability and ancientness of truth, proceeds to reject the authority of both antiquity and custom. "Christ called himself *veritas*, not *consuetudo*." The novelty of a doctrine is no evidence of its falsity. *Haereses non tam novitas quam veritas revincit*; "it is not so much their novelty, as truth, that convicts heresies; and whatever savors of opposition to truth is a heresy even though it be ancient custom." While the fundamental rule of faith remains constant, "other matters, both of doctrine and behavior admit of corrective innovation (*novitatem correctionis*), the grace of God, to wit, operating and advancing to the end."

De virginibus velandis 1.

For what kind of a supposition is this, that, while the devil is always at work and is daily adding to the ingenuities of iniquity, the activity of God either has already ceased or has stopped advancing? Whereas the reason why the Lord sent the Paraclete was that, since man's mediocrity made it impossible for him to take in all things at once, his instruction should little by little be directed and ordered and carried on to perfection by the Vicar of the Lord, the Holy Spirit. "I have still," he said, "many things to say unto you, but ye are not yet able to bear them; when that Spirit of Truth shall come, he will lead you into all truth, and will make known to you the further things that still remain [to be revealed]." But he also pronounced further concerning his [the Paraclete's] work. For what is the office of the Paraclete but this: the direction of teaching, the revelation of the Scriptures, the reformation of the intellect, the advance towards better things? Nothing is without stages of growth; all things await their due time. Finally, Ecclesiastes says, "There is a time for all things." See how created things themselves come to fruition little by little. First is the seed, and from this the shoot pushes out; then boughs and leaves gather strength, and the whole of what we call a tree expands; then the bud swells and from the bud bursts the flower, and from the flower the fruit emerges. And the fruit itself, at first crude and unshapely, passing little by little through a succession of stages, is ripened to the mellowness of its flavor. So also righteousness (for the God of righteousness and of the creatures is the same) existed at first only in its rudiments, in the form of the natural fear of God; from this it advanced through the Law and the Prophets to infancy; then through the Gospel to the fervor of youth; and now through the Paraclete it is settling into maturity.[20]

Here, it will be observed, Tertullian's conclusion rests upon two analogies. The first is the analogy between the stages of racial and of individual mental development. The minds of men in the earlier periods of history, and even in the present, are immature; their powers of understanding are limited. The revelation of truth must therefore be gradual and progressive. Even the divine Instructor must conform to this pedagogic necessity. This conclusion was pertinent specifically to man's religious history. But the argument appeals also to an analogy of wider implications—that of natural processes in general, and especially of biological processes. No living thing at its beginning is what it is destined to become; it proceeds from inferior to superior forms, and this slow progression follows a fixed sequence. In the life of creatures, everything is subject to the necessity of gradual development; in the broader and vaguer sense of a modern term, "evolution" is the ubiquitous characteristic of nature. Tertullian's chronological primitivism has here obviously given place to its opposite.

It was, certainly, in its application to religion that this assumption of an "advance toward better things" chiefly interested Tertullian; but he also sometimes expressed a belief in a more secular kind of progress in the history of mankind. *A propos* of the polygamy of the patriarchs, he remarks that "there is always a laxity at the beginning of anything," *semper initia laxantur*, a highly anti-primitivistic generalization; and though the great example of this is in the contrast between the Old Dispensation and the New, he adds: "I think, also, that even in human institutions and laws later things surpass (or prevail over) primitive ones," *posteriora pristinis praevalere.*[21] In a chapter of his *De anima*, attacking the Pythagorean doctrine of the transmigration of souls, he argues that any such theory is inconsistent with the continuous increase of the earth's

---

[20] The passage especially well illustrates the fact that in Christian theology the Third Person of the Trinity has been peculiarly the patron of the idea of progress.

[21] *Exhortatio castitatis* 6.

population: "if the living come from the dead, then there must always remain unchanged one and the same number of mankind"; and in developing the point Tertullian sees in population-growth a major cause of the past progress of civilization. In his own time, however, he assumes that the problem of over-population has arisen; with this he deals (perhaps following Varro) in a proleptically Malthusian manner: famines, pestilences and wars are necessary and therefore beneficent checks upon the tendency of mankind to multiply to excess.

De anima 30.

We find in the *Accounts of the Antiquities of Man* [22] that the human race has gradually increased in numbers, alike in the case of those peoples who have remained on their original territory, and of those who have become nomads or emigrants, or have sought lands through conquest—as the Scythians in Parthia, the Temenidae in the Peloponnesus, the Athenians in Asia, the Phrygians in Italy, and the Phoenicians in Africa; and likewise through those formal migrations which are called colonizations, by which cities, in order to rid themselves of the burden of excessive population, disgorge into other regions their human swarms. For while the aborigines still remain in their original abodes, they have at the same time lent even larger populations to other territories. Surely it is evident that the world as a whole is becoming better cultivated and better provided than in its earlier days. All parts of it are now accessible, all are known, all are open to trade; most pleasant farms have obliterated all traces of once notorious wastes; cultivated fields have subdued forests; flocks and herds have put wild beasts to flight; sandy deserts are sown, rocks are planted, marshes drained, and cities are now as numerous as were formerly scattered huts. No longer are islands feared, nor are their rocky shores dreaded; everywhere are houses and people and ordered government, everywhere [human] life. The final evidence of the fecundity of mankind is that we have grown burdensome to the world: the elements scarcely suffice for our support, our needs grow more acute, our complaints more universal, since nature no longer provides us sustenance. In truth, pestilence and famine and wars and earthquakes must be looked upon

[22] The reference is probably to the lost work of Varro *De antiquitatibus rerum humanarum*. It would appear from Tertullian's citation that Varro must have attempted some rudiments of " political arithmetic " in dealing with the question of population-growth.

as a remedy for nations, a means of pruning the overgrowth of the human race.[23]

It must be added that Tertullian's belief in progress in religion is usually—in spite of some expressions to the contrary—merely retrospective. Two other factors in his thought made this inevitable. In the first place, both his legal training and his personal temperament made him crave a definitive formulation of doctrine, a *regula fidei* needing no supplementation or future reinterpretation. We seek in order to find; we find what we have sought when we attain belief; and what is to be believed is what Christ taught. "This limit has been fixed for you by Christ himself, who does not wish you to believe anything else but what he has taught, nor even to seek for anything else."[24] Tertullian therefore is at pains to prove that the doctrines of the Church of his time are strictly identical with those of the "primitive Church."[25] This implied that the Paraclete had, after all, *not* revealed any "further things" to mankind.

But still more potent than this craving for a fixed and final standard of doctrine in preventing Tertullian from habitually and consistently extending the conception of gradual progress into the future, was his chiliasm. His outlook upon the time to come was determined almost wholly by those eschatological beliefs, derived largely from the concluding chapters of the Apocalypse,[26] which were still dominant among Christians of his time; and these beliefs were not based upon any analogy

---

[23] Tertullian's Malthusianism, it need hardly be said, was decidedly premature. Modern historians have pointed out that what was actually taking place in Italy, and in the Empire in general, in the early Christian centuries, was an alarming decrease of population. Thus under Gallienus (middle of third century) "the great city of Alexandria had no more than half its former inhabitants," and Gibbon observed, somewhat speculatively, that "if one applied this proportion to the whole world, half of the human race had disappeared." (Boissier, *La fin du paganisme* (1903), II, 368). Cf. also Tenney Frank, *Economic History of Rome*, 2d. ed. (1927), 204 ff.

[24] *De praescriptione haereticorum* 10. This writing is of earlier date than those last cited, and probably almost as early as the *De testimonio animae*. But it can not safely be assumed that the inconsistency of these passages is evidence of a conscious and deliberate change of doctrine. Tertullian troubled little about consistency, and was capable of almost any amount of rapid fluctuation between ideas that appealed to him, however incongruous with one another.

[25] *Ibid.*, 20.

[26] Chapters 20-22.

either with the natural development of organisms or with pedagogic gradualism. The future of man was not pictured as a continuation of a process of advance by successive stages, hitherto and now operative; the prospect which the accepted dogmas placed before the imagination of the pious was of two tremendous cataclysmic events, sudden and supernatural interpositions from without. The anticipation of the Second Coming, to be followed by the thousand years of human perfection and happiness "upon this earth," was naturally, for faithful believers, a cheerful one; but the immediate future to which they looked forward was one to be dreaded. For "the day of the Lord" was to come only after there should be "a falling-away, and the man of sin, the son of perdition," *i. e.*, the Anti-Christ, should appear, bringing conflicts of the nations, persecutions and manifold disasters upon Christians as well as pagans.[27] Tertullian, therefore, while he at times dilates enthusiastically upon the imminence of the Lord's coming, in other passages represents his fellow-Christians as legitimately praying for its postponement; and for the hope of its postponement he found a biblical warrant. For the crucial chapter of Second Thessalonians had spoken of "one who restrains," or holds back, the appearance of the Anti-Christ; and this restraining power was construed to be the Roman Empire. It was for this reason above all, Tertullian declares, that the Christians prayed for the Emperors and for the stability of the Empire. "For we know that the great force which threatens the whole world, the end of the age itself, with its menace of hideous suffering, is retarded only by the respite which the Roman Empire means for us. We do not wish to experience all that; and when we pray for its postponement, we are helping towards the continuance of Rome."[28] It would seem from this that Tertullian's dominant feeling—and that of most second-century Christians —about the next age to be expected for mankind was one of fear, mitigated by a not very confident hope of the possible persistence, for a time, of the *status quo*.

[27] Second Thessalonians 2, cited by Tertullian in *De resurrectione carnis* 24.
[28] *Apologeticus* 32, tr. T. R. Glover, in Loeb Lib., 154. There is a similar passage in *De resurrectione carnis* 24. The latter is a relatively late, the *Apologeticus* an early writing of Tertullian; on this matter his state of mind seems to have remained unchanged.

III

The word "nature" had long since come to designate, along with its many other meanings, the whole world of sensible objects and its ordinary processes and empirically known laws— the sense which is perhaps the most current one in contemporary usage. There is in this sense no obvious or necessary normative implication; the term is simply a summary name for things as they are, not as they ought to be. Nevertheless, even this widest and primarily descriptive signification of "nature" and "natural" early took on a eulogistic coloring (which for many it still has) and became the source of value-judgments. This seems to have come about chiefly in two ways. In the first place, the sanctity attaching to the word in its other uses—it was *par excellence* the "blessed word" of classical antiquity—was simply transferred to this use. Since "nature," in one sense, *meant* the norm of value or excellence, in moral conduct and other human activities, it was tacitly assumed that "nature," *i.e.*, the actual cosmos and its laws, must be wholly excellent, and that "harmony with" and "conformity to" it (whatever, concretely, these expressions might signify) must be a moral imperative. This semantic process of the transference of an affective tone from one denotation of the word to another is especially evident in Stoicism. In the second place, for Christians, "nature," also in the sense of the cosmos, "the creation," was the work of God, who had pronounced each of its parts good, and the whole "very good." [29] It followed that nothing is to be disparaged or condemned by man which is attributable to the divine authorship—and nothing *in* man which has been implanted in him by the Creator. True, according to the Judeo-Christian doctrine of the Fall, there are tendencies in man attributable to quite another source, and therefore evil; and a text in Genesis (3: 18) could be construed to imply that even the non-human part of the creation had been "cursed" in consequence of man's corruption. Yet these considerations did not, for all minds, especially for those decisively influenced both by Stoicism and by the implications of the Christian conception of

[29] Genesis 1: 31.

God as the Creator of nature, annul the assumptions that the sensible world is good and should be admired and enjoyed by man, and that whatever is truly "natural" in man himself, *i. e.*, a part of his original generic and divinely bestowed constitution, is also good and should not be suppressed.

Now on Tertullian, with his dual Stoic and Christian heritage of ideas, these latter assumptions exercised a potent influence; they are the presuppositions of his thinking and feeling at many points. They were in conflict with other powerful tendencies in the Christian community of his time (and of later times)— tendencies to which he was not immune. But in consequence chiefly of these presuppositions he was, at least in a large part of his writings, relatively free from the more extreme forms of otherworldliness. He had no sympathy with the *contemptus mundi* which has been characteristic of so much Christian religious thought in all ages; he inveighed against the disparagement of "the flesh"; he did not admit the total depravity of man; and at times—though by no means invariably—he argued vigorously against certain ascetic ideals and practices widely approved by his Christian contemporaries. Of these aspects of his teaching some illustrations must now be given.

One of the worst errors of the Marcionites, in Tertullian's eyes, was their scorn of the sensible world. To their thesis that "the world is unworthy of God" he replies that "God has made nothing unworthy of himself—though it was for man, not for himself, that he made the world." Even the Greeks "gave to this world's fabric the name of ornament and grace," and the pagan philosophers called the several elements divine, and still more the universe as a whole, "when they considered its magnitude and strength and power and honor and glory, and the abundance, the regularity and the [conformity to] law of those individual elements which contribute to the production, the nourishment, the ripening and the reproduction of all things . . . I will, however, come down to humbler objects. A single floweret from the hedgerows, I do not say from the meadows, a single tiny shell from any sea, I do not say from the Red Sea, a single little wing from a moorfowl, I do not say from a peacock—can you, seeing these things, pronounce the Creator to be a sorry workman?" Thus for Tertullian, one may fairly say, even "the meanest flower that blows" had something divine about it, and could evoke a mood of religious reverence. Though it would be misleading to describe this feeling as pantheistic, it is more than a simple wonder at the skill of the Creator's craftsmanship; for it is associated with a strong, if vague, sense of the ubiquity of a divine presence in nature: "all things are filled with their Author and are occupied by him"; there is "no part of space" in which "the creatures are empty of deity" (*divinitas*).[30] Tertullian, in short, was not devoid of what a later age was to call *Naturgefühl*.

From the same Stoic and Judeo-Christian premises came the strain in Tertullian's teaching in which he is unique among patristic writers. To the fashion of despising "the flesh" he was (before his final phase) profoundly antipathetic. It, not less than the soul, was willed and created by God, *aeque caro dei res est*; both are essential components of the nature of man. Tertullian has, indeed, usually been described as a materialist, and it is true that, in several passages, he adopts the metaphysics of Stoicism. "Everything that exists is a bodily existence of its own kind. Nothing lacks bodily existence except that which is non-existent." [31] Even the soul, then — "as the Stoics have no difficulty in persuading us" — is a corporeal substance.[32] But this seemingly unqualified assertion of materialism does not really express what may be called Tertullian's working theory of man's constitution. He may better be described as a psycho-physical dualist, for he habitually distinguishes soul and body and assigns to them quite distinct and incompatible attributes and functions. What he does insist upon is their inseparability (at least so long as man lives in this world), their "intimate union," and the indispensability of the body and the physical senses to all the activities of the soul and "the mind" (which is a function of the soul). Six chapters of *De resurrectione carnis* are devoted to vindicating what he calls the *carnis dignitas*, and in his zeal for this theme he even ventures to hint a doubt whether the soul is not subservient to the body, rather than the contrary.

[30] *Adv. Marcionem* I, 13, 11.
[31] *De carne Christi* 11.
[32] *De anima* 5.

De resurrectione carnis 7.

Has God combined [the soul] with, or rather, inserted and intermingled it in, the flesh? Yes; and has so closely compacted them together that it can be held to be uncertain whether the body bears about the soul or the soul the body, whether the flesh is the servant of the soul or the soul of the flesh. But it is rather to be believed that the soul is the driver and has the mastery, as nearer to God. Yet this also enhances the glory of the flesh, that it contains that which is nearest to God and makes itself a partaker in the soul's mastery (*dominatio*). For what use of nature is there, what enjoyment of the world, what savor· of the elements, that the soul does not feed upon by means of the flesh? How, indeed, can it be otherwise? Is it not through it that the soul is sustained by all the organs of the senses—by sight and hearing and taste and smell and touch? . . . Speech, too, takes place by means of a bodily organ. Through the flesh are made possible the arts, through it the studies and the talents of men, and their business and their works and their employments (*officia*) ; so that, in fine, the whole life of the soul is so bound up with the flesh that cessation of life for the soul is nothing but separation from the flesh.

This is, manifestly, a far cry from the (supposedly) Pauline assertion of an absolute "opposition" of flesh and spirit; [33] it is not a far cry from the dictum of the Victorian poet which to many readers of 1864 doubtless seemed a little bold:

> Nor soul helps flesh more, now, than flesh helps soul.

Man's sinfulness, then, for Tertullian is not attributable to the duality of his constitution; the flesh as such is not the root of evil in him. But that the race since the Fall is universally and deeply corrupted Tertullian, of course, could not and did not question. Yet that even unregenerate man is totally or fundamentally or "naturally" evil he will not admit. Doubtless

---

[33] Galatians 5: 16-17. Tertullian is aware that he is in seeming conflict with Paul here, and tries to explain it away. He admits that "the Apostle says that ' in his flesh dwelleth no good thing ' (Romans 3: 18) and declares that ' they who are in the flesh cannot please God ' because ' the flesh lusteth against the spirit ' " (Galatians *loc. cit.*). But Tertullian disposes of "these and similar statements " by a distinction which was, of course, quite foreign to the thought of Paul: " It is not the *substance* of the flesh but its acts that are described as without honor "; and for its evil acts the soul, "which compels the flesh to do its bidding," is responsible (*De res. carnis* 10).

there may be said to be in man a second or depraved nature, *alia natura quam diabolus induxit*, which is distinct from "the nature that is from God," an antecedent and in a certain sense natural evil (*naturale quodammodo*) which arises from the *vitium originis*, i. e., through men's descent from Adam.[34] Tertullian, however, introduces this distinction of two senses of "nature" only for the purpose of explaining—or explaining away—the text in Ephesians, "We were once by nature children of wrath";[35] he is arguing that "by nature" in the proper sense we are not and never were children of wrath. Despite man's inherited propensity to sin there is always present and active within him *bonum animae illud principale, illud divinum atque germanum et proprie naturale*. "For that which is from God is rather obscured than extinguished. Obscured it can be, because it is not God; extinguished it cannot be, because it is from God . . . Thus some men are very bad and some very good; nevertheless, all souls are of one kind. And so, even in the worst of them there is something good and even in the best something bad." The "divinity of the soul," then, "in consequence of its original goodness," is more or less clearly manifest in every man.[36] Though Tertullian did much to formulate and promote the doctrine of original sin, in him it was thus combined with an equal, and sometimes more than equal, insistence upon the doctrine of man's natural and inextinguishable goodness.

In keeping with these preconceptions there is a vein of hedonism in Tertullian's moral teaching. The moderate enjoyment of all the simple and direct pleasures of the senses is legitimate, commendable, and even obligatory; otherwise Nature would not have furnished us with the capacity for such enjoyment.

De corona militis 5, 8.

Our God is the God of nature, who fashioned man and, in order

---

[34] *De anima* 16, 41. Tertullian was, at least among the Latin Fathers, the originator of the theory known as Traducianism: both soul and body are transmitted from parent to offspring at the moment of conception, and all souls are thus congenitally infected with the sinfulness inherited from the first parent (*tradux animae, tradux peccati*). Cf. R. E. Roberts, *The Theology of Tertullian* (1924), 160-162, 248-251.

[35] Ephesians I: 3.

[36] *De anima* 41.

that he might appreciate and enjoy the pleasures that attach to things (*fructus rerum*), endowed him with certain senses acting, in one way or another, through the several appropriate organs [hearing through the ear, etc.]. By means of these functions of the outer man ministering to the inner man, the enjoyments of the divine gifts are conveyed through the senses to the soul. . . . Those things are proper to be used which, to meet the necessities of human life, supply what is really useful, and afford sure aids and decent comfort; such things may be regarded as inspired by God himself, who provided them beforehand for his creature, man, both for his instruction and his delight.[37]

Christians have nothing in common with the ascetic sects of the Orient (*neque Brachmanae aut Indorum gymnosophistae sumus*)" who live in forests, refugees from life. We repudiate no enjoyment of the works of God — though, certainly, we are temperate in this, lest we use them improperly or beyond due measure (*modus*)." [38]

Tertullian accordingly discountenances excessive fasting and denounces those "heretics who preach perpetual abstinence, to the point of despising the works of the Creator." It is true that orthodox Christians on certain days observe some dietary restrictions as an "offering to God"; but, Tertullian insists, they really fast very little: *quantula est apud nos interdictio ciborum* — "only two weeks in the year of eating dry food, and not whole weeks, either, Sundays and Sabbaths being omitted; in these periods we abstain from certain foods, of which we do not reject but only defer the use." [39]

But while the enjoyment by man of whatever is "natural" is good, indulgence in what is not "natural" is evil; and Tertullian's notion of what is contrary to nature is undeniably far-reaching. It forbids any alteration of things from the character which God has chosen to give to them; it extends by

---

[37] Similarly in *De spectaculis* 2, Tertullian writes: "Everyone knows, and even Nature tells us, that the things created by God and given to man are (as we Christians also teach) all good, since they are the work of a good Creator." Unhappily, many of these intrinsically good gifts have been perverted by man, through the instigation of the Devil, to wrong uses. This, in fact — "the aberrant use by [human] creatures of that which God has created," *perversa administratio conditionis a conditis* — is the very essence of sinfulness, *tota ratio damnationis*. What constitutes an aberrant use will appear in what follows.

[38] *Apologeticus* 42.

[39] *De ieiunio* 15—a late writing, it may be noted.

implication to everything artificial, though Tertullian does not carry the implication through consistently; if he had, he would have been (what we have seen that he was not) a cultural primitivist of the most extreme sort. "What God was unwilling to produce ought not to be produced [by men]. Those things therefore are not best by nature which are not from God, the Author of nature. Consequently, they must be understood to be from the Devil, the disturber of nature; for what is not God's must necessarily be his rival's." One specific moral which Tertullian draws from this premise is that dyed fabrics should not be used for clothing. The materials of garments should be left in their natural colors, since "that which he has not himself produced is not pleasing to God." It cannot be supposed that "he was unable to command sheep to be born with purple or sky-blue fleeces." But if he was able to do so, but has not, "then plainly he was unwilling." [40] The specific moral here strikes us now as trivial and silly; but other deductions from the same premise were recurrently to be heard throughout history, and may still be heard today, in arguments against one or another exercise of human "art" — of man's intelligence and skill — to add to or amend what is supposed to be the "natural" order of things. It had not occurred to Tertullian — though Democritus had made the observation before Shakespeare [41] — that "That art which you say adds to nature is an art which nature makes; . . . the art itself is nature."

From similar premises Tertullian derives a proof of the immorality of the pagan practice of wearing crowns of flowers on the head. *Maior efficitur ratio christianarum observationum, cum illas etiam natura defendit, quae prima omnium disciplina est:* "the argument for Christian observances becomes stronger when even Nature, which is the first of all teaching, supports

---

[40] *De cultu feminarum,* I, 8. The injunction against wearing dyed fabrics is here addressed to women, but it obviously applied to both sexes. Among other things which Tertullian held, apparently for the same reason, to be against nature, were play-acting and the shows of the circus, in which the faces and forms of men and women were disfigured—and shaving. "Will God be pleased with one who applies the razor to himself and completely changes his features?" (*De spectaculis* 23). This practice had similarly been condemned by the Cynic moralists as "contrary to nature."

[41] Cf. *Primitivism in Antiquity,* 207-8.

them." How then is the teaching of Nature with respect to the propriety of wearing floral chaplets to be known? By observing that, while Nature—or "our God, who is the God of nature"—evidently intended us to enjoy "the pleasures afforded by his other creatures," since he provided us with various sense-organs of which the exercise is naturally pleasurable, there is no such *natural* pleasure in wearing a wreath of flowers on the head. For the sensible pleasures attached to flowers are those of sight and smell. "With sight and smell, then, make use of flowers, for these are the senses by which they were meant to be enjoyed." But you can neither see the color nor smell the fragrance of flowers on top of your head. *Ergo:*

It is as much against nature to crave a flower with the head as to crave food with the ear or sound with the nostril. But everything which is against nature is deservedly known amongst all men as a monstrous thing; but still more among us it is condemned as a sacrilege against God who is the Lord and Author of Nature.[42]

The invocation of "nature" as a norm in this fashion could thus, with a little ingenuity, serve as a rhetorical device for damning almost any custom of the pagans which differed from those of Christians.

But the crucial and difficult issue for Tertullian arose when, holding that everything *proprie naturale* is good and designed for man's use and enjoyment, he was compelled to face the fact that human beings are endowed with sex. The glorification of virginity and the feeling of something inherently evil in sex had by the early third century become widely prevalent, and probably almost universal, in the Christian moral temper and teaching — however limited its application in practice. And with this temper Tertullian clearly was sympathetic. Yet it could not well be denied that sex and the pleasures attaching to it are "natural"; certainly God had "produced" it; and in view of the premises to which Tertullian was committed, he could not escape the question to which Pope was to give the most pointed expression in the eighteenth century:

Can that offend great Nature's God
Which Nature's self inspires?

---

[42] *De corona* 5.

And the answer which the premises required seemed evident: to reject or despise this gift of Nature could be no less than sacrilege against the Author of Nature. Scripture, moreover, taught that procreation is a duty laid upon mankind by the divine command in Eden. Logic, and the weight of biblical authority, thus pressed Tertullian towards one view on the highly practical question whether celibacy or marriage should be the rule—or at least the ideal—for Christians; the sentiment of his fellow-believers, which he shared, and an already potent tradition, pressed him towards the opposite view; and his utterances on the subject make evident the inner conflict which resulted.

In a few passages his piety towards "nature" leads him to a reverential glorification of marriage and of the sexual act, and to the praise of maternity, not virginity, as sacred. His scorn of the contrary attitude is expressed in a sharp epigram which deserves to have been remembered: *natura veneranda est, non erubescenda.*

De anima 27.

Nature is to be reverenced, not blushed at.[43] It is lust, not the act itself, that makes sexual union shameful; it is excess, not the [marital] state as such, that is unchaste; for the state itself has been blessed by God: "Be ye fruitful and multiply." Upon excess, indeed, he has laid a curse — adulteries and fornications and the frequenting of brothels. Now in this usual function of the sexes which brings male and female together—I mean, in ordinary intercourse—we know that the soul and the body both take part: the soul through the desire, the body through its realization, the soul through the impulse, the body through the act.[44]

His own marital experience, moreover, moved Tertullian to eulogize in the highest terms the union of believers — a union

---

[43] For the Latin reader there was a possible double meaning here. One of the senses of *natura* was "the genitalia"; and the word is used in this sense by Tertullian in *De anima* 46. In the text, below, "usual function" is probably the better rendering of *solemne officium*, which, however, may possibly mean "sacred duty."

[44] Cf. also *De carne Christi* 4: The Marcionites look upon the phenomena of parturition as disgusting; in doing so they "spit upon the *veneratio naturae*"; childbirth is in truth to be regarded as *pro natura religiosum*. So *Adv. Marcionem* III, 11: *Age iam, perora illa sanctissima et reverenda opera naturae*; the particular works of nature here characterized as "most sacred and deserving of veneration" are gestation and birth.

involving both flesh and spirit. In a writing addressed to his wife he exclaims: "How can we sufficiently describe the happiness of that marriage which the Church approves, which the offering confirms, and the benediction signs and seals; which the angels report to Heaven, and the Father accepts as valid! ... What kind of 'yoke' is that of two believers who share in one hope, one desire, one discipline, and the same service? Both are brethren, both fellow-servants, with no separation of spirit or of flesh—nay, rather, they are 'two in one flesh,' and where the flesh is one, so is the spirit also." [45] It was not in this tone that Paul had written—still less, that Augustine was to write—of marriage.

Nor, in truth, is it in this tone that Tertullian always or usually writes. His most frequent passages on the subject express a violent effort to reconcile the *veneratio naturae* which he had extolled, and a deference to the divine injunction in Genesis, with the feeling, which he evidently could not repress, that virginity is after all the better state. Even in the *Ad uxorem* he exhorts his wife, if she should survive him, not to marry again. To marry once is lawful, since "the union of man and woman . . . was blest by God as the *seminarium generis humani* and devised by him for the replenishing of the earth and the furnishing of the world." Nowhere in Scripture is marriage prohibited; it is recognized as a "good thing." But "what is better than this good thing we learn from the Apostle, who permits marriage but prefers abstinence." Most to be praised, then, are those who from the moment of their baptism practise continence, and those wedded pairs "who by mutual consent cancel the debt of matrimony—voluntary eunuchs for the sake of their desire for the kingdom of heaven." [46] Second marriage, however, is positively immoral; it is a kind of adultery. Tertullian assails the Marcionites for rejecting marriage altogether. "The law of nature," though it is "opposed to lechery . . . does not forbid connubial intercourse"; it condemns "concupiscence" only in the sense of "extravagant, unnatural and enormous sins." Yet Tertullian at once proceeds to assert "the superiority of the other and higher sanctity, preferring conti-

[45] *Ad uxorem* II, 8.
[46] *Adv. Marcionem*, I, 29; *De Monogamia*, 3.

nence to marriage, but by no means prohibiting the latter. For my hostility is directed against those who are for destroying the God of marriage, not those who follow after chastity." "We do not reject marriage but only avoid it, we do not prescribe celibacy (*sanctitas*) but only urge it—keeping it as a good and, indeed, the better state, if each man seeks after it in so far as he has the strength to do so; yet openly defending marriage when hostile attacks are made upon it as a filthy thing, to the disparagement of the Creator." [47]

Yet Tertullian himself is here manifestly rejecting "the God of marriage" and "the God of nature," since, if celibacy is the more perfect state, it must be the state in which the Creator intended and desires human beings to live. At best marriage could only be regarded as a concession to the weakness of fallen man—a venial sin, perhaps, but nevertheless a sin. The attempt of Tertullian to reconcile his two positions by means of a distinction between marriage as "good" and virginity as "better" only makes the incongruity of the two strains in his teaching the more evident. For it could not well be held to be morally approvable knowingly to choose "the good" rather than "the better." Tertullian himself is constrained to admit that "what is [merely] permitted is not 'good'," and that "a thing is not 'good' merely because it is not evil." [48]

Finally, in some writings of Tertullian's latest period, the *Exhortatio castitatis* and the *De pudicitia*, the ascetic strain becomes wholly dominant, and the *veneratio naturae*, so far as sex is concerned, is quite forgotten. "Flesh" *is* now represented as at war with "soul," and all sexual indulgence is condemned: "let us renounce fleshly things, in order that we may finally bring forth fruits of the spirit"; "those who wish to be received into Paradise ought to cease from that thing from which Paradise is intact." [49] Not only second marriages but even first marriages are nothing but a species of fornication, for "the latter also consist of that which is defiling" (*et ipsae constant ex eo quod est stuprum*); only virginity has no *affinitas stupri* at all. Tertullian too has in the end come to "blush at nature." He

[47] *Adv. Marcionem*, I, 29.
[48] *Ad uxorem* I, 4.
[49] *Exhortatio castitatis* 10, 13.

still, it is true, feels some obligation to reconcile his present
position with the biblical command, "Increase and multiply";
for this purpose he falls back upon the theory of progress in
the revelation of religious and moral truth. What was legitimate or even obligatory under the Old Dispensation is not
necessarily legitimate under the New. Marriage is not to be
condemned as *always* evil, because, for those living in the
former age, it was not blameworthy. You do not "condemn"
a tree when the time has come to cut it down; nevertheless you
cut it down. "So also the marital state requires the hook and
sickle of celibacy, not as an evil thing, but as one ripe to be
abolished." Tertullian has here forgotten, or abandoned, his
assertion in the *De spectaculis* that " nowhere and never is that
permitted which is not permitted always and everywhere," because the "integrity of truth" consists in this, "that it never
changes its decision nor varies in its judgment." Thus, when
he has need of the idea of progress in his apologetic for other
worldliness, Tertullian gives up his once-cherished conviction
of the universal validity and invariability of the *lex naturae.*
With his more general and fundamental reasons—or motives—
for reprobating marriage, he combines the argument, already expressed in *Ad uxorem*, that the desire for "the bitter pleasure"
of having children and leaving a posterity behind one is irrational in Christians, who know what evil days are near at hand:
"Why should we be eager to have children whom, when we
have them, we desire to send away before us, in view of the
distresses that are now imminent?" [50]

Tertullian thus presents a chapter of considerable interest
and importance in the long and curious history of the practice
of deriving epistemological and ethical norms from the conceptions which, as the result of a complex and confused series
of historical processes, had come to be associated with the word

---

[50] *Ad uxorem* I, 5. In this last, as in some other passages, Tertullian's
" eschatology has given his ethical teaching something of the character of an
Interimsethik" (R. E. Roberts, *Theology of Tertullian*, 219); but his ethics in
general, and even his latest view about marriage in particular, certainly are not
based wholly or mainly upon eschatological considerations and are not advanced
by him as having a purely provisional validity arising out of the special circumstances of the time.

"nature." [51] Since the term had dozens of different, often vague, and sometimes incompatible connotations, it could be invoked—as it still is—in support of almost any conclusion one desired to establish. Tertullian himself, as we have seen, was able, by the exercise of a little ingenuity, to appeal to "nature" in justification of opinions which, in some cases, he evidently held for quite other reasons or from other motives. The sacred word, in short, was admirably adapted, by its ambiguity, to the uses of "rationalization." Nevertheless its very ambiguity was, and in the history of Christian thought was destined to be, a positive factor in influencing the movement of ideas. Once adopt "nature" or "the natural" as the norm in general, or in certain of its senses, and it was easy to slip over unconsciously to other senses, and difficult to avoid admitting the validity of any other normative implications which had become firmly associated with the term.

In the case of Tertullian two of the implications which have been here pointed out were of especial historical importance. The first was the epistemological assumption that there is a light of nature uniformly and equally present in the minds of all men by virtue of their rationality, an awareness of a few simple and fundamental truths, of which, therefore, the principal criterion is universality, the *consensus gentium.* The second was the assumption that the primary and generic propensities and appetites of man, being due to "nature," or "the God of nature," are good, and therefore ought not to be denied their normal gratification. Both of these, as we have seen, though at times zealously affirmed by Tertullian, were out of harmony with other doctrinal and emotional strains in him and in his Christian contemporaries. The first was at variance with his craving for an external authority and his belief in the indispensability for man's salvation of the acceptance of dogmas which manifestly were not known to all men at all times, and were, in fact, in apparent opposition to the "natural" reason of mankind. The second was in conflict with the tendency to asceticism, especially in the matter of sex, common in the Church of his time, which finally gained the ascendancy in him.

[51] Cf. *Primitivism in Antiquity*, 102 ff. and Appendix.

In the resultant inner tensions and contradictions in his thought which we have observed, he foreshadowed a part of the future history of ideas in Western Christendom. For the same two oppositions, occasionally apparent but usually repressed through the greater part of the Middle Ages, became overt and clearly defined in the late medieval and early modern centuries. Tertullian's rôle was, it is true, different with respect to these two major ideas associated (in his use) with the word "nature." As the first great Latin Father he probably did much to transmit to his successors the assumption that the primary and most essential truths of religion and morals are, or may be, known to all men "by nature," i. e., independently of revelation or authority; and this was to persist in medieval theology, though the consequences later to be drawn from it were evaded. But the anti-ascetic ethical doctrine implied by the acceptance of the norm of "nature" (in the sense distinguished in the last section of this essay) was for many centuries largely abortive. And though, in the thirteenth century, it again became very much alive, and in an extreme form — most conspicuously in Jean de Meun's part of the *Roman de la Rose*—it is improbable that this revival of a sort of moral "naturalism" owed anything to Tertullian. He partially and transiently foreshadowed it, but was not a vehicle of its transmission.[52] It was rather the feeling of something essentially "defiling" in sex, the equation *sanctitas* = celibacy, expressed in his latest writings, that his influence helped to pass on to his successors.

One more foreshadowing by him of an idea destined to great

[52] In the sixteenth century, however, the strain of moderate hedonism which has been noted in Tertullian appears in some of the Protestant Reformers. Calvin's chapter in the *Institutio* on "How to use this present life and the comforts of it" contains pretty unmistakable echoes of the *De Corona*, and insists, in accord with Tertullian, that the other "creatures" were designed by God not only for man's necessities but also for his "enjoyment and delight" (*oblectamento quoque ac hilaritati*), and that it is his privilege and duty to use them for the purpose for which they were intended. "Has the Lord adorned flowers with so much beauty that delights the eye, with so sweet a fragrance which delights the sense of smell, and shall it be unlawful for us to enjoy that beauty and this odor?" The enjoyment of good food and of wine, also, is legitimate (*Institutio*, III, chap. 10, 2). Calvinism, in spite of its predominant otherworldliness, did not encourage the mortification of the flesh, and sanctioned the "natural" sensible pleasures which things afford (*naturales rerum dotes*); and in this the influence of Tertullian is probably discernible.

fortunes in a much later time may be recalled in conclusion. It was, as we have seen, in his efforts to reconcile his faith in a divine revelation contained in the Old Testament writings with the innovations of the Christian doctrine, that he was led to contradict his own assertions of the uniformity of operation of the human reason and the immutability of the "teaching of Nature," and to propound the thesis of the necessarily gradual development of man's capacity for apprehending truth, especially moral and religious truth. This same thesis was eventually to play an important part in overcoming the static universalism and uniformitarianism (also associated with the first of the meanings of "nature" which have been noted in Tertullian) of the Enlightenment. If, in one vein in his teaching, he was a precursor of Lord Herbert, Tindal and Voltaire, he also adumbrated, in the early third century, an idea which, when elaborated in the late eighteenth by Lessing, in his *Erziehung des Menschengeschlechts*, was to be regarded by many of that age as revolutionary and epoch-making.[53]

[53] Frederic H. Hedge, when he published in 1847 what is apparently the first English translation (with a few omissions) of this work of Lessing's, said of it: "This Essay is considered as one of great importance in speculative theology. It contains the germ of all that is most valuable in subsequent speculations on these subjects" (*Prose Writers of Germany*, 4th ed. (1856), 91.

BIBLIOGRAPHY

OF THE

PUBLISHED WRITINGS OF ARTHUR O. LOVEJOY

1898–1951

Compiled by

JOHN COLLINSON

NOTE.—The compiler wishes to thank Mr. Lovejoy, who pointed out a number of errors and omissions, for his cordial co-operation; and Mr. Victor Lowe, of the Department of Philosophy at Johns Hopkins University, for his painstaking help and advice.

OMISSIONS. This Bibliography is believed to be substantially complete, except that the task of searching for letters to the editors of newspapers, and unsigned articles, was not undertaken. Their inclusion would have made more striking Mr. Lovejoy's conviction that scholars should concern themselves with contemporary problems.

Mr. Lovejoy's principal books, though given detailed listings chronologically, should have separate mention:

The Revolt Against Dualism (1930)
Primitivism and Related Ideas in Antiquity [with George Boas] (1935)
The Great Chain of Being (1936)
Essays in the History of Ideas (1948)

ABBREVIATIONS

AJT	American Journal of Theology
BAAUP	Bulletin of the American Association of University Professors
BWUA	Bulletin of the Washington University Association
EO	Educational Outlook
HJ	Hibbert Journal
IJE	International Journal of Ethics
	[Became "Ethics" after v. 48, #3 (1938)]
JEGP	Journal of English and Germanic Philology
JHI	Journal of the History of Ideas
JP	Journal of Philosophy, Psychology, and Scientific Method
	[Became "Journal of Philosophy" after v. 17 (1920)]
Mi	Mind, n.s.
MLN	Modern Language Notes
Mo	Monist
Na	Nation
NR	New Republic
PB	Psychological Bulletin

PMLA   Publications of the Modern Language Association
PPR   Journal of Philosophy and Phenomenological Research
PQ   Philological Quarterly
PR   Philosophical Review
PS   Popular Science Monthly
Sc   Science, n.s.
SS   School and Society

BIBLIOGRAPHY

1898

1. The Buddhistic technical terms upādāna and upādisesa. *Journal of the American Oriental Society*, 19 (second half):126–36.

1901

1. Syllabus: Robert Louis Stevenson, moralist: a study of a contemporary chapter in the history of the evaluation of life. The Washington University Association, 1901.
2. Syllabus: The philosophy of Buddhism, four lectures. The Washington University Association, 1901.

1902

1. Religion and the time-process. *AJT*, 6:439–72.

1904

1. Ethics and international relations. *BWUA*, 2:30–61.
2. The dialectic of Bruno and Spinoza. University of California *Publications in Philosophy*, 1:141–74.
3. Religious instruction in non-sectarian colleges and universities. *EO*, 1:107–12.
4. Review: F. J. E. Woodbridge, The philosophy of Hobbes. *PR*, 13:385–86.
5. Review: S. N. Dean, trans., Saint Anselm's Proslogium etc. *PR*, 13:384–85.
6. Fourth annual meeting of the Western Philosophical Association. *JP*, 1:269–70.
7. Some eighteenth century evolutionists. *PS*, 65:238–51, 323–40. Reprinted in *Scientific Monthly*, 71:162–78.

1905

1. Review: L. Stephen, Hobbes. *PR*, 14:97–99.
2. Review: G. Hessenberg and others, eds., Abhandlungen der Fries' schen Schule, v. 1 and 2. *PR*, 14:617–19, 15:216–17.
3. School extension. *EO*, 2:202–208.
4. Fifth annual meeting of the Western Philosophical Association. *JP*, 2:377.

1906

1. Democracy in the twentieth century. *BWUA*, 4:81–102.
2. On Kant's reply to Hume. *Archiv für Geschichte der Philosophie*, Band XIX, Heft 3, p. 380–407.
3. Review: P. E. More, The Shelburne Essays. *BWUA*, 4:151–55.
4. Kant's antithesis of dogmatism and criticism. *Mi*, 15:191–214.
5. The sixth annual meeting of the Western Philosophical Association. *JP*, 3:318.
6. The influence of self-consciousness on volition, *JP*, 3:326–27.
   An abstract of 1907—5.
7. Review: A. Buchenau, trans., Leibnitz Hauptschriften zur Grundlegung der Philosophie. *PR*, 15:437–38.
8. Review: A. Rivaud, Les notions d'essence et d'existence dans la philosophie de Spinoza. *PR*, 15:436–37.
9. The fundamental concept of the primitive philosophy. *Mo*, 16:357–82.

1907

1. The mind of the freshman. *BWUA*, 5:105–37
2. The entangling alliance of religion and history. *HJ*, 5:258–76.
3. Report of the Missouri child labor committee. *Annals of the American Academy*, January.
4. Review: P. Deussen, Outline of the Vēdanta system of philosophy according to Shankara. *JP*, 4:23–24.
5. The desires of the self-conscious. *JP*, 4:29–39.
6. Increase in the President's power. *Public Questions Club of Saint Louis*, 1907, p. 99–106.
7. The General Assembly and the next generation. *Missouri State Republican*, 6:4, January 18, 1907.
   Reprinted by Children's Protective Alliance of Missouri.
8. The origins of ethical inwardness in Jewish thought. *AJT*, 11:228–49.
9. Review: O. Külpe, Immanuel Kant: Darstellung und Würdigung. *JP*, 4:554–55.
10. Kant's classification of the forms of judgment. *PR*, 16:588–603.
11. Professor Ormond's philosophy. *PB*, 4:339–49.
12. The place of Linnaeus in the history of science. *PS*, 71:498–508.
13. Review: Studies in philosophy and psychology: Commemoration Volume by former students of C. E. Garman: Part I. *PB*, 4:18–24.

1908

1. Kant and the English Platonists. In *Essays, philosophical, and psychological, in honor of William James, professor in Harvard*

University, *by his colleagues at Columbia University.* New York: Longmans, Green & Co., 1908, p. 265–302.

2. Pragmatism and theology. *AJT*, 12:116–43.

3. The thirteen pragmatisms. *JP*, 5:5–12, 29–39.

   Second part reprinted in W. G. Muelder and L. Sears, *The development of American philosophy: a book of readings.* Boston: Houghton Mifflin Co., 1940, p. 404–10.

4. Religious transition and ethical awakening in America. *HJ*, 6:500–14.

5. Review: F. C. Sharp, A study of the influence of custom on moral judgment. *JP*, 5:548–53.

6. Review: W. B. Smith, The theory of a pre-Christian cult of Jesus. *Mo*, 18:587–609.

7. Review: I. W. Riley, American philosophy: the early schools. *Sc*, 27:464–66.

1909

1. Review: E. B. Bax, The roots of reality: being suggestions for a philosophical reconstruction. *PR*, 18:75–80.

2. Some aspects of Darwin's influence upon modern thought. *BWUA*, 7:85–99.

3. The meaning of φύσις in the Greek physiologers. *PR*, 18:369–83.

4. The obsolescence of the eternal. *PR*, 18:479–502.

   Address of the president at the ninth annual meeting of the Western Philosophical Association, Saint Louis, April 9, 1909.

5. Metaphysician of the life-force [Bergson]. *Na*, 89:298–301.

6. Pragmatism and realism. *JP*, 6:575–80.

7. The argument for organic evolution before "The Origin of Species." *PS*, 75:499–514, 537–49.

8. Review: O. Külpe, Immanuel Kant, Zweite verbesserte Auflage. *JP*, 6:719–20.

1910

1. Review: A. Collier, Clavis universalis, E. Bowman, ed. *JP*, 7:77–79.

2. The service pension of the Carnegie Foundation. *Na*, 90:109.

   Reprinted in *Sc*, 31:299–300.

3. The treatment of "opposition" in formal logic. *JP*, 7:101–105.

4. A note (on 1910—3, p. 104). *JP*, 7:133.

5. Retrospective anticipations of the Carnegie Foundation. *Sc*, 31:414–15.

6. Review: H. Bergson, Time and free will. *Na*, 91:499–500.

7. Review: G. T. Ladd, Knowledge, life and reality. *Na*, 91:105.

8. Review: R. Eucken, The problem of human life. *IJE*, 20:83–88.

9. Review: E. Crawley, The idea of the soul. *PB*, 7:354–58.

10. Review: W. A. Heidel, Περὶ Φύσεως: a study of the conception of nature among the pre-Socratics. *PR*, 19:665–67.
11. Review: T. M. Johnson, trans., Proclus's Metaphysical elements. *JP*, 7:220.
12. Kant and evolution. *PS*, 77:538–53, 78:36–51.
13. The place of the time problem in contemporary philosophy. *JP*, 7:683–93.

1911
1. Christian ethics and economic competition. *HJ*, 9:324–44.
2. Review: H. E. Cushman, A beginner's history of philosophy, v. 1. *IJE*, 21:352–55.
3. William James as philosopher. *IJE*, 21:125–53.
4. Schopenhauer as an evolutionist. *Mo*, 21:195–222.
5. The meaning of vitalism. *Sc*, 33:610–14.
6. The import of vitalism. *Sc*, 34:75–80.
7. Review: R. M. Wenley, Kant and his philosophical revolution. *Na*, 93:166–67.
8. Review: B. Russell, Philosophical essays. *Na*, 93:319–20.
9. Review: E. van Biéma, L'espace et le temps chez Leibnitz et chez Kant. *PR*, 20:313–17.
10. Review: T. and G. A. de Laguna, Dogmatism and evolution: studies in modern philosophy. *PR*, 20:535–45.
11. Reflections of a temporalist on the new realism. *JP*, 8:589–600.
12. Review: H. Bergson, Matter and memory *and* Creative evolution. *Na*, 91:648–49.
13. Review: H. E. Cushman, A beginner's history of philosophy, v. 2. *IJE*, 22:111–13.
14. Buffon and the problem of species. *PS*, 79:464–73, 554–67.
15. Existence and formal logic. *JP*, 8:660–63.
16. Review: G. Santayana, Three philosophical poets: Lucretius, Dante, and Goethe. *MLN*, 26:244–47.

1912
1. Leibnitz. In *A cyclopedia of education*, 3:673–75.
2. The unity of science. In "Mathematical and physical sciences: non-technical lectures by members of the faculty of the University of Missouri, Series I." *Bulletin of the University of Missouri*, I:1–34.
3. Review: W. Fite, Individualism. *American Political Science Review*, p. 141–44.
4. The problem of time in recent French philosophy. *PR*, 21:11–31, 322–43, 527–45.
5. Review of recent works on logic. *Na*, 95:40–41.

6. Review: F. J. MacKinnon, The philosophy of John Norris of
   Bemerton. *PR*, 21:256–57.
7. Review: J. Goldstein, Wandlungen in der Philosophie der
   Gegenwart. *JP*, 9:327–30.
8. Discussion: "Present Philosophical Tendencies." *JP*, 9:627–40,
   673–84.
9. Letter from Professor Lovejoy. *JP*, 9:720–21.
   An elaboration of p. 634 of 1912—8.
10. Review: J. Ward, The realm of ends. *Na*, 94:414–15.
11. Review: E. Boutroux, Historical studies in philosophy. *Na*,
    95:594.
12. The meaning of Driesch and the meaning of vitalism. *Sc*, 36:672–
    75.
13. (with others) Discussion: The relation of consciousness and
    object in sense perception. *PR*, 21:199–204.

1913

1. On some novelties of the new realism. *JP*, 10:29–43.
2. Discussion: Secondary qualities and subjectivity. *JP*, 10:214–18.
   Reply to a criticism of 1912—8 by M. R. Cohen.
3. The metamorphosis of the Carnegie Foundation. *Sc*, 37:546–52.
4. The practical tendencies of Bergsonism. *IJE*, 23:253–75, 419–43.
5. Review: E. B. Holt and others, The new realism *and* G. S. Fuller-
   ton, The world we live in. *Sc*, 37:867–72.
6. Error and the new realism. *PR*, 22:410–23.
7. Review: A. T. Robinson, The applications of logic. *Na*, 96:481.
8. Some antecedents of the philosophy of Bergson. *Mi*, 22:465–83.
9. Realism versus epistemological monism. *JP*, 10:561–72.
10. Review: L. T. Hobhouse, Development and purpose. *Na*,
    97:163–64.
11. Preface: Some comparative statistics relating to the graduate
    department of the [Johns Hopkins] university. Johns Hopkins
    Alumni Magazine, 2:9–10.
    Followed (p. 11–22) by extracts ("chiefly from published sources")
    selected by A. O. Lovejoy.
12. Review: O. Külpe, The philosophy of the present in Germany.
    Na, 97:215.
13. Review: B. A. G. Fuller, The problem of evil in Plotinus. *Na*,
    97:438–39.

1914

1. Bergson and romantic evolutionism. University of California
   Chronicle, 15:1–61.
   Two lectures delivered before the philosophical Union of the University
   of California, September 5, 12, 1913. Reprinted at Berkeley, California:
   University of California Press, 1914.

2. On the existence of ideas: in three studies in current philosophical questions. Johns Hopkins University *Circular*, 33:178–235.
3. Review: J. H. Leuba, A psychological study of religion. · *IJE*, 34:216–20.
4. (with others) The case of Professor Mecklin: report of the committee of inquiry [A. O. Lovejoy, Chairman] of the American Philosophical Association and the American Psychological Association. *JP*, 11:67–81.
5. The profession of the professorate. The Johns Hopkins *Alumni Magazine*, 2:181–95.
6. Review: B. Croce, Giambattista Vico. *Na*, 99:46–47.
7. A national association of university professors. *Na*, 99:580.
   Also in *Sc*, 40:744–45.
8. Relativity, reality, and contradiction. *JP*, 11:421–30.
   Reply to a discussion of 1913—2 by M. R. Cohen.
9. German scholars and the "Truth about Germany." *Na*, 99:376.
   Parts reprinted in S. R. H. and J. F. M., *Sixty American opinions on the war*. London: T Fisher Unwin, Ltd., 1915, p. 104–105.
10. Review: E. B. Holt, The concept of consciousness. *PR*, 23.664–77.
11. Qualities, relations and things. *JP*, 9:617–27.
12. Professorial landsturm. *Na*, 99:656–57.

1915

1. Organization of the American Association of University Professors. *Sc*, 41:151–54.
2. Reply to Professor Darmstaedter. *Na*, 100:195–96.
   Concerns 1914—9 and 12.
3. What was the *casus belli?* *Na*, 100:246–47.
4. Review: H. M. Kallen, William James and Henri Bergson. *Na*, 100:388–90.
5. Review: F. Thilly, A history of philosophy. *JP*, 12:272–77.
6. (with others) Report of the committee of inquiry on conditions at the University of Utah. The American Association of University Professors, July, 1915.
7. Review: R. G. Usher, Pan-Americanism. *Na*, 101:16–17.
8. Review: H. S. Chamberlain, Immanuel Kant. *Na*, 101:261–62.
9. Review: J. H. Rose, Origins of the war. *Na*, 101:295.
10. As to an embargo on arms. *NR*, 4:156–57.
11. (with others) General report of the committee on academic freedom and academic tenure. *BAAUP*, 1:15–43.
12. Methods of the board of regents of the University of Utah. *SS*, 3:314–16.

1916

1. The American Association of University Professors. *Na*, 102:169–70

2. (with others) Report of the committee of inquiry [A. O. Lovejoy, Chairman] on the case of Professor Scott Nearing of the University of Pennsylvania. *BAAUP*, v. 2, #3, pt. 2, p. 1–57.

3. Review: G. Sorel, Reflections on violence. *American Political Science Review*, 10:193–95.

4. Review: D. Cheydleur, Essai sur l'évolution des doctrines de M. Georges Sorel. *MLN*, 31:360–63.

5. (with others) Reports of committees concerning charges of violation of academic freedom at the University of Colorado and at Wesleyan University. *BAAUP*, v. 2, #2, pt. 2, p. 1–76.

6. The topic for discussion at the 1916 meeting of the American Philosophical Association. *JP*, 13:573–80.

   Signed for the executive committee by A. O. Lovejoy, Chairman, and E. G. Spaulding, Secretary.

7. (with others) Report of Committee P on pensions and insurance. *BAAUP*, v. 2, #5, p. 57–76.

8. On the meaning of "romantic" in early German romanticism. *MLN*, 31:385–96, 32:65–77.

   Reprinted in 1948—1.

9. The future of the Carnegie Foundation. *Na*, 103:417–19.

10 Academic freedom. *Na*, 103:561.

1917

1. (with A. B. Hart) *Handbook of the war for public speakers*. Committee on Patriotism through Education, National Security League, New York, 1917.

2. America impartial. *NR*, 10:75.

3. On some conditions of progress in philosophical inquiry. *PR*, 26:123–63.

   The presidential address before the sixteenth annual meeting of the American Philosophical Association, December 27, 1916.

4. Progress in philosophical inquiry. *PR*, 26:537–45.

   Reply to criticisms of 1917—3 by E. Albee and others.

5. Benevolent neutrality? *NR*, 10:229–30.

6. (with others) Report of the committee of inquiry concerning charges of violation of academic freedom, involving the dismissal of the president and three members of the faculty at the University of Montana. *BAAUP*, v. 3, #5, pt. 2, p. 1–52.

7. To conscientious objectors. *NR*, 11:187–89.

8. Philosophical discussion and the American Philosophical Association. *JP*, 14:719–20.

   Reply to a criticism of 1917—3 by J. E. Creighton.

1918

1. War aims and peace aims. Johns Hopkins *News-Letter*, 22:1, 4, 7, January 14, 1918.

2. (with E. Capps and A. A. Young) Academic freedom in war time. *Na*, 106:401–402.
3. War policy of American and British labor. *NR*, 15:206–208.
4. What kind of conference? *NR*, 15:377–78.
5. Is a peace of conciliation possible? *NR*, 16:257–59.
6. (with others) Academic freedom in war time: report of the committee on academic freedom and academic tenure. *BAAUP*, v. 4, #2–3, p. 16–47.
7. German peace drives rightly named "traps." New York *Times Magazine*, 47:4, 15, July 28, 1918.

1919

1. Introduction. In *America joins the world: selections from the speeches and state papers of President Wilson, 1914–18.* New York: Association Press, 1919.
2. (with H. F. Stone) Supplementary statement concerning the plan of compulsory and contributory annuities proposed by the Carnegie Foundation. *SS*, 9:150–54.
3. Russia and the outbreak of the European war. *NR*, 18:348–49.
4. (with others) Pensions and insurance. *BAAUP*, v. 5, #6, p. 20–84.
5. Review: A. D. Snyder, The critical principle of the reconciliation of opposites as employed by Coleridge. *MLN*, 34:303–305.
6. The Left and the League. *Review of Reviews*, 1:80–81.
7. Is there a huge social surplus? *Weekly Review*, 1:163–65.
8. Washburn College and Professor Kirkpatrick: correspondence between A. O. Lovejoy and P. P. Womer. *SS*, 10:406–407. 558–59.
   Reprinted in *BAAUP*, v.5, #6, p. 9–11.
9. Annual message of the president. *BAAUP*, v. 5, #7–8, p. 10–40.
   Parts reprinted in *SS*, 10:749–56.
10. Dr. Jordan and the Carnegie Foundation. *NR*, 21:80.

1920

1. Pragmatism versus the pragmatist. In Durant Drake and others, *Essays in critical realism: a cooperative study of the problem of knowledge.* London: Macmillan and Company, Ltd., 1920, p. 35–81.
2. Review: I. Babbitt, Rousseau and romanticism. *MLN*, 35:302–308.
3. Schiller and the genesis of German romanticism. *MLN*, 35:1–10, 134–46.
   Reprinted in 1948—1.
4. Keynes and Dillon. *Weekly Review*, 2:279–80.
5. Clemenceau and the Left Bank. *Review of Reviews*, 2:359.
6. Mr. Mencken and the Armenian Massacres. *The Evening Sun*, Baltimore, May 31, 1920.

7. Review: R. B. Perry, The present conflict of ideals. *Harvard Theological Review*, 13:189–94.
8. Teachers and trade unions. *Educational Review*, 60:106–19.
9. Recent discussion of university problems: Lafayette College. *BAAUP*, v. 6, #6, p. 8–18.
10. Further discussion of unionization: Better organization of teachers without unionization. *Educational Review*, 60:329–35.
11. Letter to the editors: Proprietary professorships and academic freedom. *Weekly Review*, 3:417–18.
12. Pragmatism as interactionism. *JP*, 17:589–96, 622–32.
13. Is academic freedom desirable? *Educational Review*, 60:423–27.

1921

1. "Pride" in eighteenth-century thought. *MLN*, 36:31–37.
    Reprinted in 1948—1.
2. (with others) Report of the committee of inquiry [A. O. Lovejoy, Chairman] on conditions in Washburn College. *BAAUP*, v. 7, #1–2, p. 66–137.
3. Profit-sharing and industrial peace. *IJE*, 31:241–63.
4. Review: B. Russell, The analysis of mind. *The Independent*, 107:215–16.

1922

1. Address at the presentation of a portrait of Professor H. S. Jennings. Johns Hopkins *Alumni Magazine*, 10:81–86.
2. Pragmatism and the new materialism. *JP*, 19:5–15.
3. The paradox of the thinking behaviorist. *PR*, 31:135–47.
4. Reply to Professor Babbitt. *MLN*, 37:268–74.
    Concerns 1920—2.
5. Review: A. K. Rogers, English and American philosophy since 1800. *Christian Register*, August 31.
6. The length of human infancy in eighteenth-century thought. *JP*, 19:381–85.
7. Time, meaning and transcendence. *JP*, 19:505–15, 533–41.

1923

1. Shall we join the League of Nations? *NR*, 34:138–39.
2. "Representative ideas" in Malebranche and Arnauld. *Mi*, 32:449–61.
3. The anomaly of knowledge. University of California *Publications in Philosophy*, 4:3–43.
4. The supposed primitivism of Rousseau's "Discourse on Inequality." *Modern Philology*, 21:165–86.
    Reprinted in 1948—1.
5. Rousseau's pessimist. *MLN*, 38:449–52.

6. Review: U. Sinclair, The goose-step. Johns Hopkins *News-Letter*, 27:2, May 18.

1924

1. The discontinuities of evolution. *Essays in Metaphysics*, University of California *Publications in Philosophy*, 5:173–220.
   Second Annual Howison Lecture, delivered at the University of California, March 25, 1924.
2. Professional ethics and social progress. *North American Review*, 219:398–407.
3. Pastness and transcendence. *JP*, 21:601–11.
   Reply to a discussion of 1922—8 by J. Dewey.
4. Reply to Professor Laird. *Mi*, 33:180–81.
   Concerns 1923—2.
5. On the discrimination of romanticisms. *PMLA*, 39:229–53.
   Reprinted in 1948—1.
6. Contemporary philosophy and psychology: their common problem. *PB*, 21:565–68.
7. Reply to the editorial, "A professorial fiasco," in the *New Republic*, 39:6–7, May 28, 1924. *BAAUP*, 10:388–90.
8. (with others) Report of the committee of inquiry [A. O. Lovejoy, Chairman] concerning Clark University. *BAAUP*, 10:412–79.

1925

1. La théorie de la stérilité de la conscience dans la philosophie Américaine et Anglaise. *Bulletin de la Société Française de Philosophie*, 25:89–116, 131–32.
2. Review: N. K. Smith, Prolegomena to an idealist theory of knowledge. *PR*, 34:185–93.
3. Review: J. Harrington, Oceana, ed., S. B. Liljegren. *MLN*, 40:45–46.
4. Review: E. Wentscher, Englische Philosophie. *JEGP*, 24:605–606.

1927

1. The meanings of "emergence" and its modes. *Proceedings of the 6th International Congress of Philosophy*, p. 20–33.
   Also in *British Journal of Philosophical Studies*, 2:167–81.
2. "Nature" as aesthetic norm. *MLN*, 42:444–50.
   Reprinted in 1948—1.
3. Optimism and romanticism. *PMLA*, 42:921–45.
4. Review: W. E. Hocking, Man and the state. *Yale Law Review*, 36:723–24.

1929

1. Anti-evolution laws and the principle of religious neutrality. *SS*, 29:133–38.
   Also in *BAAUP*, 15:307–14.

2. Review: H. N. Fairchild, The noble savage. *PQ*, 8:174–75.

1930

1. *The revolt against dualism: an inquiry concerning the existence of ideas.* Chicago: Open Court Publishing Co., New York: W. W. Norton and Company, Inc., 1930.
2. A temporalistic realism. In G. P. Adams and W. P. Montague, eds., *Contemporary American Philosophy* (J. H. Muirhead, ed., Library of Philosophy series). London: G. Allen and Unwin, Ltd., New York: The Macmillan Company, 1930, v. 2, p. 85–105.
3. Academic freedom. *Encyclopaedia of the Social Sciences*, 1:384–88.
4. The dialectical argument against absolute simultaneity. *JP*, 27:617–32. 645–54.
5. Review: F. C. Sharp, Ethics. *PR*, 39:613–22.

1931

1. Review: A. Schinz, La pensée de Jean-Jacques Rousseau. *MLN*, 46:41–46.
2. The paradox of the time-retarding journey. *PR*, 40:48–68, 152–67.
   Rejoinder to a reply to 1930—3 by E. B. McGilvary.
3. The time-retarding journey: a reply. *PR*, 40:549–67.
   Further discussion of 1930—3 and 1931—2.

1932

1. The parallel of deism and classicism. *Modern Philology*, 29:281–99.
   Reprinted in 1948—1.
2. The genesis of the American Association of University Professors. *BAAUP*, 18:305.
3. Dualisms good and bad. *JP*, 29:337–54, 375–81.
   Reply to criticisms of 1930—1.
4. The travels of Peter, Paul and Zebedee. *PR*, 41:498–517.
   Further discussion of 1930—3, 1931—2 and 1931—3.
5. The first Gothic revival and the return to nature. *MLN*, 47:419–46.
   Reprinted in 1948—1.

1933

1. Address: Hitler as pacifist. American Jewish Congress, Baltimore Branch.
2. The Chinese origin of a romanticism. *JEGP*, 32:1–20.
   Reprinted in 1948—1.
3. Monboddo and Rousseau. *Modern Philology*, 30:275–96.
   Reprinted in 1948—1.
4. Dualism and the paradox of reference. *JP*, 30:589–606.
5. (with A. S. Edwards) Rollins College report. *BAAUP*, 19:416–39.
6. Review: C. W. Morris, Six theories of mind. *PR*, 42:617–26.

1934

1. Foreword. To L. Whitney, *Primitivism and the idea of progress in English popular literature of the eighteenth century* (Contributions to the history of primitivism). Baltimore: The Johns Hopkins Press, 1934.

1935

1. (with G. Boas) *Primitivism and related ideas in antiquity: A documentary history of primitivism and related ideas*, v. 1. Baltimore: The Johns Hopkins University Press, 1935.
   With supplementary essays by W. F. Albright and P. E. Dumont.

1936

1. *The great chain of being: a study in the history of an idea*. Cambridge, Massachusetts: Harvard University Press, 1936.
   The William James Lectures, delivered at Harvard University, 1933. Second printing, 1942; third printing, 1948; fourth printing, 1950.

1937

1. Milton and the paradox of the fortunate fall. *ELH: A Journal of English Literary History*, 4:161–79.
   Reprinted in 1948—1 and in M. Shorer and others, eds., *Criticism: the foundations of modern literary judgment*. Harcourt Brace and Co., 1948, p. 137–47.
2. (with A. J. Carlson) Teacher's oath laws: statement of Committee B. *BAAUP*, 23:26–32.
3. Review: V. de Sola Pinto, Peter Sterry, Platonist and Puritan, 1613–72. *MLN*, 52:423–25.

1938

1. The historiography of ideas. *American Philosophical Society Proceedings*, 78:529–43.
   Reprinted in 1948—1.
2. Harry Walter Tyler, 1863–1938. *BAAUP*, 24:219–21.
3. Professional association versus trade union. *BAAUP*, 24:347–55.
4. Professional association or trade union? *BAAUP*, 24:409–17.
5. Harvard University and Drs. Walsh and Sweezy: A review of the Faculty Committee's report. *BAAUP*, 24:598–608.
6. Abstract: The historiography of philosophy. *JP*, 35:677–79.

1939

1. Present standpoints and past history. *JP*, 36:477–89.

1940

1. Reflections on the history of ideas. *JHI*, 1:3–23.

2. Introduction [and some footnotes]. To P. Wiener, "Leibnitz's project of a public exhibition of scientific inventions." *JHI*, 1:232–40.
3. Editorial note. *JHI*, 1:503.
   Concerning an article by F. J. Teggart, *JHI*, 1:494–503.
4. Coleridge and Kant's two worlds. *ELH: A Journal of English Literary History*, 7:341–62.
   Reprinted in 1948—1.

1941

1. The meaning of romanticism for the historian of ideas. *JHI*, 2:257–78.

1942

1. On the criteria and limits of meaning. F. P. Clarke and M. C. Nahm, eds., *Philosophical essays in honor of Edgar Arthur Singer, Jr.*, Philadelphia, Pennsylvania: University of Pennsylvania Press, 1942, p. 3–23.
2. The communism of Saint Ambrose. *JHI*, 3:458–68.
   Reprinted in 1948—1.

1943

1. Review: B. Willey, The eighteenth century background. *MLN*, 58:485–87.
2. Culbertson's international armed force. *Free World*, 6:463–69.

1944

1. EM 10, G. I. roundtable: What shall be done about Germany after the war? Washington, D. C.: U. S. Government Printing Office, 1944.
2. EM 12, G. I. roundtable: Can we prevent future wars? Washington, D. C.: U. S. Government Printing Office, 1944.
3. Should there be an international organization for general security against military aggression? *Problem Analyses*. Universities Committee on Post-War International Problems, # 4.
4. The Dumbarton Oaks proposals: the enforcement of peace. *Problem Analyses*. Universities Committee on Post-War International Problems, #18.
5. Reply to Professor Spitzer. *JHI*, 5:204–19.
   Concerns 1941—1.

1945

1. (with others) A discussion of the theory of international relations. *JP*, 42:477–82.

1946

1. Goldsmith and the chain of being. *JHI*, 7:91–98.
2. A note on Peirce's evolutionism. *JHI*, 7:351–54.

1947

1. The duality of the Thomistic theology: a reply to Mr. Veatch. *PPR*, 7:413–38.
   Reply to a criticism of parts of 1936—1 by H. Veatch.
2. Analogy and contradiction: a surrejoinder. *PPR*, 7:626–34.
   Reply to a rejoinder to 1947—1 by H. Veatch.

1948

1. *Essays in the history of ideas*. Baltimore: The Johns Hopkins Press, 1948.
2. Necessity and self-sufficiency in Thomistic theology: a reply to President Pegis. *PPR*, 9:71–88.
   Reply to a discussion of 1947—1 and 1947—2 by A. C. Pegis.
3. Comment on Mr. Pegis's rejoinder. *PPR*, 9:284–90.
   Reply to a rejoinder to 1948—2 by A. C. Pegis.

1949

1. Historiography and evaluation: a disclaimer. *JHI*, 10:141–42.
2. Reply. *JHI*, 10:141–42.
   To a review of 1948—1 by T. Spencer.
3. Communism versus academic freedom. *American Scholar*, 18:332–37.

1950

1. Address at presentation of the Hollander Foundation Award to the Baltimore City Medical Society. The Hollander Foundation, Baltimore.
   On the occasion of the admission of Negro physicians to membership in the Society.
2. Terminal and adjectival values. *JP*, 47:593–608.

INDEX